D1715692

THE NEW BLACK: ALTERNATIVE PARADIGMS AND STRATEGIES FOR THE 21ST CENTURY

RESEARCH IN RACE AND ETHNIC RELATIONS

Series Editor: Rutledge M. Dennis

Recent Volumes:

Volume 10:   The Black Intellectuals – Edited by Rutledge M. Dennis

Volume 11:   The Sociology of Oliver C. Cox – Edited by Herbert Hunter

Volume 12:   Marginality, Power and Social Structure – Edited by Rutledge M. Dennis

Volume 13:   The Racial Politics of Booker T. Washington – Edited by Donald Cunnigen, Rutledge M. Dennis and Myrtle Gonza Glascoe

6402563

RESEARCH IN RACE AND ETHNIC RELATIONS   VOLUME 14

THE NEW BLACK: ALTERNATIVE PARADIGMS AND STRATEGIES FOR THE 21ST CENTURY

EDITED BY

RODNEY D. COATES
Miami University, Ohio, USA

RUTLEDGE M. DENNIS
George Mason University, Fairfax, Virginia, USA

ELSEVIER
JAI

Amsterdam – Boston – Heidelberg – London – New York – Oxford
Paris – San Diego – San Francisco – Singapore – Sydney – Tokyo
JAI Press is an imprint of Elsevier

JAI Press is an imprint of Elsevier
The Boulevard, Langford Lane, Kidlington, Oxford OX5 1GB, UK
Radarweg 29, PO Box 211, 1000 AE Amsterdam, The Netherlands
525 B Street, Suite 1900, San Diego, CA 92101-4495, USA

First edition 2007

British Library Cataloguing in Publication Data
A catalogue record for this book is available from the British Library

ISBN-13:   978-0-7623-0985-6
ISBN-10:   0-7623-0985-7
ISSN: 0195-7449 (Series)

For information on all JAI Press publications
visit our website at books.elsevier.com

Printed and bound in The Netherlands

07 08 09 10 11 10 9 8 7 6 5 4 3 2 1

Working together to grow
libraries in developing countries
www.elsevier.com | www.bookaid.org | www.sabre.org
ELSEVIER   BOOK AID International   Sabre Foundation

DEDICATION

Rodney Coates:
Dedicated to Sherrill L. Sellers, my partner in life

Rutledge M. Dennis:
Dedicated to my sons and daughter: Shay T., Imaro "Marlin", Kimya, and Zuri

And to my grandsons and granddaughters
Shay Joshua, Justin Shamar, Desiree Porcher, Shaphan, and Cierra

CONTENTS

LIST OF CONTRIBUTORS

Amy E. Ansell	Department of Sociology, Bard College, Annandale-on-Hudson, NY, USA
Diane R. Brown	Institute for the Elimination of Health Disparities, UMDNJ-School of Public Health, University Heights, Newark, NJ, USA
Reginald Byron	Department of Sociology, The Ohio State University, Columbus, OH, USA
Hiu Ha Florence Chong	Tzu Chi University in Taiwan, China
Rodney D. Coates	Department of Sociology and Gerontology, Miami University, Oxford, OH, USA
João H. Costa Vargas	Center for African and American Studies, The University of Texas at Austin, Austin, TX, USA
Rutledge M. Dennis	Department of Sociology/Anthropology, George Mason University, Fairfax, VA, USA
Ashley ("Woody") Doane	Department of Social Sciences, Hillyer College, University of Hartford, West Hartford, CT, USA

Lisette Garcia   Department of Sociology, The Ohio State
                           University, Columbus, OH, USA

Michelle Harris   Department of Sociology and
                           Anthropology, Wheaton College, Norton,
                           MA, USA

L. Adele Jinadu   Department of Political Science and Dean
                           of the Faculty of the Social Sciences,
                           Lagos State University, Lagos, Nigeria

Antoine Joseph   Department of History and Social
                           Science, Bryant University, Smithfield,
                           RI, USA

Sherry Mong   Department of Sociology, The Ohio State
                           University, Columbus, OH, USA

Aldon Morris   Department of Sociology, Northwestern
                           University, Evanston, IL, USA

Vincent J. Roscigno   Department of Sociology, The Ohio State
                           University, Columbus, OH, USA

Sherrill L. Sellers   School of Social Work, University of
                           Wisconsin, Madison, WI, USA

Charles V. Willie   Professor Emeritus Graduate School of
                           Education, Harvard University,
                           Cambridge, MA, USA

George Wilson   Department of Sociology, University of
                           Miami, Coral Gables, FL, USA

Bette Woody[†]   Department of Sociology, University of
                           Massachusetts, Boston, MA, USA

INTRODUCTION

At pivotal points in American history events, individuals and groups inter-act to define eras. As an example, more than 30 years after the end of the Civil War, W. E. B. Du Bois heralded the birth of a new class among Black Americans, a Talented Tenth, whose education, devotion, and tenaciousness toward freedom and justice for blacks would define their life and world. But the quest for newness was merely unique to this period. In the late eight-eenth century Toussaint Louverture, in expelling and defeating the French, sought a New Haiti; during the first three decades of the nineteenth century David Walker, Gabriel Prosser, Nat Turner, and Denmark Vesey all sought, through violence, to overthrow the institution of slavery; and usher in a New Beginning for Africans whose entrance in the New World began with slavery; the mid-nineteenth century world of Frederick Douglass, Harriet Tubman, Sojourner Truth, and a host of abolitionists challenged both the institution of slavery, the Southern Confederacy, and the national government to save Black Americans and the American union by engaging in the second American Revolution and by ending forever the outcast status of black citizens.

Viewed collectively, all of Du Bois' books and articles, written during the last decade of the nineteenth century and the two decades into the twentieth century, were designed to promote this New Being, this New Negro. He saw the evolution of this new person, this new group, as the reflection of an internal and deep ongoing institutional change within the nation itself, a change, which might be slowed and stalled, but never stopped. Du Bois sought to explain to the nation, and to Black Americans themselves, how the experiences, sociology, and history of the unique people as the New fit quite well with the opening of the New World and America as the First New Nation. He reasoned that if the New Nation intended to abandon the ways of the Old World which the American Revolution asserted, surely the ideology of color and oppression, created under slavery, would be abandoned. That this was not the case meant that the promise of black advancement could not rest solely with the dominant group but greater efforts must be made by blacks to assure their own liberation and freedom. But if social change must be imminent, the Old Negro must be distinguished from the New Negro. A reading of W. E. B. Du Bois' classic, Souls of Black Folk (1903) and

James Weldon Johnson's book The Autobiography of an Ex-Colored Man (1912) illustrate how each juxtaposed the Old Negro and the New Negro. Each saw Southern Blacks as the Old and Northern Blacks as the New, though the categorization of each contained both positive and negative traits. For Du Bois, the road to the new was shaped via organizations and institutions ideologically committed toward raising racial consciousness and confronting the system together with enlightened and progressive allies. In Johnson's case, the character in his novel, and it was a novel, not an autobiography, decided, since he looked "white",to "pass" over into the white world.

In the 1930s and 1940s academic intellectuals emerged as key interpreters of black life. E. Franklin Frazier, Charles Johnson, St. Claire Drake Horace Cayton, Allison Davis, Hyland Lewis, Ira Reid, and others not only documented historical and traditional patterns of black lifebut they also projected new directions in black life based on advances in education and greater political involvement. Just as the artists and writers were documenting the New Negro throughout the culture, Frazier, along with Drake and Cayton, were noting the rise and influence of a New Black Middle Class, Frazier's Black Bourgeoisie, whose emergence would reflect new class and social status relations among blacks in their segregated communities. Studies by these scholars followed Du Bois' classic Philadelphia study in documenting the diversity of black life exemplified in family and religious life, and within community organizations and institutions. Of the intellectuals during this period only Oliver C. Cox's classic, Class, Caste, and Color (1948) made a case against racial, caste, and class inequality on a structural and macro level with a quasi-Marxist perspective. With that perspective, he launched a frontal attack on American and Western racial and class inequality by situating these inequalities within the network of American and world capitalism. Cox's New Person would be one oriented toward class, not race, in as much as Cox saw racial analyses as essentially a subset of a class situation, and as such, primarily nationalistic, bourgeois, and inherently negative.

The 1950s were unique years in that many black academic intellectuals such as Kenneth Clark, Ralph Bunche, and Robert Weaver would play a major role in some of the major legal cases of this decade's beginning with the Brown v. Board of Education Decision. The other unique feature of this decade would be the emergence of religious or theological intellectuals, chief among these was Martin Luther King, Jr. These religious and theological intellectuals, like intellectuals from previous decades sought to define and promote the New Negro and the New Black. The bulk of these intellectuals would reside in the South, were born in the South, and would devote their energies toward assisting in the creation of the Civil Rights Movement (see articles by Coates and Morris). But it would not be long before voices in the background, at the end of the 1960s, impatient with the slow gains of the Civil Rights Movement, would begin to chant Black Power and boldly asserted that the Civil Rights Movement had not been able to produce the "New" New Black, one not willing to walk lock-step with liberal whites who helped to shape and define the Movement. The Black Power Movement facilitated a link to, and promoted Pan-Africanism, which yielded yet another model of the New Black, this time a Black more intricately linked to Africa and Africanisms. Thus, it can be seen that the idea of newness and the desire to be new have been key features of the emotional and social mind-set among Black Americans for as long as Black Americans have been the unique group within the American mosaic.

Rutledge M. Dennis presents the idea of the New Black by illustrating how and why black intellectuals may be seen as representatives of the New Black. He describes how the role of the intellectual was defined by Du Bois and Kelly Miller during the first decade of the twentieth century, and how Alain Locke and the creative artists of the Harlem Renaissance would stamp the name New Negro in the 1920s to both define the era and to advance the idea that a virtual social, cultural, and political revolution had sneaked up on the nation, and that while the nation was asleep, the New People had emerged. Dennis juxtaposes several models of intellectuals: the Du Bois-Miller version, the Locke version, the Harold Cruse version, the Post-Cruse version, and the version he proposes, the Dennis version. In addition, Dennis uses a theory of dual marginality to explain the process by which individuals, in this case, intellectuals, are able to move from single marginality to dual marginality, and why in a society already segmented by race and class, and representing deep dual and unequal division, but which experience varying degrees of political, cultural, and economic integration, intellectuals would live as dual marginals to a greater extent than would other segments of black communities whose contacts with whites and white culture are generally limited to the hours spent at work. Dennis asserts that the dual marginality theme entails degrees of tensions and the ability to live with contradictions, but that is the challenge facing intellectuals, and it's a challenge they cannot escape: they live in a split society, and they, with their education and keen insights must be beacons, not only to Black Americans but also to white Americans as well.

Aldon Morris reassesses the evolution of social protest and social movements on the quest for Black Liberation and the manner in which black protest has historically shaped all arguments and the general discourse on democracy, freedom, and liberation, at home and abroad. Morris asks what constituted the genius of the Civil Rights Movement, and answers that both the leaders and the participants together made the movement so successful after the leaders and the movement participants soon recognized that the social change for which they fought would only come if they could "generate massive crises within the Jim Crow order." In addition, the idea was also to stage massive national demonstrations so that foreign media would be well informed and politicians and citizens in Europe, Asia, Africa, and Latin America would know, thus connecting American national treatment of blacks to the on-going Cold War then at its peak, between the United States and Russia. Morris links the importance of the Civil Rights Movement to other movements which were inspired by it: Student; Women's; Farm Workers; Native America; Disability; Gay and Lesbian; and Environmental. He also contends that he sees no reason why the Movement could not continue to be relevant into the twenty-first century, but for it to function, it has to answer the key questions: Who is currently the enemy? Can a black protest movement emerge and be sustained if it is not anchored in the black community?, and is there a sufficient level of institutional strength in the black community to sustain a national protest movement? Though difficult, he does not see the possibilities as impossible.

The second half of Morris' paper is an important case study of racial inequality within the American Sociological Association (ASA) and why and how racial inequality within ASA prompted the emergence of a social protest movement within the association. He views racial inequality, along with gender and class inequality, as endemic within all professional national organizations in that these organizations mirror the racial, class, and gender perspectives of the dominant culture. Using data from the ASA's National Office, the book on Black Sociologists edited by Blackwell and Janowitz, and various articles published in the American Sociologists, Morris documents how the organizational structure, award system, and annual programmatic structure all represented an ASA which was as segregated as any structure had been during the nadir for blacks during the worse eras of Jim Crow. Morris presents a concise, but detective-like progression of the events, which led to the presentation of demands from black sociologists, then the creation of a caucus of Black Sociologists in 1969. This caucus was formalized into the Caucus of Black Sociologists in 1970. Later Morris compares the relative success of the Caucus, which eventually became the Association of Black Sociologists (ABA) with the controversy over the selection of a black editor of the ASA journal, American Sociological Review (ASR). A black co-editor was chosen, along with a white co-editor, and many blacks began a petition largely conducted using e-mails and electronic attachments; however, the petition did not have the necessary 500 signatures. Morris makes an interesting point in explaining the failure of the petition movement, and asks if protests and social movements can ever be successfully waged if, rather than the face-to-face encounters as was true with the national Civil Rights Movement and the Caucus of Black Sociologists, future protests had to be waged through the electronic e-mails and e-mail attachments, as was the case with the editorship conflict.

The essay by Rodney Coates begins by indicting social analysts of presenting an overly deterministic assessment of social life, with an over emphasis on social structure and an under emphasis of "the role of black agency and free will." He concludes that historically, the black response to subservient status in America falls into three main areas: passive, reactive, and direct action. In a unique view of the Civil Rights Movement Coates posits the genesis of the Civil Rights Movement as occurring with the advent of Western Imperialism, and breaks the movement into four main historical divisions, each with its own history, cultural, and sociological constellations:

The Movement in Colonial and Revolutionary America; the Movement in Ante and Post-Bellum America; the modern Civil Rights Movement, and the Post-Civil Rights Movement. It is this last Movement, the Post-Civil Rights Movement, which Coates believes to be crucial if racial justice is ever to be achieved. The key to this racial justice is the concept of Social Justice which, according to Coates, can only be achieved if the society, especially whites, recognize that race is an important legacy of America's history, and this recognition cries out for new ways of approaching the racial question. First of all, according to Coates, the notion of social justice is only possible if guilt ceases to be placed at the feet of whites, and if blacks cease to claim victim status. Such "guilt and victim-hood politics," Coates claims, "rarely lead to anything but embarrassed, reluctance on the part of the guilty, and frustration and anxiety on the part of the victim." This cycle of recrimination makes it difficult for both sides to respond in ways acceptable to the other, producing in the white community a "compassion fatigue," and in the black community a "nihilism." These negative behavioral attitudes and actions by whites and blacks must be abandoned to "restore the African to his proper place in our global universe." Lastly, Coates concludes by asserting that three central social policy outlines must be activated if the African's proper place in the universe is to be a reality: reparation, affirmative empowerment, and affirmative opportunity.

The essay by Antoine Joseph begins by revisiting the central issue in the formation of the American Republic – the meaning of democracy for the new republic, the workable plan for majority–minority power and relations, and the enactment of policies to ensure an adequate checks and balances system. At stake was the desire to avoid what many believed to be one of the negative fall-outs from this new system of democracy–the danger of "majoritarian tyranny." Joseph begins his paper with this theoretical model in order to test that model against the actual practice of majoritarian tyranny as it exists in the twenty-first century between blacks and the dominant white society. With the Katrina case as his model, Joseph sketches a brief history of the "Old Racism" of Wallace, Faubus, and Maddox, in which racism was overt and manifest, and there were few attempts to hide racist and discriminatory intent. This racism is juxtaposed to the "New Racism" in which the appeal is subtler, indirect, and covert. He cites cases surrounding the associations and utterances of Lott, Ashcroft, Barbour, Helms, the Willie Horton advertisements, and the uses of the confederate flag throughout the South as examples of this new racism, which is packaged and wrapped in the theology and politics of "conservative populism." This populism, according to Joseph, given its antigovernment intervention agenda and its opposition to social programs, has great appeal to lower and working-class white ethnics who are in direct competition with minorities for jobs, government benefits, and social services. The result has been the entrenchment of the politics of racial polarization, which precludes opportunities for class and racial cooperation. This, plus the fact that currently all three branches of the government are controlled by the Republican Party have, Joseph contends, sharpened, and made more evident majoritarian rule and majoritarian tyranny which can be seen in the unequal distribution of the nation's resources. According to Joseph, this does not bode well for the future of Black America.

In projecting educational objectives for the twenty-first century Charles Willie urges us to revisit the 1950s and 1960s, decades of social conflicts, but also decades of massive social change. He also asks that we do not forget that one of the main lessons of these two decades was that "blacks assumed responsibility for their own liberation and took to the streets with demonstrations to initiate change." Taking to the streets was, according to Willie, "an internal declaration by people of color that they are free," for as Martin Luther King, Jr. himself said of the Civil Rights Act of 1964, and Willie quotes him: "this legislation was written in the streets." Wilson questions the validity of arguments designed to compare blacks with whites and other groups with respect to how fast blacks must go to achieve parity with whites and other groups. He views such logic as unsound and unproductive. Instead, he wishes to assess blacks from their educational points of departure. That is, to gage their progress from the point from which they started. This argument is sound because Willie thinks it impossible to assume any black parity with whites and other groups until there is a decline and decrease in discrimination against blacks. He uses a similar argument against comparing correlations between education and income between blacks and whites, and his reason for objecting to this comparison is the same: We're not going to have the education–income parity with whites until income and wages discrimination against blacks disappear. He also challenges the manner in which whites shifted the education paradigm from "equal access to education" to "equal outcome from education," believing blacks were wrong to accept this shift, and should, instead, have insisted on a dual approach to the education issue, one emphasizing both access and outcome. In this argument, Willie contends that it is not education which should be criticized but the society which is "less willing to reward blacks compared to whites for increased educational attainment." Finally, Willie proposes the adoption of specific educational policies for this new century to negate the problems which have represented the negative legacies of the twentieth century: Howard Gardner's theories of complimentarity and multiple intelligences.

The glass ceiling in academia is the central theme of the paper by the late Bette Woody and Diane R. Brown. Like essays previously discussed, they analyze old and new forms of racial and gender discrimination and ask, why in the era of the advancement of women, black women encounter a "glass ceiling" in the nation's prestigious doctoral and research institutions? The authors document the evolution of increases in black women's college and university enrollment throughout the 1980s and 1990s. The startling data has been the drastic decline in black men's college and university enrollment during those same periods. The other startling data relates to the lack of advancement among black women in filling the vacuum left by the drastic decline in black men's enrollment. The authors posit the view that black women are caught in the intersection of gender and race, and as such are victimized by a "dual disadvantage" in economic status. The inability of black women to succeed in doctoral and research institutions, the authors assert, may be explained by three factors: the lack of senior faculty mentors, the 'chilly atmosphere' in the academic institution, and inappropriate sexual behavior and conversations; possible difficulties in finding peers for collaborative cooperation in writing grants and publications, and participation on committees and attendance at professional meetings; Black women may be handicapped by being shunted aside on community services committees, diversity committees, and serving extra-advisory roles to minority and women students.

The sociology of racial socialization has provided keen insights into the process by which young people are initiated into the cult of racism. As we move into the twenty-first century it is important to note the subtle and not so subtle ways, in which assumptions surrounding the idea of race is used and understood. The idea of an initiation into racial socialization is important because becoming a racist was explored by Rutledge M. Dennis in an earlier article depicting autobiographical writers who were children and youth in the 1920s, 1930s, and 1940s. In the present preliminary and exploratory study, he was interested in the process by which youth in the 1980s and 1990s navigated the minefield of race and assumptions about race. Given the rigid racial divide between blacks and whites in the 1920s through the 1960s, what whites collectively experienced about blacks and their attitudes about those experiences and attitudes reflected the racism accepted and believed. It is in this sense that racism was a religion and a dogma, believed in as fervently as one believed in any religious faith and dogma. These student journals reflect ambivalence on the part of many students, however, more than that, they reflect a changing racial consciousness over time with respect to race and Black America. The journals also reflect the fact that by the 1980s and 1990s, most white students in public schools were attending these schools with black students in varying white–black student ratio, and were participating with these students in various activities: band, choir, sports, class projects, and honor societies. They thus knew more about these students than previous generations of whites. For this reason, many were often willing and able to stand up to a parent, usually the father, who wanted them to disassociate themselves from their black classmates and friends. Why this changing racial consciousness is important for blacks in the twenty-first century has to be understood from the vantage point of future intergroup cooperation and alliances. And as suggested by Bennett's article, these same whites and/or their children may indeed form the army of those comprising a future environmental peace and justice movement. This is not to suggest that racism has or will quickly disappear. It does suggest that collective black selfinterest would dictate that blacks continue to play a decisive institutional role in all sectors of the society and continue to keep their figures on the racial and class pulse of the nation.

The essay by Ashley Duane highlights the evolution of "color-blindness" as a racial ideology as expressed through the national discourse on race, a racial discourse in which the society engages as dominant groups attempt to promote and legitimize their ideological perspectives on race and matters surrounding race. Conversely, less dominant groups challenging dominant groups' perspectives seek to undermine the dominant assessment and rally their allies and supporters for their particular version of the racial discourse, and as Duane states it, this public discourse has to be understood both as "a contested process and as a political conflict." As Duane mentions briefly, the color-blindness metaphor is often cited with reference to the well-known quote of Martin Luther King, Jr., and what Duane asserts is that racists and those who purport to deny the reality of race, seek to turn Dr. King's statement from social structural reality to one signifying "good feelings." According to Duane, those favoring an elite discourse on the ideology of race and color-blindness include the Thernstroms, Dinesh D'Souza, and Ward Connerly, and at the heart of their ideology is a denial of racism and the dangers of "reverse racism" and the "quota system." They further contend that race is merely a social construction, hence ideas of racial identity and racial consciousness, if such exists, are merely phantom and social constructs created to politically enhance the power base of specific groups. Along with disputing the theory of color-blindness Duane challenges issues currently included in the racial discourse: the emergence of the theme of "racial ambiguity" and the "demonizing of diversity."

Roscigno, Garcia, Mong, and Byron provide the reader with a unique look at data supporting the pervasiveness of workplace discrimination. Heretofore, employment problems and difficulties, as the authors assert, especially for Black Americans, have been blamed on levels of "skills deficits" and differences in human capital. According to the authors, if one accepts this position, "African Americans will earn lower wages, have less organizational power, and fewer overall economic opportunities." However, they contend, this may not be the case. Rather, discriminatory practices, arbitrary decision-making, and subjective decisions may play a much larger role than previously assumed in issues of hiring, promotion, and firings. Analyzing all cases of racial discrimination filed with the Civil Rights Commission in the state of Ohio from 1988 through 2003, they were able to assess and document examples of general harassment, racist remarks, isolation, etc. The highest percentage of racial discrimination cases involved firing, followed by harassment, lack of promotion or a demotion, and discrimination in hiring. This study supports the view of previously discussed researchers that racial discrimination is not dead, though it is often more difficult to detect.

George Wilson's essay analyzes the life-chance opportunities among impoverished and middle class African Americans. He focuses on how segregation affects life-chance opportunities for the middle class in employment and the impoverished class in residence, and his central thesis is that "employment and residence structure the racialization of life-chance opportunities." He draws on "equivalency analysis" research in racial stratification to buttress his case, for unlike many theories which assessed the class bases of racial inequality, internal colonialism, split-labor market, and competition theory, Wilson, using equivalency analysis, challenges the idea that impoverished blacks and whites encountered similar life-chance opportunities. He further contends that "permanent poverty" is more likely to be the fate of the black impoverished, who would also become economically marginal and more spatially concentrated than would the white impoverished. According to Wilson, with these forces lined against them the black impoverished might, as others have suggested, move toward fatalism, resignation, and the creation of an "oppositional culture." Despite their middle-class status and the occupational gains made during the 1970s, 1980s, and 1990s, racialization in employment has affected black economic advancement due to the middle-class blacks' inclusion into a segregate job network, residing in communities in which higher percentages of the residents are impoverished, and working in organizations where they may be expected to handle "minority issues" and minority customers. Like many other contributors Wilson juxtaposes the old racism and discrimination to the more modern forms. He alludes to matters of subtleties, institutional, and nonracial dynamics, to describe "modern racial discrimination" as Pettigrew describes it. This modern form is not based on "ill–will," but it is indirect and based on "business necessity" and self-interest." Wilson cautions the society, especially Black Americans, to remain alert to the vestiges of racism. He predicts that (1) segregation in employment and housing will not decrease; (2) the negative consequences of segregation shows no signs of weakening; (3) political intervention, once used to remedy and address social ills, is on the wane, and (4) additional research is needed to ascertain how "patterns of integration across the residential and employment spheres explains racialization across the American class structure."

L. Adele Jinadu's essay advances the view that the changing geopolitical needs of the United States and African nations must address crucial historical and contemporary issues before both can adequately shore up their relations to meet the changing demands of the twenty-first century. In outlining the areas and issues of interest to both, Jinadu begins by outlining five assumptions necessary in charting a more positive relationship between the United States and Africa: (1) Foreign relations should be a the locus for the intersection of the national interests of various state–actors or nation–states; (2) U.S.–African relations must be assessed within contexts of each political entity's domestic politics; (3) Future U.S.–African relations should highlight the role of nonstate transnational actors (private sector groups and individual citizens); (4) U.S.–African relations must be grounded in ideas of mutuality of respect and reciprocity, and (5) U.S.–African relationship in the twenty-first century must be based on shared similarities – their shared colonial experiences and their common break with colonial rule. Both the U.S. and Africa must be attentive to their mutual internal domestic political structure, for it tends to guide and shape eventual foreign relations agreements and possibilities. In the U.S., the structure of U.S.–African relations has been affected by whichever political party is in office because, according to Jinadu, Republican congresses tend to pay less attention to Africa. Since this is the case, it has meant that the only group which has advanced the case for African issues and concerns, the Congressional Black Caucus, has been weakened and their influence on African issues diminished. In addition, when Republicans control the congress they are more likely to greatly restrict financial and technical aid to Africa. In Africa the domestic policy agenda as in many countries has centered on grassroot effort to facilitate both empowerment and democracy. Secondly, the end of warfare in Angola and Mozambique has provided unique opportunities for the U.S. and Africa to begin a process of mutual reconciliation and trust. The most troubling issue for both the U.S. and Africa has been the rise of civil and ethnic wars and the conflicts between the U.S. and Africa regarding human rights violations in many African nations. Jinadu ends his essay with a call for more African American participation and involvement in African issues. More than that, he calls for an African American agenda for U.S.–Africa policy in the twenty-first century.

Recently, more attention has been devoted to the African Diaspora and transnational identities and other concerns. Joao H. Costa Vargas's unique case study of a largely African American social activist organization, the Coalition Against Police Abuse (CAPA) and its transnational linkage with the Jacarezinho favela in Rio de Janeiro, Brazil, is instructive for several reasons: Collectively, and singly, each uniquely evokes ideas of identity politics and the policy of "radical becoming." Drawing on ethnographic data from the Jacarezinho favela and CAPA in Los Angeles, Costa Vargas incorporates ideas from black feminist and critical race theorists and positions his identity politics and theory of becoming into a sociopolitical framework which assists in enhancing racial consciousness as a vehicle for ensuring social justice for marginal groups. One of the problems in the Los Angeles–Rio interface has been the historic differences in conceptualizing race and racism in the United States and Brazil. According to Costa Vargas this difference, with U.S. blacks having a more rigid definition of racial categories, and Brazilians having less rigid definitions of the relationship between color and racial categories. It would be a difference, which would persist from the beginning of their encounters until the very end. What the encounter did make possible, however, was the facilitation of a greater dialogue within Brazilian society, which enabled such issues as black beauty, interracial marriage, affirmative action, quotas, and reparations. The immediate common threads uniting the two groups were examples of police brutality, unemployment, and the lack of necessary public services. But a more central idea connecting the two communities, according to Costa Vargas, is the black radical tradition which had been the foundation of diaspora thought in the Americas.

As African and Caribbean blacks increasingly comprise greater percentages of the Black American population, more scholars are beginning to delve into subtle and not so subtle differences between Native Blacks, Afro-Caribbean, and African Immigrants. *Theorizing Heterogeneity* by Sherrill Sellers, Hiu Ha Florence Chong, and Michelle Harris analyzes the social and economic well-being between the three groups by using census data from 1990 to 2000. They assess the groups by using three theoretical models: Assimilation, Cultural, and Ethnic Penalty. The traditional Assimilation Model assumes that each immigrant group will eventually integrate into mainstream white middle-class society. The authors suggest that this process of integration is more problematic than many assume, for the question is, within which community will immigrants integrate? An ethnic community, a white middle-class community, or a black inner-city underclass community? Secondly, the Cultural perspective proffers the view that norms and values are crucial in determining the social and economic success of ethnic groups and immigrants. Lastly, the Ethnic Penalty Model focuses on the role of ethnicity in a group's mobility. The authors conclude that the latter model more accurately describes the plight of Native Blacks, Afro-Caribbeans, and African Immigrants life-chances in that the three groups have lower income, higher poverty, and higher unemployment than whites.

Finally, the essay by Amy Ansell, like many previous essays, evokes a comparison of the "old racism of apartheid" to "new forms of racism" in the postapartheid era. Ansell's research is an analysis of 154 written submissions to the Head Office of the South African Human Rights Commission as a prelude to the South African National Conference on Racism in 2000. The manner in which black and white South African's approach the idea of race leads the author to suggest the existence of "two nations of discourse." These two national discourses reflect an ideological bifurcation. Unlike the old forms of racism the new form does not project overt racial hatred, nor is it mean-spirited and suggestive of the ideology of white supremacy.

However, though unspoken, the position of whites reflect "a racially in-egalitarian status quo," but rather than racism residing in the "white mind," says the writer, it rather resides in the "socio-historical contexts which gives it purchase." The challenge to the new South Africa, the author contends, is not so much to detect those who use code words to hide their racism. Rather, it is more important to understand the process by which racism adapts and changes. Lastly, Ansell advocates that a structural analysis enables a deeper understanding of power and race relations in South Africa. Such an analysis brings into sharper focus both the construction of whiteness and the relationship between racial ideology, racial inequality, and racial dominance.

Rodney D. Coates
Rutledge M. Dennis
Editors

PART I:
THE NEW BLACK: A CONCEPTUAL FRAMEWORK

THE INTELLECTUAL AS A REPRESENTATIVE OF THE "NEW BLACK": CHALLENGES FOR THE 21ST CENTURY

Rutledge M. Dennis

When societies experience cataclysmic and revolutionary political, economic, or cultural changes, their members may use these opportunities to cleanse themselves of previous spiritual and political attributes, that is, shed their former skins and declare themselves reborn as a New People or a New Nation. Alain Locke (1925) suggested such an idea when he wrote his much celebrated essay in The New Negro. When he used the term "new," he was referring to a collective and individual belief and mood that, among blacks, a virtual "metamorphosis" had taken place "beyond the watch and guard of statistics." That this metamorphosis was visible and obvious, was beyond questioning, but also to be understood was the reality that the metamorphosis did not suddenly occur phoenix like in the midst of a barren nothingness. Rather, as Locke suggested, this "New Black" was below the radar in white America, and "beyond the watch and guard of statistics." It was a group, a people who, having lived in dank quarters for so long, was slowly moving from its enclosed cocoon, slowly emerging from its long hibernation to blossom and take creative flight.

The New Black: Alternative Paradigms and Strategies for the 21st Century
Research in Race and Ethnic Relations, Volume 14, 3–30
Copyright © 2007 by Elsevier Ltd.
ISSN: 0195-7449/doi:10.1016/S0195-7449(06)14001-5

Locke concluded that a new vigor, new spirit, new courage, new mission, and more importantly, a new consciousness, had emerged among significant portions of the black population, the general population as well as the class of educators, creators, and cultural disseminators known as "intellectuals." It was W. E. B. Du Bois (1970[1897]), however, who tapped into and alerted the world to what must have been a revolutionary idea when he first proclaimed it: that fast on the heels of the post-Civil War era, a new group, and a new class had emerged among the black population; it would be an educated cadre whose mission would be that of assisting in the elevation of a largely impoverished population, and of assisting the nation in coming to grips with its racial past and chart a new course for future generations. He announced this radical proposal in an essay published by The American Negro Academy. There he proposed the outlines for a black radical intellectual insurgence whose main responsibilities would be that of creating "race organizations" and institutions which would occupy the front-line position against racial and social injustice: colleges, newspapers, business organizations, a school of literature and art, and "an intellectual clearing house for all these products of the Negro mind which we may call a Negro Academy." Implicit in Du Bois' concept of the intellectual role was the duty of initiating and sustaining a much needed feeling of "race consciousness" among the masses of the black population which would facilitate the construction of various in-group organizational and institutional networks so vital to this cause.

Later in an article, "The Talented Tenth", Du Bois (1971[1903]) expanded upon this theme and laid the sociological and philosophical foundations for what might be seen as both a theory of black intellectuals and the accompanying explanations of the complex intricacies of the life, world, and work of intellectuals. According to him, they were to be "leaders of thought and missionaries of culture among their people." Integral to this movement would be the elite cadre's role (both interracially and intraracially) as objective truth searchers and as social activist/reformers. The 1897 speech and the 1903 paper constituted the beginning of a relatively consistent and cogent Du Boisian social, political, and economic thesis to which he basically adhered throughout his life. The central features of the thesis were his attacks on the economics and culture of capitalism, the attacks on the American political system and its acceptance of racial and social inequality, and his reiterations to black people that they must be different, be better than whites, and be willing to lead the charge for their own freedom, through alliances whenever necessary, but alone if necessary, if freedom were to be attained.

This paper is an exploratory survey of the sociology of an idea: The intellectual class as the New. We will note the continuities and discontinuities around this theme as we trace its evolution from the late nineteenth century assumptions of Du Bois, on to the reformulations of this theme in the essays and books of Kelly Miller, Alain Locke, and Harold Cruse. Finally, we illustrate how the twenty-first century has prompted a reassessment of the black intellectual role, as that role has had to be re-defined by changing social, political, and economic circumstances, both at home and abroad. Thus, a persistent theme throughout this paper is a probing of the changing situations, and circumstances which made it possible for an intellectual class to have emerged in a society rife with racial and class injustices as well as sexual injustices. Understanding the emergence of the theme and how its role was played reflected a point-counterpoint, action-reaction, and a reformist-radical stance of "one step forward and two steps backwards." Both the nation and the world, and black America, changed because of the situational variables they encountered as they responded to everyday realities.

The idea of the New Person stands out in these early speeches and articles, for it signifies Du Bois' keen analysis of the interaction of history, sociology, economics, and politics in the making of the New World and the New America. He believed similar knowledge, ideals, values, and social pressures were necessary in creating the New Negro, and since he believed the New Negro was crucial in shaping the New America, he placed great emphasis on a reshaping and remolding of the Negro Mind. This central theme is the foundation of his use of sociology, psychology, and history as they relate to the black population. This is why he frequently cited Toussaint Louverture and his attempt to create a New Haiti as a forerunner of resurgent rebels in this country who sought to remold the American social and psychological landscape. He saw David Walker's "Appeal" and the revolts by Nat Turner, Gabriel Prosser, and Denmark Vesey as heeding the call for a new freedom and the birth of the New Man, as the term was then used. Later, he described in a similar manner the anti-slavery social activism of Frederick Douglass, Harriet Tubman, Sojourner Truth, and a host of others as a signal of the birth of freedom and liberty in the country. There was anger in his speech and in the article, but despite the anger, Du Bois threw down the challenge to blacks and to whites, but more often than not, he wanted to arouse what he believed should be a deeply rooted black collective racial consciousness which he believed would overcome the existing economic and political problems confronting blacks. His exhortations to blacks during this time seemed to be more centered on touching a nerve, which might energize their collective "will power" which would then ignite a more massive "will to freedom." Quite frankly, both he and Booker T. Washington appeared to be appealing to what they wished were latent "will to endure" and "will to succeed" characteristics among blacks (see Dennis, 2006), and what they might do to make these latent feelings and ideas into manifest actions and behavior. The importance of the "will" was used to explain a variety of behavior throughout the nineteenth century and the early decades of the twentieth century. In fact, so much of the Du Boisian emphasis on collective social action seemed to have been based on the exercise of individual wills and for the group, a collective will. This he may have gotten from his teacher at Harvard, the philosopher and psychologist William James (1954[1896]), whose popular idea of "the will to believe" was consistent with similar ideas of "the will" which permeated European and American philosophical thought throughout the nineteenth century.

Of great importance here is that the two essays by Du Bois were written less than 40 years after the civil war. Both essays were expressly enthusiastic regarding the role of the educated elite (intellectuals) and why they might have no other recourse than taking on this major role, a theme repeated later in *The Souls of Black Folk* (1903). After all, they were the ones most prepared, blessed by fate, as Du Bois summarized their positions and accomplishments. Du Bois reasoned that if blacks were going to advance, those most prepared educationally, culturally, and economically would be in a better position to do so, and in the process, help others not so fortunate. Du Bois' charge to intellectuals echoes the Luke Thesis which has become a part of contemporary expectations, especially among racial, ethnic, cultural groups: that if one is able to rise out of poverty due to a series of circumstances, good fortune, hard work, etc., one is then obligated to "give back" something to the group from which one emerged. As stated in Luke 12:48: "For unto whomever much is given, of him shall be much required: and to whom men have committed much, of him they will ask the more." It is interesting to trace Du Bois' concept of the educated strata (Dennis, 1977; Dennis, 1997) from these early essay pronouncements to the late 1950s and early 1960s to note his changing views of American intellectuals and the circumstances which prompted him to change his views on the role of black American intellectuals. Tracing this evolution permits us to understand more fully the evolution of social structural forces emerging within black communities: the attachment of the vast majority of black voters to the Democratic Party, the mass migration of millions of black Southerners to the North and West, the quest for integration as a key movement within predominately black organizations, the Civil Rights Movement, the Black

Power Movement, world wars and regional wars, the politics and economics of the "cold war," the anti-colonial wars throughout Africa, Asia, and parts of Latin America, the devastations of inner city work and patterns of social relationships due to shifts in the global economy, and the resistance to limited and slow integration when it began to occur. All of these issues would play a role in the rise of intellectuals and the roles and positions they would have in the American social, political, and economic landscape.

Another early twentieth century view of black intellectuals was presented by the mathematician-sociologist Kelly Miller (1968[1908]). He largely repeated Du Bois' rationale for supporting an intellectual class, viewing "enlightened blacks" as a "superior class"(culturally, educationally, and collectively possessing a greater degree of individual and group consciousness) upon whom would be "imposed unusual responsibility and opportunity for service." Like Du Bois, Miller attributed the gains made by blacks, indeed the very survival of blacks, to the enormous efforts of teachers, physicians, ministers, and writers; like Du Bois, Miller lauded these men and women for their past and current contributions to black life. And like Du Bois, there was never the slightest hint that the intellectuals would default on their obligations. What was necessary to both Du Bois and Miller in their interpretation of the intellectual role was the linking of this class' mission to the needs of the general black population. This is why both men, though Du Bois more than Miller, saw the acquisition and development of racial and class consciousness among intellectuals as vital to their mission.

During the period when Du Bois and Miller explicated their views on intellectuals, the social and political exclusion of blacks from the larger white society was virtually complete, and the gulf between racial and ethnic groups very wide. Perhaps, for this reason, we cannot even speak of blacks as marginal since there were minimal economic ties and relationships but few social/interracial ties. Therefore, if the intellectuals described by both men were marginal, they were also marginal to their own, black, communities, and their marginality focused on the fact that they had access to higher education, knew more, and hence, thought more about their plight and the plight of fellow blacks. For these reasons, according to both Du Bois and Miller, they would be, or ought to be on the frontline of efforts to redress the grievances of their people and devise strategies and tactics to assist in group freedom.

Throughout the 1910s, a series of events occurred to alter the subtext of black life in America, thereby diverting the themes by Du Bois and Miller. However, these events would alter the political and socio-cultural landscape of the American nation and promote greater individual and collective racial

consciousness among Black America: World War I, the death of Booker
T. Washington, the creation of the NAACP, and the rise of Garveyism and
his Universal Negro Improvement Association (UNIA). As Du Bois suggested in his Talented Tenth article, this new racial and class consciousness
would more readily be achieved and demonstrated by the more educated,
the educated cadre.

In the next decade Locke (1969[1925]) would edit a volume whose title,
"The New Negro", was also the title of the first article by Locke in the book.
He, and a host of other writers in the volume, simply celebrated the birth of
The New Negro as a new type, a new personality, which would constitute
the making of a new "group sociology" whose very birth would alter the
social, political, economic, and cultural fabric and dynamics of the inner
world of blacks as well as the larger dominant white world. Commentators
in the New Negro volume wished to describe how this transformation had
occurred, the current fruits of this transformation, and what might be long-
term consequences of this metamorphosis. It is also important to keep in
mind that though Washington and Du Bois debated tactics and strategies,
both wanted to create a New Negro. If Du Bois' position entailed a rejection
of the existing capitalist economics and culture as soulless, exploitative, and
cruel, Washington thought the New Negro would be heavily grounded in
the principles of the capitalist–entrepreneur model. An interesting assertion
here is the idea that Washington, too, was an intellectual, though of a
different sort, plus the fact that he saw himself in opposition to intellectual
types. But he was clearly an organizational and bureaucratic intellectual.
What sets them apart had nothing to do with their respective desires to
create the New Man (New Person), but rather the divergent roads each saw
as making it possible to achieve that goal.

The birth of the "new" is often heralded after revolutionary wars, revolts,
and radical political and economic changes. For example, after their respective revolutions both America and France, and later Russia (Heller,
1988) and China (Smith, 1990) heralded the "new man" in order to place
distance between pre- and post-revolutionary individuals and societal values; likewise, in our own era, many writers sought to document the rise of
the "new woman" during the height of the feminist movement in the United
States. In a similar fashion, the men's consciousness movement has spawned
ideas of the "new man." During the anti-colonial era in Africa, Nkrumah
(1970[1963]) and others called for the emergence of a New Africa, which
for many was anti-Western and anti-capitalist, while for others it simply
meant abandoning Western hegemony and replacing it with their own local
version.

The use of the term "new" simply reflects a desire to move away from the old stereotypes, values, and behavior of the past, and to create, nurture, and affirm new images, and perhaps new myths and stereotypes for the present and future. The activities of the "New Negro" fell within the socio-cultural and artistic boundaries enunciated by Du Bois, in as much as the tone of the Renaissance would be dialectical: both separatist and particularistic, but also, both integrationist and cosmopolitan. But the unique feature of this social "newness" as expressed in the New Negro (1928) was that it would not only encompass the cultural and artistic, but also the social, educational, and economic, represented by the writings of social scientists such as W. E. B. Du Bois, E. Franklin Frazier, Charles Johnson, Kelly Miller, Robert Moton, Walter White, Melville Herskovits, and Elise Johnson McDougald. As expressed by sociologists, historians, and political scientists, the newness represented a bold breaking the social and emotional shackles of the past and emerging as a "whole" person. What was interesting about the New Negro volume was the general self-consciousness among the contributors that they indeed did represent a new class of black scholars and artistic and scholastic activists who were interested in demonstrating that blacks were like whites, but different, and different from whites, but similar. While discussions of the Renaissance generally focus on literary, artistic, or scholarly creativity, little attention has been devoted to the massive revolution in political and racial consciousness initiated by Marcus Garvey and his UNIA. But as Cruse (1967, 1968) documents so well in his books, Garvey and his movement would evoke a storm of protest and opposition from middle-class blacks who, generally, did not want their status, and that of the masses of blacks to move from racial segregation to isolation as black colonies in Africa as Garvey's program proposed. However, then Garvey, and later Cruse, would not pose the issue as one between integration and segregation, but rather between segregation and integration in the U.S., and "independence" in Africa, or on another level, between a pro-black nationalism and a pro-white integration.

Perhaps the defining feature of The New Negro is the generally positive position by the authors regarding the social and artistic transformation taking place and how and why they view this as a harbinger of even greater change to come. That is, viewing the history of enslavement and the post-slave experience, the writers were heralding a victory of having come through that experience. And despite the on-going brutalization of blacks in the South and the disfranchisement there, and the persistence of segregation in the North, the Renaissance and the coming of the New Negro provided a hope that even if revolutionary changes were not forthcoming, steady incremental changes would occur. This feeling permeates the entire volume.

The Harlem Renaissance would attract and involve cultural intellectuals, but that movement would be short lived. Political and organizational intellectuals would play a much larger and more sustained and consistent role in the community life of blacks in Harlem and throughout the nation. In the 1920s, intellectuals within the NAACP, the Urban League and Marcus Garvey's UNIA, and a host of socialist and nationalist organizations would have as their themes large and small variations on issues such as assimilation and separatism and cultural monism and cultural pluralism. Of great importance during this period, and perhaps a point missed or viewed as unnecessary by Harold Cruse, was the fact that this era offered blacks the first legitimate opportunity to move outside of the two established political parties, neither of which was interested in the political participation of blacks, since both parties adhered to the general racist values and policies of the society. Given this choice, and not wanting to move to the political right, it is understandable why many black intellectuals viewed parties on the left, socialists and communists, as allies in the struggle against racism, social injustice, and colonialism. Viewing Garvey as too nationalistic and too separatist, and in some cases wrongheaded, and assessing the NAACP as too non-political, parties of the extreme left espoused policies of inclusion and internationalism views which appealed to the desire of intellectuals to play decisive roles in the larger American society.

Cultural intellectual creativity and heightened class and racial consciousness were re-directed inwardly: a return to certain folk traditions and customs and the introduction of African themes in novels, plays, and poems. The interracial contacts were made possible largely as a result of the opening of Harlem as a social and sexual playground for whites who made weekend forays into Harlem to experience the other side of the racial divide. Again, it is important to note that the interracial contacts were engaged in by blacks of all classes, but the whites engaging in this contact were generally from the middle and upper classes and generally among the social and cultural elites, for it must be remembered that during this era and for many years afterward, New York was a segregated city, and as the history of clubs in Harlem and downtown New York illustrated, black performers could perform, but were not welcome or permitted in the audience as customers.

Thus, the Du Bois–Miller era, which represented a rigidly segregated world, which largely confined black intellectuals to the black world, was transcended by a world in which intellectuals moved among the elite cultural and economic world of whites in Harlem and throughout New York City, though the city itself was largely segregated. The Harlem Renaissance represented an opening of the Black Mind, the White Mind, a look into the Black

Psyche and the White Psyche, and an intense critique and observation of both the subsystems and subcultures of Black America and White America. For the first time in history, black creative artists and other black professionals were experiencing a cultural revolution of sorts, but it would be a short-lived revolution, cut short by several events and social factors (Bronz, 1964): Few blacks could afford to purchase the books and art works; white intellectuals shifted their time and energies toward the coming Great Depression, while more than 60 percent of the residents of Harlem were on public relief.

Harold Cruse's (1967) insightful and politically and historically rich book on New York intellectuals was yet another step in the unfolding of the socio-politics of intellectuals. His book would be both a critique and a crucial link between the political and racial culture of the 1920s and 1930s and illustrate how events of these eras would demonstrate continuities and discontinuities with the culture and politics of the 1940s, 1950s, and 1960s. What differentiated Cruse's interests from the interests of Locke and others in their discussions of the Renaissance were the latter's focus on artistic and cultural matters, whereas Cruse is primarily interested in, and emphasized politics and political philosophy and political and social theory. Cruse's ire was directed toward two groups and two ideologies: those whom he believed were less attentive to the black cultural agenda, but were instead lulled by the integrationist promises and policies of liberal politics on one hand, and those who were duped into adhering to socialist and communist policies on the other. Though his book is a case study of the politics of Harlem, it also gives the reader an inside look into the policies and practices of the Communist Party, U.S.A., and the various socialist parties which competed with the Communist Party, and each other, for the allegiance of both intellectuals and workers. His book is rich in the insider's perspectives, and he documents them from his then experience, because he was once a member of the party. Having had this experience he understood the problems encountered by black creative writers and artists who sought to project and develop programs and policies around black themes. This attempt opened them to charges of being nationalistic, bourgeois and regressive. Cruse's "crisis" centered on the inability of black creative artists and writers to play the cards closely associated with what they do best: the cultural card. He reasoned that since blacks in the United States will probably never acquire political or economic power, the historical and collective black strength and overall contributions to American life lies on the cultural front. For him, his book is a cautionary tale for black intellectuals in pursuit of artistic and cultural freedom. Just as he views the two American political parties as incapable of accepting the black cultural agenda, he reasoned that oppositional parties on the left were no better. The entire book repeats the theme of a major crisis among black intellectuals. Since black intellectuals, in the Du Boisian sense, are cultural creators as well as interpreters, if they have a crisis, it must have grave societal consequences. To eliminate the crisis, intellectuals must dig deeply into their cultural roots in order to ex-cavate and orient their novels, stories, songs, and poetry, and dance around cultural themes derived from the organic centers of black life.

Cruse's description of the political and theoretical turf wars of the 1930s and 1940s introduced the reader to a new phenomenon: the cultural and political marginality of the intellectual. Cruse's treatment of this marginal cultural and political class enables us to examine what would be the ambivalent role of blacks as intellectuals in predominately white political organizations, in this case, socialists and communists. Cruse presents a case of black intellectuals in white political organizations to illustrate his point that blacks will never be free to develop their cultural and political agenda within white organizations, or black organizations, especially those organizations whose strategies and pro-grams elevate class analysis over racial and ethnic analysis, socialists and com-munists, or elevate racial and social integration policies over nationalist ones.

The class–race problem was at the heart of the marginalization of black writers and artists who join the socialist and communist parties in search of an emotional and intellectual home. A similar marginalization was experi-enced by Du Bois in the 1930s in his dispute with the NAACP over his attempt to develop a black-oriented economic program, the Black Economic Commonwealth, during the depression. The integrationist policies of the NAACP could not accept what they interpreted as a Washingtonian nation-alist economic strategy, for which Du Bois was removed from the NAACP Board. This would be his last association with the organization in whose founding he participated. It is interesting that Cruse's discussion of black intellectual informs the reader of a marginality not possible in Du Bois, Miller, or even Locke et al. discussions of intellectuals. The marginality of intellectuals may not have been possible because black intellectuals were completely excluded and hence, total outsiders in the social and political arena, and marginality presupposes an existing, ongoing, relationship.

When compared to the New Negro book, the most striking feature of the Cruse book is Cruse's often personal accounts of the events and issues surrounding the political and cultural battles in New York City. There is both an attempt to set the records straight and duel with both the living and the dead over interpretations of events and happenings – past and present. But there is also much political passion and a sense of righteous indignation over what Cruse believes to be missed opportunities by past and contemporary intellectuals. What also sets Cruse's book apart from the New Negro is his argument for the importance of theory and methodology when analyzing the intricacies of black life, and to make the case that both theory and method are crucial as precursors to collective social action. It is the absence of such a theory of their own community life and culture, which entices blacks to follow the cultural and political ideas of others. For Cruse, having escaped from a dogmatic Marxism in which theory may have had a stranglehold on viewing reality, he then as a non-Marxist sought to elevate the importance of a social theory to demarcate social behavior in a society generally theoretically impoverished, a view of American society observed by Alexis de Tocqueville (1990[1835]) in the early 1830s. Essentially, Cruse's views on theory takes one back to many of the early classical theorists in sociology and the social sciences in that theories tell you where you are going, why you are going, and what you are suppose to do when you arrive. In any case, Cruse's book was published just as many radical and non-traditional events and activities were taking place throughout the country (McEvoy & Miller, 1969): the Black Student Union Movement; Black Studies Movement, Anti-War Movement, a host of Ethnic Studies Movement, and the Feminist Movement. Since his book was published in the late 1960s, he could not place into his model the large numbers of black students who would be attending predominately white colleges and universities, and the increasingly growing numbers of black faculty and staff who would be recruited to teach or become administrators at these colleges and universities.

The small, but increasing numbers of black students, faculty, and staff at predominately white schools, would slowly change the nature of the discourse on discussions of black intellectuals. Owing to these subtle changes, total outsiders were becoming semi- and quasi-insiders, and a plethora of books and studies would address the issues, challenges, and problems facing this first generation of black faculty, students, and staff who entered predominately white colleges, universities, and businesses (Johnson, 1974; Davis & Watson, 1985; Hammond, 2002).

THE POST-CRUSE INTELLECTUAL: THE RISE OF THE ACADEMIC INTELLECTUAL

A snapshot of intellectuals from Du Bois to Cruse's Crisis book reveals several major characteristics: Many of the earliest intellectuals were predominately independent novelists, playwrights, and poets. If they were academicians, they worked exclusively in predominately black colleges and universities, and in predominately black organizations and institutions, such as black newspapers, magazines, and journals. However, as mentioned earlier, a virtual structural reformation began in the 1970s as blacks began to be employed in a variety of positions and roles within white organizations and institutions, though the gains were generally small. Black faculty and staff recruitment was generally fueled by the enrollment of black students, who by the late 1960s and early 1970s were demanding the creation of Black Studies programs and departments in white colleges and universities they attended. By the early and mid-1970s, throughout the country, many black intellectuals would emerge in the organizational networks which surfaced key segments of black life and whose presence would be felt significantly in the larger society: the Black Congressional Caucus; educated and progressive members of the clergy with Ph.D.s and doctorates in theology, sociology, and social policy; clinical social workers and psychologists; clinical sociologists; administrative and organizational specialists; and a host of other occupations and positions.

This significant structural shift in black intellectual life from predominately black to predominately white institutions had radical overtones, to some extent. This limited black presence within predominately white institutions was often accompanied, in many cases, by cultural shocks and levels of social and cultural ambivalence, for both blacks and whites. For here, black Americans had to ask questions asked by earlier immigrants to the U.S.: How much of who I am, or was, must be shed to fit into white organizational culture? An even more crucial question was that of whether these formerly all-white institutions, now feeling the pressures by both students and the government to increase racial and ethnic diversity within the organization, would welcome and make room for those formerly excluded? For many blacks the question took on Faustian dimensions: How much of a Faustian deal must I make? That is, how much remolding and reshaping of the self must be made? And if I am a pathfinder, or even a "token," is that not an important role to get my feet in the door so that others may likewise make such a choice? For the academic intellectual, especially those who were among the first wave of black faculty members, as they surveyed the academic scene, with large numbers of students enrolling into the universities, they saw their presence as vital to the education of the black students. Indeed, they felt an obligation to all students, but as they communicated with these first generation black students, who had been the first in their families to have attended higher education, these faculties and black students would have so much in common. The most pronounced feature of their commonalities would be the fact that this would be the first experience for both black students and black faculty in a predominately white educational setting. For one, the world of work; for the other, the world of student. And even if the social and family background and experiences of the two were different, each knew and felt an obligation to assist each other, and though black students often wanted to see the black faculty as a part of his heritage and brought a heightened sense of understanding and despite age differences, some shared experiences, the faculty understood that special role he played, even as he understood that he had an obligation to all students.

Many of these young black academicians knew that in seven years as they faced tenure and promotion decisions, they would have to demonstrate proficiency in scholarship, teaching, and service like their white colleagues. But that reality did not prevent many of theme from taking on tasks much greater than those taken on by their white peers, chief among this overload was their involvement in service, both within and beyond the university. Many became the "unofficial" advisers to the black students on campus. They were often overburdened with committee assignments, often there to be the "black presence." This is not to belittle their presence, for quite often, they were one of the few blacks in the academic division, and other black faculties were also over-committed for committee work.

Having become a part of the white organizational culture, it was clear that there were issues of particular interest to blacks which were not being addressed by the institutions, whether college, university, or business. There may have been recruitment of faculty, staff, and students, but very few strategies and programs to retain them, few programs and events to reflect their presence on campus. That is, the organization remained culturally white with few attempts made to reflect a small but growing organizational diversity. The concept of "dual marginality" (Dennis, 2003) has been used to reflect the issues facing blacks in such an environment (a somewhat similar argument was advanced by Jarmon and Dennis (1976) with reference to the retrenchment of black organizations on predominately white college and university campuses).

According to one part of this concept, blacks are marginally a part of the organizational structure and culture. That is, living with the reality of being partially in and partially out: A part of the white structure, but not central to that structure and with great ambivalence toward the organization, for there are many unmet needs more visible once one is in the organization than could have been seen looking in from the outside. This is why throughout the 1970s and 1980s, a host of black faculty and staff organizations was created on predominately white campuses. This development is, of course, similar to the rise of Black Student Unions in the 1960s and 1970s.

This duality refers to the need to be attentive to the organizational strategies and needs of which the faculty is a part, and those special interests and needs of minority groups which institutions, on certain levels, may not always be cognizant. Indeed, having, in some cases, worked diligently to bring blacks into their institutional world, many white administrators were often less than pleased to have these blacks become their most vocal critics on the slowness of the organization in recruiting and retaining students, faculty, administrators, staff, and upper- and middle-level managers. This is why in the late 1960s and early 1970s many black caucuses were formed within the mainstream professional organizations in sociology, psychology, history, political science, and anthropology. This pattern followed Cruse's idea of creating organizational structures and networks to best address those specific ethnic group needs not known, and if known, neglected and not addressed by large professional organizations. Joyce Ladner's (1973) book on the "death of white sociology" was consistent with the general thrust of Cruse's argument that it was not enough for blacks to simply oppose racist theories and methodologies of white scholars. Rather, they must construct their own distinct and unique theoretical and methodological models – the ones emerging organically out of the unique and lived experiences of blacks.

The second part of the "dual marginality" thesis is that black intellectuals are also, in many ways, marginal to black communities. This is because, given the world of scarcity from which many blacks are born and socialized, especially in the South, and given the existing political, educational, and cultural exclusion, unless there are strong forces pulling in the opposite direction, the world and life of the intellectual will constitute a very small part of the black communal life. Segregation, when legal, created a closed black inner world. When not legal, social norms supporting segregation had similar effects: black individuals and groups had to rely primarily upon the strength of their internal institutional networks. This was made possible by the large numbers of dedicated parents, family members, teachers, ministers, and key community leaders and neighbors who made a valiant, and often successful efforts to inform children and youth by assigning the books, presenting the music, and discussing local and distant places which sought to expose students to a different world which was non-restrictive and excluded. Therefore, those who generally embark on a course leading to a life of the intellect have already begun to look and think beyond their communities. The young boys and girls who, at an early age, are obsessed with books and reading, thinking of science and scientific experiments, skilled in the use and spelling of words not often used at home, at play, or often in school. They are "of" their community, but not "in" their community. These youth have sentiments for their family members, teachers, friends, etc., but their eyes and minds have already begun to scan the world beyond their communities. These two parts of dual marginality do not constitute a love-hate dichotomy, but simply the intellectual and social directions of individuals.

Had Cruse moved beyond New York City, he would have been able to see that nationalistic and particularistic policies prevail among many black intellectuals, though he might disagree with the groups in which the nationalistic philosophies exist: churches, sororities, and fraternities, the various black caucuses within predominately white professional associations Cruse (1968, pp. 90–91) believed he found the core intellectual crisis of the black intellectual: "Detached from the Negro working class, he tries to integrate and to gain full membership in a stagnating and declining Western society ... the American Negro intellectual is unable to cement his ties with the more racial-minded segments of the Negro working class ... this would require him to take a nationalistic stand in American politics – which he is loath to do." This statement reflects a social-class split within black communities generally highlighted by the differences in the two nationalist approaches taken by Garvey and Du Bois. Each viewed himself as nationalistic, though Garvey's nationalism had a much straighter and more consistent trajectory, whereas Du Bois' would be more changeable, and as some might say, more inconsistent, because he, Du Bois, had to, as leader of the NAACP, engage in *real or practical politics*. For Garvey, nationalism meant an almost total disengagement from white society. For Du Bois, it did not entail such a separation, merely economic, educational, political, and cultural nationalism which Du Bois believed could take place within the confines of the U.S. and within separate black community enclaves. Here, one must be careful, for though the NAACP focused on the theme of integration, the integration ideal, for many blacks, was not one devoid of their sense of themselves as a "people," a major ingredient in a group's nationalism. The nationalism of NAACP members, and those who were not a part of any organization might not have the level of nationalism evoked by Garvey's UNIA, yet we cannot assume that they lacked a degree of nationalism, just as we cannot assume that each UNIA member had the degree of nationalism held by Garvey. Viewing himself as one of the inheritors of the legacy of Marcus Garvey (1968), Cruse, like Garvey, sees the middle classes and intellectuals as hopelessly addicted to social integration and lacking meaningful and intensive cultural depth. This is why he viewed the working lower classes as crucial in saving blacks from cultural and racial extinction. That point may be debatable. But what is interesting here is Cruse's projection of the black working class as the cultural savior for the black population. He does so in the contexts of a Garveyite nationalism. By doing so, he is juxtaposing this nationalistic model to a model he now inveighs against: the Marxist model, though not necessarily the Leninist model (Lenin, 1969), in which the workers will develop greater class consciousness in their struggle for autonomy and liberation. The Leninist position, predicated on the development of an educated, politically astute, intellectual elite, has much in common with Du Bois' position on race leadership, in that intellectuals, dedicated to the cause of social change, will help energize the workers and help them develop revolutionary class consciousness. In Du Bois' case, black intellectuals, because they live in a world of ideas and actions, would initiate and take their racial consciousness to black communities; this will serve as an impetus for social change.

I wish to end this segment by outlining more cogently how my concept of the black intellectual as a representative of the New Black differs from previous models of intellectuals, mainly, the "organic intellectual" of Antonio Gramsci (1971) and the "free floating intellectual" of Karl Mannheim (1936[1929]). The new intellectuals would appear to have much in common with Gramsci's organic intellectual in that they would emerge out of the group whose common experience was one of racial oppression and social exclusion. Similar to its "mission" as outlined earlier in statements by Du Bois and Miller, like Gramsci's organic intellectuals, they would work with the population to create organizations and institutions, then use these to engage in the political struggles designed to abolish race and class discrimination. It is clear to see that there can be no consistent analogy between the new black intellectuals and Gramsci's model since the latter's model was confined to issues of class power and the role of the organic intellectuals in joining in a mutual effort with the masses of workers, alongside the workers' political party, to destroy a reactionary state, in this case, Italy. Race and class issues as intertwined and, basically inseparable, prevent the new intellectuals from having a simple sociological and political landscape. In addition, Gramsci's analysis of a society in social, cultural, political, and economic turmoil does not provide a neat fit for the contemporary American model due to dissimilar world and local circumstances. What is compelling in Gramsci, and a point new intellectuals would be wise to follow, is the association and involvement of organic intellectuals in the people's everyday political and economic struggles. His views are worth quoting

(Gramsci, 1971, p. 10, as quoted in Boggs, 1976): "The mode of being of the new intellectual can no longer consist in eloquence, which is an exterior and momentary mover of feelings and passions, but in active participation in practical life, as constructor, organizer, 'permanent persuader,' and not just a simple orator ...." The arguments for organic intellectuals are very compelling, and necessary, and when compared to some of the principles laid out by Du Bois in his Talented Tenth article, the parallels are astonishing.

Mannheim's "free floating intellectual" poses less of an obstacle while comparing his model to the new black intellectual. The structure of race in America and the historical restrictions imposed on the entire black population made it unlikely that black intellectuals could create a "socially unattached" role for themselves, nor can it be assumed that they could exist in the confines of the U.S. by being on any level, unattached. In reality, in the U.S., historically, black intellectuals, like other blacks, lived and existed behind a "thick veil," with their ascribed roles and positions given them almost as a birthright. Hence, much of their lives were spent in an attempt to change the structural conditions, which historically forced them into a "racial role." The sheer urgency of their own personal social position and the position of family members, and that of the larger black community, negated any possibility of ever being a free floater. What is important in Mannheim's model that is extremely useful for new black intellectuals is his idea of "dynamic mediation" as it relates to the "peculiar social position" of intellectuals. In a society riveted by social, race, and class conflicts, Mannheim's intellectuals would make use of this "dynamic mediation" in order to "develop the social sensibility that was essential for becoming attuned to the dynamically conflicting forces. Every point of view was examined constantly as to its relevance to the present situation" (Mannheim, 1936[1929], p. 157).

Mannheim's references above to both "relationism" and "situational variables" have great relevance for new intellectuals because they suggest a manner of assessing events within an era and how, as situations change, intellectuals must return to the drawing board. Neither, however, addresses the issue of being unattached. An example of both relationism, situational variables, and the factor of time would be Du Bois' (1935) decision to advocate the creation of all-black economic and political institutions, a call for self-segregation during the depression. This plan was a model of what Booker T. Washington would have created, and Du Bois, in a series of speeches, explained that times had changed, that blacks were suffering and needed to organize themselves politically and economically. Therefore, to continue to chart a course largely emphasizing racial equality and integration was short sighted and foolish. He would resign from the NAACP as a result of this dispute. New intellectuals may face similar decisions addressed by Du Bois. As Mannheim suggested, and Du Bois demonstrated, different times may require reassessments of old committments and assumptions. For example, the intellectuals in this new century may have to reassess such issues as busing, charter schools, and integrated schools.

NOTES TOWARD A THEORY OF DUAL MARGINALITY AND INTELLECTUALS: THE DIALECTICS OF ENGAGEMENT AND DISENGAGEMENT

The preceding section of the paper explored the idea that intellectuals must live, work, and deal with situations in which they are marginal vis-à-vis dominant and more powerful groups. Since academic intellectuals have become the most notable sector in black intellectual life, as professors, researchers, scholars, administrators, and staff personnel, as suggested above, they must be well-versed, as intellectuals, in their own history, culture, social and political thought as well as be cognizant of both on-going short- and long-term philosophies and aspirations, and the general culture of the people. But if we view intellectuals as the guardian of the culture as well as those who fight for social justice and for the oppressed, a cautionary note must always be advanced in any mandate for intellectuals to be always at one with the people, either the people or group into which they were born, or for whom they fight. Though this may seem like a major contradiction, an understanding of this cautionary note may well determine the effectiveness or lack of effectiveness of intellectuals as they work with others to achieve social change. As important as it is for black intellectuals to be attached somewhere, it is also important for intellectuals to simultaneously practice a degree of disengagement. Like the engagement needed to understand the pulse of the people, a certain disengagement is often necessary if one is to rationally and objectively evaluate, judge, and move with the people so that in the process, intellectuals become the students, and are taught, and students become leaders, and teachers. To achieve this aim, intellectuals must be both engaged and disengaged, must be in their society, and fight for those in their society. But on some levels, they must fight in order to keep a certain distant and not be totally swallowed up by the very society and people they love and of which they are so much a part. For black intellectuals it means a "dual marginality" in that the intellectual is engaged with black life, history, and culture, but not so engaged that the critical eye or mind becomes submerged. Isaac Bashevis Singer (Kresh, 1979) makes an interesting comment on the engagement–disengagement theme, for while he contends that the creative individual must be both an insider and an outsider, he also affirms that the creative individual must also have roots, that he must "have an address." For this reason, Singer has always, in his literary works, chosen the particular over the universal. It is in this sense of having begun with roots, and having an address, that we understand the formative years of black intellectuals. And in Singer's use of the idea, intellectuals have a home, a place. During their formative years, they are immersed in their home, their place: the world of parents, relatives, neighbors, friends, and a host of related organizations and institutions such as churches (for a very few, synagogues and mosques), schools, boys and girls scouts, sports groups, and many other associations and groups. This remains true for the vast majority of blacks despite the fact that integration has become a reality for many individuals and families. In reading the autobiographies of black intellectuals what has become clear is that many individuals who later become intellectuals were, as youngsters, already looking beyond their immediate environment (their communities, schools, etc.) to sights, ideas, and places afar, culled from books, music played and heard, and ideas and individuals encountered on the news, television, movies, etc.

The intellectual role has been an important force in Black America. What is being asserted here is that intellectuals should inspire and inform the population and collectively add their voice to that of the people whom they purport to serve. But intellectuals must also serve a role as critics and use their skills as correctives voices to policies and positions being proposed and addressed, even within the communities they serve. Hence, they must not be reduced to being mere blind followers of the people. Instead, intellectuals must work with the people to help them sharpen, if necessary, their sense of political and social reality and assist in shaping a new vision for the future. They have an obligation, when assessing difficult situations, when asked, or not asked, to proffer a cogent, logical, and coherent argument why an act or policy should, or should not be undertaken. Nor should intellectuals blindly follow party lines. Here we have history to assist us: Under Russian and Chinese communism there were intellectuals of the left who, either freely or under coercion, betrayed their role as critical observers and actors and became party hacks and propagandists who skewed and adjusted their writings and speeches so as to be consistent with party policies, theories, and dogmas. Cruse's entire book is a denunciation of this practice, but others have had similar experiences. Georg Lukacs (1997[1922]) is a classic case, but the stories of Arthur Koestler, Ignazio Silone, Richard Wright, Andre Gide, Louis Fischer, and Stephen Spender tell of their experiences as well (Crossland, 1963). The same was true of intellectuals under Fascist and Nazi regimes. In our own society similar policies prevail: There are intellectuals of the left who are seldom critical of the national Democratic Party, its policies and platforms; likewise, there are intellectuals of the right who are seldom critical of the national Republican Party, its policies and programs. Perhaps Singer's point has some relevancy here, for having found a home and a place, at least politically, some intellectuals may be reluctant to give up the comfort of having roots, even when they disagree with the basic assumptions and policies. Or in the case of old hard-line Stalinists, they will never disavow Stalin, because they believed he offered them the only home and place they ever had, or wanted.

What is argued here is that attachment should not blind one to problems, which must be addressed. Thus the detachment side of the attachment–detachment dichotomy should not be viewed as a rejection of the people, only as a necessary and needed corrective. And if necessary, it should be done in the spirit of intellectual life as projected by both Du Bois and Cruse. Bill Cosby's recent controversial statements are in the spirit of which is expressed here. There are few who would question Cosby's love of black people, yet it is this love which forces him to address black audiences with some of the hard realities of contemporary black life which he feels must be addressed if blacks are to be a new and different people which he desires. A close reading of the speeches and books of black leaders such as Douglass, Washington, Du Bois, on to King and Malcolm X would reveal among these men degrees of engagement and disengagement to and from black communities. It is in this sense that black intellectuals must forge stronger links to their communities, but strong links should also make it possible for intellectuals to be critical when necessary.

The other side of the dual marginality theme for black intellectuals involve their relationships in organizations and institutions within the predominately white world in which they live and work, and how members of their group view them from the outside, looking in, a situation blacks share with members of other ethnic groups. One of the accusations often made against many blacks in predominately white institutions is that they have "become white." Those who have taken such a position generally cite such superficial features as speech and dress. What they do not understand is that black professor tend not to dress"down," but to dress"up," a pattern which was also true of a generation of black students on predominately white campuses until the 1980s. On predominately black college campuses, students continue to dress "up." On campus, faculty and administrators may provide advice and may serve as advisors to national civil rights groups, fraternities, and sororities, and may opt to be more involved in local non-university religious and social organizations. Thus, one of the assertions of a theory of dual marginality within majority institutional structures relates to the selectiveness with which many blacks approach these institutions and the whites with whom they work. For many the engagement–disengagement thesis prevails. For example, many blacks outside of many predominantly white institutions would be shocked to know that the very blacks whom they accuse of "acting" or wanting to be white, are often very attached to majority black local and regional organizations. The issue here is choice, and the freedom to join, or not join, and the deeply held view of many black and intellectuals to be attentive to the Luke theorem.

This dual marginality is a necessary feature of the life of black intellectuals, especially since the age of integration in which the vast majority of black intellectuals, especially academic intellectuals, work in predominately white institutions. This duality must then be viewed as natural and normal and under the existing social and racial climate, almost necessary as the American society is theoretically an open society, but it is also a highly segmented society, both with respect to race and class. Also important is the reality that black intellectuals belong to a "pariah group," a less powerful group, but it cannot be forgotten, despite their personal intellectual attributes, that they were born among the outcast and the excluded, and are viewed as a part of this group. Less powerful groups, and groups which enjoy fewer societal privileges almost always must be dual marginally, for less powerful groups must adjust to, and learn the ways and customs of more powerful groups. It is never the reverse. Since powerful groups are the source of information and opportunities, less powerful groups, if they desire to obtain some of the opportunities, then they must learn the ways of powerful groups as well as retain the understanding of their own cultural values, languages, etc., and a saying for Jewish Americans 50 years ago that there might be acculturation without assimilations, may be less true today, however, for blacks the assertion might still be true. As all studies have shown, blacks and whites continue to live, socially, in two separate worlds, and though intellectuals come into much greater contact with whites by virtue of their employment, housing, and travels, the idea that since this is the case, these intellectuals have "lost contact" with all black communities, may be more myth than reality. This dual marginality no doubt fosters a degree of tension, under certain circumstances, but one should be careful of over-exaggerating the conditions under which intellectuals must act and react. One must dismiss those who see nothing but woe, pain, and eternal confusion for black intellectuals. That they must of necessity live in two worlds may be their greatest asset. Du Bois, using himself, no doubt, as a model of intellectual behavior, knew that intellectuals must live in two or more worlds and in so doing, may be the link among people, organizations, and institutions. He believed intellectuals could do so with minimum discomfort because their vast education prepared them for the ambiguities and ambivalences of life in a racially and class-segmented society.

Unless black intellectuals of this new century are so much different from previous generations of intellectuals, there is little reason to despair. Old issues will remain such as the need to balance the individual's need for self-enrichment and the community's need for collective social action. This was the great message and challenge hurled to intellectuals by Du Bois. Cruse took black intellectuals into the murky politics of Harlem and New York City, and his discussion of "the crisis" became an enduring class contradiction from which many intellectuals thought they could not, or would not recover. As Cobb (2002) illustrates, his insightful analyses should not be dismissed, nor should they be permitted to be the Sisyphean rock upon which intellectuals are rendered immobile.

The New Black must claim the legacy of belongingness and ownership of the American physical, sociological, and emotional space, proclaiming themselves to be rightful inheritors of the American intellectual legacies of Du Bois, King, Malcolm, Washington, Douglass, Tubman, Truth, and a host of others. Intellectuals must move beyond their ethnic/racial as well as class heritage and view themselves as co-heritage partners along with Lincoln, Jefferson, Franklin Roosevelt, Debs, John Brown, and Harry Truman, despite the contradictions and ambiguities surrounding their names and images. The challenge for the twenty-first century black intellectuals is to analyze the United States, and the world, from the ground up, and to give both unique perspectives from our unique status and position as dual marginals embedded in the American reality with all the keen insights suggested by Du Bois. But intellectuals are to do this because doing so enables them to interact with the people and, hence, help move them toward greater social, political, and cultural consciousness. We still must grapple with Du Bois' prophetic pronouncement regarding color and the twentieth century, and that reality will not quickly disappear. What is important, however, is that black intellectuals working with the black population and progressive individuals and groups continue to help shape Black America and America in ways that the twenty-first century may well become The Century of the Black American.

The dual marginality of black intellectuals provides them with special skills, talents, and insights, not available to intellectuals of the majority groups, for living in both worlds offers unique insights, a view Du Bois (1995[1903], p. 3) understood when he wrote The Souls of Black Folk, for in this book he notes that "... the Negro is a sort of seventh son, born with a veil, and gifted with second-sight in this American world." Du Bois' "second-sight" is important to the dual marginality thesis, for it entails a "first sight" which is the inner world of blacks. The second sight is that ability to gain access to and obtain deep insights into the world of the other. When the concept was first broached by this writer (Dennis, 1991; see also Dennis & Henderson, 1980), black youth was the focus of the dual marginality. I had not yet developed the view which placed blacks squarely in the world of the other. Then, it was merely a yearning to join that world and a sporadic journey into that world only to return to one's own geographical home. What assisted me in sharpening my views on dual marginality was a return to my Masters thesis (Dennis, 1969; Warner & Dennis, 1970), a re-casting of Kurt Lewin's (1948, 1951) Field Theory, a re-reading of Yinger (1965), and Mey (1972), and a return to Du Bois' autobiography, Dusk of Dawn (1940). Returning to these books returned me to the idea of "situational variables," and the concept of "the social field," ideas and themes central to my thesis. Rather than one social field in which there would be both negative and positive reactions and responses, I projected two social fields, one white, one black, in which blacks would/could move from one field to another. This movement represented the increasing manner in which many blacks were able to both move between the two worlds but also live within these worlds. I viewed the two worlds as existing in a dialectical relationship, just as I viewed black intellectuals as participating in a dialectical encounter as they were in the dialectical process of both engaging and disengaging themselves to and away from both world. Du Bois gave me the best cue for defining dual marginality when he used the term "dual environment" to refer to the white and black worlds within which blacks live and must deal with daily. The process is dialectically in that tensions and contradictions which are inherent in segmented and race and class charged societies, are never resolved, and under present political and economic guidelines, cannot be resolved.

Thus, in the United States there are the constant and continual dialectics of degrees of acceptance and rejection by the larger dominant society (see Rose, 1997). My assessment of dual marginality for black intellectuals was anchored in the social and geographical positions from which black intellectuals come and their personal as well as collective circumstances, history, values, ideals, and ideas which shaped them as they grow and develop in the inner black world. Coming from their unique perspectives, it would be inevitable that tensions, contradictions, and dilemmas would follow them and new ones would develop. Like Lewin's model suggests, we could speculate that black intellectuals would be moving both toward as well as away from the black and white social fields, often simultaneously. Du Bois presents a classical case of some of the "inner contradiction and frustration" of many in the inner black world, but I believe he overstates the case in explaining black frustration in the black world. He notes that in their desire to avoid segregation, educated blacks will not sit beside blacks on streetcars, attend black churches, and refuse to join black organizations. Many will, however, he said, take every opportunity to join white political and cultural groups. While that may be true in a few cases, it is doubtful that it existed to any large degree. Du Bois himself may best exemplify this dual marginality because he was often rather uneasy in both worlds though he moved constantly between these worlds as many intellectual do today. For probably most of them, a request to give up one of their worlds would be impossible, for though the tensions and contradictions abound, they become manageable, but never disappear. Ironically, those very tensions and contradictions have the potential to serve as the generator of highly creative approaches to social problems. That means that, as is the case with true dialectics, at least the position proposed by George Simmel (Spykman, 1966), no final solution is attained, nor can it be, for the dialectics can never be resolved. It remains a permanent condition, simply reflecting the real and existing world which is unpredictable and is ever-changing. In this sense, dual marginality was not possible during the era of strict segregation when blacks could not "live" in the world of whites. It would only be possible, and will not disappear as long as the social worlds reflect power inequities and differences. Whites will not be bothered with ideas of dual marginality because the term only resonates in cases where one group has to live in a world of the "other." White political intellectuals may be bothered by the political system, but they generally do not have to live in the world of an "other," so different from themselves.

CONCLUSION

This essay sought to advance two important arguments points pertinent to an analysis of black intellectuals. First, I illustrated that a class of the highly educated and creative, those oriented toward the world of ideas, whom we call intellectuals, emerge at crucial moments in various societies. In the United States, following the defeat of the confederacy in the South, and the selective opening of opportunities in the North, a class of black Americans emerged, willing and able to challenge racial and social injustice. Du Bois and Miller spoke to and partially for this class as both thinkers sought to lay out a program and format for this class' mission, both for blacks and for the larger white society. One has to read Du Bois' early essays and books to understand the ways in which this mission was often stated in biblical terms. Also important for Du Bois and Miller was the thought that these few well-educated blacks constituted a "new breed" of thinkers and shapers of the black reality who would fashion a radically new black social imagination which would unleash a world of great and never – before – seen possibilities.

Thus, the "new men," which included women, were the products of new opportunities as the American society itself was being transformed, though black Americans would not see the full force of these changes regarding social justice until the 1960s. The second stage of the growth of black intellectuals occurred during the first two decades of the twentieth century in which there was a convergence of two important social, political, and cultural movements: the rise of Marcus Garvey's Back – to Africa Movement and the literary-cultural movement called the Harlem Renaissance. Each, in a sense, fed on the other, and each highlighted the rise of a New Black, and each separate and together encompassed the political as well as the cultural. As was true of the earlier emergence of the "new black" which was only made possible with the destruction of slavery, the migration of blacks to the North, and changing laws and mores.

Cruse's book, The Crisis, was a revolutionary text in that it challenged the heretofore untouchable theory of integration as the only option for blacks. Not only did he present an alternative for black American, but he also excoriated black intellectuals for their failure to provide workable cultural and political ideas and programs for a black population that he believes had lost its bearing and directions. But Cruse focused only on the political and cultural world of New York City, and when his book was published, the nation, and black Americans were not yet into another phase of the evolution of the Black Intellectual: the Academic Intellectual.

The second strand highlighted in this paper is the rise of academic intellectuals which was sparked by the desegregation of major white colleges and universities and by the struggles waged on predominately white campuses to establish Black and Ethnic Studies programs, and by students demands for black and minority faculty. With this level of integration of

black academicians into formerly segregated white institutions, we witnessed
the emerging prototype of yet another "new black," but this time, unlike the
experiences of earlier generations of intellectuals. This new academic black
moved from being the excluded to being the included, and the term I have
coined to describe this process is dual marginality. This term is different
from its previous uses, for as immigration and migration are now the constant realities of this new century, and as structural opportunities now
emerge within the American society, groups, and individuals, in this case,
blacks, now have opportunities, if they so desire, to live simultaneously in
two worlds, and such an existence does not, for many, become unbearable.
In fact, the idea of doing so remains one of the most challenging and ex-
citing adventures of our times.

This essay directs the reader to understand how each era presents
challenges to its citizens. Black Americans were presented with many such
challenges, but when opportunities were made possible by changing laws
and shifting social norms, classes of black intellectuals emerged to both
document and engage in the arguments surrounding the key issues of the
day. The contemporary intellectual as a representative of the new black has
demonstrated the desire to respond to the issues of the day as willingly as
intellectuals of previous era have. And just as Du Bois admitted that a
double consciousness provided blacks with the vision to see a variety of
realities, dual marginality, but providing opportunities, as Singer suggested,
to have a home and a place in both worlds, does likewise.

REFERENCES

Boggs, C. (1976). *Gramsci's marxism.* London: Pluto Press.
Bronz, S. (1964). *Roots of Negro consciousness.* New York: Libra Publishers.
Cobb, W. J. (Ed.) (2002). *The essential Harold cruse.* New York: Palgrave.
Crossland, R. (Ed.) (1963). *The God that failed.* New York: Harper & Row.
Cruse, H. (1967). *The crisis of the Negro intellectual.* New York: William Morrow.
Cruse, H. (1968). *Rebellion and revolution.* New York: William Morrow.
Davis, G., & Watson, G. (1985). *Black life in corporate America.* Garden City, NY: Doubleday
    Books.
Dennis, R. M. (1969). *A field view of prejudice and discrimination.* Masters thesis, Washington
    State University, Pullman, WA.
Dennis, R. M. (1977). Du Bois and the role of the educated elite. *The Journal of Negro
    Education, XLVI*(7), 388–402.
Dennis, R. M. (1991). Dual marginality and discontent among black Middletown youth. In: R.
    Dennis (Ed.), *Research in race and ethnic relations.* Greenwich, CT: JAI Press.

Dennis, R. M. (Ed.) (1997). *The black intellectuals. Research in race and ethnic relations series* (Vol. 10). Greenwich, CT: JAI Press.

Dennis, R. M. (2003). Towards a theory of dual marginality: Dual marginality and the dispossessed. *IDEAZ*, *2*(1), 21–31.

Dennis, R. M. (2006). The situational politics of Booker T. Washington. In: D. Cunnigen, R. Dennis, & M. Glascoe (Eds), *The racial politics of Booker T. Washington*. Oxford: Elsevier.

Dennis, R. M., & Henderson, C. (1980). Intellectuals and double consciousness. In: C. Hedgepeth (Ed.), *Afro-American perspectives in the humanities*. San Diego: Collegiate Publishing Co.

Du Bois, W. E. B. (1935). A Negro nation within a nation. *Current History*, *LXII*(June), 265–269.

Du Bois, W. E. B. (1970[1897]). The conservation of races. In: P. S. Foner (Ed.), *The American Negro academy occasional papers, No. 2, in W. E. B. Du Bois speaks*. New York: Pathfinder Press.

Du Bois, W. E. B. (1971[1903]). The talented tenth. In: A. G. Paschal (Ed.), *A W. E. B. Du Bois reader*. New York: Collier Books.

Du Bois, W. E. B. (1995[1903]). *The souls of black folk*. New York: Penguin Books.

Garvey, M. (1968). *Philosophy and opinions of Marcus Garvey*. New York: Arno Press.

Gramsci, A. (1971). *Selections from the prison notebooks of Antonio Gramsci*. London: Lawrence and Wishart.

Hammond, T. A. (2002). *A white collar profession*. Chapel Hill: University of North Carolina Press.

Heller, M. (1988). *Cogs in the wheel: The formation of soviet man*. New York: Alfred Knopf.

James, W. (1954[1896]). The will to believe. In: A. Castell (Ed.), *Essays in pragmatism*. New York: Hafner Publishing Co.

Jarmon, C., & Dennis, R. (1976). *The retrenchment of black organizations on predominately white universities*. Unpublished data. First National Black Think Tank, September 25, University of Maryland.

Johnson, R. (1974). *Black scholars on higher education in the 70s*. Columbus, OH: ECC Publications.

Kresh, P. (1979). *Isaac Bashevis Singer*. New York: The Dial Press.

Ladner, J. (1973). *The death of white sociology*. New York: Random House.

Lenin, V. I. (1969). *What is to be done*. New York: International Publishers.

Lewin, K. (1948). *Resolving social conflicts*. New York: Harper and Brothers.

Lewin, K. (1951). *Field theory in social science*. Westport, CT: Greenwood Press.

Locke, A. (1969[1925]). *The new Negro*. New York: Atheneum.

Lukacs, G. (1997[1922]). *History and class consciousness*. Cambridge, MA: MIT Press.

Mannheim, K. (1936[1929]). *Ideology and Utopia*. New York: Harcourt, Brace & Co.

McVoy, J., & Miller, A. (1969). *Black power and student rebellion*. Belmont, CA: Wadsworth Publishing Co.

Mey, H. (1972). *Field-theory: A study of its application in the social sciences*. New York: St. Martin's Press.

Miller, K. (1968[1908]). *Radicals and conservatives*. New York: Schocken Books.

Nkrumah, K. (1970[1963]). *Africa must unite*. New York: International Publishers.

Rose, P. I. (1997). *They and we*. New York: McGraw-Hill.

Smith, H. (1990). *The new Russians*. New York: Random House.

Spykman, N. (1966). *The social theory of Georg Simmel.* New York: Atherton.

Tocqueville, A. (1990[1835]). *Democracy in America.* New York: Vintage Books.

Warner, L., & Dennis, R. M. (1970). Prejudice and discrimination: An empirical example and theoretical extension. *Social Forces, 48*(4), 473–484.

Yinger, M. J. (1965). *Toward a field theory of behavior.* New York: MaGraw-Hill.

PART II:
RACE, POLITICS, AND SOCIAL JUSTICE

THE BLACK PROTEST MOVEMENT: THE LESSONS OF THE PAST AND CONTEMPORARY CHALLENGES

Aldon Morris

It is important for African Americans, as well as all Americans to take a look backward and forward as we enter a new century, indeed a new millennium. When a panoramic view of the entire history of African Americans is taken into account, it becomes crystal clear that African American social protest has been critical to Black liberation. In fact, African American protest has been critical to the freedom struggles of people of color around the globe and to progressive people throughout the world.

The purpose of this essay is (1) to revisit the profound changes that the modern Black freedom struggle has achieved in terms of American race relations; (2) to assess how this movement has affected the rise of other liberation movements both nationally and internationally; (3) to focus on how this movement has transformed how scholars think about social movements; (4) to discuss the lessons that can be learned from this ground-breaking movement pertaining to future African American struggles for freedom in the new century; and (5) to contrast a recent instance of race-based insurgency with similar protest in the civil rights period to illuminate how contemporary insurgency may differ from that of the past.

It is hard to imagine how pervasive Black inequality would be today in America if it had not been constantly challenged by Black protests throughout

The New Black: Alternative Paradigms and Strategies for the 21st Century
Research in Race and Ethnic Relations, Volume 14, 33–53
Copyright © 2007 by Elsevier Ltd.
All rights of reproduction in any form reserved
ISSN: 0195-7449/doi:10.1016/S0195-7449(06)14002-7

each century since the beginning of slavery. The historical record is clear that slave resistance and slave rebellions and protest in the context of the Abolitionist movement were crucial to the overthrow of the powerful slave regime.

The establishment of the Jim Crow was one of the great tragedies of the late nineteenth and early twentieth centuries. The overthrow of slavery represented one of those rare historical moments where a nation had the opportunity to embrace a democratic future or to do business as usual by reinstalling undemocratic practices. In terms of African Americans, the White North and South chose to embark along undemocratic lines.

For African Americans, the emergence of the Jim Crow regime was one of the greatest betrayals that could be visited upon a people who had hungered for freedom so long; what made it even worse for them is that the betrayal emerged from the bosom of a nation declaring to all the world that it was the beacon of democracy.

The triumph of Jim Crow ensured that African Americans would live in a modern form of slavery that would endure well into the second half of the twentieth century. The nature and consequences of the Jim Crow system are well known. It was successful in politically disenfranchising the Black population and in creating economic relationships that ensured Black economic subordination. Work on wealth by sociologists Melvin Oliver and Thomas Shapiro (1995), as well as Dalton Conley (1999) are making clear that wealth inequality is the most drastic form of inequality between Blacks and Whites. It was the slave and Jim Crow regimes that prevented Blacks from acquiring wealth that could have been passed down to succeeding generations. Finally, the Jim Crow regime consisted of a comprehensive set of laws that stamped a badge of inferiority on Black people and denied them basic citizenship rights.

The iron fist of southern state power, the United States Supreme Court, and white terrorist organizations backed the Jim Crow regime. Jim Crow was also held in place by white racist attitudes. As Larry Bobo has pointed out, "The available survey data suggests that anti-Black attitudes associated with Jim Crow were once widely accepted ... [such attitudes were] expressly premised on the notion that Blacks were the innate intellectual, cultural, and temperamental inferior to Whites (Bobo, 1997, p. 35)." Thus, as the twentieth century opened, African Americans were confronted with a powerful social order designed to keep them subordinate. As long as the Jim Crow order remained intact, the Black masses could breathe neither freely nor safely. Thus, nothing less than the overthrow of a social order was the daunting task that faced African Americans during the early decades of the twentieth century.

The voluminous research on the modern civil rights movement has reached a consensus: that movement was the central force that toppled the

Jim Crow regime. To be sure, there were other factors that assisted in the overthrow including the advent of the television age, the competition for Northern Black votes between the two major parties, the Cold War, and the independence movements in Third World countries that sought to overthrow European domination. Yet it was the Civil Rights movement itself that targeted the Jim Crow regime and generated the great mass mobilizations that would bring it down.

What was the genius of the Civil Rights movement that made it so effective in fighting a powerful and vicious opposition? The genius of the Civil Rights movement was that its leaders and participants recognized that change could occur if they were able to generate massive crises within the Jim Crow order-crises of such magnitude that the authorities of oppression would be forced to yield to the demands of the movement to restore social order. Max Weber defined power as the ability to realize one's will despite resistance. Mass disruption generated power. That was the strategy of nonviolent direct action. By utilizing tactics of disruption, implemented by thousands of disciplined demonstrators who had been mobilized through their churches, schools, and voluntary associations, the Civil Rights movement was able to generate the necessary power to overcome the Jim Crow regime. The famous crises created in places like Birmingham and Selma, Alabama, coupled with the important less-visible crises that mushroomed throughout the nation, caused social breakdown in Southern business and commerce, created unpredictability in all spheres of social life, and strained the resources and credibility of Southern state governments while forcing white terrorist groups to act on a visible state where the whole world could watch. At the national level, the demonstrations and the repressive measures used against them generated foreign policy nightmares because foreign media in Europe, the Soviet Union, Asia, and Africa covered them. Therefore, what gave the mass-based sit-ins, boycotts, marches, and jailing their power was their ability to generate disorder.

As a result, within 10 years, 1955–1965, the Civil Rights movement had toppled the Jim Crow order. The 1964 Civil Rights Bill and the 1965 Voting Rights Act brought the regime of formal Jim Crow to a close.

The Civil Rights movement unleashed an important social product. It taught that a mass-based grassed roots social movement that is sufficiently organized, sustained, and disruptive is capable of generating fundamental social change. In other words, it showed that human agency could flow from a relatively powerless and marginalized group that was thought to be backward, and incapable of producing great leaders.

Other oppressed groups in America and around the world took notice. They reasoned that if American Blacks could generate such an agency they should be able to do likewise. Thus the Civil Rights movement exposed a source of agency available to oppressed groups. By agency, I refer to the empowering beliefs and action of individuals and groups that enable them to make a difference in their own lives and in the social structures in which they are embedded.

Because such agency was made visible by the Civil Rights movement, disadvantaged groups in America sought to discover and interject their agency into their own movements for social change. Indeed, movements as diverse as the Student Movement, the Women's movement, the Farm Workers movement, the Native American movement, the Gay and Lesbian movement, the Environmental movement, and the Disability Rights movement all drew important lessons and inspiration from the Civil Rights movement. From that movement other groups discovered how to organize, how to build social movement organizations, how to mobilize large numbers of people, how to devise appropriate tactics and strategies, how to infuse their movement activities with cultural creativity, how to confront and defeat authorities, and how to unleash the kind of agency that generates social change.

For similar reasons, the Black freedom struggle was able to effect freedom struggles internationally. For example, nonviolent direct action has inspired oppressed groups as diverse as Black South Africans, Arabs of the Middle East, and pro-democracy demonstrators in China to engage in collective actions. The sit-in tactic made famous by the Civil Rights Movement has been used in liberation movements throughout the third world, in Europe, and in many other foreign countries. The Civil Rights Movement's national anthem "We Shall Overcome" has been interjected into hundreds of liberation movements both nationally and internationally. Because the Civil Rights movement has been so important to international struggles, activists from around the world have invited civil rights participants to travel abroad. Thus, early in Poland's Solidarity movement Bayard Rustin was summoned to Poland by its protest leaders. As he taught the lessons of the Civil Rights movement, he explained that "I am struck by the complete attentiveness of the predominately young audience, which sits patiently, awaiting the translations of my words" (Rustin, no date).

Therefore, as we seek to understand the important of the Black Freedom Struggle, we must conclude the following: the Black Freedom Struggle had provided a model and impetus for social movements that have exploded on the American and international landscapes. This impact has been especially pronounced in the second half of the twentieth century.

What is less obvious is the tremendous impact that the Black Freedom Struggle has had on the scholarly study of social movements. Indeed, the

Black freedom struggle has helped trigger a shift in the study of social movements and collective action. The Black movement has provided scholars with profound empirical and theoretical puzzles because it has been so rich organizationally and tactically and because it has generated unprecedented levels of mobilization. Moreover, this movement has been characterized by a complex leadership base, diverse gender roles, and it has revealed the tremendous amount of human agency that usually lies dormant within oppressed groups. These empirical realities of the Civil Rights movement did not square with the theories used by scholars to explain social movements prior to the 1960s.

Previous theories did not focus on the organized nature of social movements, the social movement organizations that mobilize them, the tactical and strategic choices that make them effective, nor the rationally planned action of leaders and participants who guide them. In the final analysis, theories of social movements lacked a theory that incorporated human agency at the core of their conceptual apparatuses. Those theories conceptualized social movements as spontaneous, largely unstructured, and discontinuous with institutional and organizational behavior. Movement participants were viewed as reacting to various forms of strain and doing so in a non-rational manner. In these frameworks, human agency was conceptualized as reactive, created by uprooted individuals seeking to reestablish a modicum of personal social stability. In short, social movement theories prior to the Civil Rights movement operated with a vague, weak vision of agency to explain phenomena that are driven by human action.

The predictions and analytical focus of social movement theories prior to the 1970s stood in sharp contrast to the kind of theories that would be needed to capture the basic dynamics that drove the Civil Rights movement. It became apparent to social movement scholars that if they were to understand the Civil Rights movement and the multiple movements it spun, the existing theoretical landscape would have to undergo a radical process of reconceptualization.

As a result, the field of social movements has been reconceptualized and this retheoritization will affect research well into the new millennium. To be credible in the current period any theory of social movements must grapple conceptually with the role of rational planning and strategic action, the role of movement leadership, and the nature of the mobilization process. How movements are gendered, how movement dynamics are bathed in cultural creativity, and how the interactions between movements and their opposition determine movement outcomes are important questions. At the center of this entire matrix of factors must be an analysis of the central role that human agency plays in social movements and in the generation of social change.

Thanks, in large part, to the Black freedom struggle, theories of social movements that grapple with real dynamics in concrete social movements are being elaborated. Intellectual work in the next century will determine how successful scholars will be in unraveling the new empirical and theoretical puzzles thrust forth by the Black freedom movement. Although it was not their goal, Black demonstrators of the Civil Rights movement changed an academic field.

A remaining question is: Will Black protest continue to be vigorous in the twenty-first century, capable of pushing forward the Black freedom agenda? It is not obvious that Black protest will be as sustainable and as paramount as it has been in previous centuries. To address this issue we need to examine the factors important to past protests and examine how they are situated in the current context.

Social movements are more effective when they can identify a clear-cut enemy. Who or what is the clear-cut enemy of African Americans of the twenty-first century? Is it racism, and if so, who embodies it? Is it capitalism, and if so, how is this enemy to be loosened from its abstract perch and concretized? In fact, we do not currently have a robust concept that grasps the modern form of domination that Blacks currently face. Because the modern enemy has become opaque, slippery, illusive, and covert, the launching of Black protest has become more difficult because of conceptual fuzziness.

Second, during the closing decades of the twentieth century the Black class structure has become more highly differentiated and it is no longer firmly anchored in the Black community. There is some danger, therefore, that the cross-fertilization between different strata within the Black class structure so important to previous protest movements may have become eroded to the extent that it is no longer fully capable of launching and sustaining future Black protest movements.

Third, will the Black community of the twenty-first century possess the institutional strength required for sustaining Black protest? Black colleges have been weakened because of the racial integration of previously all-white institutions of higher learning and because many Black colleges are being forced to integrate. The degree of institutional strength of the church has eroded because some of them have migrated to the suburbs in an attempt to attract affluent Blacks. In other instances, the Black Church has been unable to attract young people of the inner city who find more affinity with gangs and the underground economy. Moreover, a great potential power of the Black church is not being realized because its male clergy refuse to empower Black women as preachers and pastors. The key question is whether the Black church remains as close to the Black masses – especially to poor and working classes – as it once was. That closeness determines its strength to facilitate Black protest.

In short, research has shown conclusively that the Black church, Black colleges, and other Black community organizations were critical vehicles through which social protest was organized, mobilized, and sustained. A truncated class structure was also instrumental to Black protest. It is unclear whether during the twenty-first century these vehicles will continue to be effective tools of Black protest or whether new forces capable of generating protest will step into the vacuum. In this context, it is unclear how far-reaching technological changes will affect Black protest. In particular, it is not clear how the Internet and associated forms of electronic communications will affect protest movements.

I foresee no reason why Black protest should play a lesser role for Black people in the twenty-first century. Social inequality between the races will continue and may even worsen especially for poorer segments of the Black communities. Racism will continue to affect the lives of all people of color. If future changes are to materialize, protest will be required. In 1898, as DuBois glanced toward the dawn of the twentieth century, he declared that in order for Blacks to achieve freedom they would have to protest continuously and energetically. This will become increasingly true for the twenty-first century. The question is whether organizationally, institutionally, and intellectually the Black community will have the wherewithal to engage in the kind of widespread and effective social protest that African Americans have utilized so magnificently. If previous centuries are our guide, then major surprises on the protest front should be expected early in the millennium.

Social protest has continued to occur since the civil rights movement but in a more limited and localized fashion. It is instructive to examine such a protest because often it contains the seeds that germinate into a widespread and coherent social movement. During the civil rights movement racial equality was sought throughout the larger society. At that time, the majority of institutions discriminated against African Americans including professional social science organizations. These prestigious learned societies were not able to escape social protest aimed at achieving racial equality. The American Sociological Association (ASA) was one such organization that became the target of protest by black sociologists in the late 1960s and early 1970s. The protest that they launched resulted in significant racial change. It enabled Blacks to become participants in many aspects of the ASA that had been closed to them previously. Nevertheless, by the late 1990s Black had not gained equal access to many important positions in the ASA. Once again some Black sociologists, along with their supporters, found it necessary to protest such practices as earlier generations had done during the civil rights movement. Below, I contrast these two instances of social protests to discern how contemporary Black insurgency may differ from that of the past.

Three analytic points guide my analysis of racial inequality in the ASA. First, national social science organizations matter, despite the relative lack of scholarly attention they have received. Second, in their structure and behavior, national social science organizations tend to mirror and reproduce the social stratification system of the larger society. Thus, in the American context such organizations mirror and reproduce the class, race, and gender hierarchies of Americas. These outcomes should be anticipated despite the expectations that such organizations should be enlightened in matters of social inequality and embrace values of social justice. On the contrary, the material and symbolic interests of social scientists of the dominant group often override values of social justice in the absence of strong social-change forces. Third, social science organizations are likely to embrace values of social equality and undergo significant change when pressured to do so by formidable social protest. In the absence of such pressure they are likely to pull back on the throttles of change. They may even revert to exclusionary values and practices commonplace prior to the changes generated by social protest. This is especially true if additional changes being sought appear to threaten the fundamental structure of the privileges enjoyed by social scientists of the dominant group.

This analysis of the ASA focuses on racial equality although it is relevant to gender and class equality as well. Indeed, Pamela Roby (1992) found that widespread discrimination against women in the ASA was pronounced until women engaged in protest during the late 1960s that resulted in significant gender change. I will begin this analysis with an assessment of the importance of a national organization of sociologists. The arguments that social science organizations reproduce structures of social inequalities and change only when challenged by social protest will be demonstrated through the use of relevant historical and contemporaneous data.

IMPORTANCE OF ASA

The ASA matters to the academic discipline of sociology. It currently has over 13,000 members and its annual budget runs into millions of dollars. The founding of this national organization in 1905 signaled to the larger society and the scientific community that sociology existed as a discipline, and that sociology had come of age. Principal goals of the ASA have been to promote and defend sociology as a discipline. Moreover, the ASA has played an important role in the production of sociological knowledge by providing outlets for sociologists to present scholarly papers and disseminate their findings at its professional meetings, and through publication in its journals. The ASA has played an important role in the production and maintenance of a status hierarchy among sociologists through the dispensation of academic awards and the appointments and elections of sociologists to visible positions in the scientific community. From such platforms elite sociologist have been able to enhance their abilities to secure research funds, to address governmental bodies, and to play prominent roles in their local academic settings.

The annual meetings of the ASA enable thousands of sociologists to interact and discuss their intellectual work. In fact, such gatherings function much like a vast four-day seminar housed in hotels and restaurants. In these spaces, new ideas are born and old ones are refined and recycled. The ASA meetings also provide opportunities for sociologists to meet publishers and secure book contracts. The annual meetings cement social relationships and help sociologists develop a sense of community and shared identity. Thus, the ASA is an important tool for sociologists because it houses important material and symbolic resources. Given this reality, the issue of whether this organization serves its dues – paying constituency free of racial bias, becomes significant indeed.

RACIAL HIERARCHY INSIDE THE ASA: JIM CROW

Social science organizations tend to mirror and reproduce the social stratification system of the larger society. The structure and functioning of the ASA throughout America's Jim Crow period is fully consistent with this postulate. Indeed, it is accurate to conclude that the ASA mirrored the Jim Crow order from its founding in 1905 until the early 1970s. The power structure of the ASA comprises inseparable administrative and intellectual components. They include the organization's Executive office, its board of directors known as the Council, its offices of President, Vice-President, and Secretary. The central ASA mechanisms through which sociologists achieve visibility and recognition are its journals, Annual meetings, and academic awards. For the ASA to mirror and reproduce the Jim Crow racial order, Blacks would have to be largely excluded from its overall power structure during the Jim Crow era.

The relevant data confirms this contention. For this analysis data were obtained from ASA's National Office, from Lawrence Rhoades' (1981) history of the ASA and from secondary sources especially the volume, *Black*

Sociologists edited by Blackwell and Janowitz (1974). Data were also gathered from a variety of articles published in the spring, 1992 Volume of the *American Sociologists*.

The data reveal a pattern of Black exclusion during ASA's 64 years of existence during the Jim Crow Order. Thus, out of the 61 ASA presidents only 1 was Black; out of 109 Vice-Presidents only 2 were Black; out of 15 ASA secretaries none were Black; out of 5 Executive offices none were Black; and during these 64 years only 4 Blacks served on ASA's Council. Additionally, during the Jim Crow era ASA produced eight journals with no Blacks serving as editors.

During the same period, ASA established two major awards for academic work – the MacIver Award and the Sorokin Award. Out of 14 recipients only 1 was Black. During the 64-year Jim Crow period, Black participation in ASA's Annual meetings was nearly invisible. Blackwell (1992) found that "Toward the end of the 1960's, in the period between 1965 and 1968, the ASA had 23 constitutional, standing, and ad hoc committees. Of the 203 total members in each of those years, no more than 3 Blacks ever served in any year" (p. 12). Moreover, Blackwell revealed that "in 1968, only 1 black sociologist appeared on the program" (p. 12). In the Jim Crow period, the sociological discourse of the ASA was conducted in a white voice.

These data clearly documents that for 64 years the ASA walked in lockstep with America's Jim Crow order. Blacks were largely excluded from its decision-making bodies, from editorships of its journals, from its executive offices, from its scholarly prizes, from managerial positions, and from participation in its annual meetings. The exclusion from annual meetings was especially painful, for as Blackwell stated, "blacks felt victimized by deliberate acts of exclusion from intellectual discourse" (1992, p. 12).

Thus, for 64 years the ASA was a de facto Jim Crow organization fully congruent with the racial status quo of the times. Nevertheless, by the 1960s winds of social change roared through the larger society and it was only a matter of time before they struck the ASA.

SOCIAL PROTEST AND SOCIAL CHANGE IN THE ASA

In 1971, major racial changes occurred in the ASA. Those changes included establishing a Committee on the status of Racial and Ethnic Minorities; an ad hoc committee on the relationship of black sociologists to the ASA; a committee to develop a graduate fellowship program for minority students and to secure the necessary funds; the DuBois–Johnson–Frazier Award to honor exemplary research on minority communities. Other changes occurring during this pivotal year included the appointment of a full-time staff sociologist in the executive office to deal with fundamental issues regarding the professional development of racial minorities and women. For that year's annual meeting 15 minority scholars chaired scholarly sessions. Finally, in 1971 ASA President, William Sewell, appointed a Black sociologist to that year's all-white Council.

Clearly, in 1971 a limited but significant racial transformation occurred in the ASA. Summing up these changes, Sewell (1992) wrote that "no meeting since has had this high a proportion of its sessions planned and chaired by minority members" (p. 62). Why was this so? This was no internal revolution for in the late 1960s the leaders of the ASA had no proposals on the drawing board to address the Jim Crow practices of the organization.

Change occurred in the ASA because some of its Black members revolted and attacked ASA's racism. The civil rights and black power movements that were exploding around them during the late 1960s inspired these sociologists. This embryonic social movement of Black sociologists formed during the 1968 Annual Meeting in which only one Black was on the program.

During the Association's 1968 business meeting these insurgent Black sociologists presented six resolutions that would eventually change ASA's racial regime. These resolutions called for Black representation in ASA, for Blacks to become members and chairpersons of ASA's committees, for Blacks to become chairpersons of sections, for Blacks to become presenters of papers and serve as discussants at annual meetings, that Black people be allowed to have equal access to ASA's journals, and that Blacks become readers and referees of papers in ASA's journals. In addition, at the 1969 Annual Meeting those Black Sociologists made an additional demand: that ASA establish a Fellowship program for Black students interested in becoming professional sociologists.

At this time a Caucus of Black Sociologists formed to carry forth the challenge. As a result, ASA's Council approved the pending resolutions. However, ASA responded like most dominant groups when challenged by the oppressed; it approved the resolutions but failed to implement real change. By 1970, the social movement of Black sociologists confronted the ASA by organizing themselves into a Caucus of Black Sociologists and demanded change. As Blackwell (1992) put it, "Tensions mounted and the demand for inclusion escalated ... The session was bitter, acrimonious, contentious, and occasionally uncivil" (p. 13).

The protest was successful in part, because ASA's president, William Sewell, embraced the challenge and used the power of his office to push through many of the changes advocated by the Black Caucus.

The social protest of that period is largely responsible for the significant level of minority inclusion in the current ASA. For example, at its annual 2000 meeting, minority sociologists were visible throughout the program. At that meeting, one of the members of the original protest group – Charlie U. Smith – was awarded the DuBois–Johnson–Frazier award. The Minority Fellowship program has become a highly successful enterprise enabling significant numbers of minorities to obtain the doctorate in sociology. An African American woman is currently serving as Secretary of the Association. Minorities are currently serving on the ASA Council and currently the Vice President-elect is an African American male. The *American Sociological Review* for the first time in its history has a Black coeditor.

Clearly, a minor revolution of racial inclusion has occurred in the ASA. But the record is clear: protest triggered that revolution. Reflecting on the significance of that social protest movement, former ASA president Sewell (1992) wrote that it "demonstrated that organized and vigorous protest is the most effective means of bringing about change" (p. 57). Protest during the same period was responsible for the revolution in women's participation in the ASA. Explaining this change Pamela Roby (1992) wrote that it occurred because "within sociology, we organized, organized, organized" (p. 25). Yet, that "revolution" proved limited and unfinished. I turn now to that unfinished business and one particular response to it.

THE UNFINISHED REVOLUTION

Black exclusion as editors of ASA's academic journals has remained intact since its Jim Crow period. The journals are one of the major intellectual lifelines of the Association and the larger discipline of sociology. Yet, Blacks remain largely excluded from that lifeline. Shortly, I will deal with this form of exclusion in depth because of its consequences and the revolt it recently triggered. At this juncture it is instructive to point out that other forms of racially based academic apartheid continue to exist in the ASA.

Conferring academic awards is an important function of learned societies. Such awards help determine which kinds of scholarship is deemed worthy of honor. They also play a significant role in facilitating the upper mobility of the scholars chosen to be honored. It is rare for African Americans to win major academic awards from ASA. For example, no Blacks have ever won the prestigious "Career of Distinguished Scholarship Award." The "DuBois–Johnson–Frazier Award" appears to have become the "Career of Black Distinguished Scholarship Award" for African Americans. While the establishment of this award represents a measure of progress, legitimate questions can be raised as to whether it has had the unintended consequences of leaving white privilege intact.

The Program Committee of ASA is important because it has the responsibility of planning the annual meetings and establishing its intellectual tone. A new program committee of approximately a dozen members is appointed each year to carry out this function. A trend of academic tokenism has developed regarding Black participation on this Committee, given that during 18 annual meetings since the Jim Crow period, only 1 Black person at a time has ever served on the program committee. Five of the post Jim Crow Committees has had no African Americans. Finally, the day-to-day administration of the ASA is the responsibility of an executive director. Even though the ASA has existed for nearly a century, no Black person has ever served in this capacity. I return now to the issue of ASA journals and their editorships.

Black participation in the editorship of ASA journals has remained largely unchanged since the Jim Crow era. Since that period ASA has had 13 journals and 98 editors. Of the 98 editors only two have been Black: Jacquelyn Jackson edited the *Journal of Health and Social Behavior* from 1973–1975; Franklin D. Wilson currently serves coeditor of the *American Sociological Review* (*ASR*). Wilson was appointed to a three-year term that ends in 2002. Thus, although the ASR was founded in 1936, it would take two-thirds of a century for a Black person to become one of its editors. Unlike the overwhelming majority of his predecessors, Wilson serves as a coeditor and is accompanied in that capacity by a white colleague.

The ASR is the flagship journal of the ASA. Articles published in the ASR generate visibility, prestige, and upward mobility for their authors. By publishing in the ASR one has a chance to influence important scholarly debates and shape future research. Because of its status as ASA's premier journal, the ASR is a valuable resource that should operate in a nondiscriminatory manner. The journal's editor and its editorial board members are the key actors who determine which articles to publish, how intellectually diverse the journal will be and whether the ASR will be free of ascriptive biases including racial discrimination.

Over the last decade, the ASR has come under scrutiny by some members of the ASA who argue that the journal is intellectually narrow and has a history of excluding people of color from its editorship and as editorial board members. Internal studies have been conducted by concerned ASA members (e.g. Feagin, 1995) and elected officers of the ASA. One fact was clear as the twentieth century closed. No Black person or other persons of color had ever served as editor of ASR. It was also argued that few people of color published in the ASR because previous editors and editorial teams did not reach out equally to all ASA members and were not likely to value the kind of scholarship produced by scholars of color. These were very serious and public charges of exclusion that ASA could not ignore.

In 1995, the ASA Council responded to charges pertaining to the lack of diversity in the ASA generally and with respect to its journals in particular. The Council passed a number of resolutions to increase diversity overall in the ASA and to implement measures that would produce diversity in its journals. The Council informed editors of its journals to "take aggressive action to increase the representation of women and people of color" (Levine, 1996). The Publications Committee, an elected body of the ASA, was given the charge to solicit proposals from potential editors of ASA journals. This Committee is crucial to the diversification of the journals because historically, the Council prior to 1999 had never overruled its recommendation as to who should become ASR's editor. In the late 1990s, the Council directed the Publication Committee to take action to make sure ASA's flagship journal, the ASR, would become diversified.

In 1999, the Publication Committee made a historic recommendation to the Council. It recommended to Council that Walter Allen, a distinguished sociologist at the University of California, be named ASR's first Black editor. Moreover, Allen's proposed editorial team consisted of six members four of whom were distinguished minority scholars who held academic posts at major universities. This was a bold recommendation that would have brought instant diversity to ASR's editorial positions. These sociologists were embedded in diverse networks that would enable them to solicit manuscripts from dissatisfied members of the ASA as well as from the typical submitters. The ASR appeared to be on the brink of change given that the Council had always accepted the recommendation of the Publication Committee.

When the recommendation reached the Council some if its members were dissatisfied with the choice advanced by the Publication Committee. Those members organized themselves in opposition to the Allen recommendation arguing that Allen was not qualified to edit the ASR. Originally, the Publication Committee advanced Allen as their first choice and another white candidate as their second choice. All of the other applicant's proposals were deemed to be less meritorious and were not recommended to the Council. In an unprecedented action, those opposed to Allen and his proposed editorial team, asked to review a proposal that was not advanced by the Publication Committee. A Black and White colleague at the University of Wisconsin who sought to co-edit the ASR had developed that proposal. Following a heated debate, the Council narrowly decided to appoint the interracial team as co-editors of the ASR. Never before had the Council rejected the recommendation of the Publication Committee or appointed an editor whose proposal that Committee deemed insufficiently meritorious. The deliberations of the Council were supposed to be confidential. Those Council members who voted to reject the Allen's candidacy were confident that their unprecedented actions would not be disclosed to ASA's general membership.

THE REVOLT

The secret could not be contained. The contents of the deliberations were "leaked" by insiders who were startled by the highly unusual action. The actions of Council became widely known when a prominent member of the Publication Committee resigned and placed his resignation letter on the Internet so those interested could be informed of his reason for resigning. In that letter Burawoy wrote: "I was elected to the Publications Committee to reflect a variety of perspectives current in our discipline, and to speak for the diverse interests of its membership. In our deliberations we were following the directives of Council itself which several years ago urged the Publications Committee to insure the openness of the American Sociological Review as our flagship journal. Yet as soon as we recommend distinguished editors with new visions that we believe would enrich our discipline, we are arbitrarily over-ruled without consultation, discussion or dialogue" (Burowoy, 1999). Burawoy referred to Councils action as a "flagrant transgression of substantive democracy." Within days of Burawoy's letter, sociologists had begun a vigorous debate over this issue. Much of that debate occurred electronically and in the pages of *Footnotes* the official organ of the ASA.

Discontent over the decision was conveyed largely through e-mails and electronic attachments. Those opposed charged that the decision was racially motivated and that the Council violated its own procedures. One group of sociologists charged that Allen and his mostly minority editorial team were rejected because they were considered "too black" and "too political." They concluded that "for us ... the claim that Allen and his team are not 'qualified' smacks of elitism which is indistinguishable from white racial privilege." (Portes, 1999).

Those Council members who supported the decision maintained that the best candidates were chosen and constitutionally the Council had the power to make the final decision. Sharp battle lines were drawn between the summer of 1999 and the August 1999 Annual meeting. During this time the conflict was conveyed mostly through the electronic media. It was agreed that the insurgent sociologists would protest the decision at the Annual 1999 business meeting. That was to be the first face-to-face meeting of the protesters. Up until that time, discontent had been mobilized electronically.

At a 7:00 a.m. business meeting on August 22nd, over 300 sociologists confronted the leadership of ASA. These scholars expressed their anger and opposition over the decision and demanded change. In particular, they presented and passed a resolution that called for the Council to postpone its earlier decision so that a search and a decision on an editor could be implemented. In the end the Council tabled this resolution and stood by their earlier decision. They maintained that "the new editors were appointed based on their merit and according to current procedure and the transition of the new office has already occurred" (Quoted in Statement from the American Sociological Association Section on Racial and Ethnic Minorities, 1999). The protest group was appalled by the action of Council and vowed to continue the struggle.

Following Council's action to stand by its decision, the insurgent sociologists escalated its tactics. They drew up a petition that stated that "The current editors' term will end in the year 2001 reducing their term from three to two years. Walter Allen will be appointed editor of ASR for a three-year term beginning at the end of their term, with the transition beginning in summer of 2001" (ASA Member's Resolution, 1999). Additionally, they called for a boycott of the ASR by ASA members stating that, "In addition to signing the petition please discontinue subscription to ASR until there is a satisfactory solution to this controversy" (*ibid.*). With this action, the conflict had sharpened and could not be reconciled between the two groups through polite and civil negotiations.

The petition needed 500 signatures of ASA members in order for this effort to be successful. That number of signatures would have empowered the protesters to demand that a general vote of the membership be taken to determine the legitimate editor of the ASR. The petition drive was mobilized through the electronic media. The petition was sent to sociology departments and ASA members by way of an e-mail attachment. In the end, the protest movement was unable to generate the number of signatures required for the general vote of the membership. As a result, the action of the Council prevailed and their two choices became the coeditors of the ASR. The

Council did concede to demands to change the procedures through which journal editors were appointed and it established a task force to explore ways by which the ASR could become more diverse. In the final analysis, ASA's power structure emerged victorious over the protest movement.

TWO STRUGGLES COMPARED

It is instructive to explore why the protests of the late 1960s and early 1970s were more effective than the one to diversify the ASR three decades later. Two differences between these struggles are apparent. That is, over the decades the social environment in which the two struggles occurred had changed significantly and so had the mobilization process. These two factors affected the final outcomes.

The earlier protest occurred during the heyday of ASA's de facto Jim Crow regime. As pointed out earlier, during that period Blacks were excluded from meaningful participation at all levels of the Association. This reality could not be disguised or hidden. The transparent nature of the racial discrimination afforded the protesters with a clear-cut enemy that could be attacked and a moral high ground that legitimized and energized the protest movement. Additionally, the earlier struggle emerged during the period of a larger social movement where blatant Jim Crow practices were being overthrown especially in the South. In this environment, a learned society could lose legitimacy if it were unwilling to change practices not drastically different from those which southern segregationist were being forced to abandon. In the late 1960s, Black sociologists were able to effectively attack a Jim Crow regime that was losing its grip nationwide.

The insurgents who led the challenge during the ASR controversy faced a drastically different environment. The formal Jim Crow regime as well as its de facto counterpart in the ASA no longer existed. The opposition to the movement could maintain that their actions were based on meritorious grounds rather than racism. The presence of a number of Black and other minority sociologists in visible positions in the ASA provided a measure of credence to this view. The earlier protestors operated in an environment where racial segregationists ideologies were being openly espoused. The latter protesters confronted an environment where ideologies of reverse discrimination and color blindness were seeking dominance. No clear-cut enemy reared its head during the ASR controversy.

The opposition gained the upper hand in the controversy when they chose a Black sociologists to become coeditor despite the fact that the proposal of he and his white colleagues did not clear the Publication Committee on meritorious grounds. The view that racism played no role in Council's decision was buttressed by the fact that their action resulted in the first Black becoming an editor of the ASR. Leaders of the protest movement responded that this view "ignores that in post-civil rights America's racial issues are no longer just about us having 'symbolic representation' ... This challenge should not be undermined by attempting to handpick the minority candidates that Council believes to be most qualified" (Statement From the American Sociological Association Section on Racial and Ethnic Minorities, 1999). Nevertheless, the decision of the Council to appoint a Black person was a formidable barrier for the protestors to overcome. Whites who might have supported the petition decided otherwise because they worried that such support could be construed as racism against the Black coeditor. The division also cut into the support of some Black and minority sociologists because they were not prepared to argue that the Black coeditor was an "Uncle Tom" unworthy of being an ASR editor. They were outraged over the decision to reject Allen and his team rather than the candidacy of the Black coeditor. When the dust cleared the petition failed in part because the opposition succeeded in appearing to be above racism and the presence of a Black person on their slate eroded crucial support needed for the movement to triumph. The social environment in which they struggled had shifted significantly so that the "enemy" was able to clothe itself in an opaque garb that enabled it to appear to some as a friend rather than foe.

This changed environment allowed members of the power structure to vigorously attack the movement. In the earlier protest, the president of the ASA embraced the goals of the challengers and used his office to make changes. This is not to argue that those earlier insurgents operated in a benign environment. Indeed, Blackwell (1992) informs us that back in 1970 "those who presented the resolutions and argued for their approvals were labeled "house niggers, 'careerists', militant opportunist. In fact, a few prominent sociologists either resigned or threatened to resign from ASA membership because of the positive response to most of the resolutions" (p. 13). Nonetheless, such reactions did not prevent ASA's president from supporting the movement. By the late 1990s, that environment had changed such that the president of the ASA castigated the movement rather than embrace its goals. Indeed, Portes advised sociologist "to put a halt to this destructive process." He went on to argue that "Together we must vigorously resist attempts by mobilized activist groups to impose their will on the majority, disregarding democratic principles and properly conducted elections" (Portes, 1999). Protest movements for racial justice in the post civil rights period confront an environment far less hospitable and clear-cut than was the case during the dark days of the Jim Crow era.

It was impossible to mobilize protests through an electronic media during the civil rights movement. The technological superhighway was not available to insurgents during that era. The original ASA protest was planned and mobilized through face-to-face contact. In those gatherings, members of the aggrieved population were able to build social solidarity and to pledge to each other that they would perform the tasks required to produce effective collective action. Their discontent and mobilization were crystallized and politicized through interpersonal networks and friendship bonds.

In contrast, the ASR rebellion was mobilized largely through electronic media consisting of e-mails, attachments, and the Internet. This approach to mobilization raises the fundamental question of whether collective discontent can be effectively forged through electronic media. It is not clear that these media are effective in generating and directing the anger required for people to engage in risky collective action. It is true that electronic media can provide inexpensive modes of communications that enable members of protest groups to receive vital information swiftly. However, instant communication does not automatically translate into commitment and the concrete actions crucial for a challenge to succeed. Once the electronic buttons have been pushed, activists run the risk of relaxing thinking they have laid the groundwork for mobilization to occur. In the end, such communication may produce a "virtual movement" but fall short of the commitment and disciplined work needed to generate social change through collective action.

It is not possible to determine definitively if the petition drive during the ASA controversy would have been successful if face-to-face organizing had been the dominant mode of mobilization. However, anecdotal information suggests that few potential supporters of the movement were contacted directly and asked to sign the petition. It is reasonable to assume that the 300 people who attended the 7:00 a.m., business meeting and supported the resolution would have signed the petition. If this were true, the movement would only have had to garner another 200 signatures from the remaining 13,000 members of the ASA. Initially, the leaders of the petition drive were confident that they would easily surpass the number of required signatures. Yet, they had few firm commitments and failed to engage in the hands on organizing that would have enabled them to make realistic projections and to engage in the work needed to overcome the shortfall. In the end it appears that movement participants placed far too much confidence in "virtual mobilization" rather than the kind of hands on mobilization that occurred in Black communities, churches, colleges, and homes during the civil rights movement (see Morris, 1984; Payne, 1995). While the technological revolution can function as an asset to protest movements, it may also contain hidden liabilities that dilute the effectiveness of protest. It is quite possible that this informational revolution played a role in slowing the progress to diversify the ASR while giving the appearance that the movement was headed toward victory at a supersonic pace.

In summary, the civil rights movement ushered in profound changes on the racial front and set the stage for other types of protest movements to emerge and transform the nation. The original ASA protest belongs to that era and played a crucial role in toppling many of the Jim Crow practices of ASA. Referring to the protest of the late 1960s and earlier 1970s, ASA's 1971 President William Sewell stated, "I find it puzzling that organized protest took so long to develop and become effective in the American Sociological Association." He summed it up this way, "I must say that I do not think the recent increases in the participation of women and minority sociologists would have come about, if it had not been for those who played important roles in the caucuses. They are the ones who forced us to recognize the validity of their pleas for equal opportunity in the affairs of the association. They are the ones who will have democratized the American Sociological Association" (1992, p. 62).

The challenges faced by contemporary movements for racial justice and democracy include undressing and exposing the modern barriers that stand in the path of progress and directing new technologies to serve the interests of social change rather than the beneficiaries of an unequal status quo. The insurgents of the civil rights movement revealed that durable mobilizing and organizing efforts, along with creativity, commitment, and courage were the cornerstones of change. In the modern era these same qualities coupled with a grasp of how new technological innovations can speed up the change process, will prove crucial to effective social protest movements.

REFERENCES

Blackwell, J. E. (1992). Minorities in the liberation of the ASA? *The American Sociologist*, Spring, pp. 11–17.

Blackwell, J. E., & Janowitz, M. (Eds) (1974). *Black sociologists: Historical and contemporary perspectives*. Chicago: University of Chicago Press.

Bobo, L. (1997). The color line, the dilemma, and the dream: Race relations in America at the close of the twentieth century. In: J. Higham (Ed.), *Civil Rights and Social Wrongs: Black-White Relations Since World War II* (pp. 31–55). University Park, PA: Penn State University Press.

Burowoy, M. (1999). Letter to Alejandro Portes. *Footnotes*. American Sociological Association, July/August.

Conley, D. (1999). *Being Black, living in the red: Race wealth, and social policy in America*. Berkeley: University of California Press.

Feagin, J. (1995). Memorandum to American Sociological Association Council, January 7.

Levine, F. J. (1996). The Open Window, *Footnotes*. The American Sociological Association, March.

Member's Resolution. (1999). An E-mail sent by Dr. Bonnie Dill to American Sociological Association Voting Members, November 5.

Morris, A. (1984). *The origins of the civil rights movement: Black communities organizing for change*. New York: Free Press.

Oliver, M., & Shapiro, T. E. (1995). *Black wealth/White wealth: A new perspective on racial inequality*. New York: Routledge.

Payne, C. (1995). *I've got the light of freedom*. Berkeley: University of California Press.

Portes, A. (1999). Response from past-president Portes. *Footnotes*. American Sociological Association, November.

Rhoades, L. J. (1981). *A history of the American sociological association 1905–1980*. Washington, DC: American Sociological Association.

Roby, P. (1992). Women and the ASA: Degendering organizational structures and processes, 1964–1974. *The American Sociologist*, Spring, pp. 18–48.

Rustin, B. (No date). *Report on Poland*. New York: A. Philip Randolph Institute

Sewell, W. H. (1992). Some observations and reflections on the role of women and minorities in the democratization of the American Sociological Association, 1905–1990. *The American Sociologist*, Spring, pp. 56–62.

Statement from the American Sociological Association Section on Racial and Ethnic Minorities. (1999). Institutional Racism, ASA Council, and the ASR Editorship. *Footnotes*, American Sociological Association, November.

FROM CIVIL RIGHTS TO SOCIAL JUSTICE

Rodney D. Coates

Many scholars, particularly sociologists, responded with surprise when the "Modern Civil Rights Movement" suddenly appeared upon the social landscape (Hughes, 1963).[1] As one reads recent scholarship regarding race, racism, and various processes of racialization, it is easy to come to the conclusion that blacks merely reacted or at worst have been passive participants throughout much of their sojourn in the United States. Thus, if we look at the work of Omi and Winant (1986) it would seem that the racial state rearticulates, and reforms itself to effectively nullify agency on the part of blacks and other racialized groups. In a brilliant critique of the history of civil rights in America, Klinkner and Smith (1999) analysis affords even less agency as the state merely accommodates blacks during times of high demand or crises. From Massey and Denton (1993) we learn that the forces of racism and industrialization interacted to produce racialized, hyper-segregated ghettos in which blacks were relegated to isolation and often reacted by developing a "black street culture at odds with white culture". These debilitating behaviors are not that different from what others called "culture of poverty" (originally this term comes from Lewis 1964, but most recently it can be found in the work of Ortiz & Briggs, 2003), or Elijah Anderson's (1999) "code of the street". "When work disappears", Wilson (1996) observes that both good jobs and a large number of the black middle class move to the suburbs and poor blacks respond by developing "ghetto

The New Black: Alternative Paradigms and Strategies for the 21st Century
Research in Race and Ethnic Relations, Volume 14, 55–78
Copyright © 2007 by Elsevier Ltd.
ISSN: 0195-7449/doi:10.1016/S0195-7449(06)14003-9

specific behavior". And finally, West (1993) argues that modern capitalism and market forces have destroyed communal links between individuals and the family, church, and friendship. Thus, set adrift, blacks find themselves increasingly nihilistic as evidenced by extreme levels of lovelessness and hopelessness.

Recognizing the macro-analytical bias of these various studies, we are left with an overly deterministic set of analyses that under-emphasizes the role of black agency and free will. Simply put, it is easy to conclude that blacks have been either extremely passive or at best merely reactive in these processes. It is not that the findings, observations, and/or theoretical pronouncements are without value, but rather we need to also look at the micro-level structures, which will serve to balance our reflections. In this paper, I will therefore argue for a more robust formulation suggesting that black responses have been both varied and dynamic. And rather than one specific set of responses, we can identify at least three – passive, reactive, and direct(ed) actions.[2] It will be argued that the various civil rights movements, representing direct(ed) action, provide a clearer picture of black responses to the racial order or state.[3]

If, as Omi and Winant (1986) assert, racial elite respond to challenges to the supremacy of the racial state by a process of rearticulation, then we should also expect to see similar sets of rearticulation in the form of direct (ed) action by respective racialized non-elites.[4] Consequently, just as we can identify the racial contours of specific periods, we should also be able to identify the contours of specific civil rights movements throughout the history of the racial state. Hence, our purpose is to also identify these contours and identify the specific civil rights movements over time.

Finally, it should be understood that civil rights is just another phrase for racial justice. Given this, it is further understood that racial justice is part of a wider social justice process. Therefore, given a social justice context, we will conclude by suggesting the contours of the next social justice movement.

UNDERSTANDING THE CONTOURS OF CIVIL RIGHTS MOVEMENTS

There are those who talk of the Modern Civil Rights movement in almost mournful terms – as in the demise, or the death of the movement.[5] Fortunately, nothing can be further from the truth. The Civil Rights movement did not die; it completed its mission, and therefore had no further reason for being. This is not to suggest that there are no longer any issues that must be resolved, or problems solved – no it is just the realization that the reasons that gave rise to the Civil Rights movement were resolved in the late 1970s, and rather than sadness, there should be rejoicing for the victories won.

When one talks of the Civil Rights movement, typically they are making reference to what more aptly should be described as the "Modern Civil Rights" movement. The insertion of the "modern" helps us to understand that in actuality there have been multiple "Civil Rights" movements throughout the history of the United States. In point of fact, the movement toward Civil Rights began with the advent of Western Imperialism. The movements that we will concentrate on will be: (1) Early Civil Rights movement in Colonial and Revolutionary America, (2) Civil Rights movements in Ante and Post Bellum America, (3) Modern Civil Rights, and (4) Post Civil Rights.[6]

Early Civil Rights Movements

As the colonies racial economy developed and become more diversified, we note the development of more diversified responses in the form of directed actions and social movements among the Africans. Although certain elements of the colonial experience may be associated with religious freedom, the dominant theme of colonial America was economic. Economics, more specifically European imperialism,[7] defined the structure, values, and purpose of the early colonies. As labor shortages intensified, and the use of forced labor – European, Native American, and African – became more accessible – the relationship between the governors and the governed became more conflictual. Race and racism were created as a means of controlling the conflict, and redirecting the stress away from the racialized elite. Thus racialized labor became hierarchically arranged (codified by law) to produce segmented labor, political and social markets. With the development of these racially segmented markets, we can also speak of the development of a racial economy. This racial economy ultimately became the basis of the racial state. Through its laws, the racial state of early America defined and codified race and the institution of slavery.

With this codification, racism, in all of its ugly dimensions, was born. Each of the original American colonies, shortly after coming into being, systematically began to create systems of slavery. Virginia was the first to make slavery legal in 1661; soon the other colonies would follow. Africans responded to these laws and slavery with increased resentment, as masters feared slave uprisings.

The colonial assembly therefore adopted a rigid slave code, restricting the freedom of movement of slaves, inflicting severe penalties for even minor offenses and denying slaves civil and criminal rights (Logan, 1957, p. 9, cited by Thompson, 1965, p. 20).

As observed by Burns:

Through elaborate statutory schemes, the slave codes regulated the movement of blacks, denied any family relationships, and applied criminal sanctions according to a different and harsher standard than applied to whites. The law confirmed and guaranteed the debased situation of the slave ... (Burns, 1973, p. 159)

Of interests, is that while subjugated, these people were not without agency. To the extent that this agency became organized, and systematized then we can call it a movement. As a consequence, movements represent both process and products of collective agency. What makes a movement a civil one reflects populations within a civil (e.g. state, national, or political) jurisdiction exercising their collective agency. The fact that the populations, in early Western Imperialism, most likely to develop civil agency, were not covered as civil subjects is all the more intriguing.

But African resistance to being colonized, racialized, and forced into servitude was very real and organized. For example, African ethnic enclaves developed in most of the 13 colonies. Organized resistance, in the form of revolts, revolutions, legal challenges, and conspiracies are well documented. History reports the first slave revolt in the United States in 1526 when a group of about 100 Africans (possibly the first to come to this continent) forcefully challenged their captivity. While scholars differ in terms of location,[8] they nevertheless agree that these blacks, once free, went on to form the first permanent settlement, other than Native Americans, in the United States.

Bell argues that black protests associated with both French and Spanish colonial periods began emerging as early as 1718. During the Spanish period of New Orleans, she observes the emergence of a cohesive, assertive free black community that provided a social base for the protest tradition, and white political radicals exiled from France helped to sustain an egalitarian ideology against discriminatory and repressive legislation during the antebellum era. Free black protest reached a peak with the petition of black militiamen who claimed full citizenship and equality in 1803 (Bell, 1997).

African cultural and sociopolitical values served to define, and augment the slave revolts that enveloped New York City in 1712, the 1739 Stono rebellion in South Carolina, the 1745 New York conspiracy, the 1800 Richmond slave plot associated with Gabriel Prosser, Nat Turner's 1831 revolt in Southampton, Virginia and Denmark Vesey's 1832 conspiracy in Charleston. (Rucker, 2006) Thus, both individually and collectively, slaves carried out an extensively complex, and often subtle form of social protest. These protests took many forms to include the sabotage of machinery, tools, and personal possessions, surreptitious destruction of crops or maiming of animals, feigning ignorance, clumsiness, self-mutilation, and suicide. (Aptheker, 1943, pp. 140–149) Suttles concludes:

> For wherever slave regimes were being assailed from outside forces they were also being attacked literally at their centers by the slaves themselves. Plantation authority was confronted with repeated challenges not only as a consequence of white men's uneven economic development, political crises, and moral critiques, but also in the rebellion of slaves in their own ideological ... terms. In the period 1829–32, for example, when English and other slave powers were immersed in and traumatized by economic and political debates...there were slave revolts in Virginia, Louisiana, North Carolina, Caracas, St. Jago (Santiago), Tortola, Martinique, Antigua, and in Brazil (Suttles, 1971).

Clearly these are not isolated events, or are they random; rather they reflect deliberate organized, systematic acts of agency. These provide clear evidence of a movement where Africans challenged the state regarding their status and their civil rights. During this period several documents can also be identified, where Africans, or their agents, petitioned the courts for these same rights. Thus we note in 1774:

> The Petition of a Grate Number of Blacks of this Province who by divine permission are held in a state of Slavery within the bowels of a free and Christian Country.
>
> ... That yur Petitioners apprehend we have in common with all other men a natural right to our freedom without being depriv'd of them by our fellow men as we are a freeborn Pepel and have never forfeited this Blessings by aney compact or agreement whatever. But we were unjustly dragged by the cruel hand of power from our dearest frinds and sum of us stolen from the bosoms of our tender Parents and from a Populous Pleasant and Plentiful country and Brought hither to be made slaves for Life in a Christian land. Thus we are deprived of every thing that hath a tendency to make life enven tolerable, the endearing ties of husband and wife we are strangers to for we are no longer man and wife than our masters and mistresses thinkes proper marred or unmarred. Our children are also taken from us by force and sent maney miles from us wear we seldom or ever see them again there to be made slaves of for Life which sometimes is very short by Reson of Being dragged form their mothers Breest. Thus our Lives are imbittered to us on these accounts .... We therfor Bage your Excellency and Honours will give this its deer weight and consideration and that you will accordingly cause an act of the legislative to be passed that we may obtain our Natural right our freedoms and our children be set at lebety ... (Aptheker, 1951, pp. 6–9, cited in Grant, 1991, pp. 29–30)

These Africans challenged the state's right to make them slaves, as they deemed that they had been deprived of their "natural rights" that they had never "forfeited". They recognized their condition was made even more intolerable in that they were denied such basic rights as marriage, control of their children, or themselves. Thus, within the parameters of civil society, they protested their status, asserted their rights, and made clear their demands to the appropriate legislative authorities. We are left with a definite conclusion that Africans, in the revolutionary period, acted in concert to demand their collective civil rights. The evidence, showing a multi-faceted approach, further demonstrates the reality that this was a process, not an event. The sustained nature of this process adds further evidence to the conclusion that they reflect not a series of episodes, but a movement with clear and distinct goals, agendas, means, and ends.

Civil Rights in Early America: North

When the revolutionary war severed ties between the colonies and Great Britain, it also marked a shift in America's racially defined caste system. Separate racial trajectories can be noted between the north and the south following the American Revolution. In the north, the revolution began the process, which gradually transformed slavery into a racially stratified class system. In the south, slavery became the dominant institution through which the racial state and economy were evidence. The gradual emancipation of slavery, coupled with the disappearance of European indentured servants, served to intensify the rift between white and black labor (Horton, 1999). In the North, blacks found their position at the bottom continuously reaffirmed as whites agitated to restrict their access to better jobs (Foner, 1983, p. 211; Franklin & Moss, 1988, pp. 142–143, as cited by Tate, 1998). Preference for white workers continued to preserve racially segmented labor markets as European immigrants were encouraged (Litwack, 1961, pp. 158–159). Competition between whites and blacks was fiercest among unskilled and semiskilled positions at the bottom of the ladder (Tate, 1998). While a small middle class of black professionals developed, the majority of the Africans were marginalized among the poor (Tate, ibid., p. 768).

The mercantile dominated north-eastern cities, along with the predominance of Quakers, Catholics, and Dutch, produced a radically different political economy then the agrarian, based slavocracies of the south, with the predominance of Protestants. The contours of African civil rights' activities in the racialized North were radically different then those in the racialized South. Thus, the demands of an increasingly urban and industrialized economy, facilitated the development of a more diversified African constituency.[9]

Northern blacks increasingly saw this marginalization extended into the political, social, cultural, and educational institutions. While northern blacks experienced relatively more freedom then their southern counterparts, they nevertheless were limited. With the exception of Connecticut, black suffrage in New England was limited to those able to pay a poll tax. Throughout the north, "Blacks faced segregated public conveyances and accommodations" (Tate, *ibid.*, p. 769).

The period between 1787 and 1837 has been described by Bennett (1993) as one of the most critical periods for black America. For it was during this period that the first permanent African American institutional forms came into being. These institutions would become the formal vehicles from which the black agenda, agency, and actions would be articulated.

In 1787, when Richard Allen and Absalon Jones, and other black congregants, were forced to worship from the balcony of the St. George's Methodist Church, the second, sustained collective civil rights movement among blacks was initiated. Black responses to these racial insults were the creation of separate black institutions. Blacks responded not only by starting their own black church but also the creation of the Free African Society (i.e. the first black civil rights organization in this country). Thus a movement was born, launched by religious leaders, merging both the secular and the sacred, and served to create an effective protest strategy that advocated for both political and religious freedom. From this movement we note the development of burial and assurance societies, emigration societies, abolitionist movement, "the dissemination of ideas, political forums, fund-raisers to sustain Black institutions, escaped fugitives, vigilance committees, and antislavery protest ..."[10] (Tate, *ibid.*, p. 773). Northern free black resistance in the antebellum period relied upon:

"... Three interconnected variables: (a) the material circumstances of Black existence; (b) Northern Black institutional formation undergirding emerging indigenous leadership and protest direction; and (c) the overt and covert operations of vigilantism, dramatic slave rescues, and the Underground Railroad ..." (Tate, *ibid.*, p. 764)

Often when we speak of this period, we tend to ignore the efforts of women. In Salem, Massachusetts, Black women in 1832 established the first all female abolitionist movement. As pointed out by Yee, this movement was complex in that it served to give notice to both racial and sexual exploitation experienced by black women (Yee, 1992).[11]

Civil Rights in Early America: South

During the revolutionary era, Florida, under Spanish rule, became infamous as a haven for runaway slaves. Slaves and their Spanish and Native American allies, forged bonds, waged wars of resistance, and maintained stable communities for over a hundred years prior and during the formal founding of the United States. Africans were with the Spanish "when they explored the South Atlantic and the gulf coast, and they helped to found St. Augustine, the ancient city in 1565" (Southall, 1934, p. 77). Aided by the Spanish, African fugitive slaves found refuge in Florida, and with the aid and protection of Governor Montiano in 1739, established a viable colony near St. Augustine. (Southall, *ibid.*, p. 78). In subsequent periods, Africans and Seminoles[12] forged common bonds (of struggle, marriage, and community) that continued long throughout the 17th and 18th centuries.

Slavery defined the south, molded its social, political, and economic instructions. Every day life, custom, morality, and ethics were all conditioned and distorted by slavery. As V.O. Keys notes:

> In its grand outlines the politics of the South revolves around the position of the Negro. It is at times interpreted as a politics of cotton, as a politics of free trade, as a politics of agrarian poverty, or as a politics of planter and plutocrat. Although such interpretations have superficial validity, in the last analysis the major peculiarities of southern politics go back to the Negro. Whatever phase of the southern political process one seeks to understand, sooner or later the trail of inquiry leads to the Negro (Keys, 1949, p. 5 cited by Cook, 1976, p. 281).

The first independent black institutions developed in the South were religious in origin. Specifically, southern black converts of white Separatist (or New Light) Baptists were the first to establish separate black churches. These early churches sprang from plantation congregations at Luneburg, Virginia. Smith (1988) observes that the first urban black church originated in Savannah, Georgia with the founding of the First African Baptist Church in 1777. The first pastor, Andrew Bryan, "with a number of his followers, was whipped and imprisoned as means of putting a stop to their proceedings. But they found advocates and patrons among very respectable and influential characters, and, by well-doing, at length disarmed and silenced their bitterest persecutors" (Love, 1888). As pointed out by Genovese (1974) religion provided blacks cover for social and political activism. Therefore it was not uncommon for whites to fear the establishment of religion among the slaves.

> In the meantime, there developed among the Whites misgivings with regard to training Blacks in the Christian religion. This was due, in large measure, to the fear that as a result of becoming inducted into the Christian church, Negroes would develop a spirit of

freedom from and resentment to their status. This fear was all the more intensified as a result of the insurrection in 1831 led by Nat Turner in Virginia (McKinney, 1971 p. 457).

Nat Turner in 1831 attempted to spark a slave rebellion. Claiming religious prophesy, Turner incited over 60 black slaves to massacre over 50 whites in Southampton, Virginia. Before 1831, there had been simmering slave unrest, expressed in either individual rebellion or escapes. Large-scale revolts led by both Gabriel Prosser in 1800 and Denmark Vesey in 1822, although aborted had nevertheless sparked widespread fear throughout the south. President Jefferson called the Prosser revolt the "most serious and formidable conspiracy we have ever known of the kind" (cited by Gross & Bender, 1971, p. 490). The idea that slaves might rise up in the night and butcher, shattering the notions of the passive and happy slave, their white masters caused shock and horror throughout the south. The mood quoted by Genovese was:

> A great number of southerners at all times held the firm belief that the Negro population was so docile, so little cohesive, and in the main so friendly toward the whites and so contented that a disastrous insurrection by them would be impossible. But on the whole there was much greater anxiety abroad in the land than historians have told of, and its influence in shaping southern policy was much greater than they have appreciated (Genovese, *ibid.*, p. 595).

As Genovese concludes, this resistance represented political action, which directly challenged the power of the racial state.

Southern black women responded to sexual exploitation in a multitude of ways. Black women, in response to rape and sexual exploitation, developed what Hine's refers to as a "culture of dissemblance". This dissemblance produced a type of split personality, where black women "... created the appearance of openness and disclosure but actually shielded the truth of their inner lives and selves from their oppressors" (Hine, 1989). Although hidden, these nevertheless were the basis of more open forms of protest, rebellion, and resistance. Clearly, black women were not helpless, as witnessed by the multiple poisonings of various white families, home burnings, infanticide, and other acts of violence perpetuated by black women (Hine, 1990, pp. 659–661). Wood (1987) demonstrates that black female slaves were not without agency. They not only effectively organized their labor, but also withdrew their labor to protest, rioted, planned escapes, and otherwise showed their unwillingness to be passive.

Civil Rights leading up to the Civil War
The 30 years leading up to the civil war was characterized by the increasing mobilization, protests, and agitation of blacks in both the North and the

South. The South responded by solidifying the slave state, while in the North more draconian racial laws were enacted (Dick, 1974). In the 1857 Dred Scott case, the United States Supreme Court ruled that blacks had no rights, they could never have rights, and Congress had no power to change their status. Thus, whether slave or free, the black in America was to be forever left out civil, political, economic, and cultural rights due to others within this country. The end of the Civil War (1861–1965) brought much hope that the Nation could now heal. Not only did Congress pass the 13th, 14th, and 15th Amendments,[13] but it also passed a series of legislative enactments aimed at enforcing civil rights. Black Americans pinned their hopes of total freedom on the 13th, 14th, and 15th Amendments to the U.S. Constitution, which together granted them full citizenship. Under the 1866 Civil Rights Act a variety of civil rights that covered all citizens (regarded of race) were expanded. Under these civil rights we note prohibition of both peonage and slavery; nondiscrimination in public accommodations; the right to sue, make contracts, or serve on juries were prohibited; and finally equality in all rights and privileges covered under the Constitution and laws of the United States. The Act provided for both civil and criminal remedies, to which both private and states could be held accountable. No sooner had these enactments become law, significant racial re-articulation redefined and effectively nullified their intent.

Civil Rights After the Civil War
The Civil War helped to crystallize black agitation, in both the North and the South, for freedom, justice, and equality. With the successful conclusion of the Civil War, blacks in the North began to refocus their attention to closer to home. Ohio, in 1870, with a black population of fewer than three percent of the state's population, had one of the largest black populations in the North. Ohio was also distinguished with some of the most comprehensive and racist laws of any northern state. Continual agitation on the part of black leaders, forced moderate white leaders to pass a series of civil rights measures. Tight national and state elections during 1870s and 1880s made Ohio a swing state. Blacks leveraged their newfound voting franchise to secure integration of higher end public accommodations for black upper class, integration of public schools, and the repeal of the ant-miscegenation laws. It was also Ohio Congressman John A. Bingham, who fathered the 14th Amendment. These gains were however reversed in the next two decades, as racism swept the South, the state, and the country and more regressive "Jim Crow Laws" in both the North and the South (Gerber 1976). By the late 1880s the dream of reconstruction, was replaced by the

nightmare of Jim Crow. Plessy V. Fergusson sealed the coffin of reform, as blacks throughout the country realized the harsh realities of extreme racial backlashes, the beginning of the lynching campaigns, and the continual programs of political, economic, and cultural disenfranchisement. In the North these backlashes resulted in the creation of ghettos (Massey & Denton, *ibid.*) and in the South the extremely impoverished black belt.[14]

The battle to gain access to the totality of American liberties would be incomplete without access to public accommodations. The Supreme Court in *Plessy V. Fergusson* (1896) effectively closed the door of any hopes toward racial conciliation. In its ruling, the Court upheld a Louisiana law which stipulated that "equal but separate" railway cars for black and white passengers. The Court ignored Justice John Marshall Harlan, its lone voice of reason who argued that the action would not only create a racial caste system, but that blacks would be denigrated, and the colorblind intent of the Constitution would be nullified.

In *Plessy*, the Supreme Court declared that black Americans would retain the stigma of race and second-class citizenship, and be denied even basic access to public accommodations. This ruling, more than any other single action, led to the dissolution of good will, the dismantling of postwar Reconstruction, and the wholesale creation of the extensive apparatus of Jim Crow segregation under the misbegotten rubric of "separate but equal." It would take almost a half-century, several hundred lynchings, and countless court cases before *Plessy* would be overturned.

As observed by Washington:

> Within less than thirty years after the passage of the first of the civil rights statutes, a great part of the congressional program was nullified or reduced by the action of the courts and subsequent congresses. The "privileges and immunities" of United States citizens which the Fourteenth Amendment forbade the states to abridge were narrowly construed to refer to privileges of national citizenship.... (T)he Supreme Court construed the Fourteenth Amendment ... provide only for the enforcement of its provision against acts of the state ... not ... private individuals from violating the rights of others. (Washington 1951: 335)

Modern Civil Rights

The racial state, as a consequence of the *Plessy V. Fergusson* ruling, now mandated racial segregation. Within months after this historic ruling, seventeen southern states began to implement sets of laws – known as Jim *Crow* or *de jure segregation* that formalized and legitimized racial segregation in most institutional spaces. Among these were laws that established "separate but equal" educational facilities. While often lacking specific legislation, the

North accomplished the same effect through what has been termed *de facto segregation.*

Black migration helped restructure northern labor markets, increased labor unrest, intensified racial conflict, and served to redefine the parameters of the racial state of the late 19th and early 20th century (Brown, 1998, p. 320). Black labor, in both the North and South, faced increasing racial hostility as white labor mobilized. Through the birth of the labor movement, in the 1870s, blacks found themselves targeted in both the East and the South. Many of the early labor leaders and union recruits were "Copperheads", or pro-Confederate northern Democrats (Leary, 2005). Black skilled labor was effectively removed from competition with white skilled labor with the passage of the Wagner Act. As explained by Leary:

> Until the 1930s when the first national labor laws were passed ... unions were not legally recognized... In order to get the necessary votes in Congress, President Franklin Roosevelt had to make a deal with the "Dixiecrats," the significant number of Southern Democrats ... The Dixiecrats agreed to vote to legalize labor unions if the law excluded agricultural and domestic workers. This compromise eliminated most of the black working class in the South from legal union coverage. This compromise was intended to keep former slaves and their descendants in a state of poverty and dependence... (Leary, *ibid.*)

White skilled craftsmen and other blue collar workers effectively organized and unionized to exclude black and other racialized minorities. It was only through the organizing of A. Phillip Randolph do we see the beginnings of a black labor movement in the United States. His success however was limited to organizing among the lower skilled and menial positions with the railroads, etc.

With the advent of World War I and II, blacks demanded greater involvement in all aspects of American society. Their demands were initially met, as both industry and the military, reluctantly responded by significantly increasing the presence of blacks. These increases, however, were short-lived, as witnessed by the massive firings and layoffs at wars' end. Racial unrest, in the form of protests, riots, and political activism continued throughout the 30s and 40s.[15]

> The Negro's morale at the beginning of World War II is also partly explained by his experience in World War I. Black America had gone into that war with high morale, generated by the belief that the democratic slogans literally meant what they said.... But the image of a new democratic order was smashed by the race riots, lynchings, and continued rigid discrimination. The result was a mass trauma and a series of movements among Negroes in the 1920s, which were characterized by a desire to withdraw from white society which wanted little to do with them.

Consequently, when the appeals for black participation in the new war to save Europe were made, many blacks responded with a cold shoulder.[16] An editorial in the Crisis summarized this mood by stating:

> The CRISIS is sorry for brutality, blood, and death among the peoples of Europe, just as we were sorry for China and Ethiopia. But the hysterical cries of the preachers of democracy for Europe leave us cold. We want democracy in Alabama and Arkansas, in Mississippi and Michigan, in the District of Columbia – *in the Senate of the United States*. (Italics in original. Crisis 1940)[17]

The attack on Pearl Harbor caused blacks to espouse a different slogan. As expressed by W.E.B. Du Bois, blacks had to win the battle on both fronts, in Europe and at home (Jones, 1944).

By the 1950s, segregation had become the symbol of racial hegemony in America. Efforts in the United States since the mid-twentieth century have been aimed at reversing racial segregation. These efforts, which constitute the modern civil rights movements, were political processes that made use of civil protest, litigation, and economic sanctions to eliminate racial segregation. Racial segregation, both de jure and de facto, has historically served to restrict access to education and training, economic and political institutions, occupational and social mobility, religious and social institutions, and neighborhoods and transportation facilities. Within the United States, most desegregation activity has focused on educational institutions, public accommodation, and the military.

The *Brown* decision, by striking down legal segregation on the basis of race in public schools, reversed the Supreme Court's 1896 decision in *Plessy V. Fergusson*.

The 1954 *Brown v. Board of Education* ruling, with its aim to end school segregation, struck at the heart of the system of racial entitlements in the United States. Nothing less then a revolution was envisioned. As pointed out by Gary Orfield and Susan Eaton (1996), no one believed that merely placing black and white kids in the same classroom would end centuries of discrimination. Rather, the movement toward integration recognized that white dominance had been engineered through exclusive control of select schools. The Supreme Court ruled that racially segregated schools did indeed perpetuate racial stigmas among blacks, and that such schools were therefore inherently unequal. Yet, in striking down *Plessy*, the Supreme Court decided ambiguously that integration should take place "with all deliberate speed."

"All deliberate speed" has been described as simultaneously placing the country's feet on both the accelerator and the brake. Throughout the South, a multitude of strategies were instituted to delay, divert, or otherwise circumvent the Brown ruling. In 1956 advocates of segregation were successful in convincing Virginia's governor and state assembly to pass laws blocking the funding of school integration. One of the most striking anti-integration efforts occurred in 1957 when Arkansas governor Orval Faubus (1910–1994) ordered the state's national guard to block the doors to Little Rock's Central High School, preventing nine black teenagers from entering. Only after President Dwight Eisenhower (1890–1969) sent federal troops to the site were the nine students allowed to attend the school. Other states were equally creative. Prince Edwards County in Virginia decided to close all of its public schools rather than integrate them. Lawsuits filed on behalf of blacks throughout the South filled the courts. More definitive court rulings ensued, but the road to integration was fraught with many obstacles.

A decade after the *Brown* decision, southern schools remained 98 percent segregated. Continual agitation on the part of blacks led to the 1964 Civil Rights Act. Thereafter, courts prescribed more immediate and encompassing integration efforts. Starting in 1966 with *United States v. Jefferson County Board of Education*, the Fifth Circuit Court not only ordered integration but also remedies to redress historical segregation. In *Green v. County School Board of New Kent County* (1968), the U.S. Supreme Court ordered schools to provide immediate integration. Similar court rulings, aggressive enforcement by the federal government, and the vigilance of southern blacks eventually led to the racial transformation of schools in the South. By 1970, slightly more than 45 percent of black youths attended integrated schools.

Frustrated with the slow pace of integration, the Supreme Court in the 1971, in *Swann v. Charlotte-Mecklenburg Board of Education*, ordered the massive urban desegregation plan. In this plan, with the aid of busing, the first district wide school desegregation order was provided. Busing, as it came to be known, became very controversial as a tool to achieve integration.

Access to public space and private dwellings has long been disputed terrain in the United States. Property and the access to property has been the determinant not only of status, but also of political and social rights and privilege. In the United States, the rights to vote, hold political office, and seek legal recourse were all initially reserved for those who owned property. Thus, the first sets of laws aimed at controlling blacks included laws that not only declared them property but also restricted their ownership rights.

The 1964 Civil Rights Act put an end to segregated lunch counters, hotels, trains, buses, and theaters. This legislation owes its enactment to the courage and determination of many who became heroes of the modern civil rights movement. On February 27, 1960 four black college students in Greensboro, North Carolina, defied the laws of segregation by sitting down at a whites-only Woolworth's lunch counter and requesting service. Although they were not served, their defiance sparked similar acts in over one hundred American cities throughout the 1960s. In 1961 civil rights activists known as "Freedom Riders" began to protest the whites-only policies in public bathrooms and buses. In 1961 thirteen Freedom Riders, white and black, left Washington, DC, in two buses heading south. Pipe-toting men in Anniston and Birmingham, Alabama attacked riders on the first bus. The second bus was firebombed just outside of Anniston. Undaunted, sit-ins, freedom rides, and other forms of protests compelled a reluctant Congress and president to pass and sign into law the 1964 Civil Rights Act. This Civil Rights Act, like none before it, represented the mother lode for racial justice in America. The Act literally changed American society. Racial segregation and discrimination were prohibited in public accommodations, government, and private enterprise. Jim Crow was dead in the South, and no longer could states legislate racial segregation in housing, education, employment, or hiring.

On the heals of the 1964 Civil Rights victory, Black Civil Rights groups such as the National Association of Colored People (N.A.A.C.P.), Congress on Racial Equality (C.O.R.E.), Southern Christian Leadership Conference (S.C.L.C.) staged massive protest throughout the South. A series of protests in Selma, Alabama on March 7, 1965 resulted in hundreds of peaceful protestors tear-gassed, bludgeoned with clubs, sat upon by dogs and viscous mobs, and arrested – all under the supervision of state and local police, and caught on tape by national media. Bloody Sunday, as it came to be known, shocked the nation and prodded the president to act. President Johnson addressed the nation, calling this a sad day for America. Two days later, President Johnson sent the Voting Rights bill to Congress. On August 5, 1965 Johnson signed into law the Voting Rights Act which guaranteed blacks the right to vote. Thus, blacks finally gained the rights provided for with the 14th and 15th Amendments. The Voting Rights Act provided federal oversight for voter registration and elections in counties to determine voter eligibility or where registration or turnout had been less than 50 percent in the previous presidential election It also prohibited literacy tests and made provisions for non-English speaking Americans. With the 1970 extension it also banned the infamous poll tax. It was again renewed in both 1975 and 1982. Not only have millions of black voters benefited, but also thousands of black elected officials have been elected over this time period. As all other rights derive from the right to vote, in a Democracy there is no right more precious than the right to vote. Consequently, the Voter's Rights Act is quite possible the single,[18] most significant civil rights legislative action ever passed by the Congress.[19]

Finally, under President Johnson, a bold new vision for America, aimed at addressing the long, delayed remedies for centuries of neglect, racial exploitation, and discrimination – was launched. The Great Society Programs, finally the racial, economic, and gender rift were to be crossed. The marches, the songs, and chants, the long summer nights, and trees with their "strange fruit" – had brought a Nation to the realization that "a change" had to come. The two primary purposes of the Great society were to end poverty and provide for racial justice. Programs were established to address education and urban problems, transportation and consumer protection, environmental protection, and ultimately gender inequality. The vision, almost a reality, never totally reached the light of day. In its stead, a series of more conservative Presidents and Congresses, became engrossed in financing the military-criminal-industrial complex. The Great Society Programs, with its vision of a new day, a New America – died the death of political short sightedness.

In 1972, President Nixon, fearful of a Wallace victory, aggressively sought to ban busing. Although Congress failed to act, the United States Supreme Court provided the necessary ruling. A Detroit case, in 1974, *Milliken v. Bradley*, involving a metropolitan area resulted in the cessation of busing across the city's borders. The 1974 Supreme Court ruling ordering busing would intensify the controversies associated with integration.

Busing and forced integration generated considerable fear among many white Americans. This fear resulted in "white flight, (i.e. when whites leave typically urban areas to avoid living in proximity to blacks)" and it fuelled a conservative backlash against desegregation efforts. During the 1970s, some Republican politicians, such as Richard Nixon (1913–1994), would ride the waves of this backlash all the way to the White House and control of both houses of Congress. These conservative forces also oversaw the first set of reversals. By 1974 in *Milliken v. Bradley*, the Supreme Court blocked a Detroit area-busing plan. In this and subsequent cases, the courts ruled that local decisions regarding school integration should be respected.

As segregation was challenged in the North, the Supreme Court would institute even more radical moves, inaugurating the era of busing, teacher integration, gradual integration, and magnet schools. Although partial success may be claimed, more than 50 years after Brown, little progress has been made toward the racial integration of America's school system. White flight, private schools, and the more recent voucher movement have all served to preserve racial segregation in schools.

Post Civil Rights and The Case for Social Justice[20]

The various civil rights movements asserted certain rights that had been denied to blacks throughout their history in America. Civil rights successes include access to voting and the courts, education and accommodations, military service and political offices. No longer were lynch mobs, vigilante groups, or racist gangs accorded legal sanctions. Anti-miscegenation and redlining were outlawed, poll-taxes, literacy clauses, and the all white primary were ruled unenforceable, racially proscribed segregation and legally sanctioned job bias were replaced by court ordered integration and affirmative action. These rights, following Rawls (1985), derive from social systems where free and equal participants cooperate under where "fairness" is optimized. Thus, any thing or situation which violates ones freedom or ability to be equal, or which produces a lack of "fairness" may be deemed to be unjust. Thus, the success of the civil rights movement attacked the racial state arising from violations of the presumptions of justice. Unfortunately, the centuries of racial discrimination, segregation, and hyper-exploitation has left its scars upon the black communities throughout this country. These racial legacies cry out for justice of a different sort.

The next movement, relying upon a notion of justice, calls for new forms of social justice projects and processes which recognize the legacy of the racial state.

> It is neither just nor sensible to proscribe segregation having its basis in affirmative state action while at the same time failing to provide a remedy for segregation which grows out of discrimination in housing, or other economic or social factors. (Barksdale v. Springfield School Committee, 237 F. Supp. 543, 546–1965)

Social justice is not about placing guilt at the feet of whites, nor is it about claiming victim status for blacks. Blacks have been victimized, and they have experienced as victims in America. Whites have benefited from their whiteness, and they have experienced American guilt. Guilt and victim-hood politics, practices, and solutions rarely lead to anything but embarrassment and reluctance on the part of the guilty, and frustration and anxiety on the part of the victim. The guilty, attempting to seek absolution, are encouraged to make some gesture of atonement. Such gestures, rarely anything but tokens of attrition and contrition, always delivered with great fanfare, encourages the victim to believe that finally their remedies are forthcoming. Alas, as the guilt subsides, typically with the passage of time or the pressure of economic realities, resolve is weakened, programs are reduced and/or eliminated, and another cycle of unmet promises is recorded. Each cycle of guilt and victim identification, with its resultant policies and practices of appeasements producing even more anxieties and frustrations, culminates in another generation on both sides who loose faith in the capacity of the other to appropriately respond. These cycles, being repeated several times over the course of the American experience, has produced waves of guilt, victim identification, anxiety, and frustration. This cyclic process has produced within the white community what Kozel has described as compassion fatigue, and within the black community, what West describes (but mistakenly explains) as nihilism. The guilt cycle, producing at both extreme compassion fatigue and nihilism, can only be broken by a complete solution, a real attempt to restore the African to his proper place in our universe. What is required is nothing short of justice, social justice.

Racial justice, as a special case of social justice, requires that we find a way to mend the rift between racial groups. As I see it, such remedies would have to provide for at least three central problems created by racial state (1) reparation, (2) affirmative empowerment, and (3) affirmative opportunity. In the space remaining I shall outline these remedies.

Reparations, as racial justice, would involve the assessment of damages associated with both slavery and the continual racial discrimination, not only experienced by blacks but Hispanics, Asians, and Native Americans. It also recognizes that European Americans, most noticeably Appalachians, have also suffered racial discrimination over these same periods. Such a reparations program, by definition would be at the group and not individual level. The monies identified (variously estimated between 4–20 trillion dollars)[21] would be utilized to fund programs in both affirmative empowerment and opportunity.

Although Affirmative Action has accomplished the creation and maintenance of a modern black middle class, it has primarily benefited white middle class women. Aside from this, the overwhelmingly large number of black, yellow, brown, red, and white poor have not benefited from any form of action, affirmative or otherwise. Affirmative Action, quite the contrary, has often pitted these groups against each other in a mad squabble over fewer and fewer pieces of an ever-shrinking pie. Each generation, we note more at the table, with fewer actual Affirmative Action "slots to go around." And even as the needs expand, there are increasingly successful challenges to the legitimacy of Affirmative Action at all levels of society. If Affirmative Action actually worked, it would be worth fighting for its survival. Unfortunately, Affirmative Action has only limited utility and effectiveness for those who Wilson (1987) describes as the "truly disadvantaged" regardless of color or location.

Affirmative opportunity and affirmative empowerment are derived from the visions of Franklin D. Roosevelt and Lyndon Johnson. They, collectively, recognized that in-order for one to live out the American dream – to enjoy freedom, justice, and the blessings of liberty – they must have access to excellent education and training, health care, living wages, affordable housing, and safe neighborhoods regardless of accidents of birth, life circumstance, or historical antecedents. Put simply, affirmative opportunity is the vision that all can maximize their intellectual, creative, and personal abilities unencumbered by race, gender, class, or location. It recognizes that such accidents of birth such as poverty, race, gender, or geography, in a just society, are trivial and have no bearing upon how much we are willing to invest in their and our collective future. It recognizes that we are a nation of families, and that as a nation it is in our best collective interests to maximize all of our human potential and capital. Affirmative opportunity finally recognizes that centuries of disinvestments, disincentives, and discouragements have produced killing fields rather than fields of dreams. Alternatively, affirmative empowerment starts from the reality that we must individually and collectively take responsibilities for our actions, that is past, present and in the future. It recognizes that past decisions have served to victimize whole population groups leaving them little more than subsistence to survive on. It recognizes that in order for one to be free they must feel that they have the power to change their circumstances, change their lives, and ultimately change their destinies. Affirmative empowerment, tied to affirmative opportunity, allows for choice and agency. Both, affirmative empowerment and affirmative opportunity, financed by a social justice based reparations fund, would be available for all – regardless of race, gender, class or previous conditions of exploitation, situations of poverty, or circumstances of injustice. In order to accomplish these visions we must organize new ways of viewing, one that puts social justice at its core.

Social justice organizing transcends race, gender, culture, national origin, or class. For to not understand that these are interlinked, is not to understand the systemic nature of oppression. Oppression is also psychological, political, social, cultural, and historically specific. We must understand these interactions, in order to understand the current nature of oppression. And finally, oppression, today, as it has been for 500 years is also global, imperial, and hegemonic. Our responses must clearly be multilayered, multidimensional, and multinational. Otherwise we will be working on a small, very small piece of the monster, while its tentacles continue to engulf, re-articulate, and transmutate.

NOTES

1. Not only was there surprise, but also according to Banton (1991, p. 117) prevailing models of discrimination could not account for the emergence of the 1960s Civil Rights Movement in America or the increased racialization in England.

2. Passive acceptance results when individuals or groups offer little, if any resistance to racial actions. The lack of response suggests either acceptance or resignation. Under such situations, racialized individuals are assumed to internalize the abuse and thus identify as victims. Alternatively reactions, reflecting a stimulus/response mechanism suggests that racialized individuals while responding to particular racial events/situations, such response shows little advance or consistent planning or co-ordination among large numbers of the racialized group over time. Thus, while there may be a reaction, such reaction tends to be limited in its ability to effect change or the racial state. While both passive and reactive stances of blacks may be of interests, both time and space limits their full consideration. I shall therefore restrict my attention to what can be defined as direct(ed) actions of blacks throughout their history in the United States. By direct(ed) action, I make reference to both collective action or agency and purposeful action aimed at altering specific institutions, customs, laws, and social conventions. To the extent that such direct(ed) action is sustained both over time and geographically, then we can speak of a social movement. The particular historical periods allow us to deal with specific civil right periods or movements. See Morris (2000) for an excellent analysis of why agency, while often ignored, is critical for understanding the dynamics of the civil rights movement.

3. As noted by Tilly (1978) African American, forced to live in racially hostile environments, excluded from the political, social, and economic realms of society, engage in "defensive mobilization" (p. 73). Once mobilized, collective consciousness and social agendas are developed to produce social change (Morrison, 1987, pp. 11–13).

4. I am suggesting a synergy between these two forms of rearticulation, leaving aside the conversation regarding which came first. This derives from the original concept of articulation as provided by Karl Marx (1973). He observed that in the context of domination there may occur "a reciprocal interaction ... whereby something new, a synthesis, arises." (p. 79). Morris (1998) goes further by arguing that in the "master-slave relationship" we note a kind of "reciprocal, if unbalanced, structure that confined and channeled the behavior of slave and owner" (p. 985).

5. While varied, some have argued that the modern Civil Rights movement started with the sit-ins and boycotts, and increased in activism with the Supreme Court decision of *Brown et al. v. the Board of Education of Topeka* (1954). The decline, leading to the demise of the movement, is typically associated with the civil unrest in the period beginning in 1965 through 1968 in the aftermath of the assassination of Martin Luther King, Jr. (e.g. Schaefer, 1979, pp. 184–186), (Oberschall, 1973, pp. 206–208).

6. I am well aware that these various historical periods did not come into being in isolation of either each other, or from other global forces. For the sake of this paper, given both time and space requirements, simplicity is in order.

7. Imperialism, defined as the imposition of one political structure upon another, has its roots in ancient civilization and has no racial or ideological basis. Imperialism is about power, plain and simple. Modern colonialism is a particular form of imperialism, which results in the cultural, political, and economic subjugation of an indigenous population by another. The criterion which distinguishes modern

colonialism from other kinds of imperialism is that the former is marked by significant racial, cultural, and/or religious differences implying a superior–inferior relationship between rulers and ruled, all of which is reinforced by a political and legal system designed to maintain, if not perpetuate, this definite supremacy and subordination (Grundy, 1966, p. 63).

> Imperial colonialism represents Janus-headed systems by which European nations exploited other continents and civilizations for the maximization of profits, luxury, and resources (both human and physical). Thus from South East Asia to the southern tip of Africa, from the continent of Australia to the Americas – hundreds of millions of people were subjugated, hundreds of thousands of acres of land were dominated, and billions of dollars of resources were extrapolated.

8. Jamestown, Va., is given as the site by Daniel P. Mannix and Malcolm Cowley in their Black Cargoes: A History of the Atlantic Slave Trade, 1518–1865 (New York: Viking, 1962, p. 54). Alternatively Herbert Aptheker in American Negro Slave Revolts (New York: Columbia University Press, 1943, p. 163) argues that it is more likely that this occurred near the mouth of the Pedee River in South Carolina. (Note: Both these sites are identified in footnotes obtained in Joanne Grant's edited Black Protest: History, Documents, and Analyses, 1619–the Present.)

9. Here, the development of this constituency is both by design – for the needs of this industrial economy served to increase the need for Africans with certain skills to include reading, writing, ship building, etc.

10. Northern Black ministers, a point we will come to later, were instrumental in circumventing the religion of accommodation being preached and promoted by White missionaries of the same period. By 1895, their efforts led to the founding of the National Baptist Convention (black), which according to Washington called for Black Baptist nationalism, evangelizing Africa, and protest of white racial practices (Washington, 1986).

11. By the end of the century, Yee demonstrates, this black antislavery society would lead to the establishment of the National Association of Colored Women clubs.

12. Seminoles, which means runaway, were Indians who had escaped North American slavery (Southall, *ibid.*, p. 81). Given their common enemy it is no wonder that they became fast allies.

13. The 13th Amendment abolished slavery and involuntary servitude. The 14th Amendment provided that (1) no state shall abridge the privileges and immunities of citizens of the United States; (2) provided for due process, i.e. that no state shall deprive any citizen of life, liberty, or property without due process; and (3) no state could deny any person equal protection under the law. The 15th Amendment guaranteed citizens the right to vote regardless of race, color, or previous condition of servitude.

14. These in turn led to the Great Black Migration, the Harlem Renascence, Booker T. Washington's Southern Compromise and W.E.B. Du Bois' Talented Tenth, Marcus Garvey's Back to Africa Movement, and the Niagara Movement. While important, I classify these as actual reactions, than directed actions. Thus while important, I view them to be antecedents of the Modern Civil rights movement.

15. While some had hoped President's New Deal would facilitate black progress, nothing was farther from the truth. It is therefore significant that the Joint Committee on National Recovery and the Howard University Social Science

Department declared the New Deal to be ineffectual "…as far as the Negro is concerned, New Deal social planning generally has availed him little either because of its underlying philosophy, or because its administration has been delegated to local officials who reflect the unenlightened mores of their respective communities." ("The National Conference on the Economic Crisis and the Negro," *Journal of Negro Education* V, p. 1) (Cited by Harrell, 1968, p. 547).

   16. See also Adam Clayton Powel, Jr., "Is This a White Man's War?" (Common Sense, XI, {April 1942}, 111–113) or Horace Mann bond, "Should the Negro Care Who Wins the War?" (Annals, CCXXIII, {Sept. 1942}, 81–84 (both cited by Dalfiume, 1968a).

   17. Cited by Dalfiume (1968b, p. 95).

   18. The Supreme Court in the Yick Wo V. Hopkins (1886) stated that the right to vote is "a fundamental political right, because (it) preservative(s) … all rights."

   19. As stated by the United States Justice Department, on its web page, assessed on May 23, 2006 at url: http://www.usdoj.gov/crt/voting/intro/intro_c.htm

   20. I use social justice to cover the full range of justice projects to include racial, distributive, economic, civil, political, and cultural justice (see my Social justice and pedagogy, *Journal of American Behavioral Science*, forthcoming.).

   21. see for example Bolner (1968), Darity and Frank (2003) or Coates (2004).

REFERENCES

Anderson, E. (1999). *Code of the street: Decency, violence and the moral life of the inner city.* New York: Norton Publishers.

Aptheker, H. (1943). *American Negro slave revolts.* New York: Columbia University Press.

Aptheker, H. (Ed.) (1951). *A documentary history of the Negro people in the United States.* New York: The Citadel Press.

Banton, M. (1991). The race relations problematic. *The British Journal of Sociology, 42*(1), 115–130.

Bell, C. C. (1997). *Revolution, romanticism, and the Afro-Creole protest tradition in Louisiana, 1718–1868.* Baton Rouge and London: Louisiana State University Press.

Bennett, L., Jr. (1993). *The shaping of Black America.* New York: Penguin Books.

Bolner, J. (1968). Towards a theory of racial reparations. *Phylon, 29*(1), 41–47.

Brown, C. (1998). Racial conflict and split labor markets: The AFL campaign to organize steel workers, 1918–1919. *Social Science History, 22*(3), 319–347.

Burns, H. (1973). Black people and the tyranny of American law. *Annuals of the American Academy of Political and Social Science. – Blacks and The Law, 407*(May), 156–166.

Coates, R. D. (2004). If a tree falls in the wilderness: Reparations, academic silences, and social justice. *Social Forces, 83*(2), 841–864.

Cook, S. D. (1976). Democracy and tyranny in America: The radical paradox of the bicentennial and Blacks in the American political system. *The Journal of Politics – 200 Years of the Republic in Retrospect: A Special Bicentennial Issue., 38*(3), 276–294.

Dalfiume, R. M. (1968a). The 'forgotten years' of the Negro revolution. *The Journal of American History, 55*(1), 90–106.

Dalfiume, R. M. (1968b). The 'Forgotten Years' of the Negro Revolution. *Crisis, 47,* 94. (Lynching and Liberty. *Crisis, 47* (July 1940), 209.)

Darity, W., Jr., & Frank, D. (2003). The economics of reparations. *The American Economic Review, 93*(2), 326–329.

Dick, R. C. (1974). *Black protest: Issues and tactics.* Westport: The Greenwood Press.

Foner, P. S. (1983). *History of Black Americans: From the emergence of the cotton kingdom to the eve of the compromise of 1859,* Vol. 2. Westport, CT: Greenwood Press.

Franklin, J. H., & Moss, A. A., Jr. (1988). *From slavery to freedom: A history of Negro Americans* (6th ed.). New York: Knopf.

Genovese, E. (1974). *Roll, Jordan, roll: The world the slaves made.* New York: Pantheon.

Gerber, D. A. (1976). *Black Ohio and the color line, 1860–1915.* Urbana: University of Illinois Press.

Grant, J. (Ed.) (1991). *Black protest: History, documents, and analysis – 1619–Present.* New York: Ballatine Books-Fawcett Premier.

Gross, S. L., & Bender, E. (1971). History, politics, and literature: The myth of Nat Turner. *American Quarterly, 23*(4), 487–518.

Grundy, K. W. (1966). African explanations of underdevelopment: The theoretical basis for political action. *Review of Politics, 28,* 62–75.

Harrell, J. A. (1968). Negro leadership in the election year 1936. *The Journal of Southern History, 34*(4), 546–564.

Hine, D. C. 1990 (1979). Female slave resistance: The economics of sex. In: D. C. Hine (Ed.) *Black Women in American History* (Vol. 2., 1990, pp. 657–666). Brooklyn: Carlson. First published in *The Western Journal of Black Studies 3,* (1979), 123–127.

Hine, D. C. (1989). Rape and the inner lives of Black women in the Middle West. *Signs, 14*(4) (Common grounds and crossroads: Race, ethnicity and class in women's lives), 912–920.

Horton, L. (1999). From class to race in early America: Northern post-emancipation racial reconstruction. *Journal of the Early Republic 19*(4) Special Issue on Racial Consciousness and Nation-Building in the Early Republic (winter), 629–649.

Hughes, E. C. (1963). Race relations and the sociological imagination. *American Sociological Review, 28*(6), 869–890.

Jones, L. M. (1944). The editorial policy of Negro newspapers of 1971–1918 as compared with that of 1941–1942. *The Journal of Negro History, 29*(1), 24–31.

Keys, V. O. (1949). *Southern politics,* Vintage, Ed. New York: Alfred A. Knopf, Inc.

Klinkner, P. A., & Smith, R. M. (1999). *The unsteady march.* Chicago: University of Chicago Press.

Leary, E. (2005). Crisis in the U.S. labor movement: The roads not taken. *Monthly Review, 57*(2) (Accessed online, May 24, 2006, available at URL http://www.monthlyreview.org/0605leary.htm).

Lewis, O. (1964). The culture of poverty. In: J. J. Tepaske & S. N. Fisher (Eds), *Explosive Forces in Latin America.* Columbus: Ohio State University Press.

Litwack, L. F. (1961). *North of slavery: The Negro in the free states, 1790–1860.* Chicago: The University of Chicago Press.

Logan, R. W. (1957). *The Negro in the United States.* New York: D. Van Nostrand.

Love, E. K. (1888). History of the first African baptist church. (Accessed online on May 19, 2006, available at URL http://www.reformedreader.org/history/love/toc.htm).

Marx, K. (1973). *The Grundrisse.* New York: Random House.

Massey, D. S., & Denton, N. A. (1993). *American apartheid: Segregation and the making of the underclass.* Boston: Harvard University Press.

McKinney, R. I. (1971). The black church: Its development and present impact. *Harvard Theological Review.*, *64*, 452–481.

Morris, A. (2000). Reflections on social movement theory: Criticisms and proposals. *Contemporary Sociology*, *29*(3), 445–454.

Morris, C. (1998). The articulation of two worlds: The master-slave relationship reconsidered. *The Journal of American History*, *85*(3), 982–1007.

Morrison, M. K. C. (1987). *Black political mobilization: Leadership, power, and mass behavior*. New York: State University of New York Press.

Oberschall, A. (1973). *Social conflict and social movements*. Englewood Cliffs, N.J.: Prentice-Hall.

Omi, M., & Winant, H. (1986). *Racial formation in the United States: From the 1960s to the 1980s*. New York: Routledge and Kegan Paul.

Orfield, G., & Eaton, S. E. (1996). *Dismantling desegregation: The quiet reversal of Brown v. Board of Education*. New York: New Press.

Ortiz, T. A., & Briggs, L. (2003). The culture of poverty, crack babies, and welfare cheats: The making of the "healthy white baby crisis". *Social Text*, *21*(3), 39–57.

Rawls, J. (1985). Justice as fairness: Political not metaphysical. *Philosophy & Public Affairs*, *14*(3), 223–251.

Rucker, W. C. (2006). *The river flows on: Black resistance, culture, and identity formation in early America*. Baton Rouge, LA: Louisiana State University Press.

Schaefer, R. T. (1979). *Racial and ethnic groups*. Boston: Little Brown and Company.

Smith, E. D. (1988). *Climbing Jacob's ladder: The rise of black churches in eastern American cities, 1740–1877*. Washington, D.C.: Smithsonian Institution Press.

Southall, E. P. (1934). Negroes in Florida prior to the civil war. *The Journal of Negro History*, *19*(1, Jan.), 77–86.

Suttles, W. C. (1971). African religious survivals as factors in American slave revolts. *The Journal of Negro History*, *56*(2, Apr), 97–104.

Tate, G. (1998). Free Black resistance in the Ante Bellum era, 1830–1860. *Journal of Black Studies*, *28*(6, July), 764–782.

Thompson, D. C. (1965). The rise of Negro protest. *Annals of the American Academy of Political and Social Science*, *357*, 18–29.

Thompson, E. P. (1965). The peculiarities of the English. *The Social Register*, *2*, 311–362.

Tillie, C. (1978). *From mobilization to revolution*. Reading, MA: Addison-Wesley.

Washington, J. (1951). The program of the civil rights section of the department of justice. *The Journal of Negro Education*, *20*(3), 333–345.

Washington, J. A. (1951). The program of the civil rights section of the department of justice. *The Journal of Negro Education*, *20*(3), 333–345.

Washington, J. M. (1986). *Frustrated fellowship: The Black baptist quest for social power*. Macon: Mercer University Press.

West, C. (1993). *Race matters*. Boston: Beacon Press.

Wilson, W. J. (1987). *The truly disadvantaged*. Chicago: The University of Chicago Press.

Wilson, W. J. (1996). *When work disappears: The world of the new urban poor*. New York: Alfred A. Knopf.

Wood, B. (1987). Some aspects of female resistance to chattel slavery in low country Georgia, 1763–1815. *The Historical Journal*, *30*(3), 603–622.

Yee, S. J. (1992). *Black women abolitionists: A study in activism, 1828–1860*. Knoxville: University of Tennessee Press.

RACIAL CONFLICT IN THE 21ST CENTURY: THE FORMATION OF A STABLE MAJORITY AND THE AFRICAN AMERICAN PREDICAMENT

Antoine Joseph

The wounds remain raw, the pictures are graphic. It is now late September 2005, it has been estimated that more than 1,000 residents of the Gulf Coast, especially in New Orleans are dead. Certainly the city and the region will have to be rebuilt. But what is most remarkable is the muted, glacial, and inadequate federal response. Perhaps incompetence is the main story. After all the administration's inept management of the Iraq war might well suggest that its response to the Hurricane Katrina disaster and tragedy is just another example of George W. Bush's incompetent administration, notwithstanding their political effectiveness. And yet, one cannot help but wonder whether the large number of African American poor in New Orleans and the Gulf Coast have in any way influenced the administration's reactions. New Orleans after all is 69 percent black and 23 percent of its residents live in poverty. Was the disaster planning, which neglected to take into account the inability of the poor to get in their cars and drive out of harms way, simply sheer incompetence, or might it be that lack of

The New Black: Alternative Paradigms and Strategies for the 21st Century
Research in Race and Ethnic Relations, Volume 14, 79–107
Copyright © 2007 by Elsevier Ltd.
ISSN: 0195-7449/doi:10.1016/S0195-7449(06)14004-0

consideration of the plight of the immobile poor in emergency planning was just another way in which poor African-Americans (and poor people in general) are invisible to this administration? Perhaps impoverished African-Americans are only useful to conservative Republicans when they can be used to symbolize the need to be tough on crime or to advance a pet program such as school vouchers. Still it is hard to understand how refugees from Katrina could end up going without food or water for several days as was reported by Joseph Mathews the director of New Orleans's Office of Emergency Preparedness (Treaster & Sontag, 2005; Wilgoren, 2005). But then again, the president's mother, Barbara Bush thought the evacuees were better off as refugees in Houston because after all, "they were underprivileged anyway" (New York Times, 2005). It will be many months if not years before a comprehensive answer to the failure of policy responses to Hurricane Katrina is answered. What is clear is that the federal response to Hurricane Katrina fits into a larger pattern. A pattern, which I will describe as indicative of the existence of a stable majority problem in American politics.

The analysis to follow begins with the thesis of majoritarian tyranny, in particular the version used by Harvard Professor Lani Guinier to explain the political marginality of African-Americans. Has a stable majority developed in American politics – one hostile to the agendas and interests of African-Americans? This is certainly one way to understand the marginalization of black voters because of their isolation from the nation's dominant party. In large measure, the Republican ascendancy since the 1980 presidential election has been based on their appeal to racial conservatives. I will show that racial polarization has been a key instrument of Republican strategy, one revealed in the use of polarizing racial rhetoric and symbolism by such prominent Republicans as Trent Lott, Jesse Helms, Lee Atwater, George H.W. Bush, and Ronald Reagan. Next, I will argue that Reagan's election in 1980 ushered in dramatic shifts in macroeconomic, budgetary and criminal justice policy, policy shifts which dramatically favored key Republican constituencies at the expense of African-Americans. Such convergence of political and economic haves has created a stable and perhaps tyrannical majority.

WHAT IS THE STABLE MAJORITY PROBLEM?

The topic of majoritarian tyranny is a classic theme of political theory. As Robert Lowell (1913) put it,

> If two highwaymen meet a belated traveler on a dark road and propose to relieve him of
> his watch and wallet, it would clearly be an abuse of terms to say that in the assemblage
> on that lonely spot there was a public opinion in favor of a redistribution of prop-
> erty. ... The absurdity in such a case of speaking about the duty of the minority to
> submit to the verdict of public opinion is self-evident.

A staple of conservative classical political thought is the notion that there is
no essential distinction to be made between democracy and majoritarian
highway robbery. Democracy equals the rule of the mob, it is merely a
majoritarian tyranny. According to Macaulay, ... "the first use which the
people will make of universal suffrage will be to plunder every man in the
kingdom who has a good coat on his back and a good roof over his
head" ... "working class suffrage would bring about the end of literature,
science, commerce and that a few half-naked fishermen would divide with
the owls and foxes the ruins of the greatest European cities". Similar ap-
prehensions concerning democracy have been found among more liberal
theorists as well. "During the debate over the 1832 Reform Bill in England
(which increased the franchise to 3.1% of the total population), John Stuart
Mill foresaw the prospect of a revolution that would "exterminate every
person in Britain and Ireland who has 500 a year" (Thompson, 1979;
Hewitt, 1977).

Stable political coalitions are especially susceptible to majoritarian tyranny. James Madison believed that in the absence of strong restraints, those
in power would behave tyrannically. The Madisonian compromise between
majority power and minority rights rests most of all on constitutional in-
hibitions, upon the belief that if constitutional limitations on excessive
power are to be effective through the separation of powers, they must be
partially countervailing. The powerful must have discordant interests, separating rather than joining them. Madison's belief that a large republic will
produce so many factions as to counterbalance each other is an act of faith
(Pitkin, 1972). But, he clearly recognized that in the absence of some "social
checks" constitutional checks would be insufficient (Dahl, 1956). Ironically,
the framers of the Constitution intended to create a system that would
constrain the power of majorities. But their creation has evolved into one,
which arguably protects the interests of the majority over and against those
of minorities.

Is majoritarian tyranny alive and well in American politics? Contemporary political theorists are well aware of the theoretical prospect of majoritarian tyranny. Political scientist Dennis Mueller believes, "What is
required for redistribution to take place under majority rule is that the
members of the winning coalition be clearly identifiable, so that the winning

2

proposal can discriminate in their favor, ..." (Mueller, 1979) Robert Dahl (1982) has argued,

> "there is this strong bias against minorities in the political system the framers helped to create. Because they succeeded in designing a system that makes it easier for privileged minorities to prevent changes they dislike than for majorities to bring about the changes they want, it is strongly tilted in favor of the status quo and against reform. In their effort to protect basic rights, what the framers did in effect was to hand out extra chips in the game of politics to people who are already advantaged, while they handicapped the disadvantaged who would like to change the status quo".

Whereas Madison and John Stuart Mill believed that a balance among rival classes or factions was required to prevent majoritarian tyranny, more contemporary pluralists hold that the invariably transitory nature of democratic majorities is the key (Dahl, 1956). According to Dennis Mueller, "Implicit in the arguments supporting majority rule we see the assumption that no stable majority coalition forms to tyrannize" (Mueller, 1979). Inconstant majorities provide the essential protection against exploitation of minorities. Flexible alliances mean majorities are continually reformed from disparate groups. Cross-cutting political cleavages thereby moderate passions. In general then, the pluralist expectation that majority rule would not result in majoritarian tyranny rests upon empirical rather than philosophical criteria. *Thus, the possibility of majoritarian tyranny cannot be ruled out apriori.*

It is a common belief that the existence of constitutional safeguards is sufficient to protect legitimate minority rights, rebutting the possibility of majoritarian tyranny. But the adequacy of constitutional protections rests squarely upon the shoulders of its judicial interpreters. Traditionally, such interpreters have opted for the most minimal interpretations of such protections possible, especially when the rights of unpopular minorities are involved. As political scientist Robert Dahl properly notes, "... there is not a single case in the history of this nation where the Supreme Court has struck down national legislation designed to curtail, rather than to expand the key perquisite to popular equality, and popular sovereignty" (Dahl, 1956). Judicial protection, then, does not protect minority interests, certainly not racial minorities. According to political scientist Joel Krieger (1986),

> during the Reagan years the ability of victims of discrimination to sue the state has been reduced by the Supreme Court's use of doctrines of sovereign, judicial, and prosecutorial immunity, and by a set of more restrictive criteria for determining standing. Decisions concerning the right to bring cases involving both educational and employment policy have indicated that the court is generally unwilling to provide group remedies for group wrongs.

Thus, for most of American history, there was little judicial protection of civil rights. Moreover, since the selection of judicial interpreters is done by election winners, notions of constitutional rights will strongly reflect the sentiments of the appointers. If majorities are stable, then perceptions of constitutional rights held by judicial interpreters often reflect the majorities' view. Those who believe constitutional safeguards are invariably sufficient must also keep in mind the view expressed by two of the nine chief justices who served more than a decade. According to Charles Evan Hughes, the constitution is what the justices say it is. And then there was the recently departed William Rehnquist, who while clerking for Justice Robert Jackson in 1952 wrote a memo titled *A Random Thought on the Segregation Cases*, which favored maintaining segregated schools. Rehnquist argued in this memo that the view "that a majority may not deprive a minority of its constitutional rights ... while this is sound in theory, in the long run it is the majority who will determine what the constitutional rights of the minority are." Rehnquist went on to argue in his memo that Plessy v. Ferguson correctly interpreted the constitution and should be "reaffirmed" (Williams, 1998).

Ultimately, the strongest protection of minority rights rests neither on constitutional proscriptions nor paternalistic good intentions, but rather upon a healthy awareness of self-interest and realistic expectations that a significant degree of cycling will occur into and out of majority coalitions. Shifting coalitions are an essential component of democracies. It is the uncertainty of current winners that they will remain in the majority that provides the most valuable safeguard for minority rights. Coalitional rigidity reduces empathy – it becomes ever more difficult for those in the political majority to see themselves as likely to be in the political minority. Thus, when the stability of political coalitions is such that the alignment of opponents is largely predictable, majoritarian exploitation becomes plausible. Stable or consistent political outcomes increase distributional inequities.

Some readers will undoubtedly find this scenario to be unrealistically static that the dynamics of electoral competition prevent such rigidity. It is here that the impact of racially oriented voting comes into play, as dissimilarities between the interests of the majority of white voters and those of most black voters forestall cycling. Instead, current patterns of racial voting have made increasingly predictable winners and losers possible, providing a catalyst for majoritarian tyranny. According to Harvard Law Professor Lani Guinier, whose writings (and failed nomination as assistant attorney general for Civil Rights) has sparked much of the recent interest in this issue: in certain cases racial (and perhaps) ethnic minorities face such extraordinary obstacles to having their policy preferences taken seriously, that they are victims of "majoritarian tyranny". Black political and economic advancement is hampered by "majoritarian tyranny". According to Guinier, a system in which a permanent and homogenous majority consistently exercises disproportionate power is neither stable, accountable, nor reciprocal (Guinier, 1994). Ultimately, as minority interests are counterposed to majority interests, race influences voting by enabling the development of persistent winning coalitions without any significant representation of minority interests. Arguably, it is the exploitation of racial antagonisms in contemporary political competition, which increases the likelihood that majority rule will be tyrannical, and that the ruling coalition will be stable.

Ronald Reagan and Contemporary Republicanism

Since 1980 there has been an increasing domination of national elections by conservative Republicans. The foundation of their success has been a "southern strategy" uniting whites across class lines, paying scant attention to the interests of black voters. In large measure, Republicans have successfully exploited racial issues. It is no accident that the consolidation of this stable majority coalition occurred during the presidency of Ronald Reagan. No post war World War II (WWII) president was more hostile to black interests than Ronald Reagan. Among 20th century presidents only Woodrow Wilson aroused a comparable degree of racial animosity. Wilson, the first southerner elected president since the Civil War, oversaw the segregation of Washington, DC. Not many prominent Northern Republican opposed both the Civil Rights Act and the Voting Rights Act, as did Reagan. Reagan clearly signaled his intentions during the 1980 presidential campaign when he told an audience of roughly 10,000 white Americans in Philadelphia, Mississippi, "I believe in states' rights". These sentiments were expressed in the area where three civil-rights workers – Michael Schwerner, Andrew Goodman, and James Cheyney – were brutally murdered in 1964. In the view of civil rights legend Andrew Young, "Reagan's affirmation of state's rights looks like a code word to me that it's going to be all right to kill niggers when he's President" (Black & Black, 1992). Reagan grudgingly signed the 25-year extension of the Voting Rights Act, and he favored diminishing its scope. Reagan initially opposed, but hesitantly accepted a federal holiday honoring Martin Luther King, Jr. His administration supported the effort of Bob Jones University to retain tax exemptions despite its racially discriminatory practices. This position was rejected by the Supreme Court by an eight-to-one margin. Reagan advocated ending affirmative action, and he was the first president since Andrew Johnson to veto a civil rights bill. Furthermore, of the 366 judges appointed to the federal bench (more than half of the federal judiciary at the time) by Reagan, only seven were black (Guinier, 1994; Black & Black, 2002).

While he was careful to avoid presenting himself as a virulent racial demagogue like George Wallace, Orville Faubus, or Lester Maddox, Reagan made careful use of both racial codewords and an aggressive advocacy of policies, which have considerably harmed black Americans. In the words of political scientists Donald Kinder and Lynn Sanders, Reagan proved himself a master of "the new etiquette governing public discussion of race". "The new rules governing public discussion of race require not the abandonment of racism, but rather that appeals to prejudice be undertaken carefully, through indirection and subterfuge. Political debate on matters of race now often takes place in code. Racial codewords make appeals to prejudice electorally profitable even when, as in contemporary American society, prejudice is officially off limits"(Kinder & Sanders, 1996).

Reagan's success was partially based on his capacity to make racial appeals coolly. Relying on misleading and often deceitful anecdotes about welfare queens and food stamp chiselers, Reagan's image as a conservative but not racially bigoted candidate appealed to millions of white Americans, but very few blacks. Among major party postwar candidates, only Barry Goldwater received a smaller percentage than the nine percent Reagan received in 1984. Without standing in front of schools, barring black students, and by employing his legendary affability, Reagan helped to make racism, or at the very least racial policies which severely damaged the life chances of black Americans eminently respectable. Ronald Reagan was both the most popular president since FDR among white Americans and the most despised among black Americans. Blacks by a three-to-one margin viewed Reagan as a racist (Apple Jr., 1996; Black & Black, 2002).

Yet, perhaps the lowest depths of overt race-baiting in the postwar era (WWII) of presidential campaigning by a major party candidate was undertaken not by Ronald Reagan, but by his vice-President and successor, George H.W. Bush. The 1988 Bush campaign successfully used racially loaded imagery in the infamous Willie Horton advertisements. Willie Horton, was a black convict, who, while on a weekend furlough, raped a white woman. During the 1988 campaign, an "independent expenditure" group "Americans for Bush" spent over half a million dollars in one month for televisions ads about Willie Horton. A flier for Bush distributed by the state GOP in Maryland showed pictures of Dukakis and Horton together with the message "Is This Your Pro-Family Team for 1988?". The Illinois State

Republican Committee produced a pamphlet, which continued the message that "All the murderers and rapists and drug pushers and child molesters in Massachusetts vote for Michael Dukakis". Bush campaign manager, Lee Atwater told a group of southern Republicans just prior to the Democratic convention, "there is a story about a fellow named Willie Horton who, for all I know, may end up being Dukakis' running mate". Not long before he died, Lee Atwater confessed that the decision to politicize the Willie Horton issue was made at the top echelons of the Bush campaign team. Willie Horton told Playboy magazine that a woman who identified herself as an employee of an organization related to the Bush campaign telephoned him and wrote him letters asking that he endorse Dukakis (Blumenthal, 1990; Feagin & Batur, 2001; Noah, 1999).

According to a Bush campaign aide who helped produce the Horton commercials "Willie Horton has star quality. Willie's going to be politically furloughed to terrorize again. It's a wonderful mix of liberalism and a big black rapist" (Blumenthal, 1990). The stratagem worked well enough for some pundits to ask if the Democratic ticket consisted of Dukakis and Horton, instead of Dukakis and Bentsen!

True, George H.W. Bush and Lee Atwater's manipulative use of race appears to have been more a reflection of calculated opportunism than of deeply held conviction. But using racially loaded messages opportunistically rather than sincerely hardly constitutes mitigating circumstances. Furthermore, there is good reason to believe the Horton smear succeeded. Kinder and Sanders examined survey responses before and after the Horton story became central to the campaign. They conclude that the Horton story helped to activate racial resentments, just as Republican strategists intended. Similarly, Andrew Kohut, Gallup's poll director, believes racial intolerance was a substantial reason for whites to vote for Bush (Kinder & Sanders, 1996).

Antiblack Republican rhetoric has not been limited to presidential candidates. Recently, Trent Lott has been the subject of heightened scrutiny because of comments he made praising Strom Thurmond's 1948 segregationist "States Rights" presidential campaign. Lott argued that the nation would have been better off if Thurmond had won the election. At Senator Thurmond's 100th birthday party, he said "I want to say this about my state: When Strom Thurmond ran for president, we voted for him. We're proud of it. And if the rest of the country had followed our lead, we wouldn't have had all these problems over all these years, either" (Hulse, 2002).

In one sense, the recent uproar over Lott's comments is surprising, his views have long been "hidden in plain sight", in the words of New York

Times columnist and Princeton economics professor Paul Krugman (Krugman, 2002). Lott has been making comparable comments throughout his political career. After a speech by Senator Thurmond at a Reagan campaign rally in Jackson, Mississippi in 1980, then Congressman "You know if we had elected this man 30 years ago, we wouldn't be in the mess we are today". In 1984, Congressman Lott spoke to a gathering of the Sons of the Confederate Veterans. He followed up this speech with an interview in a magazine named Southern Partisan "I think that a lot of the fundamental principles that Jefferson Davis believed in are very important to people across the country, and they apply to the Republican Party" ... "The Republican agenda from tax policy to foreign policy, from individual rights to neighborhood security are things that Jefferson Davis and his people believed in". At a library dedication in 1998, Lott said "Sometimes I feel closer to Jefferson Davis than any other man in America". In 1979, Congressman Lott received the Jefferson Davis Medal from the United Daughters of the Confederacy for his role in the successful restoration of Jefferson Davis's American citizenship.

Nor are these merely rhetorical excesses. Lott's politics both before he entered electoral politics and after his election to Congress demonstrate behavior consistent with these views. In 1964, he led the opposition to the desegregation of his fraternity, Sigma Nu at the University of Mississippi. He was also instrumental in keeping the national fraternity segregated. In 1968, he became a top aide to one of the House's leading segregationists, William Colmer, a vociferous opponent of the 1964 Civil Rights Act and 1965 Voting Rights Act. Congressman Lott voted against the Martin Luther King holiday and the 1982 extension of the Voting Rights Act. More recently, Senator Lott cast the only negative vote against Roger Gregory's nomination as the first black to serve on the 4th Circuit of the U.S. Court of Appeals (Hulse, 2002; Applebome, 1998, 2002). Senator Lott resigned as Senate majority leader in January 2003, once it became clear he was no longer supported by the Bush administration.

However, former Attorney General John Ashcroft, has expressed similar views. In a 1998 interview in the same Southern Partisan magazine, Ashcroft called Confederates "patriots", arguing that they should not be regarded as having died for "some perverted agenda". Ashcroft helped to derail a federal judgeship for Missouri Supreme Court Judge Ronnie White, the first black on the state's supreme court. Ashcroft also accepted an honorary degree and gave the commencement speech at Bob Jones University, an institution renowned for its opposition to interracial dating and marriage (Associated Press, 2002; Powell, 2001).

We might also consider Jesse Helms infamous "white hands" advertise-
ment depicting white hands crumpling a job application while a voice-over
claims the job was awarded due to quotas (Nasser, 1996). Helms also claimed
that his Democratic opponent Harvey Gantt supported quotas favoring
blacks. Of course Helms has a well earned reputation as an old school racial
demagogue. In 1950, at the tender age of 28, Helms termed the University of
North Carolina "The University of Negroes and Communists" (Feagin &
Batur, 2001; Black & Black, 2002; Kinder & Sanders, 1996). Helms never
supported any civil rights legislation. He conducted a month long filibuster
against a holiday honoring Martin Luther King, Jr. In the 1960s, Helms
argued that the Klan was as legitimate politically as the civil rights movement.

More recently, in November 2003 former chairman of the Republican
national committee Haley Barbour was elected governor of Mississippi.
During the campaign Barbour announced that he would not ask the Council
of Conservative Citizens, an anti-Semitic white supremacist organization, to
remove his picture from their web site. Mr. Barbour argued that while some
of the groups views were indefensible, he did not want to tell any group it
could not use his picture. The Web site displays Confederate flags, and has
links to articles titled "in defense of racism" and a book, which denies the
"Holocaust". This tactic simultaneously appealed to those supportive of
racially charged sentiments while disclaiming responsibility for them on free
speech grounds. Barbour was also accused of using racial codes in linking
the gubernatorial race to the separate race for lieutenant governor. Barbour
repeatedly linked his Democratic opponent with the black candidate for
lieutenant governor (Associated Press, 2003; Dawidoff, 2003).

The views and actions of Lott, Ashcroft, Helms, and Barbour typify a
party whose electoral success in the post civil-rights era has been built on the
embrace of retrograde racial views and the evisceration of moderate Re-
publicanism. When Republicans seek to neutralize the taint of bigotry, they
rely heavily on symbolism, such as the parade of minority Republicans at
the 2000 Republican national convention, a gathering in which it seemed as
if every black Republican in attendance made an appearance on the podium.

Moreover, the successful campaigns of Ronald Reagan and the first George
Bush highlight an important trend of contemporary politics: unlike the 1950s
when a key to black advancement was the emergence of interparty competition for black votes, during the last generation, a different type of swing
voter has become the object of interparty competition. The parties have been
more likely to compete for voters with little sympathy for black Americans.

Racial antipathy to blacks proved to be a valuable common denominator
for core Republican supporters in presidential elections since 1968. Persistent,

albeit at times submerged racial antagonisms have been instrumental in the polarization of social and economic policy preferences. The coalescence of affluent, middle, and working class whites into a majority coalition has been based upon their sharing attitudes, which can be termed "conservative populism". We might also term conservative populism the protection of white skin privilege. Conservative populism helps to solidify the alliance between upper-middle and upper-income groups favoring anti-government intervention libertarianism with the antipathy to social programs resonating among working and lower class white ethnics (who are often in direct competition with minorities for jobs, government benefits, and social services).

REPUBLICAN DOMINANCE: AN ERA OF MAJORITARIAN TYRANNY?

In spite of the racially charged political rhetoric and campaigns of the last generation, the greatest damage of racial polarization has been in the harm inflicted by shifts in economic and social policy. Race has played a central role in the development of a strategy, which allows Republicans to use conservative populism to attract middle and lower class whites. In particular, conservative populism helps to combine the more traditional Republican base of economic conservatives with less affluent whites (the so-called Reagan Democrats). Furthermore, because economic and racial conservatism are more strongly aligned than in earlier eras – due to heightened partisan polarization – political campaigns that emphasize racial conservatism elect politicians committed to economic conservatism. Hence, anti-black conservative populism provides vital support for conservative economic policies, which would have difficulty in their own right.

Racial Polarization and Economic Policy

Racial polarization contributed directly and indirectly to the Reagan-era shift in economic policy, policies responsible for much of the growth in inequality through the 1980s. The net effect was to increase the income of the affluent while generating budget deficits whose magnitude has paralyzed fiscal policy – a policy which has come to be known as starving the beast – effectively ruling out expansions of public services.

Reagan advocated a "new federalism", effectively shifting policy responsibilities from the federal to the state level. The relative decreases in the distribution of federal dollars to state and local governments has meant more regressive state and local taxes are used for purposes which more progressive federal tax revenues once covered. As the incremental growth of more regressive forms of taxation becomes the major source for new revenues at the state and local levels, this regressivity aggravates the hostility to programs for low-income families financed by state and local revenues. Such hemorrhaging of state and local budgets by "new federalism" policies is a harbinger of budgetary problems, which have become chronic features of economic downturns.

Higher social security taxes have also added to the burden imposed on those of low and moderate incomes. For many of these Americans, payments of proportional social security taxes are typically higher than their payments of federal income taxes. Changes in Internal Revenue Service policy have resulted in poorer Americans being audited more often than far wealthier ones. According to reporter David Cay Johnston, "Since 1988, audit rates for the poor have increased by a third, from 1.03 percent, while falling 90 percent for the wealthiest Americans, from 11.4 percent". Eight times as many audits are conducted of the working poor as of those making 100,000 or more (Johnston, 2000, 2005). The biggest reason is increased scrutiny of the earned income tax credit, at the insistence of Republican policy makers. In 1999, 44 percent of all audits were of returns applying this tax credit. In April 2003, the I.R.S. announced its intention to increase its scrutiny of those claiming the earned income tax credit, even though the estimated taxes avoided are dwarfed in comparison to tax avoidance and evasion schemes used by more affluent individuals, corporations, and partnership investors. The I.R.S. estimates that the federal government loses 6.5–10 billion dollars annually as a result of payments to those ineligible for earned income taxes, versus 132 billion dollars to individuals evading and avoiding taxes, 70 billion dollars to offshore accounts, 46 billion dollars to corporations, and 30 billion dollars to partnership investors. The Bush administration has also announced its intention to mount a similarly aggressive effort to prevent ineligible students from receiving free or subsidized school meals (Johnston, 2001; Walsh, 2003).

The increased scrutiny of the earned income tax credit (EITC) has occurred as the EITC has become more important. It currently plays a larger role in the reduction of rates of childhood poverty than any other government program. In 1996, 8.0 percent of all persons, (8.1 percent of blacks) and 14.5 percent of all children (14.8 percent of black children) were lifted out of poverty by the EITC. Is it possible that the reason for the increased scrutiny of this program rests upon the programs disproportionate benefits for minorities, in light of the smaller proportion of poor whites moved out of poverty? Whereas the EITC lifts 5.5 percent of pre-transfer poor whites from poverty, it lifts 14.8 percent of Hispanics and 8.1 percent of blacks who were poor before the effect of government transfers from poverty (Center on Budget and Policy Priorities, 1998). Alternatively, it may simply be that Republican hostility reflects their indifference to working poor Americans, who are unlikely to vote for Republicans, if they vote at all.

While the affluent have prospered, the living standards of the non-affluent have stagnated or declined. According to the Center on Budget and Policy Priorities there has been a 28% increase in the number of working people whose income fell below the poverty line since 1978 (Thurow, 1993). Contemporary social welfare programs distinguish entitlements aiding those near to or above the midpoint of the income distribution from those targeted to the poor – a disparity that evokes the aphorism "welfare policies for the poor are poor welfare policies". Programs targeted for the poor are the ones that absorbed the bulk of the Reagan era budget cuts. In the words of Frances Fox Piven and Richard Cloward, "Non-means tested programs such as Social Security and Medicare and a variety of veteran's benefits have been dealt with delicately and cautiously. The brunt of the cuts fall on public service employment, unemployment insurance, Medicaid, public welfare, low-income housing subsidies, and the disability and food stamp programs" (Piven & Cloward, 1982).

Perhaps most offensive of all is the percentage of children living in poverty. In 1989, when Ronald Reagan left office, 19 percent of all American children and 43 percent of black children lived in families below the poverty line. By 2000, the figures had improved, with only 15.6 percent of all American children and 30.4 percent of black children living in families below the poverty line (U.S. Census Bureau Current Population Reports, 2000).

Social spending cutbacks have been greatest in programs benefiting the poor. The reductions in food stamp benefits during the Reagan era affected 20 million Americans. Seventy percent of the savings resulted from benefit reductions for those below the poverty line. In the early 1980s, 440,000 low-income working families (almost all headed by women) lost AFDC benefits. Medicaid benefits, linked to AFDC, were also reduced. Consequently, nearly a third of all children now living in poverty have no Medicaid coverage. Furthermore, cuts in low-income housing programs have pushed an estimated 300,000 more families into substandard housing. By 1985, Reagan budget cuts reduced social spending by 10 percent (Ferguson & Rogers, 1986).

Roughly half the reductions in benefits were apportioned to households with average incomes of less than $10,000; approximately 70 percent of benefit reductions went to households with incomes less than $20,000. On the other hand, households with incomes greater than $80,000 received only one percent of the reductions. The result has been a dramatic upward re-distribution of American income, leading to the most unequal income distribution since the collection of such data began.

Programs preserved from Reagan-era budget cuts have primarily bene-fited affluent Americans. The biggest government programs from which white Americans have benefited most are the ones which have been most insulated from budget cuts: (1) Social security; (2) Medicare; (3) Medicaid; and (4) mortgage interest deductions (Wines, 1994). Even Medicaid, widely perceived to provide health care for the poor, has been selectively pruned. Today, more of Medicaid pays for health care for the elderly than for children and adults under 65. In comparison, programs which serve primarily poor Americans have been slashed much more. Nonetheless, the substantially smaller government programs from which minorities benefit receive the lion's share of opprobrium.

Race, Crime, and Punishment

Government policies which deal with punishment have always been an issue which disproportionately affects the poor. Economic policy choices both influence the criminal justice system, and are influenced by criminal justice issues. High rates of incarceration alleviate a potentially serious unemployment problem, especially of young black men (Tilly & Tilly, 1998). The rate of incarceration in the United States is the highest of industrialized nations. In 2002, for the first time in history, more than 2 million people were incarcerated in U.S. jails and prisons. Roughly 12 percent of black men between the ages of 20 and 34 are currently incarcerated, in comparison to 1.6 percent of white men in the same age group. The expense of administering the American criminal justice has grown so dramatically that in a number of states more money is spent on prisons than on higher education. The nation's inmates cost an average of $22,000 per year. In 1999, 147 billion was spend on criminal justice at all levels of government. This total is more than four times the total in 1982. The costs of the criminal justice system: police, prisons, and courts increased every year in the 1990s, although crime rates declined (Butterfield, 2002, 2003; Broder, 2003).

Young blacks growing up in impoverished circumstances within densely populated pockets of poverty receive powerful messages, messages that deeply circumscribe their life chances, and affirm their marginality. For poorly educated young black men, the alternatives to criminal activity often appear unpromising. Penal policy is also a method of regulating labor, in which prisoners assume a status of marginality. When released, the efforts of many former inmates to "go straight" are frustrated by increased restrictions on the type of jobs they can fill. According to Andrew Hacker, "In New York City, an uproar arose when it was discovered that some of its school janitors had served terms in prison. In other cities, people with prison records are barred from becoming taxicab drivers and security guards, even though they are position suitable for those seeking a fresh start" (Hacker, 1997). In the 1990s ex-felons have been barred from living in public housing and prohibited from jobs in a number of occupations. According to journalist Fox Butterfield, "In New York, there are more than 100 prohibited job categories, including plumbing, real estate, barbering, education, health care, and private security" (Butterfield, 2002). Drug felony convictions now include prohibitions on receiving student loans, welfare or food stamps.

The marginality of young black men simultaneously threatens and secures the social order. Politicians frequently capitalize on the misdeeds of black youths to win electoral support from those made anxious in part by media images and political campaigns. Finally, criminal convictions permanently bar many young black men from the mainstream of American life. Having a felony criminal conviction makes one ineligible for many desirable occupations, consigning ex-felons to a status of semi-permanent "limited" citizenship. A byproduct of imprisonment often includes the removal of black men from the electorate. An estimated 1.4 million black men, 13 percent of the total black male population cannot vote because of their criminal records. Nine states bar felons from voting for the remainder of their lifetimes (Sengupta, 2000).

The Racial Politics of Death

Perhaps the most dramatic example of racial inequality in criminal justice policy occurs in the utilization of the ultimate penal measure: the death penalty. For many years blacks received the death penalty for criminal offenses for which whites would not. It was quite common after Reconstruction for blacks found guilty of an inter-racial rape to receive the death penalty, a penalty they might not in fact survive to receive, as white mobs frequently broke into jails in order to lynch the offending party (in many cases a mere accusation was sufficient for a lynching to occur).

Between 1930 and 1964, 455 men were executed for rape in the United States. Almost all were executed in southern states. Of the 455 executions, 405 were black men, almost all were charged with raping white women (Kennedy, 1997; Clymer, 2003). In fact, the arbitrary racially biased utilization of the death penalty was crucial to its being judged unconstitutional.

The Warren Supreme Court strongly discouraged the implementation of the death penalty. During the 1940s an average of 128 executions were carried out each year, during the 1950s an average of 72. By the 1960s the pace of executions had dropped considerably. By 1963 the number of executions was down to 21, 15 in 1964, seven in 1965, one in 1966, two in 1967, and then none between 1968 and 1976 (Powe, 2001). The obstacles to the death penalty were at one time anchored by Supreme Court Justices Thurgood Marshall, William Brennan, and Harry Blackmun. But no justice today endorses the emphatic rejection of the death penalty as did Justices Marshall and Brennan, who believed that "the death penalty is an affront to a civilized society". Since the resumption of executions in 1976, its legislative and political supporters have been more careful to apply it in ways that appear superficially to be more even-handed. Executions are on the rise, 100 people were executed in the initial 12 years following the resumption of executions in 1976, 82 were executed in the first 10 months of 1999 (Greenhouse, 1999). But appearances of even-handedness do not alter the racial inequities, which are common in the application of this ultimate penalty.

Racial prejudice strongly permeates the utilization of the death penalty. Blacks are more likely to receive the death penalty, especially when they commit eligible crimes against whites. A comprehensive review undertaken by the Justice Department reveals significant racial disparities in the use of the death penalty in federal cases. Accordingly, "In 75 percent of the cases in which a federal prosecutor sought the death penalty in the last five years, the defendant has been a member of a minority group, and in more than half of the cases, an African-American" (Bonner & Lacey, 2000).

The death penalty is also a punishment with an unacceptably high-error rate. Since 1976, more than 80 death row inmates have been freed from prison. In spite of an error rate of roughly 15 percent of the total number of executions, the political champions of the death penalty are currently advocating speeding up its application. The Supreme Court, Congress, and many states have made it much more difficult for defendants to have their appeals heard (Berlow, 1999).

Certainly, the increased use of the death penalty in recent years cannot plausibly be attributed to increases in crime. Fewer, not more, people are becoming crime victims. Justice Department reports a steady decline since 1975 in the percent of households who report they have been touched by crime, from one out of three when the National Crime Survey started in 1975 to one out of four in 1988. Additionally, the rate of violent crime declined by one-third between 1992 and 2001 (Orestes, 1990; Willing, 2003).

The most common justification for the death penalty is deterrence. How-ever, there is little justification for this belief. Rather, those states that chose not to enact the death penalty since 1976 have not had higher homicide rates. Of the 12 states without capital punishment, 10 have homicide rates below the national average (Bonner & Fessenden, 2000). Homicides rates have been 50–100 percent higher in states with the death penalty than in those without it. But in spite of the absence of credible evidence showing a deterrence effect, support for the death penalty has grown stronger. In fact, federal and state judges can attend conferences to consider ways to expedite its implementation with little notice (Firestone, 1999).

The death penalty is a cheap and easy way for politicians – Democrats as well as Republicans to show their toughness on crime. Elected governors boast about signing execution warrants. Support for the death penalty helped then Arkansas governor Bill Clinton neutralize the label of being soft on crime during his 1992 presidential campaign (Berlow, 1999). Support for the death penalty permits an expression of racial antagonisms in a well understood if not always explicit code. The death penalty symbolizes the portrayal of black candidates as weak, while the image of young blacks on crime rampages have been common devices used in political campaigns. Perhaps just as pernicious as the racialization of the death penalty are the racial disparities, which afflict the contemporary war on drugs.

Race, Civil Liberties, and the War on Drugs

We have witnessed in recent years the "outing" of politicians and public officials, especially but not exclusively those running for national elective office or needing Senate confirmation regarding their past behavior in the areas of sex, drugs, and other aspects of personal behavior. When estab-lished politicians admit to drug use well in the past, it is reasonable to consider such admissions irrelevant to a candidate's current fitness for office.

But is it really irrelevant when these admissions come from those most committed to the current war on drugs? During the 2000 presidential campaign George W. Bush, was subjected to such prurient interest. For President Bush in particular, such allegations raised an interesting question. As journalist Joe Conason thoughtfully articulated-the debate is long overdue on "why drug abuse among the rich is a "disease" while among the poor it is a crime". Are the laws that send thousands of people to prison every year for drug possession administered fairly? Is justice served by incarcerating young, nonviolent drug offenders? Should the courts mandate treatment rather than imprisonment for people who make the kind of "mistake" that the Republican front-runner has now all but admitted?" (Conason, 1999).

Yet, unlike the kid glove treatment often meted out to affluent drug users, those most likely to face arrest, prosecution, and harshly punitive sentencing are young black and Hispanic males. President Bush has been a zealous advocate of harsh drug policies. While running for governor, he opposed Governor Ann Richards suggestion to increase treatment programs, claiming that "incarceration is rehabilitation". Hence, more state funds should be allocated to prisons than to treatment. As governor, Bush "tightened the state's drug-sentencing laws, okayed the housing of 16 year olds in adult correctional facilities and slashed funding for inmate substance-abuse programs" (Bryce, 1999). The result is that 13 percent of those incarcerated in state prisons are in jail in Texas. Of course, George W. Bush's stance is entirely consistent with the war on drugs as practiced in this country over the last 30 years. Those most negatively affected by the war on drugs have clearly been young Black and Hispanic males. They suffer from racial profiling, longer sentences, and higher rates of incarceration.

Recent episodes of gun violence have brought attention to the dramatic contrast between the federal government's obsession with drugs and its relaxed attitude toward gun control. Consider, for example, that in 1981 President Reagan, at the urging of the National Rifle Association (NRA), announced that the Bureau of Alcohol, Tobacco, and Firearms (A.T.F.), the federal agency charged with overseeing compliance with gun regulation, was to be abolished. While he later reconsidered and withdrew this plan, the agency has been repeatedly hamstrung. Representative John Dingell a Michigan Democrat who is a member of the National Rifle Association's board of directors arranged for the gun industry to be exempt from the Consumer Product Safety Commission. Dingell termed firearms agents a "jackbooted group of fascists who are perhaps as large a danger to American society as I could pick today" (Butterfield, 1999). A.T.F. director John W. McGaw justifies the lenient treatment of gun dealers by calling gun trafficking a "victimless" crime, even though half of the crimes in which guns were used that have been successfully traced by the A.T.F. were to just 389 dealers. One can only wonder if the racial characteristics of crack users and gun users were reversed, would the federal government continue its anti-drug campaign? While the Drug Enforcement Agency budget (adjusted for inflation) has climbed from slightly over 200 million dollars to 1.4 billion dollars in the last 25 years, the A.T.F. has gone from the same slightly more than 200 million to approximately 500 million. The only way this makes sense is if you believe the N.R.A. slogan, "guns don't kill people, people do", while drugs similarly must destroy lives without the intervention of their users.

Or, consider the contrast between the treatment of drunk drivers and drug users. An estimated 22,000 Americans annually die due to drunk drivers, while drug related deaths kill an estimated 21,000. Drunk drivers are most often white males. When arrested, they are most often charged with misdemeanors. When convicted they receive fines, suspensions of their licenses, and community service. Drug offenders are, in comparison, disproportionately low-income, and black or Hispanic (The Sentencing Project, 1993).

It is to no one's surprise that the war on drugs provides a clear example of political agendas that produce comprehensive racial disparities. The zeal to prosecute drug cases and the often unrepresentative symbols used to promote antidrug policies encourage policies which increase the harshness of penal policy, while enhancing enormously the political value (to candidates and elected officials) of appearing to be being tough on crime. Media images of the drug crisis employ stereotypes emphasizing the ethnic and racial differences between those responsible for drug use and the "innocent" majority. Although drugs are widely used in middle and upper middle class neighborhoods, most police action occurs in poor black sections (Treaster, 1990). A study by The Sentencing Project in Washington, DC found one in four black men between 20 and 29 years of age to be under the jurisdiction of the corrections system, most commonly due to drug convictions. "Drug use cuts across racial lines, but drug enforcement focuses on the inner cities and blacks, said Mark Mauer, the Sentencing Project's assistant director" (Tackett, 1990). And, let us not forget that it was a New York detective unit whose primary mission was to search for illegal drugs, which cost unarmed Amadeou Diallo his life. Diallo was guilty of the crime of standing in the vestibule of his apartment building while being struck by 19 bullets.

The disparity in sentencing policies for cocaine versus crack (a cocaine derivative) is controversial because the contrasting treatments of crack versus cocaine are a prime cause of current racial disparities in imprisonment. Far harsher sentences are being handed out for possession of crack used primarily by minorities, than for possession of cocaine used by many white Americans. This disparity was originally based on the faulty premise that crack cocaine was 50 times as addictive as powder cocaine. Blacks constituted 30 percent of powder cocaine defendants versus 84 percent of crack cocaine defendants in fiscal year 2000. While, surveys of drug use suggest that more whites than blacks use crack, the war on drugs concentrates on poor urban neighborhoods. As a result more blacks are sentenced to prison. Thus, nearly twice as many black Americans are being imprisoned as white

Americans, even though there are five times more white drug users than black ones. In 1996, 62.7 percent of drug offenders sent to prison were black, while 36 percent were white (Coyle, 2002; Egan, 1999; Holmes, 2000). Whereas 8.3 percent of 25–29-year-old black men were inmates, only 0.8 percent of white men in the same age group are inmates. Certainly there are those who believe that such disparities are justified by the greater propensity of crack users to resort to violent crime. Harvard Law Professor Randall Kennedy has argued that the racial disparities in sentencing may well be the result of reasonable judgments made by legislators to address a serious problem, and that harsher sentences for crack have the often ignored benefit of increased safety for black communities victimized by crack offenders.

The passage of time has clearly shown that the furor over crack was excessive, and that crack did not become the epidemic many proponents of differential sentencing had prophesied. Atty Eric Sterling, while serving as a lawyer for the House Judiciary Committee helped to draft several laws meant to respond to the drug crisis, has stated "that there was a level of hysteria that led to a total breakdown of the legislative process". The disparity continues because as James Alan Fox, dean of the college of criminal justice at Northeastern University puts it, "For politicians the drug debate is driven by the three R's – retribution, revenge, retaliation – and that leads to the fourth R, re-election" (Egan, 1999). Consequently, there are more people imprisoned for drug offenses in the United States – about 400,000 that are imprisoned for all crimes in England, France, Germany, and Japan combined (Egan, 1999).

The Rehnquist Court and a Conservative Judicial Majority

An increasingly conservative Supreme Court, the most conservative since 1937 has been a formidable force in the conservative shift in public policy. The replacement of racial liberals and moderates with conservatives sparked a decisive change in the Court's orientation, particularly since William Rehnquist replaced Warren Burger as chief justice. The conservative shift in desegregation cases, for example, is highlighted by the case of the Board of Education of Oklahoma City v. Dowell. The court found resegregation based on private choices permissible (Patterson, 2002). The rightward shift in voting rights is highlighted by Shaw v. Reno (1993), wherein the Courts conservative majority in a 5–4 ruling overturned redistricting in North Carolina favorable to minorities.

In the pivotal Adarand v. Pena case, that Justice Clarence Thomas issued the memorable phrase "government cannot make us equal", in support of the majority position striking down an affirmative action program. Justice Thomas's remarks echoed those of Justice Henry Billings Brown in Plessy v. Ferguson (1896), "if one race be inferior to the other socially, the Constitution of the United States cannot put them upon the same plane" (Thomas, 1997). Justice Thomas has also expressed serious reservations about the wisdom of the Brown ruling and the pro-integrationist course of action which followed it.

The Rehnquist Court has become a vital member of a dominant national Republican coalition, consistently favoring the interests of Republican constituencies at the expense of their opponents. Since Reagan, Republican administrations have given priority to creating conservative majorities on appellate courts. President Clinton, by contrast did not give a high priority to appointing liberals. On the 13 federal appeals courts, for example, Republicans have a majority in seven, Democrats in just two. These courts, directly below the Supreme Court are considered to be crucial barometers of the prevailing judicial winds because the Supreme Court decides fewer cases than ever and also because most cases that come before federal appeals courts are decided by three judge panels (Sontag, 2003; Lewis, 2002).

The direction of the court reflects a rejection of the Warren Court's legacy. Rather than protecting the disadvantaged, a common theme of the Warren Court's rulings, the Rehnquist Court's majority has become a part of the Republican majority coalition. Their decisions have followed a consistent pattern – one shared by the executive and legislative branches – of a redirection in government policy favoring the interests of those constituencies found regularly on the winning side at the expense of those regularly among the losers.

The Presidential Election of 2000

It may never be possible to fully answer whether disparate racial treatment on Election day changed the outcome of the election. There were reports that blacks were routinely stopped and asked for identification while whites were allowed to remain in the voting lines without showing any identification. A predominantly black precinct in Duval County had a long line of people waiting to vote. Meanwhile police began to hand out tickets for loitering. Some polling places were shut at the official closing time even though black voters were still in line (McCarthy, 2000).

The heart of the case of unequal treatment of black voters rests upon more tangible evidence, evidence that cannot easily be dismissed as anecdotal. In numerous cases, arbitrary decisions to void ballots were made, especially in majority black voting districts ignoring clear and unambiguous evidence of the intent of the voter. "Ballots in majority black precincts were voided at a rate three-times higher than those in non-black precincts. Nearly one in every 10 ballots in majority black precincts went unrecorded. In majority white precincts, the discard rate was less than one in 38. A prime reason, a higher proportion of black voters live in counties that use error-prone punch card machines" (Viglucci, Dougherty, & Yardley, 2000). Predominantly black areas were plagued with technological deficiencies in their election apparatus. "Heavily Democratic and African-American neighborhoods in Florida lost many more presidential votes than other areas because of outmoded voting machines and rampant confusion" (Rubinton, 2000). Of the 20 precincts with the highest voided ballot rates, 19 were in Duval County in northern Florida. According to Anthony Salvanto, a researcher at the University of California at Irvine perhaps 1,700 Miami Dade County voters' presidential ballots were invalidated because they incorrectly punched the chad beneath that of their chosen candidate. In many cases their mistake was due to a misalignment of punch card ballots and voting machines. With the proper alignment, Vice President Al Gore would have gained 316 more votes in Dade County alone (Viglucci, 2001).

Vice President Gore also lost a significant number of votes in counties that voted for George W. Bush due to questionable rulings by local canvassing boards. These boards threw out more than 1,700 votes in which the intention of the voter could be easily discerned. Many ballots were voided because voters selected either Bush or Gore, and then wrote in the candidate's name. These ballots were read by counting machines as double votes, and were thereby discarded by canvassing boards. These ballots clearly indicated the intent of the voter, and if the canvassing boards counted those votes, George W. Bush's margin of victory would have fallen by 366 votes, two-thirds of the official margin of 537 votes (Roy & Damron, 2001).

A recount conducted in Orange County, Florida shows that Al Gore would have gained 203 votes if a hand recount had occurred. Voting machines rejected 799 ballots for having either no votes or multiple votes. This county used paper ballots that were to be marked with special pens. The most common reason for rejection of ballots was due to voters using unapproved pens, i.e., not the pens provided in the voting booth. Consequently machines did not detect votes on ballots, which were filled in with black ink. While adhering to this rigid principle in counting votes cast on election day, the county counted absentee ballots (which generally favored Republicans) on machines which were much more sensitive to the voters choice. There were also hundreds of ballots, which were discounted because they were marked in the wrong places. The candidates names were circled or a bubble marked "PRES" was filled in, rather than the approved procedure of coloring in an arrow which pointed to the correct name (Mintz & Keating, 2000).

More recently, a post election study conducted by the National Opinion Research Center (NORC) at the University of Chicago came to the conclusion that the Supreme Court did not cost Al Gore the election. Rather, a recount of the ballots in the counties the Gore campaign requested would have narrowed but not prevented Bush's victory, depending on the criteria used. But that resolves only one kind of irregularity, and confirms the flaws in the Gore post-election strategy to examine four Democratic counties rather than push for a recount of the entire state. What if a full recount of the entire state had been ordered? Examining a broader group of 175,010 rejected ballots shows that the results might very well have resulted in a Gore victory. According to the NORC analysis, the cumulative effect of counting correctly marked paper ballots, and poorly marked paper ballots and disqualified but fully punched punch card ballots would have given Gore another 554 votes and thus the election (see Fessenden & Broden, 2001).[1]

Examining 2,490 ballots from Americans living overseas that were counted as legal votes after election day, the New York Times found 680 to be questionable. The ballots possessed a variety of flaws: some lacked postmarks, others were postmarked after the election, others lacked witness signatures, or were mailed from towns and cities within the United States, and in some cases were cast by voters who had already voted. These ballots should not have been counted, yet they were accepted in counties, which favored President Bush. Clearly the Bush campaign aggressively pushed to count these votes, and the Gore campaign conceded because many of these ballots were cast by members of the armed forces (Barstow & Natta, 2001). In truth, since the election was a statistical dead heat, small changes in the interpretation of valid ballots could have changed the winner.

And let us not forget the role of Katherine Harris, the Florida secretary of state, who made a number of critical decisions, each of which without exception helped George Bush and hurt Al Gore. In the 36 days it took to settle the Florida election, Ms. Harris made numerous crucial decisions – blocking manual recounts, enforcing strict deadlines for counting, and applying liberal standards for counting absentee ballots. Each move helped George Bush to pickup hundreds of essential votes (Nagourney & Barstow, 2000). Or, consider the rowdy demonstrations by protestors in Miami-Dade County, many of whom subsidized by the Republican party, including employees of such prominent Republicans as Tom Delay, the House majority whip and Senate majority leader Trent Lott (Hiaasen, 2000). Although, ultimately irrelevant due to the Supreme Court ruling disallowing the recount, the decision by the local canvassing board to stop counting ballots may well have been influenced by these protests.

Problems of a substantial racial gap in voided votes emerged in other states as well. In predominantly black Fulton County, which includes Atlanta, one of every 16 ballots was invalidated. In nearby Cobb and Gwinnett counties, which are predominantly white and Republican, and use modern equipment the invalidation rate was one in 200. In Chicago's Cook County, which normally has a nullified vote rate of 2 percent, the void rate for Election 2000 was 5 percent. A prominent reason for this dramatic increase in voided ballots was that Republican majorities in the state legislature passed a new election law, which prevented voters from voting straight party tickets. Consequently in Chicago's Cook County voters confronted a ballot with 400 candidates that was 21 pages long. The result was that the rate of disqualified ballots was one in 12 for Cook County precincts that were more than 70 percent black, but only one in 20 ballots in county precincts that were less than 30 percent black. Furthermore, the Republican dominated state legislature refused to allow Cook County to use ballot counting machines which would catch many errors, even while nearby counties were allowed to use similar technology to reduce their error rate. As a result 120,000 ballots in Cook County did not count, 70,000 in Chicago, and 50,000 in surrounding communities (Mintz & Keating, 2000).

This issue of ballot spoilage had a serious disparate impact on minorities. According to the House Committee on Government Reform "voters in low-income, high minority congressional districts throughout the country were three times more likely to have their votes for president discarded than those in more affluent, low-minority districts, and were twenty times more likely to have their votes for Congress go uncounted". A study by Harvard University's Civil Rights Project "found a strong relationship between ballot spoilage and a sizeable black population; specifically as the black population in a county increases, the spoiled ballot rate correspondingly increases. ... In Florida, racial disparities in ballot spoilage across counties persisted even when comparing counties with identical income, education, and other factors" (The Civil Rights Project, 2002, p. 8).

True, the U.S. Supreme Court, slightly more than a month later, cast the decisive vote, ruling on a 5–4 basis that recounts of the Florida vote were violations of the 14th Amendment's equal protection clause, thereby awarding victory to George W. Bush the Republican candidate. Yet the Supreme Court's declaration only increased the speculation – did George W. Bush really win the election among the electorate, or did he merely win the election on the court? As legal scholar Ronald Dworkin points out, "It is therefore, difficult to find a respectable explanation of why all and only the conservatives voted to end the election in this way, and the troubling question is being asked among scholars and commentators whether the Court's decision would have been different if it was Bush, not Gore, who needed the recount to win – whether, that is, the decision reflected not ideological division, which is inevitable, but professional self-interest (Dworkin, 2001). It is certainly reasonable to ask whether these events further confirm an overall trend, of a conservative Republican coalition, one including both elected officials and Supreme Court Justices, using questionable methods to assure their preferred outcome?

Were the messy circumstances of the 2000 election exceptional? Consider other evidence: only three African-Americans have been elected to the U.S. Senate: Edward Brooke in 1966, Carol Moseley-Braun in 1992, and Barack Obama in 2004. Only one black Virginia L. Douglas Wilder was elected governor in any state during the 20th century. Qualified and promising black Americans have found their electoral careers ended by a "race ceiling". Twenty-five years after the passage of the Voting Rights Act there were only five black Democrats out of 116 southern representatives. The doors to the pinnacles of state and national political power have usually been shut to blacks. There is, however, some evidence of slow progress. The number of African-Americans in the House of Representatives grew from 26 to 39 members during the 1990s, while membership in state legislatures grew from 430 (5.8 percent) to 557 (7.5 percent) over the same period (Clymer, 2001; Black & Black, 2002). Moreover, the number of black elected officials increased from 1,469 in 1970 to 8,936 by 1999. Yet, most black Americans are elected as local politicians in majority black districts. The list of talented black leaders facing a "race ceiling" when they seek higher office includes both titans of the civil rights struggle such as Andrew Young to quieter moderates such as Harvey Gantt and Tom Bradley (Sack, 2001; Sonenshein, 1995). Each failed when seeking offices beyond the confines of majority black-congressional districts or cities with large black populations.

Toward a Stable Majority?

Ultimately, the decline in the redistributive impact of government programs in the last 35 years parallels the increasing stability of a majority political coalition. Economic policies, which produce declining social welfare spending and an increasingly regressive tax structure, have facilitated a dramatic increase in wealth inequality in the United States. Parsimonious social and draconian criminal justice policies also help bond social and economic conservatives whose economic interests diverge, while sharpening racial polarization. A byproduct of focusing economic and social grievances on problems attributable to racial minorities is to characterize young black men as a class of potential Willie Hortons. Declining redistribution in the public sector and growing inequality in the private sector are perhaps the clearest indicators of the declining political influence of America's have-nots. These trends provide very strong circumstantial evidence to support the thesis that the growing convergence of political and economic haves has spawned majoritarian tyranny.

Racial polarization has been essential to the formation of a stable majority coalition. The dominant coalition and party in American politics has become more conservative and more homogeneous, reducing the need for politicians to reach across racial lines. Conservatives dominate all three branches of the national government. The key swing constituencies (white southern conservatives and northern white ethnics who may be nominally Democratic, but who have often voted Republican in national elections) have had a disproportionately large influence on political calculations. Politicians desirous of winning elections pay more attention to these voting blocs. The dominant national coalition mirrors the attitude of these swing voters on a number of key issues, but especially in their racial resentments and anti-tax conservatism. When the effects of the (long-term) Republican dominance of the Presidency, the gradual but nonetheless considerable translation of control of the presidency into conservative judicial majorities, and the perhaps more tenuous, but frequently right oriented coalitions that are strongest in the Congress, it is apparent that there is no branch of the national government in which moderate or liberal economic, political, and social interest groups are as strong or stronger than are competing conservative interest groups.

Classical democratic theorists believed the populace would either be sufficiently homogeneous to prevent divisions in interests from becoming pervasive, or that cycling would prevent rigidities from becoming stable. Race has come to define predictable axes of political power and economic redistribution. Thus, the tragedy that has befallen the victims of hurricane Katrina is an understandable consequence of the redirection in government policy which has severely damaged the life chances of America's urban poor.

NOTE

1. Organized by a consortium of news organizations which included The *New York Times*, *The Washington Post*, *The Wall Street Journal*, *CNN*, *The Tribune Company*, *The Palm Beach Post*, *The Petersburg Times*, and *The Associated Press*.

REFERENCES

Apple, R. W. Jr. (1996). G.O.P. tries hard to win black votes, but recent history works against it. *New York Times*, September 18.

Applebome, P. (1998). Impeachment republicans, 130 years later: Dueling with the heirs of Jeff Davis. *New York Times, December 27*(section 4), pp. 1, 4.

Applebome, P. (2002). Lott's close walk to the south's history of segregation. *New York Times, December 13*, p. A22.

Associated Press. (2000). Ashcroft: Confederates were 'patriots'. *Miami Herald, December 28*, p. 12A.

Associated Press. (2003). Candidate won't press racist group on his photo. *New York Times, October 18*, p. A10.

Barstow, D., & Van Natta Jr., D. (2001). How Bush took Florida: Mining the overseas absentee vote. *New York Times, July 15*, pp. 1, A15, A16.

Berlow, A. (1999). The wrong man. *Atlantic Monthly, November*, pp. 66–91.

Black, E., & Black, M. (1992). *The vital south*. Cambridge: Harvard University Press.

Black, E., & Black, M. (2002). *The rise of southern republicans*. Cambridge, MA: Harvard University Press.

Blumenthal, H. (1990). *Sidney pledging allegiance*. New York: Harper.

Bonner, R., & Fessender, F. (2000). States with no death penalty share lower homicide rates. *New York Times, September 22*, A1–A23.

Bonner, R., & Lacey, M. (2000). Pervasive disparities found in the federal death penalty. *New York Times, September 12*, A18.

Broder, J. (2003). No hard time for prison budgets. *New York Times, January 19*, 5.

Bryce, R. (1999). *Salon magazine, August 24*.

Butterfield, F. (1999). Limits on power and zeal hamper firearms agency. *New York Times, July 22*, A1–A12.

Butterfield, F. (2002). Freed from prison, but still paying a penalty. *New York Times, December 29*, 18.

Butterfield, F. (2002). Study finds steady increase at all levels of government in cost of criminal justice. *New York Times, February 11*, A14.

Butterfield, F. (2003). Prison rates among blacks reach a peak, report finds. *New York Times, April 7*, A11.

Center on Budget and Policy Priorities. (1998). Strengths of the safety net: How the EITC, social security, and other government programs affect poverty, March 9.

Clymer, A. (2001). Shaping the new math of racial redistricting. *New York Times, July 15*, (Section 5) p. 16.

Clymer, A. (2003). Louisiana senate renews debate on death penalty. *New York Times, August 31*, p. A14.

Conason, J. (1999). *Salon Magazine, August 24*.

Coyle, M. (2002). Race and class penalties in crack cocaine sentencing. *The Sentencing Project.*

Dahl, R. (1956). *A preface to democratic theory*. Chicago: University of Chicago Press.

Dahl, R. (1982). On removing certain impediments to democracy. In: I. Howe (Ed.), *Beyond the welfare state* (pp. 71–98). New York: Schocken Books.

Dawidoff, N. (2003). Mr. Washington goes to Mississippi. *New York Times, October 19* (Section 6), pp. 48–54.

Dworkin, R. (2001). A badly flawed election. *New York Review of Books, January 11*, 53–55.

Egan, T. (1999). War on crack retreats, still taking prisoners. *New York Times, February 28*(1), pp. 20–21.

Feagin, H. V., & Batur, P. (2001). *White racism* (2nd ed.). New York: Routledge.

Ferguson, T., & Rogers, J. (1986). *Right turn: The decline of the democrats and the future of American politics.* New York: Hill and Wang.

Firestone, D. (1999). Judges criticized over death-penalty conference. *New York Times, August 19,* p. A16.

Fessenden, F., & Broden, J. (2001). Study of disputed Florida ballots finds justices did not cast the deciding vote. *New York Times, November 12,* pp. A1–A16, A17.

Greenhouse, L. (1999). Death penalty gets attention of high court. *New York Times, October 30,* pp. A1–A10.

Guinier, L. (1994). *The tyranny of the majority.* New York: The Free Press.

Hacker, A. (1997). *Money.* New York: Touchstone.

Hewitt, C. (1977). The effect of political democracy and direct democracy on equality in industrial societies. *American Sociological Review, 42.*

Hiaasen, C. (2000). Rioting by GOP tourists. *Miami Herald, November 29.*

Holmes, S. (2000). Race analysis cites disparity in sentencing for narcotics. *New York Times, June 8,* p. A16.

Hulse, C. (2002). Lott faces growing attacks over praise for Thurmond. *New York Times, December 11,* p. A23.

Johnston, D. C. (2000). I.R.S. more likely to audit the poor and not the rich. *New York Times, April 16,* p. A1.

Johnston, D. C. (2001). Rate of all I.R.S. audits falls; poor face intense scrutiny. *New York Times, February 6.*

Johnston, D. C. (2005). *Perfectly legal.* New York: Portfolio.

Kennedy, R. (1997). *Race, crime, and the law.* New York: Vintage.

Kinder, D., & Sanders, L. M. (1996). *Divided by color.* Chicago: University of Chicago Press.

Krieger, J. (1986). *Reagan, Thatcher and the politics of decline.* New York: Oxford University.

Krugman, P. (2002). Gotta have faith. *New York Times, December 17,* p. A35.

Lewis, N. A. (2002). First the senate, now the court of appeals. *New York Times, December 1* (Section 4) p. 3.

Lowell, R. (1913). *Public opinion and popular government.* New York: Longmans.

McCarthy, S. (2000). Was Jim Crow in action at Florida's election sites? *Newsday, November 20,* p. A28.

Mintz, J., & Keating, D. (2000). A racial gap in voided votes. *Washington Post, December 27,* p. A01.

Mueller, D. (1979). *Public choice.* Cambridge: Cambridge University.

Nagourney, A., Barstow, D. (2000). G.O.P.'s depth outdid Gore's team in Florida. *New York Times, December 22,* pp. A1–A22.

Nasser, H. El (1996). Helms is victor in race-tinged negative contest" *USA Today, November 6,* p. 14a.

New York Times (2005). The former first lady: Barbara Bush calls evacuees better off. *July 9,* p. A22.

Noah, T. (1999). *Did Gore hatch horton?* Slate: Chatterbox November 1.

Orestes, M. (1990). The political stampede on execution. *New York Times, April 4,* p. A10.

Patterson, J. (2002). *Brown v. board of education.* New York: Oxford University Press.

Pitkin, H. F. (1972). *The concept of representation.* Berkeley: University of California.

Piven, F. F., & Cloward, R. (1982). *The new class war.* New York: Pantheon Books.

Powe, L. (2001). *The Warren court and American politics.* Cambridge, MA: Harvard University Press.

Powell, M. (2001). The rebels of the right: Some politicians still seek to "Explain" the confederacy. *Washington Post, January 16.*

Roy, R., & Damron, D. (2001). "Small counties wasted more than 1,700 votes. *Orlando Sentinel, January 28*, p. A1.

Rubinton, N. (2000). Media underreported Florida's obstacles to "voting while Black." *Minnesota Star Tribune, December 10.*

Sack, K. (2001). Pressed against a race ceiling. *New York Times, April 5.*

Sengupta, S. (2000). Felony costs voting rights for a lifetime in 9 states. *New York Times, November 3*, p. A18.

Sonenshein, R. (1995). Can Black candidates win statewide elections? In: T. Rueter (Ed.), *The politics of race: African-Americans and the political system* (pp. 307–324). New York: ME Sharpe.

Sontag, D. (2003). The power of the court. *New York Times, March 9* (Section 6), p. 44.

Tackett, M. (1990). Minor drug players are paying big prices. *Chicago Tribune, October 15* (Section 1) p. 9.

The Civil Rights Project. (2002). Harvard university. *Democracy spoiled: National state and county disparities in disfranchisement through uncounted ballots* (pp. 1–12).

The Sentencing Project. (1993). Does the punishment fit the crime? Drug users and drunk drivers, questions of race and class: Executive summary. May 1993.

Thomas, B. (1997). *Plessy v. Ferguson.* New York: Bedford.

Thompson, D. F. (1979). *John Stuart Mill and representative government.* Princeton: Princeton University.

Thurow, L. (1993). *Head to head.* New York: Warner.

Tilly, C., & Tilly, C. (1998). *Work under capitalism.* Boulder, CO: Westview Press.

Treaster, J. B. (1990). Is the fight on drugs eroding civil rights? *New York Times, May 6*, E5.

Treaster, J. H. & Sontag, D. (2005). Pleas for help. *New York Times, February 9*, pp. A, A18.

U.S. Census Bureau Current Population Reports. (2002). Children below poverty level by race and Hispanic origin: 1970 to 2000. No. 669.

Viglucci, A. (2001). 1,700 Dade voters mispunched chads. *Miami Herald, January 6*, p. 1A.

Viglucci, A., Dougherty, G., & Yardley, W. (2000). Blacks votes were discarded at higher rates, analysis shows. *Miami Herald, December 12.*

Walsh, M. W. (2003). I.R.S. tightening rules for low–income tax credit. *New York Times, April 25*, pp. A1–C4.

Wilgoren, J. (2005). In tale of two families, a chasm between haves and have-nots. *New York Times, May 9*, pp. A1–A10.

Williams, J. (1998). *Thurgood Marshall American revolutionary.* New York: New York Times Books.

Willing, R. (2003). Inmates over 2 million, a record for USA. *USA Today, April 7*, p. 13a.

Wines, M. (1994). Taxpayers are angry, they're expensive too. *New York Times, November 20*, p. e5.

PART III:
THE WORLD OF WORK

RACIAL DISCRIMINATION AT WORK: ITS OCCURRENCE, DIMENSIONS, AND CONSEQUENCES

Vincent J. Roscigno, Lisette Garcia, Sherry Mong and Reginald Byron

ABSTRACT

The literature on racial inequality at work has denoted the role of human capital differences, labor market variations in opportunity and especially the economic consequences of workplace racial segregation. Although discrimination is typically inferred as a mechanism, it is seldom treated as a focus in its own right. Drawing from a unique dataset of all racial discrimination cases filed in the state of Ohio from 1988 to 2003, the authors analyzed various dimensions of workplace racial discrimination (i.e., institutional access, mobility, and harassment), as well as the ways in which they unfold in actual workplace settings. Expulsion is the most common form of workplace racial discrimination, followed by general racial harassment. This is notable, given that much prior research has tended to focus on issues of hiring and promotion. Qualitative analyses of case material reveal how discretionary, and often arbitrary, criteria play a part in discriminatory behavior, with consequences for hiring, firing,

The New Black: Alternative Paradigms and Strategies for the 21st Century
Research in Race and Ethnic Relations, Volume 14, 111–135
ISSN: 0195-7449/doi:10.1016/S0195-7449(06)14005-2

*promotion, and demotion. Harassment, in contrast, appears to be aimed
at racial hierarchy maintenance, and often has quite significant consequences for the social psychological well-being of its victims. We conclude
by highlighting these general lessons and how they inform prior work, and
discuss the implications of our arguments and analyses for future research.*

INTRODUCTION

Racial inequality at work remains prevalent 40 years after the Civil Rights
Act and despite significant gains for African Americans in educational attainment. Indeed, minority unemployment remains about double that for
whites, wage inequalities persist, and African Americans continue to be
concentrated in low-status, service-sector work with little room for occupational mobility. Although most concede that minority human-capital
deficits may account for some outcome differences, studies have consistently
found that income and wage deficits (e.g., Cotter, Hermsen, & Vanneman,
1999; Marini & Fan, 1997; Tomaskovic-Devey, 1993; Tomaskovic-Devey &
Skaggs, 2002), employment disparities (Cohn & Fossett, 1995; Wilson,
Tienda, & Wu, 1995), and inequalities in promotion and authority
(McBrier & Wilson, 2004; Smith, 2002; Wilson, 1997; Wilson, Sakura-
Lemessy, & West, 1999) remain even in face of human capital controls. But
why?

Some attribute persistent inequalities to labor market sectoral differences.
Cohen (1998), for instance, in his multilevel analyses of race and gender
inequalities across labor markets of the U.S., finds that income disparities
vary rather systematically as a function of local economic conditions. A
similar point has been made by Wilson (1978) in his historical overview of
African American secondary sector employment in large, inner city areas of
the U.S. More proximately meaningful, however, may be the extent to
which minorities are segregated. Kaufman (1986, 2002) recently found significant segregation of African Americans into lower-skilled, race-typed jobs
involving menial tasks and poor working conditions. Tomaskovic-Devey
(1993) comes to a similar conclusion and suggests that these patterns are
likely due to *social closure* processes wherein minorities are sorted into jobs
that require fewer educational credentials and offer less job training. Such
analyses have proven incredibly useful in terms of specifying the prevalence
and consequences of segregation for race groups, the general devaluation of

minority work, and corresponding wage and mobility inequalities. Yet, until recently, little insight has been offered on the potentially discriminatory processes that may contribute to the very outcomes that have received so much attention.

Limited attention to discriminatory processes, while largely driven by data limitations, may also very well be a consequence of theoretical conceptions of stratification and how it manifests. Indeed, while organizational or geographic variations in levels of inequality provide insights into macro-level sociological outcomes and relations with, for instance, racial competition across neighborhoods or segregation at work, they tend to offer less insight into the micro-mediational processes that are most assuredly playing a role (Feagin & Eckberg, 1980). This article, by providing explicit conceptualization of stratification as a dynamic, interactive process, reflects a commensurable extension of prior work and explicit effort to address the call for "mechanism-oriented" analyses of stratification and its origins (Reskin, 2000, 2003) – a call that has been echoed in recent analyses and overviews of the workplace inequality literature (e.g., McBrier & Wilson, 2004; Huffman & Cohen, 2004; Vallas, 2003). Drawing from a unique dataset of approximately 35,000 workplace racial discrimination cases filed in the state of Ohio from 1988 to 2003, we address the occurrence, dimensions, and consequences of racial discrimination at work. The quantitative data are quite rich and allow for straightforward analyses of discrimination type and form of injury. The qualitative material, drawn from case files, goes much further and provides rare insight into the interactional dimensions of discrimination as well as its costs relative to more conventional and objective measures of inequality (e.g., wage disparity, levels of unemployment, etc.). Indeed, analyses suggest that discrimination is not only about gaining objective or material advantage in the world of work. Rather, it also involves racial hierarchy maintenance during interaction.

RACIAL STRATIFICATION AND WORK

Extensive research over the past several decades has examined workplace racial inequality, and sociological work on the topic is clear. The gap between African Americans and whites in terms of wages, organizational power, employment opportunities, and quality of life has not narrowed significantly. And, notably, these gaps remain even in the face of declines in educational inequality and human capital differences (Feagin, 1991; Hughes

& Thomas, 1998; Kessler, Mickelson, & Williams, 1999; Kirschenman & Neckerman, 1991).

Traditionally, neo-economic theorizing and status attainment research have identified differences in human capital as the principal cause of labor market disadvantages, particularly those of African Americans. The assumption here is that individual investments, such as education, can increase productive capability and, thus, worth and compensation (Kingston et al., 2003). Kaufman (2002) refers to this as the "skills deficit" argument, noting that some workers have differing (i.e., lower) levels of human capital that will result in differential labor market opportunities. If one accepts this premise, it might historically make sense that African Americans will earn lower wages and have less organizational power and fewer overall economic opportunities.

The biggest problem with the aforementioned explanation, however, is its "methodological individualist" orientation, wherein societal outcomes are seen as rooted largely in individual behaviors. A solitary focus on human capital simply overlooks the role of inequality in institutional processes, generally, along with closure enacted by institutional and dominant group actors that reifies existing stratification hierarchies. Moreover, all individuals are presumed to have equal opportunity, for instance, in compulsory schooling or work experience. Those disadvantaged in the labor market are viewed as lacking characteristics that make them more desirable employees (Bibb & Form, 1977). Finally, human capital investments are often assumed to be fixed across all segments of the labor market (Beck, Horan, & Tolbert, 1978). This assumption is problematic because research has documented how the social organization of labor varies across industrial sectors and the ways in which economic and social rewards correspondingly follow (Kaufman, Hodson, & Fligstein, 1981).

Labor market sectoral differences and levels of workplace segregation seem more paramount. In recent years an abundance of the work and stratification literature has highlighted the structure of the labor market and its relationship to inequality (e.g., Beggs, 1995; Coleman, 2002; Mason, 2000). This body of work has highlighted the effects of economic structures on the racial wage gap (e.g., Huffman & Cohen, 2004; McCall, 2001), the role of racial competition on group economic well-being, and the role of business concentration on black employment (e.g., Coleman, 2002). It has been less successful, however, in explaining the overall receptiveness of industrial sectors to non-white workers (notable exceptions include Royster, 2003; see also Beggs, 1995). Correspondingly, recent analyses and overviews of the literature have suggested that sorting mechanisms, including discretionary decision-making and discrimination by employers and co-workers, may be partially responsible.

THE POSSIBILITY OF RACIAL DISCRIMINATION

There is good reason to suspect that attention to discrimination itself will contribute to our understanding of minority-group well-being and experiences in the world of work. Research pertaining to downward race and gender mobility by McBrier and Wilson (2004), and employment exits by Reid and Padavic (2005) suggest that discrimination, specifically, arbitrary and subjective decision-making within firms, may be key. Although Huffman and Cohen's (2004) and Peterson and Saporta's (2004) recent analyses of race and gender wage disparities, respectively, do not measure or analyze discrimination directly, they come to the conclusion that discrimination in worker allocation and exclusion is likely playing a part in persistent disparities that they find.

The possibility of discrimination as an important, although seldom directly studied, mechanism is bolstered further by recent analyses of employer attitudes by Moss and Tilly (2001). These researchers demonstrate that, like subjective biases and stereotypes in the more general population, employers too may hold biased views and consequently make skewed hiring, promotion, and firing decisions (see also Kirschenman & Neckerman, 1991). Experimental and audit designs highlight the centrality of employer preconceptions more directly, especially the ways in which subjective biases translate into *discriminatory behaviors* both in the hiring process and while on the job (Pager, 2003; Laband & Lentz, 1998; Neumark, Bank, & Van Nort, 1996; Yinger, 1995).

Such biases toward African Americans might include, for instance, the view that they are more inclined toward criminality or less stable as employees owing to parenthood, each of which may influence hiring and promotion decisions. For African-American women, employer biases may include the fit between the employee and gender-typed work, or an expectation that a prospective or existing employee may become pregnant or be less committed owing to motherhood. This may lead to exclusion, stagnation in mobility, or sexual harassment, particularly when expectations are violated (e.g., Gruber, 1998; Gutek & Cohen, 1987; Padavic & Orcutt, 1997). Providing in-depth analyses of such interactions at work, the various dimensions of discrimination and their potential costs would provide much-needed insight into the nature of workplace relations and the social processes implicated in the reproduction of racial boundaries and inequalities (Vallas, 2003).

DISCRIMINATION, ITS DIMENSIONS, AND CONSEQUENCES

A sound understanding of inequality brings together awareness of structure and action and their potentially reinforcing and/or conditional nature (Giddens, 1984; Lawler, Ridgeway, & Markovsky, 1993). For our purposes, this entails not only consideration of prior research on race disparities at work but also serious consideration and theoretical development pertaining to the very social processes that create and reinforce those disparities (Vallas, 2003). Without doing so, conceptions of stratification production and persistence remain overly structural, with little room for, or acknow-ledgment of, agency – agency on the part of gatekeeping actors within institutional and organizational contexts, as well as that often exercised by those victimized by inequality.

The work literature provides a solid starting point. Researchers have sought to explain the residual, once human capital differences are accounted for, and denoted how varying structures of local opportunity and levels of organizational segregation (in the case of workplaces) matter, and in im-portant ways. Yet, much remains to be explored, particularly in terms of *how such patterns are recreated at a more proximate level* – a point with which much recent scholarship concurs (e.g., Charles, 2003; Reskin, 2003; Vallas, 2003). We believe clear conceptualization of discrimination, its di-mensions, and its various consequences is also important.

Whether undertaken by sociologists or by fair hiring and housing advo-cacy groups, much of the research on race stratification and work tends to highlight, rather indirectly, objective elements of discrimination (e.g., whether or not one gets a job, whether or not one is promoted, wage differences, etc). Discrimination, both sociologically and legally, however, involves much more than this. It also embodies differential treatment once employed, and it is on this point that research has been limited to but a small handful of experiential and retrospective analyses.

Feagin (1991), for instance, provides insight into the day-to-day and often informal aspects of discrimination in his analyses of experiences reported by 37 African Americans across several U.S. cities. In particular, and be-yond forms of general white avoidance and antagonism toward African Americans, he notes various forms of discriminatory treatment in public spaces. Consistent with the theoretical goals outlined previously, he delineates the interactive character and process-oriented nature of discriminatory acts as well as African Americans' varying responses to such behavior. His account sheds light not only on day-to-day discriminatory realities, but also the distinctly interactive aspects of discriminatory behavior whose aim is status and hierarchy maintenance rather than systematic institutional exclusion.

Although studies such as Feagin's can be critiqued on the basis of retrospective bias, reliance on perceptions of discrimination experiences, and/ or small samples, they nevertheless add a much-needed social and interactional dimension to our understanding and conceptualization of stratification maintenance (see also West & Zimmerman, 1987). Moreover, they explicitly direct attention toward discrimination beyond its purely objective and easily measurable manifestations.

We conceive of discriminatory acts as multi-dimensional: (1) shaping institutional access, (2) influencing mobility differentially, and (3) reifying racial hierarchy through interaction and harassment in general. One of the more important of these, at least historically, has been the *limiting of institutional access* either through exclusion (not hiring) or purging through expulsion (firing). Recent work by Pager (2003) and Pager and Quillian (2005), which relies on audit tests of employers, reveals the contemporary importance of hiring discrimination. Less overall attention has been given to expulsion, although it may be just as important. With regard to *mobility*, much recent work has suggested that discrimination via managerial discretion is likely occurring, yet few, if any, have been able to systematically detail and examine such behavior.

No work of which we are aware grapples seriously with the issue of *general harassment* and racial hierarchy maintenance in the arena of work. This is quite unfortunate, in our view. Although the consequences of general harassment may not affect victims in terms of shaping their objective work status (e.g., getting the job, promotion, or salary increase), there is good reason to suspect that such discrimination holds quite significant social-psychological consequences for its victims. As suggested in a small body of work, even "subtle" discriminatory and differential treatment can be quite consequential to overall well-being of minorities, who often adopt strategies to cope with, avoid, and resist discriminatory actors, interactions, and processes (see, for instance, Krieger, Rowley, Herman, Avery, & Phillips, 1993; Williams, 1995; Williams & Collins, 1995).

Analyses of discriminatory processes, especially when coupled with first-party interpretations of what occurred and the consequences – one of the goals of the current project – would shed significant light on the discrimination's multiple dimensions and costs. Moreover, such analyses will likely provide a more grounded view of discrimination response. Indeed, as Feagin's (1991) analysis of minority discriminatory experiences reveals, racial ethnic minorities on the receiving end of discriminatory actions, despite suffering negative outcomes, are far more than passive recipients. Rather, they are active agents – agents often engaged in complex strategies of coping, avoiding, and confronting the discrimination they face.

DATA

Our main sampling frame includes all cases of racial discrimination in employment filed with the Civil Rights Commission of the state of Ohio (OCRC) between 1988 and 2003. Since 1988, the base data for each case have been input into a database file, a copy of which was made available to the authors. These data include a case ID number; the charging party's race and sex; the respondent (e.g., employer name) and their location; the basis of the charge (e.g., race, gender, religion, etc.); the harm or injury that occurred (e.g., exclusion, promotion, firing, sexual harassment, etc.); the industry (for employment cases), the outcome of the investigation; and a host of geographic identifiers (zip codes, Metropolitan Statistical Area codes, and county Federal Information Processing Standards codes). Cases that are filed with the OCRC are typically doubly filed with the Equal Employment Opportunity Commission (EEOC), although this federal agency often relies on OCRC findings unless the case falls into an already existent EEOC investigation, litigation, or national initiative. Thus, the data provide both a rich body of discrimination suits from a state that, given both the heterogeneity in its industrial structure and significant minority composition in quite large urban areas (i.e., Cincinnati, Akron, Cleveland, Toledo, Dayton, Columbus), is a reasonably generalizable case in point.

Since the project aims to contribute to stratification literature in general, but specifically that pertaining to race, analyses are limited to cases in which the self-reported basis of the charge itself is race/ethnicity and the charging party is African American. The resulting data equate to 34,829 employment cases of race discrimination. It would, however, be erroneous to assume that a discrimination *claim* necessarily implies that discrimination occurred. The OCRC's case determination (and a probable cause finding in particular) will help distinguish cases with little supporting evidence from those with significant and supporting evidence in favor of the charging party's claim. Along with probable cause findings, settlement of a case in the charging party's favor (prior to litigation) is often deemed as supporting evidence from the point of view of legal scholars who both study and testify in discrimination suits. Thus, we limit analyses to the 7,891 "serious" cases wherein probable cause determinations were reached or favorable settlements for the charging party were brokered by a neutral third party (OCRC or District Attorney's office) whose job it is to collect evidence, eyewitness accounts, and case histories, and to weigh the preponderance of all evidence following Department of Housing and Urban Development (HUD) and Equal Oppurtunity Employment Commission (EEOC) guidelines.

Our focus on "serious" cases will certainly have the effect of underestimating discrimination by excluding cases where there simply was not enough evidence, or many cases that are never reported. Nevertheless, it bolsters confidence and the ability to conclude that the *processes* uncovered pertain directly to serious cases of discrimination (rather than alleged or perceived discrimination). Indeed, seldom, if ever, has research been able to qualitatively document discriminatory processes within workplaces, and with the confidence afforded by neutral, third-party civil rights investigative reports and conclusions.

The authors were also granted by the OCRC permission to review and use material from case files. In legal terms, once a case is filed with OCRC and a final case determination is reached, the case file and the information contained within become public information, available to any citizen or agency – a point that both charging parties and respondents are made aware of. These files, of 20–120 pages each, on average, include the following:

- Detailed, first-hand accounts of what occurred from the charging party's viewpoint, often in his or her own words
- A response and/or explanation from the respondent as to what happened
- Witness statements as to what occurred
- Whether the charging party or respondent are represented legally or by an advocacy group
- Who carried out the discrimination (i.e., supervisor, owner, co-workers, landlord, bank, etc.)
- A deposition of testimony, taken by the Attorney General's office, if the case reached that point, and
- The occupation of the charging party, or occupation in question.

Such qualitative material is important to our theoretical aims, denoting the various processes of discrimination, its consequences for individuals on the receiving end, the way discriminatory actors justify their actions, and the ways in which organizations mitigate, encourage, or turn a blind eye to what

is occurring. Correspondingly, the authors systematically gathered qualitative materials from a random subsample of 800 cases, exploring specifically
the previously noted dimensions of discrimination experienced. We draw
largely from this material to highlight the processes, forms, and consequences of discrimination.

ANALYTIC STRATEGY AND RESULTS

Our analytic focus centers principally on the dimensions of workplace racial
discrimination, generally, and the specific ways they play out on an interactional level in the day-to-day work of minorities. We begin by analyzing,
using conventional quantitative tools, the general distribution of racial discrimination cases across our sample of "serious" discrimination complaints
($n = 7,891$). Given our principal concern and theoretical interest in dimensions of discrimination and how discrimination is actually enacted, however,
the preponderance of our analyses is qualitative, and highlights how discrimination plays a part in institutional access, mobility, and general racial
harassment.

RACIAL DISCRIMINATION AT WORK: VARIATIONS, AND DIMENSIONS

No industry is exempt from discrimination. Fig. 1 reports basic descriptives
pertaining to the percentage of all serious racial discrimination cases (7,891)
across economic sectors during the 15-year time period considered. As the
reader will note the highest number of serious cases is in the low-wage service
sector (38.2%), followed by the core industries sector (29.7%), the high-wage
service sector (19.2%), and the public sector (12.9%). Although these patterns
make intuitive sense, given the poorer overall organization in the low-wage
service sector, less formalized procedure, and a correspondingly lower level of
managerial constraint, the pattern observed may very well be a function of
black over-representation in lower-status service-sector work.

Discrimination, as we suggested earlier, takes on distinct forms with potentially unique consequences. Fig. 2 reports the breakdown of serious cases
by discriminatory form. Institutional access is captured by exclusion (i.e.,
hiring discrimination) and expulsion (i.e., firing, layoffs, etc.). Mobility is
described as upward (i.e., promotional discrimination, wages, etc.) and

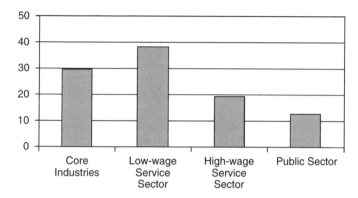

Fig. 1. Percentage of Serious Cases Filed Across Sectors.

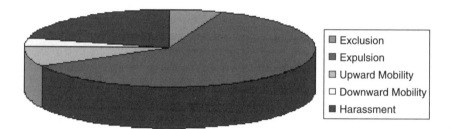

Fig. 2. Percent of Claims Filed by Form of Discrimination.

downward (i.e., demotions). Finally, and quite unique to this study, is our ability to capture general harassment, including general differential treatment, racist remarks, isolation, etc., each of which has as its goal hierarchy and boundary maintenance, and does not necessarily drive the victim out of the organization or alter their objective position within the organization.

Most notable is the very high rate of discrimination in the form of expulsion. Expulsion or firing accounts for nearly 61% of "serious" racial discrimination cases, followed by harassment, which accounts for 21% of these cases. This is particularly interesting given that much prior stratification research focuses on hiring and mobility. Simply, the "action" in terms of discrimination may be disproportionately occurring in ways that have been largely unexamined within sociological literature. These patterns are replicated, nearly identically, when we examine all workplace racial discrimination cases in the state (34,829). But what is actually occurring in these situations? How do the various forms of discrimination occur and what are the consequences for victims? To address these questions of process, we turn to qualitative case materials. We organize our discussion around dimensions of discrimination – institutional access, mobility, and harassment – outlined earlier.

Discrimination in Institutional Access: Hiring and Firing

In terms of claims where hiring discrimination is the principal injury, our data indicate that this is the fourth most common form of discrimination. Approximately 6% of the cases claim discrimination in hiring as the primary injury. Although this number seems low, it is consistent with the possibility that individuals often do not file claims for discrimination in hiring because they do not know who got the job. Here, recognizing discrimination may be quite difficult. Notably, however, sometimes the discrimination does become obvious. Consider the case of William Hawkins, a young black man seeking employment with a landscaping company, GreenGrass, Inc., where he submitted an application for employment. Over the course of nearly a year, he was continually told there were no openings. Interestingly, he had a friend employed at the same company who kept informing him of openings.

> Every time I went down and said, 'Bob, man, I'm ready – I need to get in here," Bob would always somehow tell me that this person either out-qualified me in one way or the other. But my friend Mike Foote was assuring me all along that he had to train these people, that these people had no more qualifications than I did, and on a couple of occasions they didn't even have the qualifications that I had. Bob was hiring people as I was looking for a job, while he was telling me that he was doing no hiring, he was continuously hiring people and putting them into work and not letting me know that he was doing this.

Not only was William told that there were no openings, but he encountered other obstacles as well. During the course of the year in which he sought employment with GreenGrass, Inc., William's initial employment application was lost, and he was asked to complete a second application. William was asked to provide his driver's license so that a background check and check of his driving record could be made. He was asked to submit a urinalysis, which was also lost, and he had to take a second test. According to the investigative report, no other employee was subjected to such obstacles. And, clearly, the emotional costs were high.

> I was very much hurt by Bob's actions, having taken out all this time, all these months, putting my all into trying to impress him, to get him to like me, to get him to see that I was very much qualified to do the job, that I was no different than anybody else. And to find out at the very end that Bob had been trying to pull my leg all along, or more or less

he had been trying to stop me from putting the application in and trying to put up roadblocks to discourage me from continuing my quest for a job at GreenGrass.

William is not alone in his experiences of discrimination in hiring, and one does not always have to know someone employed at the organization to determine if discrimination has occurred. Such was the case with Otis Phillips, a security guard for Rubber City, Ohio, who sought employment as a police officer in the city. He completed the paperwork and was awaiting the results of his background investigation (a common practice for recruitment of civil servants) when he was told that his name had been removed from the police recruit eligibility list owing to a poor credit history. Otis alleged that he was "aware of a younger white applicant, Chris Childs, who also has a poor credit history and he has not been removed from the Police Recruit Eligibility list." In fact, the officer who conducted the background check on Chris Childs had this to say:

After completing this applicant's background investigation there are several areas of concern:

1. This applicant has a very poor credit rating, he has 9 accounts up for collection. He has many civil judgments rendered against him. He attempted to file bankruptcy. It appears that he will not pay his bills at all.
2. This applicant has worked 13 different jobs. He doesn't seem to last too long at any job.

The oral board should take a very close look at this applicant to determine if he should be accepted for the position of police recruit.

Yet, a review of his employment file by the OCRC revealed that the officer who conducted his background check made these comments in his employment file:

The only negative thing found is the fact that the applicant is currently under a Chapter 13 judgment as a result of two divorces. He is currently meeting his financial obligations which should be completed in $2\frac{1}{2}$ years. Despite his advanced age for an applicant, he appears to possess the necessary physical and mental skills for the position.

Civil rights investigators ultimately concluded that Mr. Phillips was not held to the same standard as Mr. Childs, and that this was due to his race. Again, we see that the employer in this case did not overtly discriminate against Mr. Phillips. Rather, employer actions were relatively covert, and efforts were made to justify the discrimination as reasonable and based on different criteria.

As interesting and prevalent as hiring discrimination and the blocking of institutional access may be, more predominant in our data is institutional expulsion (i.e., firing). Indeed, over 60% of the claims filed allege that the complainant was wrongfully dismissed owing to their race. Although such claims might be highly represented because they represent situations in which employees feel harmed and are seeking retaliation against the employer, we remind the reader that our data represent claims in which a probable cause determination was reached. They are, therefore, not frivolous or merely retaliatory. Take, for instance, Shirley Milhouse, an administrative assistant at River City Cultural Center. The Center happened to be experiencing a budget shortfall and had to lay off a certain portion of its staff. Well before her termination, Shirley noticed that something was going on in the office around her, prompting her to write a letter to the director nearly a year before her termination. She noted: "…every attempt is being made to replace and demote me on both a professional and personal basis." Her concern was generated by the fact that several of her job responsibilities were delegated to her co-workers. As her concern increased, Milhouse discussed it with the director and requested a transfer, to no avail. Several months later she was terminated. In her charge affidavit, Milhouse stated that she felt that she had been denied equal terms and conditions of employment and subsequently terminated owing to her race, because:

> Respondent knew as early as January 1992 about the pending budget cuts and probable layoffs. In June 1992 Richard Steele [supervisor] had Nancy Davis' [white co-worker] job reclassified from Administrative Assistant to Curator effective April 1992. I had held the position of Administrative Assistant longer than Davis but, due to her job reclassification, I was no longer eligible to bump her when the layoffs occurred. I was the only Black employee in administration and my duties were divided among the white employees who were retained.

Rule-breaking also appears to be used as a mechanism to fire employees, and it is in this regard that there is evidence that black employees are more severely sanctioned than their white counterparts. Some African Americans in our data were terminated owing to mistakes or their involvement in work-related accidents. Yet, whites who made the same mistakes were not similarly sanctioned. Ed Taylor, a hylo driver in a manufacturing business, was terminated after damaging some equipment while driving. Although whites had caused much worse damage, including breaking a water main, they were merely given verbal warnings or allowed to change jobs. Similarly, Ben Goodwell, an operator in a manufacturing business, was fired by his supervisor for "improper conduct" when he failed to properly "report off" when leaving his equipment, and for taking a break in a restricted area. The civil rights investigator in charge of the case determined that all employees routinely took breaks in this area and that the supervisor was using this excuse to fire Mr. Goodwell. Indeed, the case file substantiated that there was a racially hostile environment, that only four of the 105 employees were black, and that Goodwell's supervisor had used racial slurs toward him. When Goodwell had taken a day off for personal reasons, for example, his supervisor had joked to other employees that he was "probably selling watermelons."

There is also evidence that lack of employee training may be a contributory factor. Jake, a truck driver employed by a company that had no written personnel policy and no progressive discipline policy, was one of only two black employees and was fired after only two weeks on the job. As he notes:

> Nobody showed me how to drive the truck, nobody never got into the truck with me and said, here, we're going to see whatever,... this is that. They didn't even let me see how the gears work, I went out and checked myself...

Although he was discharged for poor work performance and taking too long on runs, Jake tells a different story – he was harassed, and "forced to drive a truck that was unsafe". Employees who were witnesses testified that they had overheard members of management make "derogatory racial remarks" about Jake, and that they, too, had trouble with the truck. Jake believes that management was upset with him for speaking up about the safety problems, and although he testified that management had never made racial remarks to his face, he had overheard them in the office one day:

> Q: Did they mention your name?
>
> A: Yes.
>
> Q: What were they talking about?
>
> A: Well I heard, what I heard said was who does this nigger think he is, he thinks he can just come in here and drive the truck and stay gone all day and not expect us to say anything about it.

African Americans in management positions are not necessarily impervious to these processes, and may experience discrimination through exclusion from networks, withholding of information, and the undermining of their authority. Brad, the General Manager of a retail franchise, was discharged even though he had never been warned and had never been written up for disciplinary reasons. There were allegedly customer complaints against him, but he said he was never told about them. During his employment, he was left out of networks, and was not allowed the same authority and decision-making powers as white General Managers:

> On several occasions, I was made to travel to Corporate Headquarters ... just to find out the meeting was canceled. *Everyone* [charging party's emphasis] else was notified. Upon

my hiring I was told I could hire and fire. I was told I would have my own (new) store. I was not allowed to hire *anyone* [charging party's emphasis] and was told by ... [the District Manager] that I didn't need to hire anyone. I began with a staff of three, when one quit, I couldn't hire anyone. Immediately after I received the old store they changed the hours of operating. About two week [s] later, Stan quit. This forced me to work a 7-day work schedule ... I was finally allowed to take applications, I was not allowed to hire however. I had to call [Corporate Headquarters] set up an appointment for them to come down and interview ... No other manager was told that they could not hire! The general manager before me was afforded a staff of three. Not I!

Holding African Americans to higher performance standards and punishing them more harshly for policy violations are also evidenced in several of the cases. Phil Simpson, a store manager, charges that he was fired by a racist district manager for low sales performance, but that a white store manager who had worse performance was retained. Phil also claimed that the district manager falsely accused him of stealing cash and store merchandise. A chief of police was fired for failure to follow the official policy to purchase a home within the city limits of his community, but there is evidence that other city administrators had lived outside the city limits, and not been sanctioned. A boy's head basketball coach for a state school filed a claim because his contract was not renewed, despite favorable recommendations by the (white) school principal and (white) superintendent. He was the only black teacher in his district, and claims that the school renewed the contract of the (white) track coach "despite conduct and procedure problems." He states, "I was not advised of any shortcomings on my part nor was I given an opportunity to correct any problems of which I was not aware." Several witnesses, including one school board member, praised his performance.

Such cases speak of the strong role of subjective, particularistic criteria in decision making that has to do with hiring and firing. Often, as some of our cases reveal, racism is explicit and undergirds discriminatory decision making. In others, racism is not explicit. Here, justifications for firing revolve around mistakes and poor performance, and justifications for not hiring center on the applicants' competence for the position. The outcome, however, is nevertheless, racial and discriminatory in nature.

Discrimination in Upward and Downward Mobility

About 12% of all cases relate to upward and downward mobility issues. Here, the charging party was not excluded from the workplace organization nor was she/he officially pushed out. Rather, objective job status was impacted, either through lack of promotion or through demotion. This form of discrimination is particularly more apparent among those in higher status positions (managers and professionals) than in the lower occupational rungs, perhaps owing to greater mobility prospects to begin with. It seems likely that mobility may become more of an issue, as those who are upwardly mobile run into glass ceilings, or ride escalators "down" the hierarchy (McBrier & Wilson, 2004). To some degree, similar to cases of institution exclusion or expulsion reported earlier, subjective criteria often play a role, particularly in terms of employer's and manager's views of what are believed to be important "hard" or "soft" work skills.

As a case in point, a probation officer was denied promotion to supervisor because he "didn't interview well," while a White worker without the necessary job qualifications was given the position. A state rehabilitation specialist was denied a promotion given to a less qualified White person because he ranked fifth in the oral interview and could not "provide proof" of his technical degree. This is particularly noteworthy because the employee had left the technical college 27 years before, and the employer had accepted the credential for the past 23 years.

There is other evidence that "particularistic criteria" may play a role in prioritizing informal work relations over objective criteria in promotion decisions. Marvin Smith, a police officer, was denied reassignment to zone car patrol because he "could not find two other officers who would work with him." A further analysis of this case, however, reveals a story very different from that of a typical worker who had problems relating to others. The officer had been continually harassed by co-workers, including the posting of lurid cartoons of him in sexual situations. Medical examinations showed Smith to be under continued strain, and he eventually suffered a nervous breakdown.

Formal policy also periodically facilitates employer bias and blocks promotion opportunities. Jason Wright, a security guard, was unaware that there were opportunities for promotion to a supervisory position at the retail business he worked for, and was upset when a less-qualified white employee was promoted. Jason maintained that blacks were not "put in any decision-making position." When he asked about the promotion, the Director of Loss Prevention informed him that he was "against affirmative action" and believed in "people working on their own merits." According to Jason:

> I asked him about the criteria ... and, how did he get the position over me or any other blacks in the company who had been there much longer than him ... His comment was, in effect, ... that remark about laying his wallet down and [it] being there when he get [sic] back and ... I said, "Do you know what you're saying? Like you're laying your

wallet down, say like, like blacks are going to steal from you or something' ... I said, 'Do
you know what you're saying?' He said, 'It was his prerogative or at his discretion to
make what promotions that he wanted to and the way he see fit [sic], it was best for the
department,' or something to that effect.

Others, such as Shawn Sullivan, were either not informed on internal opportunities for promotion or were not allowed to interview for them despite
having "more seniority, experience and qualifications" than the White employee who was transferred from another facility and hired.

Demotion discrimination, although represented seldom among cases in
our data, is similarly often justified in particularistic ways by managers
rather than on the basis of a formal procedure. Craig Benham, a sales
manager in the retail industry, was demoted and discharged for "poor
performance" by Jones, his white Regional Manager. He had not, however, been previously notified of any performance problems. Benham
stated:

I was the only Black Store Manager and Sales Manager employed by the Respondent ... I am aware that Jones set my sales goals much higher than the previous Sales
Manager's at the same location. Respondent immediately replaced me with Tim Smith,
White, who had much lower performance reviews than I. I became aware from co-
workers that Jones was trying to fire me prior to my discharge.

Setting sales quotas higher for Benham was thus a mechanism to hold him
to higher performance standards than his white colleague. In effect, he was
demoted for not outperforming his white colleagues.

Notably, the effects of demotion are not only objective in terms of job
position or rewards (e.g., salary). They are also painfully emotional. Such
was the case for Frank Thompson, an African American who works at a
large manufacturing plant. He communicates his feelings after a demotion
for doing something that white employees did routinely, while also noting
psychological consequences he is experiencing:

I know that I did not violate the company car policy procedure as used at Acme
Manufacturing and I am aware of numerous other management personnel at the higher
echelon than myself who have either done what I did, or much worse[,] and have never
been disciplined or reprised by demotion, loss of wages, or anything else ... I am concerned with [sic] the embarrassment that my family and I have suffered in the past few
weeks, which has affected my eating and sleeping habits ... I feel that I deserve to keep
my dignity and respect...

McBrier and Wilson's (2004) minority vulnerability thesis should be considered here in relation to downward occupational mobility. The thesis
contends that minorities are especially vulnerable to lay off – or presumably
demotion decisions – because they are not as protected from downward

mobility as are White employees. It is quite likely that rule violations, minor infractions, and arbitrarily applied penalties may indeed serve as mechanisms that facilitate the demotion or firing of otherwise qualified African Americans.

Discriminatory Harassment and Differential Treatment

Seldom explored sociologically have been general processes of harassment, racial boundary creation, and hierarchy maintenance within the workplace. Indeed, most scholarship on workplace racial stratification typically focuses on aggregate differences in wages, employment, etc., while leaving relatively unexplored general processes of harassment. We suspect this is partially due to data limitations, although we also suspect that the focus on tangible positional and monetary outcomes, while useful, has distracted from interactional processes of discrimination that affect minorities on an ongoing basis – interactional processes that hold quite significant consequences for minority individuals' sense of safety, comfort, and overall psychological well-being. Our data allow us to directly confront this dimension of discrimination.

General harassment at work, including differential treatment, isolation, direct racist treatment, etc., still occurs in the world of work at a level that is quite striking. As noted earlier in Fig. 2, general harassment constitutes the second largest portion of discrimination claims at about 21%. While mobility and exclusion/expulsion appeared earlier to be driven by the use of particularistic criteria that advantages whites, harassment seems to occur in everyday interactional settings on the job, where the intent seems to be racial hierarchy maintenance. Take, for instance, Buddy Johnson, a policeman in a large urban area of Ohio. Johnson had been reassigned to various shifts within his department before he wound up as a patrolman assigned to the local hospital. He relates what occurred soon after:

> ...on June 26, 1987, I had been reassigned from general duty to "intake officer"...one Friday afternoon, Lt. Dooley came into the E/R lobby, where I was sitting, walked over to me, bent over to my ear, and in a very low voice stated to me, 'You know Buddy, you're a very lucky nigger.'

Importantly, his experience not only relates an individual encounter and how it made him feel, but also organizational culpability, if not complicity. He talks about this instance and several others with the city administration but with no remedy to the hostile environment in which he worked:

> ...this is a regular routine. The various city administrators promise I won't be harassed any longer, then soon after the oral promise I am subjected to every indignity imaginable. It is late in my career and I would like to be able to enjoy the remaining years.

General laborers and unskilled workers who filed on harassment claims report differential treatment, such as being passed over for overtime or being subjected to racial slurs. The case of Michael, a custodian in a state agency, however, shows how severe such harassment can be and how it may interfere with carrying out one's job duties. After being harassed and experiencing racial slurs by co-workers and a supervisor, he believes his written reprimand for failure to dispose of trash was racially motivated:

> In order to get to the dumpster, I am required to go the long way around, even though there is a shorter route through the gate ... [The Caucasian coordinator and Caucasian supervisor] have refused to unlock the gate in order to allow me to dump trash. They have, however, unlocked the gate for Caucasian employees when they required access to complete their job duties. Additionally, Caucasians have missed trash barrels and have not been reprimanded.

Higher status, however, does not ensure that harassment and differential treatment will not occur. Indeed, such cases are even more highly represented among semi-skilled and skilled employees, perhaps owing to the fact that they are moving into traditionally white male employment. Such workers are apt to experience unfair, negative evaluations, are asked to perform jobs that others are not, or are given unfair workloads. John Mullins, a diesinker in the metal industry, filed harassment charges because unfair, negative job evaluations kept him from the apprentice program. B. Smith, a mechanic, suffered racist comments from co-workers and managers, was denied training, left out of meetings, and had his lunch time changed so he would have to eat alone. Matthew Montgomery, a grounds maintenance foreman for a landscaping company, believes he was "forced to do more work than whites" and was denied raises that White co-workers with his same seniority received. Other workers claim that they were paid less than whites, were not granted the same opportunities for overtime, or were not properly trained. Consider Chad Brewster, a catalog coordinator for an auto parts manufacturing company:

> For the past year a six-page letter with 114 racial jokes has been circulating throughout respondent's facility. A picture of various types of monkeys has been posted on the bulletin board, which included a picture of myself. It was posted in plain sight for all employees to view. [Also posted was] a 'nigger application' for employment, a letter to a 'Jungle Bunny Hunter', and a picture of a black female giving birth to a baby who is listening to a radio.

Racial stereotyping of black men as threatening also played a role in some cases. Tim Hughes, a computer operator for a state government facility, was given a verbal reprimand for failure of good behavior because he was on a different floor from where he usually worked and was not wearing a badge. Security was notified that "a black man was causing a problem." Another case involved a foreman who believes that he was placed on probation because his supervisor did not approve of his relationship with a white female.

Harassment among upper-tier workers is less common and certainly less explicit. Chet Watkins, a senior product-training specialist in the communications industry, for instance, was denied overseas assignment and replaced by a White employee. Dan Jones, a tax examiner for a government agency, claims that he was given low evaluations and denied training. He also claims that blacks were consistently passed over for promotion and that errors were placed in his personnel file. Such discrimination nevertheless has the same effect. It isolates the target individual, creates incredible amounts of emotional strain, and makes being at work difficult, even when racism or racist comments are not overt. As one victim comments:

> Now there was nothing I could pinpoint, and say that he is actually doing it because he stayed within the scope of what a supervisor might do. But since he had never done it before I felt that way and I felt that he was probably trying to get me to be subordinate to him and–but I wasn't going to fall into that trap ... He stayed within a supervisor position ... – I mean, it wasn't – it wasn't nothing overbearing that you could put your finger on and that you could – that you could say, hey this man did this. It — it was very subtle.

CONCLUSION

Sociological research on the foundations of racial inequality at work has gone a far way in documenting racial disparities in income, unemployment, and occupational position, most often relying on aggregate data. Although it often concludes that discrimination is likely partially to blame, research on discrimination at work and its manifestation in everyday work life is quite rare. This article, drawing on quite unique data to the field, has examined racial discrimination at work as well as the various dimensions of that discrimination. Importantly, qualitative analyses of the dimensions outlined – institutional access, mobility, and harassment – reveal how the process often unfolds, how discretionary decision making by powerful actors plays a role, and what the multiple costs are for victims: costs associated with job status and emotional and psychological well-being.

A few notable findings warrant more sociological attention. First, although issues of hiring, firing, and mobility discrimination, in general, are quite important to minority workplace experiences and to their economic status, general racial harassment is important as well, accounting for nearly a quarter of the "serious" discrimination cases filed over the 15-year time period. Acknowledging discrimination's various dimensions and disentangling them is important, in our view, not only for fleshing out what minorities may be experiencing within workplaces, but also because each holds unique implications for the victims. Are they excluded from the institutional altogether? Are their mobility and, thus, economic prospects, affected in fundamental ways? And, should harassment be treated with any less importance, especially given its obvious impact on social-psychological well-being? Our results suggest that all dimensions warrant attention, although perhaps for unique reasons.

Secondly, discrimination occurs very often through interaction, and specifically through the use of particularistic criteria by more powerful status actors (e.g., managers and supervisors) during the processes of hiring, firing, promoting, and demoting. Others, using more quantitative modeling of racial stratification at work (e.g., McBrier & Wilson, 2004; Wilson & McBrier, 2005) have noted this possibility, suggesting that employers will often use "soft skill" criteria that will systematically disadvantage minorities and that may have little actual relevance to the job in question. Although we are 40 years beyond the passage of the Civil Rights Act and many businesses have formal non-discrimination policies and even grievance procedures, it remains the case that there is significant slippage between what is organizationally pronounced and what occurs in everyday interaction and decision making.

The research presented in this article is admittedly but a starting point in addressing discrimination at the workplace explicitly, its various dimensions, and its costs for victims on multiple fronts. The data we have presented is unique in these regards, and we encourage other scholars to tap into similar local, state, and national data sources to capture the complexity of this phenomenon and its varied manifestations. Although discrimination, as it occurs in the "real world" is significantly underestimated – and we caution scholars from making claims about discrimination's extent – such data nevertheless can provide, perhaps for the first time, grounded sociological accounts of the day-to-day unfolding of discriminatory treatment and its impact on groups and individuals. Moreover, such analyses are clearly warranted and will only complement what we have already learned from more quantitative work on group-level economic and workplace disparities.

REFERENCES

Beck, E. M., Patrick, M. H., & Charles, M. T. II. (1978). Stratification in a dual economy: A sectoral model of earnings determination. *American Sociological Review, 43*, 704–720.

Beggs, J. J. (1995). The institutional environment: Implications for race and gender inequality in the U.S. labor market. *American Sociological Review, 60*, 612–633.

Bibb, R., & William, H. F. (1977). The effects of industrial, occupational and sex stratification on wages in blue-collar markets. *Social Forces, 55*, 974–996.

Charles, C. Z. (2003). The dynamics of racial residential segregation. *Annual Review of Sociology, 29*, 167–207.

Cohen, P. N. (1998). Black concentration effects on black-white and gender inequality: Multilevel analysis for U.S. metropolitan areas. *Social Forces, 77*(1), 207–229.

Cohn, S., & Fossett, M. (1995). Why racial employment inequality is greater in northern labor markets: Regional differences in white-black employment differentials. *Social Forces, 74*, 511–542.

Coleman, M. (2002). Contesting the magic of the marketplace: Black employment and business concentration in urban context. *Urban Studies, 39*, 1793–1818.

Cotter, D. A., Hermsen, J. M., & Vanneman, R. (1999). The effects of occupational gender segregation across race. *Sociological Quarterly, 44*, 17–36.

Feagin, J. R. (1991). The continuing significance of race: Antiblack discrimination in public places. *American Sociological Review, 56*, 101–116.

Feagin, J. R., & Eckberg, D. L. (1980). Discrimination: Motivation, action, effects, and context. *Annual Review of Sociology, 6*, 1–20.

Giddens, A. (1984). *The constitution of society*. Cambridge: Cambridge University Press.

Gruber, J. E. (1998). The Impact of male work environments and organizational policies on women's experiences of sexual harassment. *Gender & Society, 12*, 301–320.

Gutek, B. A., & Cohen, A. G. (1987). Sex ratios, sex role spillover and sex at work: A comparison of men's and women's experiences. *Human Relations, 40*, 97–115.

Huffman, M. L., & Cohen, P. N. (2004). Racial wage inequality: Job segregation and devaluation across U.S. labor markets. *American Journal of Sociology, 109*, 902–936.

Hughes, M., & Melvin, E. T. (1998). The continuing significance of race revisited: The study of race, class, and quality of life, 1972–1996. *American Sociological Review, 63*, 785–795.

Kaufman, R. L. (1986). The impact of industrial and occupational structure on black-white employment allocation. *American Sociological Review, 51*, 310–323.

Kaufman, R. L. (2002). Assessing alternative perspectives on race and sex employment segregation. *American Sociological Review, 67*, 547–572.

Kaufman, R., Randy, H., & Neil, F. (1981). Defrocking dualism: A new approach to industrial sectors. *Social Science Research, 10*, 131–148.

Kessler, R. C., Kristen, D. M., & David, R. W. (1999). The prevalence, distribution, and mental health correlates of perceived discrimination in the United States. *Journal of Health and Social Behavior, 99*, 208–230.

Kirschenman, J., & Neckerman, K. M. (1991). We'd love to hire them, but...: The meaning of race for employers. In: C. Jencks & P. E. Peterson (Eds), *The urban underclass* (pp. 203–232). Washington, DC: Brookings Institution.

Krieger, N., Rowley, D. L., Herman, A. A., Avery, B., & Phillips, M. T. (1993). Racism, sexism, and social class: Implications for studies of health, disease, and well-being. *American Journal of Preventative Medicine, 9*, 82–122.

134   VINCENT J. ROSCIGNO ET AL.

Laband, D. N., & Bernard, F. L. (1998). The effects of sexual harassment on job satisfaction, earnings, and turnover among female lawyers. *Industrial and Labor Relations Review, 51*, 594–607.

Lawler, E., Ridgeway, C., & Markovsky, B. (1993). Structural social psychology and the micro-macro problem. *Sociological Theory, 11*, 268–290.

Marini, M. M., & Fan, P. L. (1997). The gender gap in earnings at career entry. *American Sociological Review, 62*, 588–604.

McBrier, D. B., & Wilson, G. (2004). Going down? Race and downward occupational mobility for white-collar workers in the 1990s. *Work and Occupations, 31*(3), 283–322.

McCall, L. (2001). *Complex inequality: Gender, class and race in the new economy.* New York: Routledge.

Neumark, D., Bank, R. J., & Kyle, D. V. N. (1996). Sex discrimination in restaurant hiring: An audit study. *The Quarterly Journal of Economics, 111*, 915–941.

Padavic, I., & Orcutt, D. (1997). Perceptions of sexual harassment in the Florida legal system: A comparison of dominance and spillover explanations. *Gender & Society, 11*, 682–698.

Pager, D. (2003). The mark of a criminal record. *American Journal of Sociology, 108*, 937–975.

Pager, D., & Quillian, L. (2005). Walking the talk? What employers say versus what they do. *American Sociological Review, 70*, 355–380.

Peterson, T., & Saporta, I. (2004). The opportunity structure for discrimination. *American Journal of Sociology, 109*, 852–901.

Reid, L. L., & Padavic, I. (2005). Employment exits and the race gap in young women's employment. *Social Science Quarterly*, forthcoming.

Reskin, B. F. (2000). The proximate causes of discrimination. *Contemporary Sociology, 29*, 319–329.

Reskin, B. F. (2003). Including mechanisms in our models of ascriptive inequality. *American Sociological Review, 68*, 1–21.

Royster, D. A. (2003). *Race and the invisible hand: How White networks exclude Black men from blue-collar jobs.* Berkeley: University of California Press.

Smith, R. A. (2002). Race, gender, and authority in the workplace: Theory and research. *Annual Review of Sociology, 28*, 509–542.

Tomaskovic-Devey, D. (1993). *Gender and racial inequality at work: The sources and consequences of job segregation.* Ithaca, NY: ILR Press.

Tomaskovic-Devey, D., & Skaggs, S. (2002). Sex segregation, labor process organization, and gender earnings inequality. *American Journal of Sociology, 108*, 102–128.

Vallas, S. P. (2003). Rediscovering the color line within work organizations: The 'knitting of racial groups' revisited. *Work and Occupations, 30*, 379–400.

West, C., & Zimmerman, D. H. (1987). Doing gender. *Gender and Society, 1*, 125–151.

Williams, D. R. (1995). Poverty, racism and migration: The health of the African American population. In: S. Pedrazza & R. Rumbaut (Eds), *Immigration, race and ethnicity in America: Historical and contemporary perspectives.* CA: Wadsworth.

Williams, D. R., & Collins, C. (1995). U.S. socioeconomic and racial differences in health: Patterns and explanations. *Annual Review of Sociology, 21*, 349–386.

Wilson, F. D., Tienda, M., & Wu, L. (1995). Race and unemployment: Labor market experiences of black and white men, 1968–1988. *Work and Occupations, 22*, 245–270.

Wilson, G. (1997). Pathways to power: Racial differences in determinants of job authority. *Social Problems, 44*, 38–54.

Wilson, G., & McBrier, D. B. (2005). Race and loss of privilege: African American/white differences in the determinants of layoffs from upper-tier occupations. *Sociological Forum, 20*, 301–321.

Wilson, G., Ian, S.-L., & Jonathan, P. W. (1999). Reaching the top: Racial differences in mobility paths to upper-tier occupations. *Work and Occupations, 26*, 165–186.

Wilson, W. J. (1978). *The declining significance of race: Blacks and changing American institutions.* Chicago: University of Chicago Press.

Yinger, J. (1995). *Closed doors, opportunities lost: The continuing costs of housing discrimination.* New York: Russell Sage Foundation.

RACIALIZATION OF LIFE-CHANCE OPPORTUNITIES AMONG IMPOVERISHED AND MIDDLE-CLASS AFRICAN AMERICANS: THE ROLE OF SEGREGATION IN EMPLOYMENT AND RESIDENCE

George Wilson

ABSTRACT

Assessments of the race/class determinants of life-chance opportunities for African Americans have not adequately considered the "racialization" of socioeconomic attainment within discrete categories of the American class structure. This essay integrates findings concerning how the spheres of employment and residence structure the racialization of life-chance opportunities at the impoverished and the middle-class levels: it documents that a common set of causal underpinnings structure inequality at both class levels – segregation along both spheres is a source of African Americans' inferior life-chance opportunities relative to White class peers. Nevertheless, the causal underpinnings appear to exert different influences across class categories: at the impoverished level, segregation in the residential sphere, and at the middle-class level segregation in the

The New Black: Alternative Paradigms and Strategies for the 21st Century
Research in Race and Ethnic Relations, Volume 14, 137–156
Copyright © 2007 by Elsevier Ltd.
ISSN: 0195-7449/doi:10.1016/S0195-7449(06)14006-4

employment sphere, emerge as particularly critical underpinnings of African Americans' inferior life-chance opportunities. The implications of the findings for utilizing traditional class analyses in assessing the life-chance opportunities for African Americans as well as identifying the causes of racial differences in representation within class categories are addressed.

By all sociological accounts the growing and unprecedented socioeconomic differentiation among so-called "unmeltable" (Novak, 1975) minority groups, including, most notably, African Americans, in recent decades has introduced growing complexity into the dynamics of racial stratification (see Farley, 1996). Specifically, the increasing differentiation is responsible for the expansion of sociological analyses of racial stratification that encompass a broad range of levels of the American class structure from the poor to the relatively privileged, a group commonly referred to as constituting a "middle class" (Landry, 1987; Feagin & Sikes, 1992).

The dominant interpretation of this new socioeconomic differentiation by sociologists is that it has become associated with growing "bifurcation" (Farley & Allen, 1987, p. 112) of economic opportunities for African Americans across the American class structure. Specifically, prominent theoretical formulations such as the thesis about the "declining significance of race"(Wilson, 1978) and the "growing polarization formulation" (Farley & Allen, 1987) constitute explanations for increasing "class rigidity" (Featherman & Hauser, 1978) among African Americans, i.e., the growing effects of social class in structuring "life-chance opportunities" (Weber, 1968). Accordingly, the socioeconomic standing and trajectory of African Americans across discrete class levels more closely resemble those of White class peers than African Americans at other levels of the class structure (Wilson, 1978; Farley, 1996; Hout, 1984; Pomer, 1986).

In fact, there is considerable empirical support for the notion that in recent decades "class-boundedness" (Farley, 1996) has increasingly defined the socioeconomic attainments of African Americans (see Hout, 1984; Pomer, 1986; Wilson, 1997; Wilson & Royster, 1995). Specifically, among African Americans in the post-1965 "civil rights era", the effects of class account for socioeconomic attainments on both an intra- and intergenerational basis. For example, by the late 1970s, the occupational standing of African Americans depended on socioeconomic criteria to a greater extent than was true two decades earlier: those who beat the odds and attained a level of occupational success were able to hold on to those positions to a greater extent than in the past (Wilson, 1997; Hout, 1984). Further, the effect of socioeconomic origins on destinations among African Americans have increased between the early 1960s and later decades; African Americans who moved up in socioeconomic status in the 1970s and 1980s compared to the 1960s were drawn disproportionately from relatively advantaged socioeconomic origins (Pomer, 1986).

These findings, however, should not preclude documenting the ways in which life-chance opportunities are "racialized" (O'Connor, 2001), i.e., race operates as a basis for their distribution. In this vein, one body of sociological research assesses how discrimination across stratification-relevant institutional spheres in daily life, namely, employment and residence, explain life-chance opportunities at a nuanced level – among those who, by conventional measures (e.g., income, occupation), are similarly situated in the American class structure. This body of research examines the impact of race primarily at two levels of the American class structure – the impoverished and the middle class: literally dozens of studies have now been published analyzing the dynamics of racial stratification across the employment and residential spheres at each of these class levels (for reviews see Wilson, 1997; Royster, 2003; Zubrinski, 2001).

Unfortunately, however, this research has remained nonintegrated in crucial ways. Specifically, the failure to synthesize findings across the institutional spheres of employment and residence on an intra-class basis as well as synthesize findings across class lines has impeded progress along a relatively new and important area of research in racial stratification – "equivalency analysis" (Mcbrier & Wilson, 2004) – i.e., the dynamics of racial inequality among incumbents who occupy similar class positions. This synthesis, in fact, is the basis of a mature understanding of equivalency issues, which, in turn, is integral to arriving at an ultimate determination regarding how race and class structure life-chance opportunities for African Americans.

This essay examines how the spheres of employment and residence structure the racialization of life-chance opportunities at both the impoverished and the middle-class levels. Emerging from this examination is a two-pronged thesis. First, a common set of causal underpinnings structure racialization at both class levels: segregation by race in the employment and residential spheres is a source of African Americans' inferior life-chance opportunities relative to White class peers. Nevertheless, these causal underpinnings appear to exert different influences across class categories: at the impoverished level segregation in the residential sphere, and at the middle-class level segregation in the employment sphere, are particularly critical underpinnings of African Americans' inferior life-chance opportunities. Second, the operation of segregation-induced racialization in the spheres of employment and residence has crucial stratification-based, theoretical consequences. Specifically, it suggests it is necessary to modify the use of social class in assessing stratification dynamics of African Americans: the combined effect of inferior socioeconomic attainments and a disproportionate reliance – particularly in the employment sphere – on politically mediated sources of economic opportunities, vis-à-vis the private labor market upon which Whites rely, indicates there is an element of the dynamics of caste that link the life-chance opportunities of African Americans across class categories.

THE DYNAMICS OF RACIALIZATION AT DISCRETE LEVELS OF THE CLASS STRUCTURE

Background

Sociological analyses of the class bases of racial inequality have traditionally focused on explaining the unequal distribution of groups across social-class categories (McKee, 1992; Collins, 1997). In this vein, exclusionary mechanisms central to a broad range of theoretical perspectives such as internal colonialism (Hechtor, 1972), split-labor market (Bonacich, 1973), and competition theory (Lieberson, 1980) have been enunciated to explain the over-representation of African Americans at low levels of the American class structure. Overall, common to these formulations is that differences in class representation along racial lines are viewed as "a form of inequality manifest in gross positional differences but driven by the forces of racism and prejudice endemic to American society" (McKee, 1992, p. 133).

Until relatively recently, within-class variation in life-chance opportunities across racial groups had received far less attention, presumably, for two reasons. First, there has historically been a lack of representation of African Americans in selected class categories including the relatively privileged middle class. Second, African American and White incumbents in class categories are assumed to be similarly situated along major stratification-relevant criteria (see McKee, 1992; Wilson, Sakura-Lemessy, & West, 1999). Accordingly, sociologists have assumed that African American and Whites, who share a similar class position, achieve similar "returns" in the form of both workplace-based rewards and investments in real estate to traditional stratification-based "supply side" factors such as human capital credentials (Blau & Duncan, 1967) and occupational and educational-driven aspirations (Featherman & Hauser, 1978) as well as "demand side" factors including allocation outcomes pursuant to labor-market segmentation (Hodson & Kaufman, 1982) and the dynamics of deindustrialization (Wilson, 1987; Kasarda, 1983).

Racialization among the Poor

A first body of sociological literature challenges the notion that African Americans and Whites in poverty face a similar set of life-chance opportunities. In this vein, sociological research conducted pursuant to the "rediscovery" of poverty among sociologists as a pressing social issue in the post-1980 period documents that there is systematic variation in life-chance opportunities along racial lines at the low end of the American class structure. Specifically, studies comprising this line of research include ethnographies (Royster, 2003; Edin, 1993: Anderson, 1990; Dunier, 1992; Newman, 1999), treatises, and case studies (Wilson, 1996, 1987; Massey & Denton, 1993; Gans, 1995; Ellwood, 1988) as well as survey-based analyses (Hernandez, 2001; Freeman, 1991; Duncan & Brooks-Gunn, 2001; Danziger, Sandefur, & Weinberg, 1994; Zubrinski, 2001; Jencks & Mayer, 1990; Krysan & Farley, 2002; Farley & Frey, 1994; Johnson & Oliver, 1991; Kasarda, 1990, 1983; Kirschenman & Neckerman, 1991; Bane & Ellwood, 1986; Blank, 1989, 1993; Gottschalk, 1994; Corcoran, 2001; Newman, 1999; Corcoran & Adams, 1997) and delineate poverty from nonimpoverished status typically on the basis of income or employment criteria.

Studies comprising this line of research have documented that African Americans tend to experience both more protracted impoverishment than Whites and more extreme economic deprivation in poverty than Whites. First, African Americans in both urban and rural areas, on average, are more likely than Whites to experience "permanent poverty" (Gottschalk, 1994; Corcoran & Adams, 1997), i.e., poverty that is characterized by relatively long and uninterrupted duration. In particular, permanent poverty has pronounced inter- and intra-generational consequences: impoverishment persists across the individual lifecourse and is also likely to be transmitted from parents to children (Bane & Ellwood, 1986; Blank, 1993, 1986). Conversely, poverty experienced by Whites is more often "temporary" (Gottschalk, 1994); poverty is relatively finite in duration over the life-course and it is not as likely to be transmitted across generations (Gottschalk, 1994; Corcoran, 2001; Corcoran & Adams, 1997; Duncan & Rogers, 1991). Second, African Americans are more likely than Whites to experience "dire" (Danziger, Sandefur, & Weinberg, 1994) poverty, i.e., a socioeconomic status characterized by extreme marginality. For example, studies have found that controlling for family size and family composition, the household income of impoverished African–American families in the last decade or so fell, about 30 percent below the federally mandated poverty line, while the household income for the average poor White family during the same time span fell about 10 percent below the poverty line (Jargowsky, 1997; Corcoran, 2001; Freeman, 1991).

Studies that make up this line of research, further, have identified underpinnings of the economic marginality experienced by African Americans, relative to Whites: a hallmark of the poverty experienced by African Americans is its spatial concentration (Massey & Denton, 1993, 1987; Jargowsky, 1997). Specifically, studies of trends in residential segregation by social class among African Americans and Whites have consistently found the African–American poor is, on average, approximately one-half as likely as impoverished Whites to live in neighborhoods that have at least a moderate non-poor presence, i.e., the non-poor exceeds 20 percent of the neighborhood population (Zubrinski, 2001; Massey & Denton, 1993). These findings, in fact, are consistent across the last two decades in both central city and suburban areas of virtually all major metropolitan areas and in both older housing stocks constructed before the passing of late 1960s and early 1970s federal antidiscrimination laws in housing as well as stocks constructed after the advent of the antidiscrimination laws (Krysan & Farley, 2002; Farley & Frey, 1994; Johnson & Oliver, 1991).

Significantly, these studies have also demonstrated that, as poverty increases in concentration, a wide range of disadvantageous "neighborhood effects" (Sampson, Morenoff, & Gannon-Rowley, 2002; Jencks & Mayer, 1990) are triggered, i.e., local conditions, primarily demographic and economic, that negatively impact on the life-chance opportunities of its residents. In this vein, concentrated poverty is associated with inferior local/neighborhood opportunity structures, namely, firms/businesses that provide limited prospects for stable and remunerative long-term employment as well as mobility-related institutions such as schools and training/vocational facilities that provide opportunities to become competitive in a labor market increasingly predicated on acquiring skills at an early career stage to achieve favorable career trajectories (Johnson & Oliver, 1991; Duncan & Brooks-Gunn, 2001). In addition, concentrated poverty limits the access of the African–American poor to the kinds of integrated and "socioeconomically viable" (Massey & Denton, 1993) informational networks that increase awareness of favorable employment opportunities (Johnson & Oliver, 1991; Kirschenman & Neckerman, 1991) as well as precludes opportunities to demonstrate qualities as workers to employers that combat invidious stereotypes regarding lack of productivity and fitness for work that impede opportunities in the labor market (Kirschenman & Neckerman, 1991; Wilson, 1996). Finally, concentrated poverty is associated with the rise of detrimental social psychological states such as dampened career aspirations and the formation of counterproductive values ranging from fatalism, resignation, and the formation of an "oppositional culture" (Ainsworth-Darnell & Downey, 1998; Downey & Ainsworth-Darnell, 2002) that represent a strategy for coping with limited prospects for socioeconomic advancement (Wilson, 1996; Anderson, 1990).

Finally, studies of race-based stratification among the poor document that prospects for achieving mobility out of impoverished status differ among African Americans and Whites. In this vein, African Americans in poverty, largely by virtue of residing in neighborhoods with disadvantaged neighborhood effects, face an inferior set of opportunities in the private labor market. Accordingly, they are reliant disproportionately upon one source – government-sponsored programs – to provide training to acquire skills that can be utilized in the labor market (Freeman, 1991). Conversely, the route to social mobility is broader for impoverished Whites. In addition to government intervention, Whites are able to rely upon an additional source – the private labor market – as a means of attaining social mobility.[1] In this vein, geographic proximity to firms/businesses with internal labor markets and career ladders that are part of either the manufacturing sector or the favorable sector in the burgeoning service-based portion of the American economy provides training opportunities, relatively favorable returns to human capital investments, and ultimately, social mobility through placement in positions that afford career status (Johnson & Oliver, 1991; Newman, 1999).

Racialization among the Middle Class

In the last two decades or so a developing sociological literature has also established that there is variation in life-chance opportunities on the basis of race at the relatively privileged middle-class level. This research, which encompasses both case studies (Collins, 1997, 1993; Fernandez, 1981, 1975;

Patillo-McCoy, 1999; Landry, 1987; Brown & Erie, 1981) and survey-based analyses (Wilson, 1997; Wilson et al., 1999; McBrier & Wilson, 2004; Kluegel, 1978; Thomas, 1995; Wilson & McBrier, 2005; Smith, 2001; Smith & Elliott, 2002), has been timely: it uncovers race-specific dynamics at a time when African Americans have increased their representation in occupationally based positions typically used to define the middle class – specifically, professionals, managers, and administrators – at a more rapid rate than Whites in the post-1980 period (Farley, 1996; Farley & Allen, 1987; Wilson et al., 1999).[2]

An integration of existing studies documents that a parallel set of dynamics across the same institutional spheres identified in studies of the poor are responsible for racialization in socioeconomic outcomes among African Americans vis-à-vis White class peers. However, in these studies, the employment sphere emerges as predominant. In this vein, sociologists have demonstrated that the dynamics of socioeconomic attainment in the employment sphere for African Americans are rooted in the politically mediated nature of their rise into, and placement within the middle class. Specifically, to combat discrimination in the private sector, the government has historically provided a "niche" for African Americans within the middle class job structure (Collins, 1997; Wilson, 1997). Indeed, several studies document that the majority of the African–American middle class spend the majority of their careers in the public sector (Patillo-McCoy, 1999; Brown & Erie, 1981). Nevertheless, the public sector as the locus of privilege for African Americans has had detrimental socioeconomic consequences. For example, the public sector offers progressively lesser economic returns relative to the private sector as work careers unfold (Brown & Erie, 1981; Wilson, 1997). Further, job responsibilities in the public sector tend to focus on providing services to the poor, and, therefore, do not provide contact with the kind of customers/clients, namely, the non-poor, that allow them to be perceived by prospective employers in the private sector as potentially attractive recruits (Collins, 1997, 1993).

In addition, relatively privileged African Americans who work in the private sector tend to perform politically induced "racialized labor" (Collins, 1993), i.e., engaging in job functions that are "directed at, used by, or concerned with, minority group members" (Collins, 1997, p. 54). Specifically, in predominantly White-owned and managed firms in the private sector, African Americans perform work-based functions that are tied into satisfying the consumer needs of minority customers/clients as well as in community/equal employment opportunity capacities (Collins, 1997, 1993). Significantly, racialized labor places African Americans on inferior-rewarded, "peripheral" (Collins, 1997) mobility tracts vis-à-vis performing "mainstream labor" (Collins, 1997), i.e., servicing the needs of a relatively lucrative, predominantly White client base (Collins, 1993; Brown & Erie, 1981). To date, performing racialized labor, relative to mainstream labor has been found to translate into inferior earnings "returns" for investments in human capital credentials, restriction to internal career ladders that include race-based "glass ceilings" as well as positions with circumscribed reward-relevant job characteristics such as limited span and scope of supervisory responsibility and job autonomy, and high rates of downward occupational mobility out of the middle class (McBrier & Wilson, 2004; Farley & Allen 1989; Wilson, 1997; Smith, 2005).

Finally, studies document that irrespective of allocation into the public or private sectors African Americans are disadvantaged because of reliance on racially segregated job networks (Wilson, 1997; Collins, 1993). In particular, restricted access to integrated job networks precludes African Americans from demonstrating to employers the informal, "particularistic" criteria such as loyalty, trustworthiness, and leadership potential that are important in structuring employment evaluations (Kluegel, 1978; Smith, 2001; Fernandez, 1975; Wilson, 1997). Accordingly, the lack of opportunities for African Americans to demonstrate requisite informal criteria constitutes obstacles for overcoming deep-rooted stereotypes regarding suitability for, and productivity at, work that adversely impact on employment trajectories (Wilson et al., 1999; Kluegel, 1978; Pettigrew, 1985).

Segregation in the residential sphere also plays a role in structuring racialization of socioeconomic outcomes among the middle class. In this vein, studies document that the African–American middle class tends to reside in neighborhoods composed of higher proportions of the poor than neighborhoods in which the privileged White reside (Denton & Massey, 1987). In other words, African Americans have limited ability to translate "socioeconomic assimilation" (Denton & Massey, 1987), i.e., substantial financial resources, into "spatial assimilation (Denton & Massey, 1987), i.e., neighborhoods with significant proportions of middle-class residents. Significantly, the constraints on residential options among the African–American middle class that results in living in close proximity to other African Americans is associated with inferior residential investments in terms of both "buying high" as an initial financial outlay and low levels of appreciated value in real estate with the passage of time (Galster, 1990; Massey & Denton, 1993). However, because of their accumulation of human capital and financial resources the African–American middle class, relative to the African–American poor, is able to partially offset the detrimental

consequences associated with residing in locales that contain disadvantaged
neighborhood effects: perhaps, most important, relatively privileged African
Americans – unlike the African–American poor – are not restricted to the
"neighborhood/local opportunity structure" (Anderson, 1990, p. 145) that
contains a disproportionate number of low-level service sector firms (see
Patillo-McCoy, 1999; Anderson, 1990; Dunier, 1992).

Overall, the dynamics of racialization triggered by segregation in the employment and residential spheres at both the impoverished and middle-class
levels are summarized in Table 1.

DISCUSSION

*Employment, Residence, and Racialization among the Impoverished and
the Middle Class*

Assessments of the race/class determinants of life-chance opportunities
for African Americans by sociologists have not adequately considered the
"racialization" of socioeconomic attainment within discrete categories of
the American-class structure. This essay has integrated findings concerning
how the spheres of employment and residence structure the racialization
of life-chance opportunities for African Americans at the impoverished and
the middle-class levels: it documents that a common set of causal underpinnings structure inequality at both class levels – discriminatorily induced
segregation along both spheres is a source of African American' inferior life-
chance opportunities relative to White class peers. Nevertheless, the causal
underpinnings appear to exert different influences across class categories:
at the impoverished level, segregation in the residential sphere, and at the
middle-class level segregation in the employment sphere, emerge as particularly critical underpinnings of African Americans' inferior life-chance
opportunities.

Significantly, the grounding of racialization in segregation at both class
levels makes it necessary to identify the roots of segregation. In this vein,
segregation in both residential and employment spheres has been identified
as being associated with the subtle, institutional, and ostensibly nonracial
dynamics that characterize "modern racial discrimination" (Pettigrew, 1985;
Pettigrew & Martin, 1987) rather than by the ill will and intentionality
associated with traditional "jim crow" racism (Bobo, Kluegel, & Smith,
1997). Above all, modern discrimination is characterized by its indirect
character: it encompasses facially neutral practices – based on such

Table 1. Racialization at the Impoverished and Middle-Class Levels.

Institutional Spheres	Poor		Middle Class	
	African American	White	African American	White
Residence	Deleterious Neighbor effects	Non-deleterious Neighbor effects	Deleterious Neighbor effects	Non-deleterious Neighbor effects
Employment (Economic status)	Unemployment		Public sector concentration	Private Sector concentration
	Underemployment		Racialized jobs	Mainstream jobs
	Employment in service sector with no career ladders	Employment in service + manufacturing sector with career ladders	Segregated networks	Integrated networks
(Source of mobility)	Politically mediated	Politically mediated Private labor market	Politically mediated	Politically mediated Private labor market
Life chance Consequences	Permanent poverty Extreme marginality	Temporary poverty Non-extreme marginality	Fewer rewards Career instability	Greater rewards Career stability

phenomena as "business necessity" and forms of "self-interest" that when applied in a uniform manner incorporate the legacy of discrimination and produce results that have a disproportionately negative impact on African Americans (Pettigrew, 1985; Bobo et al., 1997). Further, these practices are often rooted in a relatively modern and benign constellation of stereotypes regarding the culture/motivational deficiencies of African Americans (Pettigrew, 1985; Bobo et al., 1997; Wilson et al., 1999).

In the sphere of employment, a similar set of dynamics associated with modern racial discrimination account for the restriction of the African–American poor to the low-end service sector economy as well the African–American middle class in public sector jobs and marginalized slots in the private sector. For example, "business necessity" associated with the perceived need to ensure continued patronage of valued White clients/customers (Wilson, 1997; Fernandez, 1981) as well as statistical discrimination emanating from stereotypes about the work ethic of minority group workers (Tomaskovic-Devey & Skaggs, 1999; Pettigrew, 1985) puts a premium on allocating both the African–American poor and middle class into marginal slots relative to White class peers (Collins, 1997; Wilson, 1997). The one conspicuous difference in determinants of racial segregation in the employment sphere across class categories derives from the effects of segregation in the residential sphere: the African–American poor have experienced particularly circumscribed economic opportunities by virtue of residing in neighborhoods that have experienced most keenly the negative effects (e.g., predominance of low-level service sector jobs) of deindustrialization (Anderson, 1990).

The roots of segregation in the residential sphere at both the impoverished and middle-class levels also lie in the subtle dynamics associated with the modern form of discrimination. For example, the legacy of racial inequality manifested in differences in accumulated wealth across racial groups, who occupy similar class positions, results in a wider "residential labor market for Whites than African Americans (Conley, 1999; Oliver & Shapiro, 1996).[3] Further, forms of "self-interest" such as the perceived need to maintain the value of real estate investments among White homeowners (Galster & Keeney, 1988) and the desire of brokers/realtors to maximize economic returns in real estate transactions (Galster & Keeney, 1988) result in discriminatory practices – triggered primarily by real estate agents – that restrict African Americans to a relatively limited range of residential options (Galster, Freiberg, & Houk, 1987). These practices include "racial steering" (Galster, 1990) in which African Americans and Whites are directed toward separate housing stocks that are unequal in terms of the value of their financial investment and "blockbusting" (Galster, 1990) in which realtors sell previously White-owned property to African Americans at inflated prices pursuant to targeting a transformation in neighborhood composition from predominantly White to African American (Massey & Denton, 1993; Goering, 1986).

Consequences of Racialization for Social-Class Analysis

An additional issue that derives from the analysis of racialization concerns the applicability of utilizing the term, "social class", in assessing stratification dynamics across racial lines. Traditional conceptualizations of social class, namely, those in the Marxian and Weberian tradition, posit that class position is based on two criteria: level of socioeconomic rewards and a source of the rewards. Specifically, studies in the Weberian tradition, maintain that "a set of shared life-chance opportunities"(Giddens, 1970, p. 209) constitute the essence of class position: life-chance opportunities refer to "a market situation in the private labor market" (Giddens, 1970, p. 210) that is "separate and apart from members of other class groupings" (Giddens, 1970, p. 211). Similarly, studies in the Marxian tradition maintain that class position designates a level of ownership and control over private economic resources (Wright, 1997; Robinson & Kelley, 1979).

Significantly, there is a basis in the application of the criteria integral to the Marxist and Weberian conceptualizations for concluding that social class captures the dynamics of stratification for Whites but not African Americans. First, as this essay has maintained, African Americans receive an inferior set of socioeconomic rewards relative to Whites at both the impoverished and middle-class levels. In fact, the level of disadvantage "within class categories as it unfolds on both an intra- and intergenerational basis continues to be substantial" (Farley, 1996, p. 62). Second, socioeconomic standing and trajectories for African Americans is premised on a "politically driven interventionist economy" (Brown & Erie 1981, p. 313) designed to overcome discrimination in the private labor market. Specifically, the African–American poor tend to suffer from an economic plight that requires "radical state-based intervention to ensure subsistence and impart skills necessary to become meaningfully integrated into the labor market" (Anderson, 1990, p. 84). For the African–American middle class, politically induced dynamics "are indispensable to the creation of niches within the middle-class job structure that drive careers and economic trajectories"(Collins, 1997, p. 116). Conversely, for Whites across the class structure, life-chance opportunities are structured along lines that conform to the tenets of traditional conceptions of social class, i.e., they are determined by the more reward- and mobility-friendly dynamics in the private labor market.

Nevertheless, these findings regarding the economic marginality experienced by African Americans relative to White class peers must be balanced against those from another line of sociological research documenting that class effects account for a basic divergence in the life-chance opportunities for African Americans across lines of social class. In this vein, not only do the effects of class account for inferior socioeconomic trajectories for the African–American poor vis-a-vis relatively privileged racial peers (Pomer, 1986; Featherman & Hauser, 1978), there is evidence that in the civil rights era, the gap in economic opportunities among the African–American population across class lines is progressively widening pursuant to the "bifurcating effects" (Farley & Allen, 1987, p. 53) of continued deindustrialization, economic segmentation, and the implementation of affirmative action programs (see Farley, 1996; O'Connor, 2001).

Overall, a plausible resolution to these contrary findings involves retaining social class as appropriate usage with the proviso that across the class structure what E. Franklin Frazier (1957) called "quasi-caste dynamics" play a role in determining the life-chance opportunities for African Americans. Frazier, nearly five decades ago, recognized that the newly emerging population of African–American professionals and successful businessmen had dissimilar socioeconomic trajectories from the African–American poor, yet were linked with them in facing exclusion from participation in the mainstream labor market, namely, the private sector where the most favorable socioeconomic rewards and trajectories lie; this link among incumbents across social-class categories, according to Frazier, is a product of one of the central tenets of caste, a shared restriction in mobility opportunities that operates on an ascriptive basis – namely, race.

CONCLUSION

The dynamics of racialization that emerge from this analysis contribute to the debate about the relative effects of race and social class in structuring life-chance opportunities among African Americans in the post-1965 civil rights era. This debate has been contentious as manifested in scholars having tended to argue that the influence of one dominates the other (see Wilson & Royster, 1995). In fact, the contentiousness has made it difficult to adopt a broader, more inclusive posture which – based on the totality of evidence form sociological research – assigns an important role to both as causal factors in determining life-chance opportunities in the post-1965 civil rights era (Pettigrew, 1985). Overall, the findings presented in this essay build on previous sociological research and suggest one way in which both can be assigned an important causal role. Specifically, class tends to play a crucial role in structuring the broad parameters of socioeconomic attainments and trajectories. Simultaneously, however, one of the ways in which minority status operates – as documented in this essay – is that it serves to restrict attainments relative to Whites within these parameters, thereby, establishing a link with other African Americans irrespective of class status.

In addition, worthy of mention is that the manner in which racialization operates in the spheres of employment and residence also appears to have broader implications: it helps to explain the unequal distribution of racial groups across class categories, the traditional thrust of class-based research on racial stratification. For example, the relatively high rates of downward mobility among relatively privileged African Americans – pursuant to, for example, placement in racialized job slots – restricts representation in the middle class and swells ranks at lower-class levels, including the impoverished (see McBrier & Wilson, 2004; Corcoran, 2001). Similarly, relatively low rates of upward mobility out of poverty on both an intra- and inter-generational basis – pursuant to, for example, dynamics responsible for both "permanent" and "dire" forms of impoverishment – has the same detrimental consequences for the representation of African Americans at both class levels.

Further, not to be overlooked is that the findings from this essay do not bode well for African Americans. First, segregation in the employment and residential spheres shows little signs of abating. For example, in the residential sphere, discriminatory real estate practices that contribute to residential segregation have proven to be resistant to change: the continuing viability of racial steering and blockbusting is a product of derived economic benefits as well as notorious lax enforcement of antidiscrimination laws in housing (see Galster, 1990). In the employment sphere, dynamics that underlie the placement of the African Americans in marginalized slots relative to White class peers also persist: social psychologists have struggled to identify how to reduce the prevalence of invidious racial stereotypes (Pettigrew, 1985) and judicial rulings by majority of federal district courts have made it increasingly unlikely that segregation as an unintended consequence of practices that constitute a "business necessity" will be deemed violative of equal employment opportunity law (Fernandez, 1981). Second, the detrimental consequences of segregation appear to be increasing. For example, the acceleration of deindustrialization is producing a growing concentration of firms constituting the low end of the service sector in which African Americans reside, thereby exacerbating negative stratification-based trajectories, particularly for the African–American poor (Newman, 1999; Johnson & Oliver, 1991). Third, political intervention, which has played a disproportionate role in providing opportunity for African Americans relative to Whites across the American class structure is waning: in recent decades the cumulative effect of growing insensitivity toward the plight of the poor, fiscal crisis in government funding, and perceptions that government has become too large and intrusive is serving to constrict the already relatively marginal life-chance opportunities for both the African–American poor and middle class (Quadagno, 1994; Edsall & Edsall, 1991).

Finally, it is important to point out that more research is needed to enhance our understanding of the extent to which patterns of integration across the residential and employment spheres explains racialization across the American class structure. In this vein, research is needed to assess dynamics for other minority groups such as Latino and sub-Latino as well as Asian and sub-Asian groups. In recent decades, these populations have come to more directly compete with other groups as they have increasingly abandoned residential and occupational enclaves pursuant to attempting to expand occupational and housing options (Zubrinski, 2001; O'Connor, 2001). Further, researchers need to undertake analyses at additional levels of the class structure such as the working class, i.e., manual workers, who occupy a position between the impoverished and the middle class. Systematic analyses of race-based stratification dynamics among the working class continue to be rare compared to other class categories (Horton, Allen, Herring, & Thomas, 2000). Finally, temporal analyses, i.e., longitudinal and trend designs are needed to assess the extent to which racialization is a product of period effects and exerts variation across stages of the work-career as there is documented variation in levels of segregation across institutional spheres and the stratification-relevant importance of segregation on these bases (Farley, 1996; Krysan & Farley, 2002; O'Connor, 2001). Overall, when this research is undertaken it promises to shed light on one of the most important issues in the sociological analysis of racial stratification – the extent to which ascription operates as a cleavage that defines inequality in contemporary American society.

NOTES

1. The majority of government-sponsored programs continue to be income rather than race targeted (see O'Connor, 2001).
2. This is the most widely used conceptualization of the middle class in the racial context (see Patillo-McCoy, 1999; Wilson et. al, 1999).
3. It is recognized that racial differences in wealth accumulation is a fundamental determinant of intra-class differences in life-chance opportunities across racial groups. The wealth gap, which captures the legacy of racial discrimination has created large differences in financial resources that have widespread consequences. In this essay, wealth differences are considered only to the extent they help to account for segregation in the institutional spheres under consideration – employment and residence.

REFERENCES

Ainsworth-Darnell, J., & Downey, D. (1998). Assessing the oppositional culture explanation for racial/ethnic differences in school performance. *American Sociological Review, 63*, 536–553.

Anderson, E. (1990). *Streetwise*. Chicago: University of Chicago Press.

Bane, M. J., & Ellwood, D. (1986). Slipping into and out of poverty: The dynamics of spells. *Journal of Human Resources, 21*, 1–23.

Blank, R. (1989). Analyzing the length of welfare spells. *Journal of Public Economics, 39*, 245–273.

Blank, R. (1993). Why were poverty rates so high in the 1980s? In: D. Papadimitriou & E. Wolff (Eds), *Poverty and prosperity in the USA in the late twentieth century* (pp. 15–53). New York: Macmillan.

Blau, P., & Duncan, O. (1967). *The American occupational structure*. New York: John Wiley.

Bobo, L., Kluegel, J., & Smith, R. (1997). Laissez-Faire racism: The crystallization of a kinder, gentler, antiblack ideology. In: S. Tuch & J. Martin (Eds), *Racial attitudes in the 1990s* (pp. 15–44). Westport, CT: Praeger.

Bonacich, E. (1973). The split-labor market: A theory of ethnic antagonism. *American Sociological Review, 38*, 212–231.

Brown, M., & Erie, S. (1981). Blacks and the legacy of the great society: The economic and political impact of Federal social policy. *Public Policy, 29*, 299–330.

Collins, S. (1993). Blacks on the bubble: The vulnerability of Black executives in a White corporation. *Sociological Quarterly, 34*, 429–447.

Collins, S. (1997). *Black corporate executives: The making and breaking of a Black middle class*. Philadelphia, PA: Temple University Press.

Conley, D. (1999). *Being Black but living in the red*. Berkeley, CA: University of California Press.

Corcoran, M. (2001). Mobility, persistence, and consequences of poverty for children. In: S. Danziger & R. Haveman (Eds), *Understanding poverty* (pp. 58–83). New York: Russell Sage Foundation.

Corcoran, M., & Adams, T. (1997). Race, sex, and the intergenerational transmission of poverty. In: G. Duncan & J. Brooks-Gunn (Eds), *Consequences of growing up poor* (pp. 461–518). New York: Russell Sage Foundation.

Danziger, S., Sandefur, G., & Weinberg, D. (Eds). (1994). The historical record; trends in
    family, income, inequality and poverty. In: *Confronting poverty* (pp. 18–50). Russell Sage
    Foundation Press.
Denton, N., & Massey, D. (1987). Residential segregation of Blacks, Hispanics, and Asians by
    socioeconomic status and generation. *Social Science Quarterly, 47,* 197–211.
Downey, D., & Ainsworth-Darnell, J. (2002). The search for oppositional culture among Black
    students. *American Sociological Review, 67,* 156–164.
Duncan, G., & Brooks-Gunn, J. (2001). Income effects across the life span: Integration and
    interpretation. In: G. Duncan & J. Brooks-Gunn (Eds), *Consequences of growing up
    poor.* New York: Russell Sage Foundation pp. 410–596.
Dunier, M. (1992). *Slim's table.* Chicago: University of Chicago Press.
Edin, K. (1993). *There's a lot of money left at the end of the month: How AFDC recipients make
    ends meet in Chicago.* New York: Garland Press.
Edsall, T., & Edsall, M. (1991). *Chain reaction: The impact of race, rights, and taxes on American
    politics.* New York: Norton.
Ellwood, D. (1988). *Poor support: Poverty in the American family.* New York: Basic
    Books.
Farley, R. (1996). *The new American reality.* New York: Russell Sage Foundation.
Farley, R., & Allen, W. (1987). *The quality of life and the color line in America.* New York:
    Russell Sage Foundation.
Farley, R., & Frey, W. (1994). Changes in the segregation of Whites from Blacks in the 1980s.
    American Sociological Review, 59, 23–45.
Feagin, J., & Sikes, M. (1992). *Living with racism: The experience of the Black middle class.*
    Philadelphia, PA: Temple University Press.
Featherman, D., & Hauser, P. (1978). *Opportunity and change.* New York: Academic Press.
Fernandez, J. (1975). *Black managers in White corporations.* Lexington, MA: Lexington Books.
Fernandez, J. (1981). *Racism and sexism in White corporations.* New York: Wiley.
Frazier, E. F. (1957). *The Black bourgeosie.* Chicago: University of Chicago Press.
Freeman, R. (1991). Employment and earnings of disadvantaged young men in a labor shortage
    economy. In: C. Jencks & P. Peterson (Eds), *The urban underclass* (pp. 45–72).
    Washington: The Brookings Institution.
Galster, G. (1990). Racial steering by real estate agents: Mechanisms and motives. *Review of
    Black Political Economy, 19,* 39–63.
Galster, G., & Keeney, W. (1988). Race, residence discrimination, and economic opportunity.
    Urban Affairs Quarterly, 24, 87–117.
Galster, G., Freiberg, F., & Houk, D. (1987). Racial differentials in real estate advertising
    practices. *Journal of Urban Affairs, 9,* 199–215.
Gans, H. (1995). *The war against the poor.* New York: Basic Books.
Giddens, A. (1970). *Capitalism and modern social theory.* London: Cambridge University Press.
Gottschalk, P. (1994). The dynamics of intergenerational poverty and welfare participation. In:
    S. Danziger, G. Sandefur, & D. Weinberg. (Eds), *Confronting poverty* (pp. 85–108).
    Cambridge: Harvard University Press.
Hechtor, M. (1972). *Internal colonialism.* New Haven, CT: Yale University Press.
Hernandez, D. (2001). Poverty trends. In: J. Duncan & J. Brooks-Gunn (Eds), *Consequences of
    growing up poor* (pp. 18–34). New York: Russell Sage Foundation.
Hodson, R., & Kaufman, R. (1982). Economic dualism: A critical review. *American Sociological
    Review, 47,* 727–739.

Horton, H. D., Allen, B., Herring, C., & Thomas, M. (2000). Lost in the storm: The sociology of the Black working class, 1850–1990. *American Sociological Review, 65,* 128–137.

Hout, M. (1984). Occupational mobility of Black men: 1962–1973. *American Sociological Review, 98,* 575–592.

Jargowsky, P. (1997). *Poverty and place.* New York: Russell Sage Foundation.

Jencks, C., & Mayer, S. (1990). The social consequences of growing up in a poor neighborhood. In: L. Geary (Ed.), *Inner-city poverty in the U.S.* (pp. 38–71). Washington: National Academy Press.

Johnson, J., & Oliver, M. (1991). Economic restructuring and Black male joblessness in U.S. metropolitan areas. *Urban Geography, 12,* 542–562.

Kasarda, J. (1983). Entry-level jobs, mobility, and urban minority unemployment. *Urban Affairs Quarterly, 19,* 21–40.

Kasarda, J. (1990). Structural factors affecting the location and timing of urban underclass growth. *Urban Geography, 11,* 234–264.

Kirschenman, J., & Neckerman, K. (1991). We'd love to hire them, but; the meaning of race for employers. In: C. Jencks & P. Peterson (Eds), *The urban underclass* (pp. 26–61). Washington: The Brookings Institution.

Kluegel, J. (1978). The causes and consequences of racial exclusion from job authority. *American Sociological Review, 43,* 285–301.

Krysan, M., & Farley, R. (2002). The residential preference for Blacks: Do they explain persistent segregation? *Social Forces, 80,* 937–980.

Landry, B. (1987). *The new Black middle class.* Berkeley, CA: University of California Press.

Lieberson, S. (1980). *A piece of the pie.* Cambridge: Harvard University Press.

Massey, D., & Denton, N. (1993). *American Apartheid.* Cambridge: Harvard University Press.

McBrier, D., & Wilson, G. (2004). Going down: Race and downward mobility for white-collar workers in the 1990s. *Work and Occupations, 31,* 283–322.

McKee, J. (1992). *Sociology and the race problem.* Philadelphia, PA: Temple University Press.

Newman, K. (1999). *No shame in my game.* New York: Russell Sage Foundation.

Novak, R. (1975). *The unmeltable ethnics.* Chicago: University of Chicago Press.

O'Connor, A. (2001). Understanding inequality in the late twentieth century metropolis: New perspectives on the enduring racial divide. In: A. O'Connor, C. Tilly & L. Bobo (Eds), *Urban inequality: Evidence from four cities* (pp. 1–33). New York: Russell Sage Foundation.

Oliver, M., & Shapiro, T. (1996). *Black wealth/White wealth.* New York: Routledge.

Patillo-McCoy, M. (1999). *Black picket fences: Privilege and peril among the Black middle class.* Chicago: University of Chicago Press.

Pettigrew, T. (1985). New Black–White patterns: How best to conceptualize them. *Annual Review of Sociology, 11,* 329–346.

Pettigrew, T., & Martin, J. (1987). Shaping the organizational context for African American inclusion. *Journal of Social Issues, 43,* 41–78.

Pomer, M. (1986). Labor market structure, intragenerational mobility, and discrimination: Black male advancement out of low-paying occupations. *American Sociological Review, 51,* 650–659.

Quadagno, J. (1994). *The color of welfare: How racism undermined the war on poverty.* New York: Oxford University Press.

Robinson, R., & Kelley, J. (1979). Class as conceived by Marx and Dahrendorf: Effects on income inequality and politics in the U.S. and Great Britain. *American Sociological Review, 44,* 38–55.

Royster, D. (2003). *Race and the invisible hand*. Berkeley, CA: University of California Press.

Sampson, R., Morenoff, J., & Gannon-Rowley, T. (2002). Assessing neighborhood effects: Social processes and new directions for research. *Annual Review of Sociology, 28*, 443–478.

Smith, R. (2001). Particularism in control over monetary resources at work: An analysis of racioethnic differences in the authority outcomes of Black, White, and Latino men. *Work and Occupations, 28*, 15–33.

Smith, R. A. (2005). Do the determinants of promotion differ for White men versus women and minorities? An exploration of intersectionalism through sponsored and contest mobility processes. *American Behavioral Scientist, 48*, 1157–1181.

Smith, R., & Elliott, J. (2002). Does ethnic concentration influence employees access to authority? An examination of contemporary urban labor markets. *Social Forces, 81*, 255–279.

Thomas, M. (1995). Race, class, and occupation: An analysis of Black and White earnings for professional and non-professional males, 1940–1990. *Research in race and ethnic relations, 8*, 139–146.

Tomaskovic-Devey, D., & Skaggs, S. (1999). An establishment-level test of the statistical discrimination hypothesis. *Work and Occupations, 26*, 422–445.

Weber, M. (1968). *Economy and society*. New York: Vantage Press.

Wilson, G. (1997). Pathways to power: Racial differences in the determinants of job authority. *Social Problems, 43*, 38–54.

Wilson, G., Sakura-Lemessy, I., & West, J. (1999). Reaching the top: Racial differences in mobility paths to upper-tier occupations. *Work and Occupations, 26*, 165–187.

Wilson, G., & Royster, D. (1995). Critiquing Wilson's critics: The declining significance of race thesis and the Black middle class. *Research in Race and Ethnic Relations, 8*, 57–75.

Wilson, G., & McBrier, D. (2005). Race and loss of privilege: African American/White differences in the determinants of layoffs from upper-tier occupations. *Sociological Forum, 20*, 301–321.

Wilson, W. (1978). *The declining significance of race*. Chicago: University of Chicago Press.

Wilson, W. (1987). *The truly disadvantaged*. Chicago: University of Chicago Press.

Wilson, W. (1996). *When work disappears*. Cambridge: Harvard University Press.

Wright, E. O. (1997). *Class counts: Class studies in comparative perspective*. New York: Cambridge University Press.

Zubrinski, C. (2001). Process of residential segregation and its consequences. In: A. O'Connor, C. Tilly & L. Bobo (Eds), *Urban inequality: Evidence from four cities* (pp. 217–272). New York: Russell Sage Foundation.

PART IV:
RACE, IDENTITY, AND RACIAL CONSCIOUSNESS

THE CHANGING POLITICS OF COLOR-BLIND RACISM

Ashley ("Woody") Doane

During the past decade, a range of scholars have analyzed "color blindness" as the dominant racial ideology for the defense of white supremacy (e.g., Carr, 1997; Bonilla-Silva, 2001, 2003; Doane, 2003; Brown et al., 2003). In brief, "color blindness" incorporates a series of claims regarding the current nature of race relations in the United States, beginning with the assertion that as a result of the Civil Rights Movement and the decline of prejudicial attitudes among whites, racism is no longer a structural phenomenon and the only racism that persists in contemporary American society involves isolated "hate crimes" and other actions of the few remaining prejudiced individuals. This leads to the conclusion that race and racism no longer "matter" in American society with respect to social and economic participation. From this platform, it is then possible to argue that persisting racial inequality is either the result of happenstance or due to dysfunctional and socially pathological behaviors on the part of minority individuals and communities. Politically, "color blindness" has been employed to support the position that race-based policies for the amelioration of segregation or racial inequality are unnecessary, "unfair" to whites and in violation of basic principles of equal treatment in a democratic society.

My objective in this chapter is not to debunk the myth of "color blindness." That has been done effectively elsewhere, most notably by Eduardo Bonilla-Silva (2001, 2003), Joe Feagin (2000), and the authors of

The New Black: Alternative Paradigms and Strategies for the 21st Century
Research in Race and Ethnic Relations, Volume 14, 159–174
Copyright © 2007 by Elsevier Ltd.
All rights of reproduction in any form reserved
ISSN: 0195-7449/doi:10.1016/S0195-7449(06)14007-6

Whitewashing Race (Brown et al., 2003). Instead, I will examine what I believe is the continuing *evolution* of "color-blind" racial ideology, as proponents refine their presentation to confront new challenges and pursue new political objectives. In my opinion, understanding the changing politics of "color blindness" is essential for both the sociology of race relations and the practice of anti-racist politics.

RACIAL IDEOLOGIES AND RACIAL DISCOURSE

Ideologies are the belief systems or mental models that individuals and groups use to interpret or explain their environment. As Michael Omi and Howard Winant (1986) observed in their influential book *Racial Formation in the United States* (p. 68), the racial understandings of society are constantly being transformed as a result of political struggle. Moreover, racial ideologies are grounded in "racialized social systems" (Bonilla-Silva, 2001, p. 37), where the political, economic, and social institutions of society are intertwined with hierarchically ordered racial categories. As racialized groups struggle to maintain or to challenge systems of domination, ideologies play a key role as individuals and groups seek to mobilize supporters, gain compatriots, and neutralize or discredit opponents.

One of the best vehicles for studying racial ideologies is *racial discourse*, which I define as the collective text and talk of society with respect to issues of race. Discourse provides a central connection between macro-level racial ideologies and the micro-level understandings of individuals. Elite, media, and social movement discourses shape the social and cultural environments in which individuals acquire knowledge and in which they attach meaning to situations (Gabriel, 1998; van Dijk, 1993). For individual actors, discursive frames shape the mental models or "common sense" beliefs through which individuals interpret social reality. With respect to racial issues, these individual mental models or social representations – whether or not they are clearly articulated – are used to "explain" causes of phenomena (e.g., segregation, racial disparities in poverty and incarceration) and shape individual political attitudes (Potter & Wetherell, 1987). Yet this macro–micro relationship is inherently reciprocal. While individual beliefs are shaped by larger social forces, it is also true that the discursive acts of individuals and groups influence (i.e., reinforce or transform) larger level cultural understandings and political ideologies (Fairclough & Wodak, 1997). Consequently, the analysis of public discourse is essential to understanding racial ideologies and racial attitudes.

I contend that discourse is best understood as a contested process and as *political* conflict. As individuals and groups make claims about the nature of the racial order, they do not operate in a vacuum, but in a particular set of social and political circumstances or "political opportunity structures" (Meyer & Staggenborg, 1996). Thus, claims about race occur in response to specific racial events – e.g., affirmative action cases, school desegregation cases, claims of police brutality, disasters such as Hurricane Katrina – or longer term social trends. Discursive acts represent the material and political interests of individuals and groups and are generally directed toward strategic goals. Discourses of dominant groups work to legitimize and reproduce dominance by minimizing the extent of inequality, marginalizing claims of subordinate groups, and moving to make dominant group understandings normative for the larger society (Doane, 1997). At the same time, dominant discourses are not unopposed, but may be challenged by subordinate groups and even by dissident factions within the dominant group. In this political conflict, each side attempts to define the terms of the debate and to frame issues in a manner that will advance their material interests and political objectives. As Anne Esacove (2004) observes, this creates a process of "dialogic framing," where movements and countermovements respond to each other's discursive strategies by adopting new tactics. In essence, we are left with an ideological and rhetorical chess match, where each actor's move is influenced by the preceding moves of the opposition.

COLOR BLINDNESS AND U.S. RACIAL POLITICS

As I noted at the beginning of this chapter, color blindness is currently the dominant racial ideology for the defense of white supremacy. While discussion of color blindness per se is a relatively recent phenomenon, its roots run deep. Color blindness has slowly emerged over the past three to four decades since the end of the Civil Rights Movement. From the vantage point of the present, it has become commonplace to assert that the Civil Rights Movement transformed racial politics in the United States. In addition to the dismantling of legal segregation and the passage of civil rights legislation, the Civil Rights Movement constituted a broad-based movement for racial justice and an attack upon the existing system of racial stratification in the United States. Such a challenge to the racial order did not go uncontested. Once the Civil Rights Movement changed its focus from segregation to economic inequality and de facto segregation, the political landscape began to change. As Omi and Winant (1986) and Stephen Steinberg (1995) have observed, subsequent decades saw a shifting of racial politics, a "racial reaction" or "backlash" that sought to defend the structural advantages enjoyed by white Americans.

Yet such a conservative countermovement faced formidable challenges. One of the accomplishments of the Civil Rights Movement was the discrediting of traditional and overt expressions of racism. In the face of the institutionalization of civil rights and the ascension of a more egalitarian discourse, it was now no longer possible to defend the status quo by using direct assertions of white supremacy. What slowly emerged was the use of code words (e.g., "law and order," "neighborhood schools," "reverse discrimination"), general appeals to egalitarian principles, and the denial of racism that constituted the core of the color-blind frame. Such approaches were often coupled with more general conservative projects such as the attacks on "big government," welfare, and liberalism in general. This eventually made it possible to oppose racial equality without appearing to be "racist" – or at least being able to maintain a facade of plausible deniability. Even a resurgence of extremist and white supremacist groups served a purpose by enabling the white mainstream to buttress its anti-racist credentials by condemning their behavior and contrasting it with color blindness. Throughout the 1970s, 1980s, and 1990s, this "backlash" or "reaction" continued to gain momentum to the extent that what we now call color-blind racism is the dominant racial ideology in the United States (Bonilla-Silva, 2001, 2003; Brown et al., 2003).

I believe that the ascendancy of color blindness is a result of its resonance with a majority of white Americans. The claims that racism is a "thing of the past" and that "race no longer matters" are appealing in the post-civil rights era. To say that individuals are "color blind" and that "everyone is the same" makes it possible for practitioners to claim the legacy of the Civil Rights Movement (as evidenced by the usurpation of Martin Luther King Jr.'s well-known quote that he dreamed of a society where his children "would not be judged by the color of their skin but by the content of their character"). But color blindness is about more than good feelings. Adherence to this set of principles enables whites to maintain and defend significant social and economic advantages. Persistent residential and school segregation and economic inequality can be explained away as coincidence, natural choices, or even the failure of peoples of color to take advantage of the "equal opportunities" presumed to be available in color-blind America. Attempts to redress racial inequality may now be decried as violations of general principles of meritocracy and free choice (on "abstracted liberalism," see Bonilla-Silva, 2003, pp. 30–36) and the victimization of innocent whites (Doane, 1996, 1997). In essence, color blindness is a package of what Joe Feagin and Hernán Vera (1995, pp. 13–14) termed the "sincere fictions" that make it possible for whites to act in defense of white privilege while responding with indignation to allegations of racism (Doane, 1996).

While color blindness may appear to be a platform from which whites can claim to act in race-neutral ways, the social realities are more complex. Clearly, there are times when whites are "raced" either through "momentary minority" status (Gallagher, 1997, p. 7) or during "racial events" such as the trial of Los Angeles police officers for the beating of Rodney King, the O. J. Simpson trial, the killing of Amadou Diallo by the New York Police, and the recently decided Michigan affirmative action cases (Doane, 2006, p. 259). Many white Americans may employ racist dialogue (Myers, 2003) or racialized cultural explanations for inequality. And as Heather Johnson and Howard Shapiro (2003) demonstrate, there are times when whites act in overtly race-aware ways such as when choosing neighborhoods and schools. Nevertheless, color blindness provides whites with "storylines" (Bonilla-Silva, 2003) to rationalize their actions or to lay the ultimate blame on minority group members.

While much of the discussion of color-blind racial ideology focuses upon its content and effects, it is important to recognize that color blindness has not just emerged from social interaction, *it has been deliberately produced!* Beginning in the 1960s, new right and neoconservative politicians and intellectuals launched a multipronged attack upon liberal policies, an endeavor in which race played both a direct (busing, affirmative action) and an indirect role (Omi & Winant, 1986; Steinberg, 1995). By virtue of access to media and adeptness in framing issues (e.g., developing catchphrases such as "reverse discrimination" and "quotas"), this elite discourse was tremendously successful in shaping public understandings regarding racial issues. We have also become increasingly aware of the role of conservative foundations and think tanks in funding legal attacks on affirmative action, media campaigns, the activities of conservative authors such as the Thernstroms and Dinesh D'Souza, and, of course, Ward Connerly's American Civil Rights Institute and similar organizations (Stefancic & Delgado, 1996; Alterman, 1999; Cokorinos, 2003). In sum, much of color blindness is a political project.

Although color blindness has received the most analytical attention, it is important to emphasize that it is not the only ideology employed in contemporary racial discourse. Color blindness is opposed by what I have described (Doane, 2006) as *systemic racism* ideology. In general (although it has many variants), systemic racism ideology has emerged from past challenges to the U.S. racial order, including the Civil Rights Movement. At the core of systemic racism ideology is the assertion that racism is institutional and pervasive in American society. Proponents also often claim that anti-racist social movements and substantial institutional changes are necessary in order to achieve a more racially just society. While systemic racism is the most significant oppositional ideology, color blindness is also opposed by minority nationalist or separatist ideologies and by white supremacist ide-ologies (cf. Berbrier, 1998; Daniels, 1997; Ferber, 1998). Contemporary ra-cial politics, then, involves contestation between these opposing ideologies, with color blindness in a hegemonic position.

THE EVOLUTION OF COLOR-BLIND RACIAL IDEOLOGY

As I noted above, ideologies or social understandings are dynamic in nature. They are created strategically in an attempt to frame problems and outline solutions. They evolve in response to changing circumstances and opposing discourses. Color blindness is no stranger to this process, as its major claims and modes of articulation evolve in accordance with the exigencies of racial politics and in response to competing claims about race.

There have been consistent patterns in color-blind racial discourse. The frames of color blindness rationalize (explain, deny, obscure) the existence and nature of racial inequality in the United States. Strategically, they seek to make it impossible to make a case for systemic racism or to strive (with any legitimacy) for changes in the existing racial order. Claims of racism are either deflected or dismissed. The frames and storylines of color blindness have been well-mapped out elsewhere (Bonilla-Silva, 2001, 2003); conse-quently, my objective in this chapter is to highlight what I see as two im-portant new trends in the evolution of color blindness: the escalating attack on the concept of race and the "demonization" of diversity.

ATTACKING THE CONCEPT OF RACE

Given that the dominant message of color blindness is that race no longer matters in the United States, it is not surprising that color-blind ideology would include an attack on the idea of race. If race can be removed as a legitimate subject of conversation or object of analysis, and if the concept of race itself can be made invalid, then opposing discourses are placed beyond the pale of acceptable political discourse (and lumped along with claims of white supremacy and biological superiority). We might also expect that such a frame would have some resonance with larger publics, as discrediting race is very compatible with the notion that race no longer matters and "we are all the same." As I follow the evolution of this frame, I find three overlapping themes: (1) the claim that racial categories are racist; (2) the appropriation of the idea of race as a social construct; and (3) the belief that racial ambiguity makes race irrelevant.

Racial Categories are Racist

The claim here is simple: that it is racist to classify people by racial categories or to suggest that race matters in human interaction. This claim appears to have deeper historical roots. Ronald Takaki (1987, p. 231) cites Reagan era Attorney General Edwin Meese by saying that "counting by race is a form of racism" in a speech attacking affirmative action. In a study of a debate over racial balance in a school district in the 1990s, I (Doane, 1996, p. 39) recorded one participant making the following claim:

> Now it is clear that our School Board's agenda goes beyond equitable distribution of our town's educational resources. Their agenda categorizes us, the people of the town of West Hartford, by the pigment of our skins, by the amount of money that we make, by the language our parents speak, and then gerrymanders our school districts to create their misguided version of what is meant by equal access – homogenized ratios.

> To some of us who believe that people should be judged on their strength of character, and who believe that racism will not be eliminated until our nation, states, and towns become color blind, this agenda is repugnant.

The core of the writer's claim is that it is inappropriate ("repugnant") to be conscious of race or to employ racial categories in public policymaking (in this case, school desegregation).

The claim that racial categories are racist was extended further in an "op-ed" column by radio commentator Judy Jarvis (1997, p. A13) in which she criticized the inclusion of racial and ethnic questions in the 2000 United States census:

> But discrimination is no longer the worst problem we face in trying to get along and get ahead on our diverse country. The constant focus on our differences is. Children are being taught that they have more that divides them as Americans than unites them: from the Census Bureau's adding racial and ethnic categories, to universities' obsession with segregated dorms and social clubs; from state laws that ask employers to count color, to disastrous bilingual programs that ensure failure for so many students who are placed in them.

Why don't we cry out against these bigoted policies? Why don't we tell the politicians
who support them that more harm than good comes from well-intentioned programs
based on color, sex, and ethnic counting?

For Jarvis, racism (bigotry) is not only to take race into consideration in
policymaking, but also even to *count* by race or ethnicity or to collect racial
data. Moreover, this type of racism is, in her opinion, a more serious problem than discrimination (which is assumed to be minimal) as it promotes a
focus on differences and foments racial conflict.

Jarvis' claim that the use of racial categories was "racist" foreshadowed
subsequent developments in U.S. racial politics. In 2001, Ward Connerly
and the American Civil Rights Coalition initiated a campaign to promote a
California state ballot initiative, Proposition 54, which if passed would for-
bid California state and local government agencies (with a few exceptions)
from classifying citizens or collecting data using categories based upon race,
ethnicity, and national origin. When he introduced this campaign, Connerly
(2001a) asserted that

Race classifications have never helped anyone. The Holocaust, South African apartheid,
India's caste system – every time a country has adopted these divisive race classifications
they have only served to suppress the group out of favor. It is time California learned
this history lesson and became truly colorblind.

Similar claims were made by other supporters of Proposition 54. During the
final days of the campaign, one op-ed writer (Custred, 2003) argued that

Passing Proposition 54 will be the beginning of the end for the racial classification system
that has plagued this country since its founding. Beginning in the 17th century, the
government divided citizens by race to perpetuate slavery. In the 19th century, America
was torn apart in a war to determine how much say the government had over a person
based on his skin color... Every time the government has recognized our skin color, it
has led to evil consequences. Proposition 54 is a chance to end this historical stain and
take the first, measured step toward a colorblind government that has no place for race
in American life or law.

In both cases, the problem is framed as race consciousness or the use of
racial categories, and the claim is made that racial categories are a root
cause of such historical evils as slavery and apartheid. The proffered solution is a "truly color-blind" society where race is no longer taken into
account. While Proposition 54 was defeated by California voters in October
2003, the issue of banning the use of racial categories remains alive.
Connerly has announced plans to propose a revised initiative in California
(Schevitz, 2003) and non-compliance with racial data collection is becoming
increasingly widespread (Jenkins, 1999). This has significant political implications. If the collection of racial data is eliminated, then it will become

difficult, if not impossible, to provide credible evidence of patterns of discrimination or even to assess the relative degree of racial inequality. Claims of racism could then be dismissed as having no factual basis. As a result, white advantages will become unassailable – a position made possible by a discourse employing the language of "color blindness" and antibigotry.

The Appropriation of the Idea of Race as a Social Construct

For more than half a century, anti-racist social scientists have sought to attack biological racism and claims of racial superiority–inferiority by advancing the notion that race is not a valid scientific classification system and that it only has meaning as a socially constructed category. From the seminal work of Ashley Montagu (1997[1942]) to the recent television series "Race: The Power of an Illusion" (California Newsreel, 2003), this argument has been successfully employed to undermine traditional racist ideology. In addition, the notion of racism as a social construct has then been employed to emphasize that race has a *sociological* reality – that it is embedded in social structures and used by dominant groups to maintain systems of racial stratification. This view of race has increasingly been used to challenge the racial status quo.

More recently, the core anti-racist claim that race has no biological reality and is socially constructed has been appropriated within the "color-blind" frame that race no longer "matters." The crux of the argument is that since race is a fiction and has no scientific validity, racial categories and race-based policies are absurd and divisive. For example, in a syndicated newspaper column, Jeff Jacoby (1999) uses examples of the different numbers of racial categories cited by racist scientists (e.g., Bernier, Linnaeus, Blumenbach, Coon, etc.) to suggest the absurdity of the U.S. Census race question. He then goes on to assert that

> The difference between ancestry and race is that one is real and one is largely fiction. Race is a social construct, not a biological fact. The genes of whites, blacks, and "native Hawaiians" are indistinguishable. Of course there are physical variations among populations that originated at points far apart on the globe. But the idea that those variations are racial is a relatively recent one.

Thus, the problematic nature of racial science becomes part of the "color-blind" argument.

This argument is also apparent in claims proffered by Debra Dickerson (2004) in her book *The End of Blackness*. As part of a manifesto for black self-help and the need to change group values, she incorporates the claim that race is a "bankrupt scientific and social construct." The conclusion is clear: absent the idea of race (or blackness), the problem of racism will disappear. The failed science of race becomes further ammunition for the attempt to remove race as a valid topic for public discourse.

The appropriation of race as a social construct was extended by Ward Connerly (2001b, emphasis added), who in an op-ed piece warning the British against using a race question in their census, asserted that

> There were other Americans, among whom I count myself, who wanted to scrap our system of racial classifications. We wanted our government to recognise that *race is a social construct conjured up by politicians and social activists, to prop up a dying regime of preferential treatment and victimhood.* There racial categories, we argued, no longer reflect the reality of our existence, and worse, they exacerbated the conflicts that exist in society.

If we examine this argument closely, it is evident that Connerly is not only maintaining that race is a social construct, but he is also asserting that race is created (or at least maintained) by leaders who presumably benefit from the "regime of preferential treatment and victimhood." In other words, if we did not have "politicians and activists" raising questions about race, then race would no longer exist.

Racial Ambiguity Makes Race Irrelevant

Historically, the existence of racial ambiguity has also been used to highlight the social construction of race (e.g., Davis, 1991). The lack of logic in assigning multiracial individuals to a particular race and the existence of multiple social protocols for classification of multiracial individuals has long been used to undermine "scientific" notions of race. As is the case with the idea of race as a social construct, this issue has also been "flipped" by proponents of color blindness to buttress their arguments. This argument has two main thrusts: that the existence of multiracial individuals highlights the absurdity of racial categories and that the expanding multiracial population is making race irrelevant in social interaction.

A prime focus for this frame was the decision by the United States Census Bureau to permit individuals to check off more than one box (category) in responding to the race question on the 2000 Census. The existence of 63 racial categories and combinations, and the fact that many respondents rejected all of these to select "other," is given as further evidence of the futility of racial categories and classification (Kicklighter, 2001). This is used to buttress further the claim that the social construction of race makes race meaningless. Furthermore, the increasing number of multiracial persons and "soaring rates of interracial friendship and dating" (Jacoby, 2001) are eliminating any meaningful racial distinctions. In a syndicated article, "The Rise of the Blended American," Jeff Jacoby (2001) approvingly quotes Ben Wattenberg's claim that the separatists are being "defeated in the bedroom." The implication is that as intermarriage rapidly expands, race will fade away.

The idea of the end of race has also found its way into popular culture. Recent writers (La Ferla, 2003; Arlidge, 2004) have touted the emergence of "Generation EA: Ethnically Ambiguous" in marketing and media. The proliferation of multiracial models and the ascendancy of celebrities such as Jessica Alba, Tiger Woods, and Vin Diesel is combined with the "currently fashionable argument that race itself is a fiction" (La Ferla, 2003) to herald the dawn of a new era. Under such circumstances we hear respondents make statements such as "the salience of color across society is reducing" and "the barriers between black and white are really coming down" (Arlidge, 2004). In the EA world of fusion and crossover appeal, race is no longer relevant.

DEMONIZING DIVERSITY

Over the past 25 years, the word "diversity" has become a ubiquitous catchphrase with almost iconic status in American society. Following the Supreme Court decision in the *Bakke* case, which included Justice Powell's decision that affirmative action plans were permissible when there was a "compelling interest in promoting diversity," the idea of the positive value of "diversity" became a lynchpin of public racial discourse. During the past two decades, "diversity training," "workforce diversity," and "diversity awareness weeks" have become part of the social mainstream. The general acceptance of this idea was evident in the wide range of *amicus* briefs filed by corporations and even the military in support of the University of Michigan's affirmative action programs in the 2003 Supreme Court cases (*Gratz v. Bollinger* and *Grutter v. Bollinger*).

As a catchphrase, "diversity" has enjoyed a number of political advantages. While it is often assumed to refer to increasing the presence of peoples of color, its vagueness has allowed it to be defined and interpreted in ways convenient to speakers and audiences. From a "packaging" standpoint, I believe that the widespread acceptance of "diversity" reflects its positive connotations (inclusion as opposed to desegregation) and its relative innocuousness (promoting diversity does not require a commitment to structural change or addressing racial inequality). Beyond the fact that it "feels good," diversity has been successfully promoted as beneficial to everyone and creating more positive work and educational environments. It is no exaggeration to say that "diversity" has been *the* most successful catchphrase created by those claiming to be racial progressives.

Not surprisingly, the "success" of "diversity" has made it a target for advocates of color blindness. This is undoubtedly particularly due to its use as a rationale for the maintenance of affirmative action programs, but it also reflects its success and visibility in programming. As innocuous as "diversity" may seem, the positive valuation of difference is in direct conflict with the color-blind credo that race no longer matters. At the same time, the broad appeal of "diversity" has made it difficult to attack, especially as it has not been used to present any meaningful challenge to the racial status quo.

Over the past few years I have identified a range of strategies that have been used to undermine the political popularity of diversity. One technique has been the use of pejorative labels, such as the "diversity industry" or the "cult of diversity" to attempt to cast diversity in a more negative light. There have also been attempts to dilute diversity (by expanding its parameters beyond race) or to co-opt the term. The former was reflected in a Department of Justice diversity initiative that stressed geographic and economic diversity. The latter is evident in attempts by conservatives to claim that the paramount diversity issue is political or intellectual diversity – especially on college campuses (cf. Hebel, 2004; Horowitz, 2004; Briggs, 2003; Steyn, 2003). Thus far, these tactics have had limited impact.

More interesting, however, have been a range of attempts to re-frame diversity from the color-blind perspective by condemning it for calling attention to race. These strategies can be classified as follows:

1. *Diversity = Racism.* This is an attempt to frame diversity as racism because of its emphasis upon race. Sometimes this is in the form of a general attack ("once called Jim Crow, today diversity"); other times there is the more specific implication that proponents of diversity are engaging in racist essentialism. For example: "The overriding message of 'diversity,' transmitted by the policies of a school's administration and by the teachings of a school's professors, is that the individual is defined by his race" (Schwartz, 2003). In essence, diversity is being attacked for violating the norms of color blindness.

2. *Diversity is Racism against Whites.* This is an attempt to frame diversity in the same vein as "reverse discrimination" – one of the most successful catchphrases of the racial backlash. For example: "Diversity is a code

name, a euphemism for a racial preference system where chosen minority groups are given preferences because of their skin color. The gentle veneer of the world 'diversity' shrouds an illegal, dishonest, and hypocritical racial agenda" (Diversityblows.com, n.d.). In some cases, the charge is more direct: "during the past 30-odd years we have lived in an overtly racist society – racist against whites. In the sociocultural game of musical chairs, whites are left standing. This is true in academia and in the job market. This is Marxism 101 in action. 'Diversity actually means replacement at any cost'" (Briggs, 2003). And from David Duke's website: "Let us put it bluntly: to 'celebrate' or 'embrace' diversity, as we are so often asked to do, is no different from *deploring an excess of whites*" (Jackson, n.d., emphasis in the original). The common theme in each quotation is the redefinition of diversity as discrimination against whites.

Strategically, to re-frame "diversity" as racism or to dilute it by emphasizing "diversity of ideas" or "intellectual diversity" is to make it into a "contested concept" (Doane, 1996). If the attack on diversity is successful and it can be cast in negative terms as divisive or "racist," then the logical solution would be to advocate dropping any emphasis on diversity in favor of color blindness – as was advocated by several opponents of diversity. Likewise, if diversity is cast as one of many forms of diversity, along with diversity of geography, economic position, and ideas, then it loses whatever efficacy it has had as a tool for anti-racist mobilizing (or at least keeping racial issues on the radar of the larger society). In any event, the ongoing attacks on diversity are part of the continuing evolution of racial politics in the United States.

CONCLUSION: THE FUTURE POLITICS OF COLOR BLINDNESS

Racial ideologies in general – and color blindness in particular – are dynamic. They constantly evolve in response to changing circumstances and to the ebb and flow of racial politics. I have argued that color blindness is part of a larger process of racial backlash dating back to the 1960s – a rearticulated defense of white benefits in face of the challenges and successes of the Civil Rights Movement. Color blindness is successful because it resonates with the hopes and fears of white Americans, and because it requires no action (all one has to do to retain the façade is to continue "not being racist"). I have also asserted that color-blind racism has been deliberately produced. This is not to create a "conspiracy theory," but to recognize that color blindness did not evolve organically – it was produced by conservative academics, intellectuals, and activists well funded by conservative foundations.

In the course of this chapter, I have outlined what I believe are several emerging discursive strategies – the attack on racial categories, the appropriation of the claim that race is a social construct, and the use of the new racial "ambiguity" – to buttress the claims that race no longer matters in the United States. Each of these represents a new strategic tack by the proponents of color blindness in their quest for advantage in the ongoing political struggles around racial issues. In the same vein, the attacks on diversity represent an attempt to neutralize what has been an effective weapon on the part of those seeking greater racial inclusiveness. The common theme running throughout these arguments is that the ultimate solution to America's racial problems is the adoption of the color-blind platform: the elimination of racial categories, the abandonment of any race-based social policies to address persistent segregation or racial inequality, and the eventual removal of race from public discourse. Carried to its extreme, color blindness creates a one-dimensional context in which it becomes increasingly difficult to conceptualize, let alone challenge, the continuing significance of institutional racism – much in the manner that the government of Oceania in George Orwell's *1984* (1961[1949]) sought to eliminate "thought crime" by eliminating any challenging vocabulary.

I do not believe that the defeat of Proposition 54 is the end of attacks on the collection of racial data. While a majority of Californians rejected the measure, 36% of the electorate voted in support of the initiative. Similarly, I am not necessarily encouraged by the observation that many of the quotations presented above come from outside of mainstream media and political discourse. It is but a short journey from the extreme to the mainstream. If we have learned nothing else from the study of the racial backlash and conservative political movements in general, we should remember that they are well funded and able and willing to take the long view in promoting their political agenda. Consequently, it is critical to keep tracking the changes in racial discourse.

REFERENCES

Alterman, E. (1999). The 'right' books and big ideas: Conservative foundations lavishly subsidize authors while the left loses out. *The Nation*, November 22, pp. 16–21.

Arlidge, J. (2004). The new melting pot. *The Observer*, January 4, p. 19.

Berbrier, M. (1998). 'Half the battle': Cultural resonance, framing processes, and ethnic affectations in contemporary White separatist rhetoric. *Social Problems, 45,* 431–450.

Bonilla-Silva, E. (2001). *White supremacy & racism in the post-civil rights era.* Boulder, CO: Lynne Reinner.

Bonilla-Silva, E. (2003). *Racism without racists: Color-blind racism and the persistence of racial inequality in the United States.* Lanham, MD: Rowman & Littlefield.

Briggs, T. (2003). Colleges may favor diversity over equality. *Los Angeles Times,* July 5, pp. 2, 24.

Brown, M., Carnoy, M., Currie, E., Duster, T., Oppenheimer, D. B., Shultz, M. M., & Wellman, D. (2003). *Whitewashing race: The myth of a color-blind society.* Berkeley, CA: University of California Press.

California Newsreel. (2003). Race: The power of an illusion. Episode I: The difference between us. Christine Herbes-Sommers, director, producer, and writer. Video.

Carr, L. G. (1997). *Color-blind racism.* Thousand Oaks, CA: Sage.

Cokorinos, L. (2003). *The assault on diversity: An organized challenge to racial and gender justice.* Lanham, MD: Rowman & Littlefield.

Connerly, W. (2001a). Connerly announces racial privacy initiative. April 11. Downloaded on January 8, 2004 from http://www.racialprivacy.org/content/press/april11_2001.php

Connerly, W. (2001b). If justice is blind, the colour of your skin is of no importance. *The Daily Telegraph,* April 26, p. 28.

Custred, G. (2003). Prop. 54; the true inheritor of Prop. 209. *San Diego Union Tribune,* October 1, p. B7.

Daniels, J. (1997). *White lies: Race, class, gender, and sexuality in White supremacist discourse.* New York: Routledge.

Davis, F. J. (1991). *Who is Black: One nation's definition.* University Park, PA: Penn State University Press.

Dickerson, D. (2004). *The end of blackness.* New York: Pantheon.

DiversityBlows.com. n.d. Diversity is a lie. Downloaded on October 17, 2003 from http://diversityblows.com

Doane, A. W., Jr. (1996). Contested terrain: Negotiating racial understandings in public discourse. *Humanity & Society, 20*(4), 32–51.

Doane, A. W., Jr. (1997). Dominant group ethnic identity in the United States: The role of 'hidden' ethnicity in intergroup relations. *The Sociological Quarterly, 38,* 375–397.

Doane, A. W., Jr. (2003). Rethinking whiteness studies. In: A. W. Doane & E. Bonilla-Silva (Eds), *White out: The continuing significance of racism* (pp. 3–18). New York: Routledge.

Doane, A. W., Jr. (2006). What is racism? Racial discourse and the politics of race. *Critical Sociology, 32,* 255–274.

Esacove, A. (2004). Dialogic framing: The framing/counterframing of 'partial-birth' abortion. *Sociological Inquiry, 74,* 70–101.

Fairclough, N., & Wodak, R. (1997). Critical discourse analysis. In: T. van Dijk (Ed.), *Discourse as social interaction* (pp. 258–284). London: Sage.

Feagin, J. (2000). *Racist America: Roots, current realities, and future reparations.* New York: Routledge.

Feagin, J., & Vera, H. (1995). *White racism.* New York, NY: Routledge.

Ferber, A. (1998). *White man falling: Race, gender, and white supremacy.* Boulder, CO: Rowman & Littlefield.

Gabriel, J. (1998). *Whitewash: Racialized politics and the media.* London: Routledge.

Gallagher, C. A. (1997). White racial formation: Into the 21st century. In: R. Delgado & J. Stefancic (Eds), *Critical White studies: Looking behind the mirror* (pp. 6–11). Philadelphia, PA: Temple University Press.

Hebel, S. (2004). Patrolling professors' politics: Conservative activists and students press campaigns against perceived bias on campus. *The Chronicle of Higher Education*, February 13.

Horowitz, D. (2004). In defense of intellectual diversity. *The Chronicle of Higher Education*, February 13.

Jackson, T. n.d. What is racism? Downloaded on October 17, 2003 from http://www.duke.org/library/affirmative/whatis.html

Jacoby, J. (1999). The absurdity of census' question 6. *The Times Picayune*, August 16, p. B5.

Jacoby, J. (2001). The rise of the blended American. *The Boston Globe*, July 9, p. A11.

Jarvis, J. (1997). A bigoted way to tally Americans. *The Hartford Courant*, November 3, p. A13.

Jenkins, A. (1999). See no evil: Bans on data collection are thwarting antidiscrimination efforts. *The Nation*, *268*(24), 15–19.

Johnson, H. B., & Shapiro, T. M. (2003). Good neighborhoods, good schools: Race and the 'good choices' of White families. In: A. W. Doane & E. Bonilla-Silva (Eds), *White out: The continuing significance of racism* (pp. 173–187). New York: Routledge.

Kicklighter, K. (2001). Census' expanded racial identities open up a can of 'miscellaneous'. *Atlanta Journal-Constitution*, March 25, p. 1G.

La Ferla, R. (2003). Generation E.A.: Ethnically ambiguous. *New York Times*, December 28, pp. 9, 1.

Meyer, D., & Staggenborg, S. (1996). Movements, countermovements, and the structure of political opportunity. *American Journal of Sociology*, *101*, 1628–1660.

Montagu, A. (1997[1942]). *Man's most dangerous myth: The fallacy of race* (6th ed.). Thousand Oaks, CA: Alta Mira.

Myers, K. (2003). White fright: Reproducing White supremacy through casual discourse. In: A. W. Doane & E. Bonilla-Silva (Eds), *White out: The continuing significance of racism* (pp. 129–144). New York: Routledge.

Omi, M., & Winant, H. (1986). *Racial formation in the United States*. New York, NY: Routledge & Kegan Paul.

Orwell, G. (1961[1949]). *1984*. New York, NY: Signet.

Potter, J., & Wetherell, M. (1987). *Discourse and social psychology: Beyond attitudes and behavior*. London: Sage.

Schevitz, T. (2003). If Prop. 54 fails, Connerly says he plans revamped version. *The San Francisco Chronicle*, October 7, p. A15.

Schwartz, P. (2003). The racism of 'diversity.' Downloaded on October 17, 2003 from http://lists.indymedia.org/pipermail/imc-editorial/2003-March/010638.html

Stefancic, J., & Delgado, R. (1996). *No mercy: How conservative think tanks and foundations changed America's social agenda*. Philadelphia, PA: Temple University Press.

Steinberg, S. (1995). *Turning back: The retreat from racial justice in American thought and policy*. Boston, MA: Beacon Press.

Steyn, M. (2003). O'Connor makes catchphrase law of the land. *Chicago Sun-Times*, June 29, p. 37.

Takaki, R. (1987). To count or not to count by race and gender? In: R. Takaki (Ed.), *From different shores: Perspectives on race and ethnicity in America* (pp. 231–232). New York: Oxford University Press.

van Dijk, T. A. (1993). *Elite discourse and racism*. Newbury Park, CA: Sage.

EVOLVING WHITE RACIAL CONSCIOUSNESS

Rutledge M. Dennis

INTRODUCTION

In an earlier study of Black Middletown youth (Dennis, 1991), the research question focused on patterns of socialization within a small community. However, by inference, it included the patterns of socialization within the larger dominant community. This paper continues the focus on youth and socialization, but shifts attention to white youth. In this sense, it both complements and supplements the chapter published in a volume devoted to the impact of racism on white Americans (Dennis, 1981). In that volume, we examined how some writers described their racial "coming of age" in their autobiographies and the consequences of negative racial socialization on their subsequent social and psychological development. This exploration was conducted in part to test the hypothesis proposed by Kenneth Clark (1955), which asserted that racial socialization in the United States was largely an "unconscious" and "unplanned" feature of the socialization of white children within their families. The data presented in the 1981 edition depicted the lives of those who spent their formative years during the overtly racist decades of the 1920s, 1930s, and 1940s. The 1981 chapter also illustrated that, at least for those individuals, racial socialization was indeed an aggressively conscious process. Learning to be a racist just does not "simply happen". Rather, there is a rigorous rite of passage as those autobiographical writers attest.

The New Black: Alternative Paradigms and Strategies for the 21st Century
Research in Race and Ethnic Relations, Volume 14, 175–194
Copyright © 2007 by Elsevier Ltd.
ISSN: 0195-7449/doi:10.1016/S0195-7449(06)14008-8

The earlier article drew on elements of parental socialization and the issues around which racial socialization was pronounced; we concluded that formal parental instruction was a pivotal factor in the development of negative racial attitudes and behavior among children and youth, a point emphasized by Gordon Allport (1954). Hyman (1969) appears to agree with Allport, but his statement that "perhaps the unprejudiced white parent, with the best will in the world, does not quite know how to socialize his child to a relationship which is utterly novel in his own experience. It is perhaps a problem in innocence rather than evil, and a problem that may be declining with time". Indeed, Pettigrew (1981) has documented the rise in racial tolerance in more recent years, but even with that decline, there continues to exist large numbers of individuals and groups, as Pettigrew himself admits, to make racism a continuing problem. It is the proportion of prejudiced parents whose intents may be more akin to "evil" rather than "innocence" which makes it necessary to continue to assess the import of racial socialization and its impact on intragroup as well as intergroup relations.

This paper is part of a larger study of the racial socialization of youth. George Bernard Shaw (1974) and Ted Clark (1975) have written of the confrontation of parents and youth along intensely aggressive lines; they contend that one of the issues in the Contest of Wills between youth and parents is that youth is more susceptible to, and move in directions of, "social [racial] change", whereas parents seek to continue ongoing tradition. In his usual tongue-in-cheek manner, Shaw (1974, p. 364) notes that " ... on the whole[,] children and parents confront one another as two classes in which all the political power is on one side; and the results are not unlike what they would be if there were no immediate consanguinity between them, and one were white and the other black, or one enfranchised and the other disenfranchised ... " Clark (1975, p. 2) gives a similar view in more strident tones: " ... people have turned against young people, in effect hating them. Converting socialization into a coercive, oppressive depersonalization of the individual, society has attempted to eliminate the fear young people engender; this fear lies in young people's potential for social change."

With rare exceptions, there are few systematic studies of racial socialization (Crapanzano, 1985; Burnam & Reynolds, 1986; McIntosh, 1989; Blauner, 1990; Hacker, 1992). Generally, when race is included in studies of white socialization, it is treated as a minor issue. Moreover, when racial attitudes and behavior are linked, the subject of the study is more likely to be the socialization of black children into racial awareness and less likely to be that of white children and their racial socialization.

In another paper (Dennis, 1988), I contend that one of the reasons researchers have been successful in documenting the black response to race may be that blacks are much more open to discussing their feelings on the matter with white and black researchers. White respondents, on the other hand, may be less inclined to be forthright when discussing race, especially if the interviewer is black and their views are racist. If whites generally do not articulate their attitudes and beliefs about race candidly, it makes all the more difficult attempts to study the racial socialization of dominant and powerful groups. At a time when we are witnessing an increased racial balkanization in so many areas of daily life (employment, residence, education, and politics), it is even more imperative to focus on patterns of racial socialization, be they subtle or not. The point is that race does matter.

Children are instructed in racial matters, and this instruction may have long-term consequences not only for those currently being socialized, but also for future generations. It is this concern that is the central theme discussed in this paper. The claim being made here is not that youth should not be socialized in racial matters; rather, it is that the "kind" of socialization and the "ideology" of that socialization are manifestly important. This latter point was emphatically made by Pieter le Roux (1986, p. 184) in his autobiographical sketch, *Growing up an Afrikaner*. He asserts that racial and political socialization are one and the same and are not casual: "It is argued that this process of indoctrination is far more consciously undertaken..."

This study has several foci: First, it seeks to update the data on racial socialization; second, we explore and isolate the issues around which white racial socialization becomes important for both children and parents; third, we want to ascertain which parent plays a more crucial role in the racial socialization process; last, we analyze the racial environment in which racial socialization may be either neutral, pro-racist, or anti-racist. This includes situations in which the environment for racial socialization may alternate, at different times, between neutral, pro-racist, and anti-racist.

METHODS

The data for this study were obtained from three undergraduate Social Problems classes in a large urban university. I became interested in the use of personal journals as educational tools. For four consecutive semesters, I asked students to explore a particular theme in their journals to reflect on the type of socialization they had received on issues such as race, class, gender, or religion. Students had the option of focusing on race, class, gender, or religion. Those who were not comfortable sharing their thoughts in a journal were instructed to write an 8 to 10 page paper on racism, sexism, or religious intolerance. They were also informed that they would not be penalized for not submitting journals.

More than 95% of the students (N = 75) chose to write journals, and of those, more than 98% chose to write on racial socialization. That they selected race over the other themes may be due to a number of factors: (1) Race may have been an intimate part of their upbringing and home, and they were eager to discuss it; (2) the class represented a forum which enabled many to reflect on race, a subject generally not discussed at home; and (3) students taking a class in social problems may be more likely to discuss their racial socialization at a time when increased racist conflicts and problems are surfacing in society. Since I was primarily interested in the racial socialization of white youth, I did not draw from the sample of the black students in the class though they too wrote about their racial socialization. Finally, it must be noted that this study is not based on a representative sample of white students or youth; it merely constitutes case studies and illustrations of racial socializations.

Students were instructed to focus on key agents or agencies in the socialization process. They were also asked when they were first aware of race as an issue in their life at home, school, church, or at work; what were the particular incidents and situations that made race pivotal; how did their parents and relatives act and react to racial situations; and what specifically did their parents and relatives tell them about race or about those who belong to members of certain races. It was suggested that journal headings, such as the family, schools, the church or religion, peer groups, and the media, would assist the organization of the journal. Above all, students were assured of the confidentiality of the contents of their journals, and that if items from their journals were ever cited, their identity would be protected. The sample for this study constitutes only a small part of all the journals. Of the 45 journals used for this paper, 17 were written by males and 28 by females. The gender differential reflects two facts: (1) Female college and university enrollment often exceed that of males, and (2) female enrollment often greatly exceeds male enrollment in sociology and the social sciences. The remainder of the paper will be devoted to an analysis of the agents and agencies of racial socialization.

THE FAMILY

In nearly all societies, the family is the primary socializing agency. The structure of authority within the family provides the child his first experience of an authority relationship, and the values and expectations implicit in that experience are often translated directly into more impersonal settings – notably, the political system itself. For example, in this analysis of political socialization in Israel, Fein (1967, p. 111) notes the importance of the family as a formal agency of socialization:

> Nor is the family's role in political socialization limited to the implicit lessons it teaches about obedience, allegiance, trust, reward, and the like. The family is also an explicit teacher, providing the child with basic information about the world of politics, and shapes his attitudes and opinions of things political.

Though Fein's work pertains to political socialization rather than racial socialization, its applicability to both seems appropriate. In their review of the literature on political socialization, Niemi and Sobieszek (1977) stated that until the mid-1960s, studies tended to support the position of the family as the key socializing agency. Now, they assert, we tend to give the family too small a role in the socializing process. More recent studies, by Foster (1986), le Roux (1986), Crapanzano (1985), McIntosh (1989), and Blauner (1990), all contain written accounts of the process by which socialization takes place in a highly race-oriented society. The data from the student journals support those whose findings indicate the strong racial socializing role of the family. For example, 57% of all student journals named their families as the source of their racial socialization. Of those naming the family as the racial socializing agency, 80% were females. Only 40% of the males named their families as crucial racial socializers. Many of the students mentioned more than one agency in their racial socialization.

EFFECTS OF RACISM ON WHITE YOUTH

The 1981 review of the racial socialization of whites who were children or adolescents during formal racial segregation in the South enabled us to note the particular areas on which race and racism were centered. The student journals provide an opportunity to compare current themes and concerns with historical ones. A careful examination of the journal content suggests that the main effects of racism on white youth are largely unchanged. They are: (1) ignorance of other groups and their values and culture; (2)

stultifying group conformity; (3) split social consciousness; and (4) moral confusion and social ambivalence.

Ignorance of Others

One of the most damning consequences of racism is that it both causes and promotes the social, psychological, and physical separation between groups. Such a separation promotes isolation and insulation in which mutual ignorance prevails. William Wilson (1987) analyzes the consequences of this isolation for the community, but he does not attribute the isolation to racism. This racial divide was described by a male student who noted that he grew up frightened and afraid of black people and all aspects of their history and culture as a result of the racial socialization given by his father. As he stated: "Whenever there were assembly events whose themes were about black people, this was especially true of Black History Month, my father would send a written note to excuse me from attending these events. He was opposed to my learning anything about or by blacks. I have since broken away from those fears, but for a long time, my father's beliefs controlled my thoughts." This journal writer does not specify "why" his father adhered to such racial views. It is, however, reasonable to assume that if a parent views another group along totally negative lines, that parent would not encourage the son or daughter to attend student programs and activities which might challenge these negative assumptions. Another student, a female journal writer, related a somewhat similar incident in her family. Her father disliked blacks so much he would not permit his children to watch special programs about blacks or even "The Cosby Show".

One male cited his experience which shed much light on how "folk knowledge" and widely accepted views on racial matters create a fractured reality and contribute to a continuation of racial myths and distortions. This student wrote that before he saw "Roots", he often assumed, owing to subtle and not-so-subtle messages from family members and friends, that all blacks were slaves and had to endure their general inferior status in the United States because they were evil. As he said: "'Roots' made me aware of the fact that I did not know how the racial situation in the U.S. got to be this way. Seeing "Roots" made me look at blacks and whites in a new light; it made me understand that a lot of the racial things my family and friends talked about often had no basis in reality." In a society which is increasingly plural (in terms of race, language, religion, etc.), knowledge of the other is just good common sense. As these student journal entries demonstrate, we may eventually pay a high price for our inability to know, understand, and respect each other. Ignorance of others cannot promote cooperation, a key factor in promoting the common good.

Studying Group Conformity

Since the racial policies of the United States and South Africa were very similar at different phases of their historical development, it is instructive to note the similarities with which race became the source and center of the social conformity in both nations (see Baker, 1983; Stone, 1985; Wilson, 1973). Pieter le Roux's brief autobiographical sketch provides an excellent example of the success of racial indoctrination and how racist ideology serves as a "united racial front" to force group conformity among whites:

> Racist ideology went unchallenged because we never heard dissenting voices: it seemed to be rational, and it seemed to serve the interests of all of us. Whereas at least some parents would differ quite strongly from the official dogma with regard to church and party political issues, and whereas puritan morality was often not accepted by all, not a single parent or teacher (not even the history teacher accused of being a communist) believed in a non-racial society (le Roux, 1986, 202).

The reasons adults conform to prevailing racial ideology is often no different from the reasons youth do: The desire to be accepted by family members, friends, neighbors, etc. The pressure to conform to the prevailing racial ideology is often strong and unrelenting and hits the would-be nonconformer on all sides as demonstrated by the journal entry of one male student:

> When I was growing up my first contact with blacks occurred with "white flight", when whites left the neighborhood and blacks moved in. At first, I played ball with many of the black guys and considered them my friends. Then my white friends began to call me "nigger lover". My father also did not approve of my playing with blacks. He was always saying that blacks were "no good" and had "no usefulness" to others. In order to keep my white friends whom I had known all my life, and to keep from hearing my father's mouth all the time, I dropped my black friends. I'm ashamed to say that I also became a racist.

The central theme of the above journal entry typified one of the key themes permeating most of the journals, that of the need to "take sides". Journal writers were consistently confronted with the challenge: Whom do you favor; to which group will you give your loyalty? No area of group life presents these questions in more stark terms than the area of interracial socializing and dating. Quite a few of the female journal writers who had

had good relations with their white friends and with their families suddenly found themselves facing a barrage of heavy criticism when they ventured into interracial dating. One student's statement represents a common experience for those who dared to date interracially: "When my friends found out that I had dated a black guy they began calling me a 'nigger lover'. There was so much pressure from my friends and family that I broke off the relationship. Members of my family had already warned me that if I continued to date black guys they would disown me." Such sentiments bespeak a concept of racial solidarity which is pivotal in directing racist conformity. We have seen, and continue to see, this group solidarity being played out, not only in the area of race, but also in language, religion, and politics (see Davis & Watson, 1985; Dooley, 1985; Early, 1994). Another example of racism as conformity is related by a student whose younger brother apparently felt the need or was expected to conform to racist peer group pressures:

> My parents taught all of us to be free of prejudice and to be open minded about other races. My brother went to military school, and when he began coming home for school breaks, I noticed that he began talking about "niggers". It really shocked me because my parents did not raise us that way and would not approve. I told him that I did not like that language and asked him why he had started talking this way. He just looked at me and laughed and started telling jokes about how blacks looked and how they acted ... so after one very expensive year at a very exclusive military school where you would expect decent moral teaching, my brother has been void of all the upbringing my parents tried to bestow.

Race, like religion and language, appears to promote among many an "us" against "them" value. It is territorial like all animals, but it is a social and psychological territoriality, and addresses the manner in which groups tend to view other groups in ways comparable to a zero-sum theory.

Social and Racial Schizophrenia

The discordance between the American creed and the American deed in racial issues has been analyzed by many social scientists. This discordance has resulted in a societal fragmentation or, as some would say, social schizophrenia. Studies and analyses as widely diverse as Cruse (1987), Hacker (1992), West (1993), and Bell (1992) have attempted to analyze racial schizophrenia and its consequences for the larger society. Historically, there was never a moment in the nation's history without a social and racial split from slavery to the present. Today, this schizophrenia is pronounced in the area of race and ethnicity. This social, racial, and emotional schizophrenia was aptly described by a transplanted male Northerner who wrote:

My family was not prejudiced. My parents raised me to judge people on their personal merit. There really are prejudices in the South, and it is very evident how surroundings can affect a person. After four years in Richmond I find myself saying things I don't really mean, especially in the car; saying things where I know no one will hear me ... I generally don't think I'm prejudiced, but being around so much prejudice[d] people, I find myself constantly doing so. It's very saddening to me, but it is so subconscious that I didn't consider it all that bad ... it's when the people "really" believe in their un-educated statements that I say there is a problem.

The dual theme was cited by many writers who knew their views on race and ethnicity were schizophrenic, but not all students were aware of the extent of their racial schizophrenia. Take the quote presented below. First, the stu-dent writes of how well he gets along with other groups, how he does not consider any one group to be superior to another, but he ends this discus-sion on a note that the reader knows that he does, in fact, view groups differently:

First, I learned the culture and lifestyle of the black man at an early age so I can relate to them. Second, I live in an area which is very peaceful[,] and delinquent kids do not roam the streets ... [the] most important factor ... is I am a Catholic Christian and believe that all men are created equal and none are superior to others. Some groups behave rather unintelligently, but their culture is to blame for their intellectual disabilities, they cannot be blamed.

The much longer journal entry below seems to encapsulate not only the racial divide within the community, but more importantly, the divide felt and perceived by the individual journal writer as he reflects on his elemen-tary, middle, and high school years and tells the reader when, for him, the racial duality began:

I don't recall my parents saying anything about different races when I was growing up, but I know I had no concept of racism when I was a child. As I grew older, I accepted the racist attitudes of my peers. In elementary school I had many black friends that I played with regularly. These were children who would come home with me and we would get together and do things out of school. We did not pay attention to the color of the skin at the time. It was in middle school that I noticed the start of a definite split between the races ... It was here that small segregated groups formed. It was also in middle school that we really noticed for the first time, and acted upon it, a difference in skin color. I still had black friends in middle school, but we slowly drifted apart. There weren't as many things we had in common. It was also here that most of the blacks were placed in lower level classes ... This is where I began to perceive that they were there because they weren't smart enough to do the other work ... blacks and whites began to almost totally separate from each other ... [then there was] ... the showing of Roots ... During this time, it wasn't wise for whites to be friends with blacks...

This writer has provided a perceptive view of how he moved from having black friends in elementary school to the separation between him and his black friends during middle school and, with that estrangement, how skin color became the issue dividing the friends with whom one played. Finally, this writer goes on to link black skins with lower intelligence given the large percentage of blacks in lower level classes.

Moral and Social Ambivalence

Racism eats away at the moral values and social objectives toward which societies strive. But this racist ideology co-exists, often quite comfortably, with the highly principled goals (democracy, freedom, liberty) which serve as driving forces in our society. But the co-existence of highly principled social values alongside a racist ideology presents problems for children and youth who are unable to understand why color distinctions are being made and what color has to do with friendships and playing. In other words, as the journal writer in the above cited quote said, at an early age, he did not see color, or if color were seen, its importance was lost on those who had not yet been taught that one is supposed to view color as significant. To illustrate this point, note the moral confusion and ambivalence of a female student when she recalled her father's opposition to her associating with black female students while attending elementary school:

> My father was opposed to my associating with black girls, so I could never invite my black friends home to play in my backyard. Whenever I wanted to play with my black friends we had to meet in the school's playground. I just couldn't understand this, and I was always asking my mother why I couldn't bring my black friends home to play. She just said that if I brought my black friends home to the house, my father would be very angry. I could not understand why my father, whom I loved, would be against my having a playmate over to my house to play. Every time we would talk about the issue, my mother would say that you should never be prejudice[d] against anyone because of their race or religion. She said we must look at a person's character and morals, not their color.

In the example above, the moral confusion resulted from the fact that the youngster was receiving mixed signals, a negative message from the father and a positive message from the mother. To another male student, the issue of his own racist upbringing, by his father, did not come to a head until he joined a local church and was then confronted with the moral dilemma of continuing to adhere to his father's racist teachings or accepting a Christian view. As he described it:

> I grew up a racist. My father was a racist and was always talking about blacks in a very negative manner. All of that had an influence on me when I was young. But when I

joincd the church and realized the evil of racial prejudice, I became more open minded. I have a five-year-old daughter, and I teach her that racial prejudice is bad.

The message racist parents convey to their children – that it is acceptable, and even necessary, to view another group with extreme contempt – has to be difficult for children and youth, especially since the same individuals you are to despise attend classes with you as well as participate with you in a variety of school activities, and may, in some of the examples presented earlier in this paper, be your friends. The church in the example given above enabled the student to resolve and confront the racial issue and to eventually oppose racism. But not all churches play a positive role in opposing racism. One female student wrote of the criticism and ostracism she received when she came to her church with a black male who was a fellow student at her high school. Many members of the congregation informed her that they disapproved of her actions and her behavior in inviting him to her church. She stopped attending that church, but in her journal she noted the shock from being told that a fellow Christian was not welcome to worship in the church. She said she was torn between doing what she felt was right and supporting a racial position held by many in the church that was un-Christian.

IRRATIONALITY

One of the themes which reverberate throughout the journals is that of the irrational responses by some parents on matters of race. Even when journal writers were already aware of the racial sentiments of their parents, they expressed astonishment at the level of anger and hate when the issue of race was raised within certain contexts. One of the situational circumstances evoking this anger and hate occurred when blacks were in close physical contact with the children of racists. In the overwhelming number of cases presented in the journals in which irrationality can be noted, it is the male, generally the father, who is apt to behave more adamantly. Several illustrations highlight this relationship between gender and racial intolerance. As one female student noted:

> I was getting married and told my parents that I wanted my best friend, who was my roommate in college, and who also was black, to be a part of my wedding party. I was stunned by the anger of my father. He reacted with such rage that it frightened me. He said there would be no wedding; he would not pay for anything. He also said he would not show up at a nigger-lover's wedding. He said he couldn't believe that he had raised a daughter who would "cohabitate" with "darkies". He would not speak to me for quite a while.

Another student wrote that though both her parents were racists and always told racist jokes and attempted to make fun of blacks, her father was more racist than her mother. This student noted that her mother worked in an office and was interested in having an end-of-the-year party for her co-workers. A black male works in her office, and since all the co-workers get along well, she was going to extend an invitation to him as well. The student said: "My father raised holy hell. He said, 'Hell no. You are not having a party here as long as that nigger works in your office. As long as this is my house, there will be no niggers here to party'." As in the previous quote, it was the white male who was more rejecting of having a black present at a social gathering in which they, the males, had the power to control. The male as the more active racist is consistent with previous findings by Foster (1986) and Wilson (1983) regarding racist indoctrination within families. This pattern is also demonstrated in yet another example provided below, where it is the male who is most resistant to interracial friendship, especially if that friendship entails dating. As the student said:

> Both my parents were racists. I had a good friend who was black, but my parents would not permit her to stay overnight in our house, though my white friends could. I also could not date black guys. They said all blacks were dumb, but I started talking to one of the black guys who was really smart, but that made no difference to them. So I dated him anyway. My father got very angry with me. Eventually, my mother wanted to meet the guy, but my father would not let her meet him. It really almost became a big issue between them.

These journal entries would lead one to view the father as the most dominant figure in the racial socialization of children. But even if fathers were not alone in setting the tone of racial training, it is apparent that they are more vocal in voicing their opposition to interracial situations; they were also, at least in the examples presented by journal writers, more uncompromising in their racial positions. One male student wrote that the irrationality of racism was deeper than many of us think. He mentioned that while he was quite young, his parents had informed him that whites were superior to all other races, especially blacks. Nor does he believe that his own racial indoctrination was unique. Rather, he believes that most of his friends were given the same "message" by their parents.

A reading of the journals, both of those who wrote very little and those who wrote much, reveals the persistent theme of the "superior" white and the "inferior" black, not as subtle dogma but rather as a very direct and conscious theme. It is no wonder then that both youth and parents are shocked in the evolution of youth–parent relationship: Many youth conclude that the negative racial information they had been fed by parents may be largely false; parents are often unsurprisingly shocked by the liberation of their children from the racial indoctrination they have given them. Much of the anger from fathers may simply derive from an attempt to put the "genie" back in the racial bottle and the difficulties of doing so once their children have had opportunities to interact with those who had been deemed the pariah.

The first-hand experiences of the journal writers, often when they were children or later as youth and young adults, offer startling insights into the many ways race and racism have an impact on white youth. We have quoted at length those who have gone into great detail about their encounters with others around racial matters. I wish to round out the theme of "irrationality" by listing some of the situations recounted by the writers on the irrationality surrounding race and racism that they experienced:

1. "I worked at a sheet metal company. The company needed another employee. When blacks applied for the job, they were told that the position was already filled. The employer said he would 'rather go out of business than have the government force him to hire blacks'."

2. "In high school, most of the blacks were in vocational education. Black students were steered there by the high school guidance counselors."

3. "In our high school there was opposition to white girls dating black guys, and whenever dating occurred 'bad rumors' would quickly spread about the girl. My sister started dating a black guy and the rumors immediately started. She discontinued dating him."

4. "A local store owner always kept an 'Out of Order' sign on the bathroom door. He allows whites to use the bathroom, but when blacks ask to use the restroom, the store owner points to the sign."

5. "Some local farmers keep fences with locked gates around their ponds. They don't allow blacks to use their ponds as fishing holes, but they tell local whites to make copies of their keys so that they can fish whenever they want."

6. "There was this teacher in high school who gave grades based on race and sex. The white males got the best grades no matter how poorly they performed in tests and we white males were always given the benefit of the doubt. Blacks were always getting the failing grades, and if they got good grades, they had to work harder than the white males. During one grading period, I failed all my exams in two classes and still received Bs for that grading period."

7. "There was only one black female in my elementary school classes. The teacher, who was white, would periodically allow us to re-arrange our

seats, but no matter where the black girl moved, the teacher would make her move her seat to the back of the class. Furthermore, the teacher would not call on her when she raised her hand to respond to a question; she would also keep her in class as punishment so that she would not be able to play with the other children at playtime. At the time I knew that she was being treated differently, but I was too young to understand why."

8. "In high school, there was an open party in which anyone could come. Four of my friends went, one of whom was black. When we got to the door, my black friend was told that he could not come into the house because no blacks are welcomed to the party. We all left."

9. "After graduating from high school I began looking for an apartment in the Fan section of Richmond. At one apartment, the landlady handed me a list of house rules. One of the rules included, 'No Black Visitors Allowed'."

10. "The KKK [Ku Klux Klan] was trying to recruit members in our community when I was in high school, and they were trying to apply pressure on my father to join. My parents were afraid to be friendly either to KKK members or to blacks for fear of reprisal."

11. "I knew a popular girl in high school who had a black date for the prom. Her father did not know that his daughter's prom date was black. When the guy came to the door to pick her up, the father slammed the door in his face and told him to 'date his own kind'."

The above quotes constitute only a portion of the racial experiences students entered in their journals. Many of the journal writers who received negative racial indoctrination while young recognized at an early age that this indoctrination was irrational. But being young, they were in no position to counter or refute the adult perpetrating the racist ideology. There were those, on the other hand, who accepted the racist ideology and admit in their journals to having been racist. This latter group, looking back on their youth, tends now to interpret their racial socialization as having been irrational. One of the most persistent feelings that emerges from the former group, of those who knew they were being socialized negatively and rejected this socialization, was that they were cornered and powerless. There was also an even stronger feeling of shame for their parents, usually fathers, for living in the past, and not being able to move beyond their own racial training. There was also subtle, and often not so subtle, anger toward fathers for attempting to control and dominate their children's lives in areas of interpersonal and intergroup relations.

TYPES OF RACIAL SOCIALIZATION

It is apparent from the data presented above that the journal writers were describing three types of racial socialization: Pro-racist, non-racist (or neutral), and anti-racist.

The case studies and illustrations presented in this paper clearly demonstrate the inordinate degree to which racial socialization occurs as a very conscious act in the vast majority of families, if these student journal writers are to be believed. This study, like my previous exercise, was designed to analyse the hypothesis advanced by many, that racial indoctrination occurs as an "unconscious act" rather than as a conscious one. We may interpret the term "unconscious act" to mean the subtle and hidden approaches and languages used to refer to race, race relations, and situations involving those of different cultures and races. Certain patterns are reflected in the journals of those relating the incidents and situations of their pro-racist socialization. The vast majority of journal writers mentioned their fathers as the chief pro-racist indoctrinator, even when both parents may have socialized the children against associating with members of other groups. Those students raised in pro-racist homes noted that the pro-racist diatribe often began very early. What was most interesting among those raised in pro-racist homes was the degree to which many of them recounted opposing their father's demands that they not associate with black students either at school or in the community. However, in most cases where students sought to oppose their father's racial decree, persistent pressures forced them to bend to the racial demands. Among females from pro-racist homes, the themes most likely to incur the wrath of the father was interracial dating, the appearance of a black at a family social gathering (a party or wedding), black female students at overnight sleepovers, and black female students playing in the yard after school, having black friends, and speaking up for blacks whenever they were criticized by the father. Among males from pro-racist homes, the issues generating the father's wrath include playing ball with black guys, attending Black History Month celebrations, having black friends in school, and associating with blacks after school.

A second type of socialization is a non-racist or race neutral socialization. Students raised in race-neutral homes noted that the issue of race was seldom discussed, and if mentioned, only as "news" or happenings. Data for this brief survey indicate that those from non-racist or race-neutral homes are in an extreme minority. Students from these homes mention that their own racial socialization, in which there were pro-racist values, came from friends in school or the community.

The third type of socialization is an anti-racist socialization. Students raised in anti-racist homes wrote the following: "My parents raised me to disregard prejudices and evaluate people on a personal basis"; "My parents raised us to be open minded and respectful of other races"; "My mother told me that black people were just people of another color but made by God just like me"; also, "My parents taught us not to judge people based on race or other physical characteristics." It is instructive that of those from anti-racist homes, four of the five from such homes were born and lived their formative years in the Northeast. As a result of their own racial socialization, these students did not have elaborate racial history stories, though many did relate racial incidents at school or in the community. Students receiving anti-racist socializations were not as rare as those receiving neutral or non-racist socialization.

The following table might provide a useful model for analyzing racial socialization and its possible relationship to subsequent social behavior toward racial and ethnic groups (Table 1).

Table 1 above suggests possible co-relation between early racial socialization and social behavior. That is, one may have experienced a racist socialization, yet one's later behavior may be pro-racist, non-racist, or anti-racist. The same is true for those given non-racist or anti-racist socialization. But even here there are some problems because even in homes with pro-racist socialization, there may be occasions, as noted in some of the journal entries, when anti-racist sentiments may be cited. For example, several of the writers noted their parents' racist indoctrination and that these same parents might occasionally say that they "really feel sorry for blacks because they are treated so badly". So there may be moments of ambivalence in the utterances of parents despite an overall pro-racist sentiment or environment. But such ambivalences, according to the journals, were very rare indeed. What was not so rare was the movement of journal writer's sentiments and behavior from pro-racist to anti-racist or even non-racist. This suggests that at any one moment, individuals may be passing from one type of behavior

Table 1.   Correlation of Early Racial Socialization and Subsequent
Social Behaviour.

Racial Socialization	Pro-Racist	Race Neutral	Anti-Racist
Pro-Racist			
Race Neutral			
Anti-Racist			

to another. For example, an individual raised in a non-racist or anti-racist environment might, as some journal entries show, display pro-racist behavior if he has experienced what he believes to be negative situations with members of another race, or if he has joined a peer group whose views are pro-racist.

We are seeing many paradoxes here. The first is that children and youth may receive pro-racist socialization yet resist that socialization when they encounter members of the "pariah group" whom they like as friends. Another paradox is that irrespective of the type of racial socialization, behavior toward members of another group may not be consistent with racial training but may be more tied to what acting individuals may perceive as negative or positive interpersonal or intergroup contact with individuals and groups of another race. Finally, as a few of the journal writers reiterated, behaving in a pro-racist, non-racist, or anti-racist manner places the individual in a very distinct group, a reference group, to which the individual will be linked and identified. If we then view the various groups representing a type of racial identification or racial membership, we might cite both Simmel (1956) and Lewin (1948), who delineated the importance or criss-crossing and multiple-group membership and the inherent values of such affiliations. They both emphasize that individuals are capable of multiple, often simultaneous, allegiances in their group affiliation. Such behavior, they note, may not simply reflect degrees of the individuals' internal contradiction, but may, instead, reflect individuals' responses to a variety of situations and events in their immediate environment.

DISCUSSION

This paper is an analysis of the effects of racism on white children and youth. We sought the effects of racism as the incidents related by students in their journals. From the data presented, it is clear for the vast majority of journal writers that conscious racial indoctrination was a reality for them. From these journals we might assume that a sizable percentage of the white population continues to promote pro-racist sentiment while, simultaneously, racial progress and change may be evident in many other areas of life. As we analyze the journals we note that one of the objectives of pro-racist socialization is to continue the ideology and reality of segregation. A concomitant objective of the desire to separate children by race was to re-affirm the philosophy and politics of race superiority, that is, white supremacy.

The fact that these racial situations and racial indoctrination occurred in the 1980s and 1990s may be surprising to some. A few might insist that the era of formal racial segregation is a thing of the past as is the philosophy and politics of racial segregation. Racism, individual and institutional, must be viewed as one views a philosophy of religion in that for many it is a belief system and a way of life. For many, the old ways are difficult to shed. Especially among pro-racist families, parents may tell their children repeatedly about the racial incidents and situation in their early life as justification for retaining old customs and attitudes about race. Since these situations mean very little to their children, parents, as reflected in many journal entries, then threaten their children on many levels to force compliance, which may or may not succeed.

Finally, what emerges in the journal writings is that most students have reached a degree of accommodation with their parents, specifically, their fathers. It is obvious from their writings that students who were raised in pro-racist homes, according to their journals, have distanced themselves from their father's racial views. It is also obvious that they still want to maintain a close relationship with their family. Though the data used in this study are not a representative sample, it does suggest that race continues to play an inordinate role in the socialization of children and youth. Our findings also suggest that if race is so paramount as a socializing theme in so many families, racism does indeed shape the behavior and actions of dominant group members who may be in a position to control and determine the life chances of the non-dominant group. One of the male journal writers said he was socialized at home to be a racist, and as far as he could tell, most of his friends were also socialized by their parents to be racists. It is this collective understanding about race that makes racism an object of rigid group conformity.

One sees in the journal entries the personal struggles of the writers who opposed their pro-racist fathers and friends. Very few of the youth were able to withstand the strong pressures to disassociate themselves from blacks. Consequently, most of the youth, under great duress, abandoned their friendships and relationships with blacks. On the societal level, institutional racism may simply mirror what racist fathers tell their children: Blacks do not belong in certain positions, simply because they just do not belong there. A great part of the continuation of the ethos of racism is the attitude and behavior of many whites in so many areas of life that blacks simply do not belong and are, therefore, not entitled to similar opportunities offered to whites. Thus, despite the many changes in intergroup relations during the past 30 years, the level of negative racial socialization began in the home and may continue in schools, churches and synagogues, at work, and in the various youth peer groups and activities. As we move into the 21st century, we must continue to confront issues tackled in the 20th century: review school segregation, the existence of poor and ineffective urban schools, discrimination in purchasing homes, receiving mortgage loans, purchasing cars, etc. What is encouraging in the journals is the number of individuals who have resisted efforts to force them to adopt the world of the racist. That some youngsters resist is not only a testament to their individual valor and strength, but also a tribute to many individuals and groups who have waged battles against racism and who have sought pro-active strategies to defeat it in every realm of American life.

REFERENCES

Allport, G. (1954). *The nature of prejudice.* Reading, MA: Addison-Wesley.

Baker, D. (1983). *Race ethnicity and power.* London: Routledge and Kegan Paul.

Bell, D. (1992). *Race, racism and American law.* Boston: Little, Brown and Company.

Blauner, B. (1990). *Black lives, White lives.* Berkeley: University of California Press.

Clark, K. (1955). *Prejudice and your child.* Boston: Beacon Press.

Clark, T. (1975). *The oppression of youth.* New York: Harper and Row.

Crapanzano, V. (1985). *Waiting: The whites of South Africa.* New York: Random House.

Cruse, H. (1987). *Plural but equal.* New York: Willaim Morrow.

Dennis, R. M. (1981). Socialization and race: The white experience. In: B. P. Bowser, & R. G. Hunt (Eds), *Impacts of racism on white Americans* (pp. 71–85). Newbury Park: Sage Publications.

Dennis, R. M. (1988). The use of participant observation in race relations research. In: C. Marrett, & C. Leggon (Eds), *Research in race and ethnic relations*, Vol. 5. Greenwich, CT: JAI Press.

Dennis, R. M. (1991). Dual marginality and Black Middletown youth. In: R. M. Dennis (Ed.), *Research in race and ethnic relations*, (Vol. 6, pp. 3–25). Greenwich, CT: JAI Press.

Davis, G., & Watson, G. (1985). *Black life in corporate America.* Garden City: Doubleday.

Dooley, P. J. (1985). *Organizational transformation: A case study of the crusade for voters.* M.S. thesis, Virginia Commonwealth University.

Early, G. (1994). *Daughters.* New York: Addison-Wesley Publishing.

Fein, L. (1967). *Politics in Israel.* Boston: Little Brown and Company.

Foster, D. (1986). The development of racial orientation in children: A review of South African research. In: S. Burman & R. Reynold (Eds), *Growing up in a divided society* (pp. 158–183). Johannesburg: Raven Press.

Hacker, A. (1992). *Two nations: Black and White, separate, hostile, unequal.* New York: Scribers.

Hyman, H. (1969). Social psychology and race relations. In: I. Katz & P. Gwin (Eds), *Race and social sciences* (pp. 3–48). New York: Basic Books.

Lewin, K. (1948). *Social conflicts.* New York: Harper and Brothers.

McIntosh, P. (1989). White privilege: Unpacking the invisible knapsack. *Peace and Freedom,* *July/August,* 10–12.

Niemi, R., & Sobiedzek, B. (1977). Political socialization. *Annual review of sociology, 3,* 209–233.

Pettigrew, T. (1981). The mental health impact. In: B. P. Bowser & R. G. Hunt (Eds), *The impact of racism on white Americans* (pp. 97–118). Newbury Park: Sage Publications.

le Roux, P. (1986). Growing up and Afrikaner. In: S. Burman & P. Reynolds (Eds), *Growing up* *in a divided society.* Johannesburg: Raven Press.

Shaw, G. B. (1974). A treatise on parents and children. In: T. Talbot (Ed.), *The world of the* *child* (pp. 362–386). New York: Jason Aronson.

Simmel, G. (1956). *Conflict and the web of group affiliation.* Glencoe, IL: Free Press.

Stone, J. (1985). *Racial conflict in contemporary society.* Cambridge: Harvard University Press.

West, C. (1993). *Race matters.* Boston: Beacon Press.

Wilson, M. (1983). *Ethnic attitudes of South African primary school children.* Unpublished B.A. Hons. thesis, University of Cape Town.

Wilson, W. J. (1987). *The truly disadvantaged: The inner city, the underclass and public policy.* Chicago: University of Chicago Press.

Wilson, W. J. (1973). *Power, racism, and privilege.* New York: Macmillan Company.

PART V:
KNOWLEDGE, CULTURE, AND THE
POLITICS OF EDUCATION

THE EDUCATION OF BLACK AMERICANS IN THE 21ST CENTURY

Charles V. Willie

In an article entitled "The Civil Rights Movement and Educational Change", Meyer Weinberg, a historian, had this to say:

> Since 1940 the single most important factor in the lives of African Americans has been the rise of the civil rights movement. In the main, it was a movement of black people led by black people and has been deeply responsive to the historic goals and aspirations of blacks in America. In 1963, when Francis Keppel, U.S. Commissioner of Education, declared "Thank God for the Civil Rights Movement," he was giving voice to the growing realization that the movement was becoming the principal engine for educational change in the country (Keppel, 1964). Marching blacks and their allies demanded a series of changes: dissolution of structures of segregation ... guarantee of equal education; employment of black personnel on all levels of schooling ... ; democratization of educational policy making by ... authorities ... through black and other minority participation; and eradication of institutional and personal racism from curriculum, instructional materials, student learning, employment and promotion practices, distribution of school funds, and other areas of schooling. The kinds of changes demanded by the civil rights movement were not, of course, well received by many (Weinberg 1991, p. 3).

Of the Civil Rights Act of 1964, the great energizer for change, Martin Luther King, Jr. said, "This legislation was written in the streets" (King, 1965). There was no continuous positive action of redress until blacks assumed responsibility for their own liberation and took to the streets with

The New Black: Alternative Paradigms and Strategies for the 21st Century
Research in Race and Ethnic Relations, Volume 14, 197–207
Copyright © 2007 by Elsevier Ltd.
ISSN: 0195-7449/doi:10.1016/S0195-7449(06)14009-X

demonstrations to initiate change. Liberation and emancipation, of course, are not synonymous. The Emancipation Proclamation of 1863 was an external experience, a declaration by others that slaves were free. The civil rights revolution of the 1950s and 1960s in the United States was an internal experience, a declaration of people of color that they were free.

Martin Luther King, Jr. and his colleagues demonstrated in Birmingham, Alabama in 1963. They issued a "manifesto" demanding an end to segregation in all areas of community life and a warning that demonstrations and boycotts would continue until demands were met. From there, Dr. King took the movement to the streets of St. Augustine, Florida in 1964; to Selma, Alabama in 1965 to demand voting rights; and to Chicago the same year to protest segregated housing. The James Meredith March Against Fear in Mississippi on highway 51 in 1966, completed by a host of civil rights groups after Meredith was shot but not killed by the white enemies of freedom, demonstrated that blacks would no longer be intimidated by the violence of whites. In 1967, Dr. King began planning for the Poor People's Campaign in Washington, DC.

Dr. King's ultimate gift, the sacrifice of his life in 1968 in Memphis, Tennessee where he participated in a demonstration with the union of garbage collectors, spurred the nation to decisive action regarding the implementation of educational equity for people of color. After Dr. King's death, many institutions, including foundations and public and private educational institutions, developed minority-student recruitment programs.

Earlier, Congress had passed the Civil Rights Act of 1964, the Voting Rights Act of 1965, and amendments to these statutes in 1966 and 1967. Then in 1968, the Handicapped Early Education Assistance Act and the Fair Housing Act were passed. This legislative action indicated that demonstrations against discrimination were having a beneficial effect for people of color and other subdominant power groups.

Between 1965 and 1975, blacks were not waiting on whites to fashion equitable educational and human rights remedies. Dr. King and other civil rights leaders increased pressure for change through continuous organized demonstrations. Public laws for educational equity were enacted by the Congress, largely because of these demonstrations in the streets. In an Ebony magazine article, Dr. King wrote, "when marching is seen as part of a program to dramatize an evil, to mobilize the forces of good will, and to generate pressure and power for change, marches will continue to be effective" (King, 1966). "Marching feet", he said, "announce that time has come for a given idea" (King, 1966).

The civil rights movement led by Dr. King and others was very successful. Blacks, other minorities, women and disabled individuals, and students for whom English was not their first language now receive a much larger piece of the educational pie. At the same time, the disproportionately large piece of that same educational pie began to diminish slowly for white men.

Now, it appears, whites are striking back with a potent weapon – organized media propaganda. Because white males control the media, they have decided to use it to disseminate a distorted message that the educational system, which has been pressured into accommodating the interests and concerns of individuals other than the dominant people of power is drifting toward mediocrity and, therefore, is in need of a new set of standards. However, the facts do not support this assertion.

I view the educational system in the United States today as superior to the educational system of a generation ago and of earlier times. It is truly universal at elementary and secondary levels and more inclusive in higher education; it is also more flexible and accommodating to the needs of female students, racial and ethnic minorities, physically challenged students, bilingual students, and students with learning disabilities.

In the final years of the 1970s, there were changes in federal initiatives that favored dominant people of power. Federal higher education grants for low-income and minority students began to diminish. Limited federal resources for programs for the disadvantaged were further diluted by increasing the income range of people eligible to participate in such programs. In 1978, student financial-assistance programs were modified to give middle-income as well as low-income college students access to governmental assistance. By 1988, only about one-sixth of the billions of dollars spent by the Department of Education went directly to college students. And about one-fifth went to banks to subsidize student loans.

By the end of the 1980s, federal government policy clearly favored loans over grants, which is to say, the federal government preferred to assist middle-income over low-income students. These retrenchments for subdominant people of power came during a period when blacks and other minorities were not pressing for change as hard as they had been pressing in the past. What we recognize in the discussion here and elsewhere in this article is not minorities and low-income people failing to benefit from education, but a failure on the part of the federal government to assist its citizens of limited resources with grants (rather than loans) to meet costly college expenses.

As we move through the first decade of the twenty-first century, it is appropriate to take stock of successes and failures in overcoming racial oppression in the United States. On balance, the push for civil rights that began the direct action phase with a boycott in Montgomery, Alabama in the 1950s, has been a resounding success. This is especially true in the area of education, largely because blacks, not whites, assumed the leadership for social change.

The demographic changes in the United States are remarkable. Of college graduates, a generation ago (in 1960) before legislation mentioned in this paper was passed, only 3 percent of black adults over 25 years of age were college graduates compared to 8 percent of white adults over 25 years. Today (1997) the proportion of black college graduates continues to lag behind the proportion of white college graduates. However, the proportion of blacks 25 years of age and older who have finished college (13 percent) is four times greater than the proportion of black college graduates a generation ago (in 1960) before the passage of the Civil Rights Act of 1964. And while one-quarter of white adults have attained a college degree today (in 1997), their rate of increase is only three times greater than it was a generation ago in 1960 (U.S. Census Bureau, 1999, p. 169); the white rate of increase is smaller than that found among blacks.

An analysis of high school data is more remarkable. Back in 1960, 43 percent of all whites – 25 years and older – had graduated from high school; today their proportion has reached 93 percent, an increase of 50 percentage points. But among blacks of a similar age group, the increase of high school graduates from 22 percent in 1967 to 87 percent today (1997) represents an increase of 65 percentage points, a rate of increase far greater than that found among whites (National Center for Educational Statistics, 1998, p. 17). It is my judgment that these increased rates of educational attainment among blacks that outdistanced the rates of increase in educational attainment among whites were largely because of Brown v. Board of Education (1954 and 1955) and subsequent legislation and other court decrees to implement the school desegregation mandated by law.

In 1997, there were 394,000 black high school graduates of which 60 percent (or nearly one-quarter of a million) enrolled in college (National Center for Educational Statistics, 1998, p. 208). There was not enough space in existing historically black colleges and universities to accommodate the number of blacks who wanted to enroll in colleges and universities. To fulfill the aspirations of this increased number of black students seeking a college education, integrated colleges and universities became a necessity. If desegregation had not been required by law, the increased number of black people who wanted a college education could not have been accommodated.

The U.S. Statistical Abstract reports that black adults with a bachelor's degree only earn 70 percent more income than black adults with a high school diploma only. But the income of blacks with only a college degree tends to be one-fifth less than that received by whites with a similar education. There is an economic benefit connected with more education for whites as well as blacks. But blacks and whites with similar levels of education do not receive similar amounts of income (Willie & Reddick, 2003, pp. 154–155).

One way of assessing the progress of blacks in education today and in the future is to determine how far they have progressed from where they started rather than how far they must go to attain parity with whites or any other group. The attainment of parity with whites in income cannot be fully achieved by blacks without eliminating discrimination against blacks by whites.

Whites shifted the paradigm from a focus on equal access to education to equal outcome from education. And blacks were wrong to have embraced this paradigmatic change in focus as a legitimate way of assessing racial progress for blacks. Instead, blacks should have insisted on maintaining a dual foci on both access and outcome, not one or the other. It is from this perspective that affirmative action must be considered as a way of overcoming racial discrimination. In the future, we must study the effects of integration and other experiences of inclusion upon behavior in specific population groups as well as their relative effects with reference to the majority population.

By 1997, 83 percent of white adult persons (25 year of age and older) and 75 percent of black adult persons (of similar age) had graduated from high school (U.S. Census Bureau, 1998, p. 169); only 8 percentage points separated these racial populations with reference to this gross indicator of educational attainment. Yet, the mean earnings for all black people of $21,978 lagged 31 percent below the $28,844 mean earnings figure for white people (U.S. Census Bureau, 1999, p. 478). Among blacks and whites who had terminated their formal education with a bachelor's degree only, a diminished but persistent and significant difference of 22 percent that favored whites existed between the average earnings of these racial groups. This contemporary finding seems to confirm an observation made by Herman Miller of the U.S. Census Bureau nearly a generation ago that "schooling does pay off for nonwhites ... [but] to a far lesser degree than for whites" (Miller, 1971, p. 167).

Actually, circumstances other than the amount of formal education received may contribute to the income gap between blacks and whites. We say this because the data clearly indicate that more education is associated with higher income for blacks. And, of course, the same is true for whites. The average income for blacks who did not complete high school in 1997 was $13,110 compared with an average of $31,955 for blacks with a bachelor's degree only. College-educated blacks had an average income that was 144 percent greater than the average income of blacks without a high school education (U.S. Census Bureau, 1998). This fact means that more education is associated with a better income for blacks. In this respect, education does well for blacks and whites, since whites with only a bachelor's degree earned about 154 percent more than whites without a high school education (U.S. Census Bureau, 1998, p. 168). The problem, therefore, is not that education is less beneficial for blacks, but that discrimination continues to limit the income opportunities of blacks even when they have education that is similar to whites.

Clearly, whites are more generously rewarded than blacks as they attain more education. For example, in 1997 the average income for white people without a high school education was 17 percent greater than the average income for black people with a similar lower level of education; the average income for white people with a bachelor's degree only was 22 percent greater than the average income for black people with a bachelor's degree only; and the average income for white people with a master's degree only was 35 percent greater than the average income for black people with this level of educational attainment (U.S. Census Bureau, 1998, p. 168). Thus, it is not education that has failed blacks; rather, it seems that the society is less willing to reward blacks as it has rewarded whites for increased educational attainment.

Knowledge of these findings was one reason that I offered a counter hypothesis in my debate with sociologist William Wilson several years ago regarding whether race was declining in significance. I suggested that "the significance of race is increasing especially for middle-class blacks who, because of school desegregation and affirmative action and other integration programs, are coming into direct contact with whites for the first time for extended interaction" (Willie, 1989, p. 20). There is clear and present evidence revealed in this discussion that the income gap between black and white racial groups tends to increase as the level of educational attainment in both groups increases. Thus, discrimination must be considered, in part, as an explanation for the income gap between blacks and whites. Likewise, discrimination also must be considered as an explanation for the achievement gap between blacks and whites on tests "that rely heavily", as stated by Gardner, on a blend of logical and linguistic abilities" (Gardner, 1985, p. x).

Christopher Jencks and Meredith Philips discuss the achievement test score gap as if it is an essential measure of education quality. In their edited book, a gaggle of scholars attempt to explain why the gap in performance on tests between black and white students remains and how the gap may be closed. However, the wrong issue is being discussed. Jencks and Phillips state that "If selective colleges based their admission decisions solely on applicants predicted college grades, their undergraduate enrollment would currently be 96 or 97 percent white and Asian" (Jencks & Phillips, 1998, p. 8). Then they state without evidence that "if selective colleges could achieve racial diversity without making race an explicit factor in their admission decisions, blacks would do better in college ... " (Jencks & Phillips, 1998, p. 8).

This conjecture by Jencks and Phillips is at odds with the findings of Bowen and Bok who report that several students of color with SAT scores below 1000 and with less impressive academic credentials (who were recruited explicitly because of their race and their potential as scholars) were very satisfied with their college experience (Bowen & Bok, 1998, p. 194). In fact, "Black graduates rated their undergraduate experience in several elite colleges more highly than did their white classmates (Bowen & Bok, 1998, p. 210). Moreover, these black graduates of selective schools "were much more likely than their white classmates to have taken on leadership positions in virtually every type of civic endeavor after graduating from college (Bowen & Bok, 1998, p. 168). Despite the racial gap in average achievement scores and other academic credentials, these black students had a positive outcome because they had equal access to a good education made possible through deliberate recruitment efforts of these selective colleges. These findings reveal that "making race an explicit factor in ... admission decisions" did not harm black students in the Bowen and Bok study.

Neil Rudenstine, former president of Harvard University, has said, "whatever problems we still face as a society ... we know that they would be even more severe, divisive and profound if the nation had not made a sustained commitment to opening doors of higher education to people of all colors, religions, and economic backgrounds" (Harvard University, 1999, p. S15). Among Harvard's approximately 6,500 undergraduates, 34 percent identify themselves as being of Asian, African American, Hispanic, or Native American origin and approximately half are women (Harvard University, 1999, p. S14).

It seems to me that the goal of higher education must change from that of seeking the brightest and best students or from that of closing the test-score gap between minority and majority students to that of "seek[ing] students who have the potential to contribute something distinctive and important to the enterprise of learning" (Harvard University, 1999, p. S14), and to their communities after graduating from college.

If education is for the purpose of equipping people with knowledge and virtue to manage their society, then it is almost impossible to justify excluding anyone from the opportunity to receive an education since ignorance harms not only the individual but the total community. The growing movement to overcome inequality of opportunity because of race now encompasses age, sex, physical or mental status, and eventually will include social class or wealth. And this is as it should be. The record shows that schools of good learning can be and have been of good help to all sorts and conditions of people.

Langdon Gilkey, a U. S. citizen who saw people stripped bare of pretensions in an interment camp of 2,000 women, men and children that was located in Asia during World War II, kept a rather lengthy journal and formed this opinion about the moral basis of knowledge and rationality: "Rational behavior in communal action is primarily a moral and not an intellectual achievement, possible only to a person who is morally capable of self-sacrifice. In a real sense ... moral selflessness is a prerequisite for the life of reason – not it's consequences" (Gilkey, 1966, p. 93). Gilkey's elaboration of this idea brings the issue of the purpose of education into perspective.

> Technological advance ... spells "progress" only if [people] are in fact rational and good. A [person] motivated only by self-interest, a [person] subject to brutal or vicious prejudices and passions, one who can kill and maim with ease if [one's] security is threatened, is no technologist in whom to have confidence ... A realistic view of [people] tends to undermine the confidence a technological culture has in its own progress. Since we all want to believe in something, our secularized culture has tended to adopt an idealistic view of [people] as innately rational and good, as able to handle [themselves] and [their] history with the relative ease with which [they] dealt with nature. Consequently, the scientist rather than the politician, the knower rather than the moralist, has seemed to us to be the guarantor of security and peace, the harbinger of a better world. As I learned in camp, this vision is a false dream: the things we long for – peace, prosperity, and a long life – depend to a far greater degree on the achievement of harmony and justice among [people] than they do on the latest inventions from our laboratories, valuable as the latter may be. That achievement of harmony and justice confronts us as a race, not with problems of technological know-how or scientific knowledge so much as with the problems of political and moral decisions (Gilkey, 1966, pp. 95–96).

The wisdom of Langdon Gilkey, derived form his prison camp experience indicates that our current emphasis on standards and achievement imbalances the purposes of education and may even misdirect it, if not corrected by the multiple interests and assets of a diversified student body. Thus, Daniel Bell's recommendation that "high-scoring individuals [on the Intelligence Quotient scale] ... should be brought to the top in order to make the best use of their talents" should be rejected as connoting a definition of education that is too limited (Bell, 1973, p. 608), (Willie, 1982, pp. 16–20). "Rational behavior in communal action", as indicated by Gilkey, "is primarily a moral and not an intellectual achievement". The most intelligent people may or may not be sufficiently selfless to make rational and appropriate decisions for the public good. The purpose of education, then, is to provide learning opportunities for the acquisition of knowledge and wisdom for the making of public and personal decisions that sustain community. A community-sustaining education, therefore, focuses on equity as well as excellence; not one or the other but both.

This purpose has nothing to do with the notion that "equality of output" is the most important educational goal, as discussed by James Coleman (1968, p. 106) and Daniel Bell (1973, p. 620). What anyone achieves or produces because of greater natural or cultivated capacities should work for the good of the least fortunate, according to John Rawls (1971, pp. 302–303). And cultivated contributions by the meek and humble should also benefit the high and the mighty. Moreover, we know that a heterogeneous population is better capable of adapting to or modifying an environment effectively than one that is homogenous. Why then should public policy about education emphasize equal results when a polymorphic society of people with different talents is better? It is equality of access and quality output together about which desegregated educational policy should be concerned; not one or the other but both.

If we devote ourselves to developing educational institutions that are genuinely diversified and that are available to a diversified population, such institutions will benefit all of us. We will do this if we adopt Howard Gardner's "theory of multiple intelligences" and my "theory of complementarity" as ways of understanding the future role of education.

Gardner states that "human cognition ... includes[s] a far wider and more universal set of competencies than has ordinarily been considered ... and ... that ... most ... of these competencies do not lend themselves to measurement by standard verbal methods, which rely heavily on a blend of logical and linguistic abilities" (Gardner, 1985, p. x). Gardner defines intelligences as "the ability to solve problems or to create products that are valued within one or more cultural settings ... " (Gardner, 1985, p. x). He states that "an individual's facility with one content has little predictive power with his or her facility with other kinds of content. In other words, Genius ... is likely to be specific to particular contents ... " (Gardner,

1985, p. xi). An important claim of Gardner's theory is that "each intelligence is relatively independent of the others" (Gardner, 1985, p. xi). He concludes that "an analysis of cognition must include all human problem-solving and product-fashioning skills and not just those that happen to lend themselves to testing via standard format" (Gardner, 1985, p. xii).

Gardner's theory recognizes kinesthetic intelligence as well as spatial, musical, and linguistic intelligence. Also, he mentions logical intelligence and personal intelligence – people who understand themselves well and people who understand others well. Since "learning is considered a requirement for survival" in some societies (Gardner, 1985, p. 336), it is important to cultivate all kinds of intelligences and not just linguistic and logical–mathematical intelligences. Gardner's theory of multiple intelligences alerts us to the need to respect and nurture the development of many different skills, all of which are important in the adaptation and survival of human populations.

The theory of complementarity alerts us to the reciprocity that exists between people, between groups, and between people and groups. Also it warns against separating policies and practices that should always coexist such as excellence and equity in education. It is appropriate that any person or group in society should be open to the knowledge and wisdom and assistance of another person or group because none is self-sufficient (Willie, 1994, p. 66). Thus, dominant power groups should be in the presence of and learn from subdominant power groups; likewise, subdominants should co-mingle with and learn from dominants (Willie, 1994, p. 73). Individuals who have learned from their opposites can cope more effectively with role changes and new status situations (Willie, 1994, p. 74). The theory of complementarity recognizes the interdependence of people and of groups in human society and what they do for each other. For this reason, the different intelligences that different people possess should be cultivated for self-satisfaction and for the benefit of the whole society. Finally, the theory of complementarity recognizes that our differences are as important as our similarities.

The ideas and principles of education discussed in this article must be accepted and emphasized in the future if the unique competencies found among people of color are to be cherished and cultivated for the benefit of the total society. The theory of complementarity indicates what should be done with the multiple intelligences (mentioned in Gardner's theory) that exist in a society of pluralistic populations. They should be accepted, respected, and integrated for our mutual enhancement. Each individual who excels in one intelligence has something to give and receive from another, since none is excellent in all intelligences. This should be the mantra of minorities, whoever they are, as we move into and through the twenty-first century. For I say unto you, this is the century of pluralism, globalism, and interdependency. We who try to go it alone will fail.

REFERENCES

Bell, D. (1973). On meritocracy and equality. In: K. Jerome & A. H. Halsey (Eds), *Power and ideology in education* (pp. 607–635). New York, NY: Oxford University Press.
Bowen, W., & Bok, D. (1998). *The shape of the river: Long term consequences of considering race in college and university admissions.* Princeton, NJ: Princeton University Press.
Coleman, J. (1968). Equality of educational opportunity. *Integrated Education*, (September–October), *6*(5), 19–28.
Gardner, H. (1985). *Frames of mind: The theory of multiple intelligences.* New York, NY: Basic Books.
Gilkey, L. (1966). *Shantung compound.* New York, NY: Harper and Row.
Harvard University. (1999). The educational value of diversity. *Fortune* (June 21), *139*(12), S14–S15.
Jencks, C., & Phillips, M. (Eds) (1998). *The Black/White test score gap.* Washington, DC: Brookings Institution Press.
Keppel, F. (1964). Thank God for the civil rights movement. *Integrated Education* (April–May), 269–270.
King, M. L. (1965). Let justice roll down. *Nation* (March), 200, 269–270.
King, M. L. (1966). Nonviolence the only road to freedom. *Ebony* (October), *21*, 27–30.
Miller, H. (1971). *Rich man, poor man.* New York, NY: Thomas Crowell Co.
National Center for Educational Statistics. (1998). *Digest of educational statistics 1998.* Washington, DC: US Government Printing Office.
Rawls, J. (1971). *A theory of justice.* Cambridge, MA: Harvard University Press.
U.S. Census Bureau. (1998). *Statistical abstract of the United States.* Washington, DC: US Government Printing Office.
U.S. Census Bureau. (1999). *Statistical abstract of the United States.* Washington, DC: US Government Printing Office.
Weinberg, M. (1991). The civil rights movement and educational change. In: C. W. Willie, A. M. Garibaldi & W. L. Reed (Eds), *The education of African Americans* (pp. H3–H6). Westport, CT: Auburn.
Willie, C. V. (1982). Educating students who are good enough. *Change*, (March), *14*(2), 16–20.
Willie, C. V. (1989). *Caste and class: Controversy on race and poverty, round two of the Willie/Wilson debate.* Dix Hills, NY: General Hall.
Willie, C. V. (1994). *Theories of human social action.* Dix Hills, NY: General Hall.
Willie, C. V., & Reddick, R. J. (2003). *A new look at Black families* (5th ed.). Walnut Creek, CA: AltaMira Press.

GLASS CEILINGS IN ACADEMIA: AFRICAN AMERICAN WOMEN SOCIAL SCIENTISTS

Diane R. Brown and Bette Woody[†]

ABSTRACT

This article asks whether a "glass ceiling" prohibits African American women from achieving mainstream academic faculty teaching and research careers in the social and behavioral sciences. While African American women made dramatic strides in completion of doctoral degrees in a diversity of specializations, they have failed to date to obtain a presence in the nation's prestigious doctoral and research institutions. Indeed evidence is growing that the precipitous decline in African American male graduate enrollments and doctoral completions, has not helped employment opportunity for African American women. The result is a loss for African American women when the academic payoff could increase, but even worse is the overall reduction in an African American presence on U.S. higher education faculties. At a time when other minorities and women are expanding, this decline in African American faculty impacts student enrollments by further shrinking the pool of mentors critical to shaping future faculty of color. Research particularly in neglected areas associated specifically with African American status, is also impacted through loss of its most committed scientists. Explanations for these changes to date are limited, since most analysis of academic labor market centers on the

The New Black: Alternative Paradigms and Strategies for the 21st Century
Research in Race and Ethnic Relations, Volume 14, 209–234
Copyright © 2007 by Elsevier Ltd.
ISSN: 0195-7449/doi:10.1016/S0195-7449(06)14010-6

experience of White males and neglect the special experience of minority and women academics. This report reviews dominant theory and data available on the employment of African American women faculty with a focus on the social and behavior sciences. Available data suggest the causes are found in multiple barriers, which discourage young African American women to explore academic careers. For those who attempt to do so, there is limited access to career building employment where research funding, mentors and networks contribute to scholarly output.

1. INTRODUCTION

Despite dramatic achievements in the past 30 years, African American women remain severely underrepresented on the faculties of prestigious research universities reflecting a "glass ceiling" which halts career mobility and stifles scholarly contributions of an important segment of American academic talent. African American men and women currently make up 12 percent of the U.S. population and around 6 percent of undergraduate enrollments but only about 4 percent of total U.S. college and university faculty (Journal of Blacks in Higher Education, 2006). These figures however, do not tell the whole story. While African American women are in many ways the "success" story in academic achievement with major gains in doctoral achievement, they are underrepresented compared to either African American men or White women at less than 1 percent of total U.S. faculty. Indeed, African American male college and graduate enrollments tumbled during the 1980s, causing an overall decline in African American higher education enrollments. African American male doctorates declined by 44 percent between 1976–1977 and 1989–1990, according to data from the U.S. Department of Education, Office of Education Statistics, EPDES in 1992. By contrast, African American women undergraduate and graduate enrollments grew. Doctorates earned by African American women thus expanded by nearly one third over the same period from 38.9 to 53 percent of total doctorates earned by African Americans. However, in contrast to other women, African American women failed to acquire new faculty positions in proportion to the increase in earned doctorates.

Contradictions are also found in the quality of appointments of African American women faculty. African American women gained a substantial presence in the faculty recruitment pool in social and behavioral sciences comparing favorably to other populations. Yet African American women were less likely to be hired by doctoral and research institutions, in mainstream discipline departments and in tenure track faculty and research positions, thus suffering higher unemployment and lower pay rates (Committee on Science, Engineering and Public Policy, 2006). This study examines the employment status of African American women faculty in the social and behavioral sciences and asks: *Is there a gap between doctoral achievement and employment and productivity which leads to tenure and promotion and what is a realistic expected payoff for doctoral education for African American women?*

2. BACKGROUND THEORY AND EVIDENCE OF AFRICAN AMERICAN WOMEN IN THE ACADEMIC MARKETPLACE

Two main conceptual frameworks underlie research on higher education labor markets (Kulis, Shaw, & Chong, 2000; Fairweather, 1995). The first focuses on human capital theory and labor market processes, where the academic labor market is dominated by an elite, high-prestige competitive bid process played out at the national level. A recent variation includes the same human capital emphasis, but encompasses a market consisting of many submarkets based on geographic regions or factors. A second broad theory takes into account institutional and behavioral issues along with some human capital assumptions. Human capital theory applied to higher education suggests that under free market conditions, high demand and scarce skills would tend to command higher position status and wages. But limited, esoteric or hyper specializations can also reduce demand. External market wages in non-academic professional fields such as business, economics or applied health fields, may also influence wages. Underscoring these basic factors, higher education tends to be governed by at least two principal submarkets, one national and a second, regional in nature. While the national market is dominated by competition among institutions for scholars trained at prestigious research universities, simultaneously, regional markets compete within for local talent, or may "open" recruitment to national and even international candidates (Kulis et al., 2000). In the institutional paradigm, human capital is formed from graduate training and discipline cultures which create "desired" candidate characteristics (Blau, 1973; Jencks & Reisman, 1968). At the same time, the cultures of academic disciplines influence and shape status hierarchies in conformity with traditional academic programs and university expectations. Thus, personnel decisions ranging from the development of recruitment criteria to interpretation and ranking of the quality of scholarship or validating a particular degree, frequently reflect these cultures and may bias and screen out less "traditional" scholars. Non-traditional candidates may also fail to embrace the "preferred" research subjects or theories, or may be less aligned with core discipline notables, or may simply not be the "right race or sex" (Blackwell, 1987; Jacobsen & Newman, 1997). Research on the barriers which keep high achieving women students out of science and math teaching careers because of "unfriendly" cultures confirm such effects (Keller, 1985; AAUP Committee W, 1996; Ferber & Nelson, 1993).

Crucial to defining the institutional factors including discipline cultures are assumptions about effects of disciplines which reinforce basic values, norms and traditions which appear benign, but which can produce substantial bias in decisions. Key among impacts are those on recruitment, hiring and tenure. For example, limits to an open market may be achieved by setting up an overall framework, which is skillfully matched to preferred candidates, or simply designed to "weed out" those who do not represent a clear match between candidate characteristics and department preferences, such as the interest of the tenured professorate. Hiring success is enhanced for doctoral students socialized to disciplines as part of the doctoral degree process, or those "introduced" to hiring departments by mentors and supporters. Moreover, as competition becomes more intense, increasingly faculty are even encouraged by departments to "push" colleagues in other institutions to hire their advisees (Kulis et al., 2000; Blau, 1973; Jencks & Reisman, 1968). However, the elite research institution market is limited, subtle in communicating rules and essentially closed. The higher the perceived prestige of the institution, the less likely it is to be "open" to recruits outside a narrow core of "prestige" peer institutions (Kulis et al., 2000).

The advantage of such systems for discipline cultures is that they carry over into the tenure and promotion processes. Well-sponsored junior faculty bring benefits in the form of continued access to research funding, to former mentors, to editors of leading publications, to conferences and panels and ongoing collegial relationships. They help solicit department funds, share the mentoring role easily and generally, are less likely to pose major problems in evaluating performance for tenure and promotion. While lower status institutions tend to be more open, they are still likely to imitate discipline orientations and expectations and in many cases, may duplicate national bidding in regional settings (Kulis et al., 2000). Non-traditional candidates may find themselves as disadvantaged in regional settings as in the national market (Blackwell, 1987). Traditional explanations offered by the research community to explain the gap between doctoral degree achievement rates and the employment experience of African American women have scarcely been influenced by increasing challenges made to bolster the case of White academic women. Traditional theory focused on human capital quality asserted that factors such as work interruption, or lower educational achievements such as academic research output, represented lower productivity and reduced competitive position of women and minorities compared to White male candidates. This traditional approach is increasingly challenged as inadequate to explain the "growing exceptions" of high performance despite violations to the human capital rule, as well as evidence of multiple submarkets within the academic labor market, whether based on discipline criteria, regional preferences, which act as barriers to minorities and women (Bielby & Bielby, 1988; Ferber & Nelson, 1993; Kulis et al., 2000). The hypothesis that women make poor choices in electing personal life style (i.e. work interruption, family) over the male pattern of career paths, has been challenged as a model of rational or economic choice which inevitably costs women and institutions in the form of reduced output (Drago & Williams, 2000; Williams, 1999). Other research on productivity has generated similar results in challenging the idea that minorities and women are less productive and are poorer performers than men (Bielby & Bielby, 1988; Ferber & Nelson, 1993; Merritt & Reskin, 1997). Irrespective of causes, women and minorities continue to have limited access to faculty positions, particularly in top universities.

3. AFRICAN AMERICAN WOMEN FACULTY: GAINS OR LOSSES

The history of African American women in university teaching shows a long and arduous struggle. As part of the small African American faculty pool, African American women were historically restricted to employment in a small number of segregated institutions and within this market, further subordinated to the preferences of hiring institutions for African American male faculty (Shaw, 1996; Bowles, 1923; Cooper, 1891). College teaching was limited to teaching "women's courses" in domestic science or occasionally specialty courses such as music and languages and typically in non-tenured lecturer or adjunct positions. A key barrier, lifted completely only in the 1970s, was access to most doctoral and professional programs. Until the 1960s, African American women were tracked and strongly "encouraged" to pursue graduate education only in applied fields such as education (Berry, 1996). These factors cumulatively along with perceptions of discrimination in the higher education job market, may explain why so few African American women ventured outside of traditional 'African American women's" fields. This is true despite a recent trend by young African American women to concentrate in more diverse fields at the baccalaureate level (Trent, 1991; U.S. Department of Education, 1992).[1]

The number of African American women obtaining doctorate degrees grew rapidly during the 1980s, expanding by 26 percent between 1976 and 1990 to reach nearly 2 percent of total doctorates awarded and 62.2 percent of those awarded African Americans. But hiring and promotion rates of African American female faculty remained flat and even declined during the period. By 1995, the proportion of African American women faculty in U.S. higher education institutions reached only slightly more than one percent. This understates the proportion of African American women in the recruitment pool as well as the impact that may be felt in African American student–faculty ratios and in professional contributions to research. The relative underdevelopment of human capital in both minority and female doctoral pools translates into a low presence of minorities and women in many disciplines and in reduced rewards from less competitive fields where there are larger doctoral pools (Blau & Ferber, 1986; Anastasia & Miller, 1998; Committee on Science, Engineering and Public Policy, 2006).

The low presence of African American women on college and university faculties is usually explained by one or more of three main causes: (1) a small recruitment pool; (2) over-concentration of African American women in low-demand fields and disciplines; and (3) perception by African American women of limited access or poor treatment in higher demand, non-traditional disciplines such as the sciences and business. The small size of the African American female doctoral pool corresponds to the recent entry of African American women into college teaching careers. Other reasons are the attrition rate from undergraduate through doctoral study. While there have been impressive gains in college enrollments for African American women, this has yet to translate into an increase in graduate training rates similar to other minority women (Trent, 1991). During the mid-1990s, for example, African Americans of both genders made up 12 percent of the total population, 11 percent of the labor force, and 10 percent of full time undergraduates. But because of attrition, African Americans made up only 4 percent of graduate student enrollments. This graduate enrollment figure further contracted to 3 percent of doctoral degree completions in 1989–1990 (U.S. Department of Education, 1992). In addition, completion of doctorate degrees by African Americans dropped dramatically in the 1980s following declines in college completion by African American males. The dramatic 22 percent drop in undergraduate enrollments was almost entirely due to the 44 percent drop off by African American men. This change was soon felt in a reduction in African American graduate enrollments from 4.2 percent in 1972 to 4 percent by 1984. While some improvement was felt in an increase in total doctorates earned by African Americans from 3 to 3.7 percent between 1989–1990 and 1997–1998, this gain was accounted for almost entirely by the growth in doctorates earned by African American women (Kulis et al., 2000). Thus, African American women made up 62 percent of graduate student enrollments and 52 percent of doctoral completions in 1989–1990, a better outcome than that of African American men, but worse than that of White women and other women of color. For example, while African American women earned a majority of graduate, professional and doctoral degrees earned by African Americans, they earned fewer doctorate degrees than Asian Pacific women and lagged behind White women in percentage gains in doctoral degrees completed in the 1970s. Thus, in the period from 1976–1977 to 1989–1990, the number of doctoral degrees awarded African American women increased 26.7 percent, compared to gains of 57 percent by White women and actual declines by African American men and White men of 30.4 and 25 percent, respectively (U.S. Department of Education, 1992). By the academic year 1989–1990, African American women surpassed African American men in total doctoral degrees earned, with 612 completed compared to 566 by African American men (U.S. Department of Education, 1992). The shift to a mostly female faculty recruitment pool helped stabilize size of the African American doctoral pool. However to date, this size gain did not translate into changes in faculty recruitment patterns. In other words, African American women are still less likely to be recruited than other populations for faculty positions.

The second likely cause for the lack of African American women faculty is the distribution of African American women across field disciplines, particularly their disproportionate concentration in a few, low-demand fields. African American women made modest gains in diversification into less traditional fields and disciplines in the past decades, but an exaggerated concentration still remains in education programs. This is somewhat contradictory, since at the undergraduate level, African American women are more likely than White women to venture into non-traditional fields, including computer science and business management. Table 1 indicates the comparative field distribution of African American women undergraduates for 2003–2004.

Table 1. Bachelor's Degrees Conferred by Title IV Institutions, by Selected Race/Ethnicity, Selected Field of Study, and Gender: United States, Academic Year 2003–2004 (%).

Field of Study	White Men	Black Men	White Women	Black Women
Agriculture, agriculture operations, and related sciences	1.51	0.50	1.03	0.33
Architecture and related services	0.89	0.50	0.47	0.20
Biological and biomedical sciences	3.83	3.06	4.55	4.37
Business, management, marketing, and related support services	25.05	27.06	17.07	24.14
Communication, journalism, and related programs	4.47	4.84	6.22	5.20
Computer and information sciences and support services	6.08	8.46	1.09	3.37
Education	4.43	3.64	12.63	5.73
Engineering	8.15	5.19	1.37	1.36
Health professions and related clinical sciences	1.62	2.37	8.44	8.65
Liberal arts and sciences, general studies, and humanities	2.20	3.40	3.21	4.17
Mathematics and statistics	1.22	0.79	0.78	0.53
Physical sciences	1.90	0.95	0.94	0.76
Psychology	3.04	3.85	8.00	8.47
Social sciences	9.29	9.69	7.26	9.06
Visual and performing arts	5.09	4.00	6.25	2.67

Source: U.S. Department of Education (2004). National Center for Education Statistics, Integrated Postsecondary Education Data System (IPEDS): Fall, 2004.

With regard to doctoral degrees, data from the U.S. Department of Education for 2003–2004, indicate that nearly half or 42.5 percent of total doctoral degrees awarded African American women were in the field of education (U.S. Department of Education, 2004). While representing a decline from the rate of over 60 per cent in the 1970s, this single concentration clearly competes with more field diversity for African American women. Changes in fields by African American women are reflected in current trends in doctoral field distribution and in the undergraduate pipeline. As Table 2 indicates, earned PhDs by African American women in the sciences were significant in 2003–2004, but as is the case with women generally, social science fields, the life and health sciences dominated clearly over physical sciences and engineering. Thus, while African American women are still underrepresented in physical sciences, mathematics and engineering and in some interdisciplinary growth areas such as environmental science, urban planning and public policy, these trends point up visible gains in field diversification.

A key problem to field diversification for African American women is maintaining the diversification at the undergraduate levels into graduate programs. Data on undergraduate majors indicate that African American women who major in science and mathematics do not continue at the same rate into doctoral programs. Enrollment patterns of professional and master's degrees indicates that African American women may choose to enter programs which offer vocationally oriented graduate degrees such as health services, MBAs or enter medical or law degree programs. Thus, even more than is the case with African American men, African American women appear less attracted to faculty and research career paths than professional and managerial careers now open to them. At the same time, it is also important to note that contrary to many myths, African American women are not less likely to complete rigorous courses as evidenced by their specializations at both undergraduate and professional degree levels. Other stumbling blocks may reduce their ability to choose doctoral education, including adequate information about teaching and research careers, the presence or absence of likely mentors or role models, or the perception that there is more discrimination in doctoral programs and in employment once degrees are obtained. This is a subject which should be further pursued.

The intersection of gender and race is a unique problem confronting African American women and other women of color which in labor force terms, asks the nature of advantage or disadvantage in career payoffs. The question of how these dual characteristics are treated, has received only limited attention in research to date, owing in part to the absence of data for

Table 2. Doctoral Degrees Conferred by Title IV Degree-Granting
Postsecondary Institutions, by Race/Ethnicity, Selected Field of Study
and Gender: United States Academic Year 2003–2004 (%).

Field of Study and Gender	White	Black
Agriculture, agriculture operations, and related sciences		
Men	1.64	0.95
Women	0.66	0.22
Architecture and related services		
Men	0.25	0.42
Women	0.24	0.17
Biological and biomedical sciences		
Men	12.21	6.97
Women	9.85	4.95
Business, management, marketing, and related support services		
Men	2.98	5.17
Women	1.50	2.70
Communication, journalism, and related programs		
Men	0.85	0.42
Women	0.94	1.35
Computer and information sciences and support services		
Men	1.89	1.48
Women	0.51	0.22
Education		
Men	12.30	31.26
Women	21.33	42.52
Engineering		
Men	10.24	6.86
Women	2.43	1.80
English language and literature/letters		
Men	2.83	1.80
Women	3.78	2.42
Health professions and related clinical sciences		
Men	6.00	4.22
Women	15.79	8.72
Liberal arts and sciences, general studies, and humanities		
Men	0.22	0.11
Women	0.31	0.17
Mathematics and statistics		
Men	2.13	0.74
Women	0.84	0.06

Table 2. (*Continued*)

Field of Study and Gender	White	Black
Physical sciences		
Men	10.23	3.91
Women	3.61	1.69
Psychology		
Men	8.90	6.65
Women	16.95	14.45
Social sciences		
Men	6.69	5.81
Women	5.28	4.27
Visual and performing arts		
Men	3.00	1.27
Women	3.04	0.84

Source: U.S. Department of Education (2004). National Center for Education Statistics, Integrated Postsecondary Education Data System (IPEDS): Fall, 2004.

rigorous study, and in part to the lack of a good theoretical framework which might permit consideration of female labor more holistically (Burbridge, 1997). For unexplained reasons, government data-collecting agencies have been reluctant to over sample or target special research initiatives to examine minority women's work and career experience, or better understand their role in technical, professional and managerial roles.[2]

Several studies of African American women in the workplace have examined a variety of factors which might explain to varying degrees, how race and gender may operate jointly to pose a "dual disadvantage" in economic status. Some important work centers on the phenomena, which Bergmann called "crowding" or high concentrations of women in certain categories of occupations. Accordingly, crowding is defined as a higher proportion of employment in an occupation than the proportion of total employment in all occupations, which may increase competition and suppress wages (Bergmann, 1974). While African American women's employment was historically restricted by sanctioned discrimination, more recently despite an end to bias, statistical trends show a re-concentration of African American women in a narrow range of newer White collar and service occupations, with relatively low pay and restricted mobility (King, 1992; Malveaux, 1982). In examining overall improvements in the labor market status of African American women, researchers found gains which were

partly off-set by new forms of stratification into jobs with marginal status
(Bergmann, 1974; Malveaux, 1982). The counterpart to market stratification
in academic fields may be concentrations in field specializations (AAUP
Committee W, 1996). Other research on race and gender interface has focused on differences in work-family roles assumed by African American
women, which contrasts substantially with that of White women. Wallace
(1980) noted the very distinct role and market position of middle class
African American married women in raising African American household
income through market work. As Burbridge (1997) has noted, the family-
work roles of African American women demand a contrasting approach to
the usual study of White women, because the link between work and family
income is so strong.

Other research has served to document still other sides of the race-gender
interface sometimes postulating a job sub-stratification of African American
women. Sokoloff (1992) examined race and gender inequalities among
White and African American women in the professions and noted a need for
structural analyses to determine why different groups are affected differently
by race and gender. In the same vein, Woody's (1992) analysis focused on
the phenomena of relative concentrations in industrial sectors with the rapid
expansion of new services in the 1970s. This analysis found that the combination of marginal labor force status of African American women and
rapid job growth in sectors such as retailing, services and White-collar industry could easily force African American women into increasingly stratified employment. This was true even in quasi-professional occupations such
as those in health care and education. The resulting subcultures of the new
work were found to be short lived with high turnover and generally isolated
from mainstream job mobility (Woody, 1992). In additional to "crowding"
and hiring into newer marginal jobs, the "race-gender" problem may also
have spawned a sector discrimination problem where African American
women experience a high dependency on government and nonprofit sectors
for employment. This was the conclusion of Burbridge (1997) in suggesting
that African American women are highly dependent on "third sector" government and nonprofit organizations compared to other populations. While
such employment has contributed to an improved employment status of
African American women, compensation and mobility may be undercut by
such reduced choices in a limited set of market opportunities. Research by
Power and Rosenberg (1997) further confirmed this in findings that improved services jobs by African American women did not translate into job
mobility at the same rate experienced by White women. In addition, a discussion of Black women in the academy indicates that they experience more

stress than their male counterparts (Black Issues in Higher Education, 2005). Finally, remedies such as affirmative action, contrary to myth of "dual advantage" have been generally found to have more positive effects on White women and minority men than minority women (Kulis & Miller, 1988; Bradley, 2005).

Research on the psychological impacts of dual discrimination of race and sex provides an additional path for assessing how and why African American women, particularly in professional and academic positions, may face unique pressures and strains related to the dual "race-gender" interface in work which is less routine, more intellectual content based, and where success is externally measured on less widely agreed rules (Thompson & Dey, 1998). While dual discrimination effects themselves have yet to be fully understood, research on African American women professionals has examined the impacts on psychological adjustment and gender conflict. Brown and Keith (2003) work documented mental health impacts of professional work on African American women and found stress levels key in maintaining performance. Thompson and Dey (1998) measured stress levels using a statistical sample of male and female African American faculty and found high stress levels directly associated with what they term "multi-marginality" of being "underrepresented by race, scholarly agenda and the larger academic and social communities". Their research concluded that while both sexes scored high on dimensions of stress experienced, African American women faculty in universities and four year colleges experienced greater levels of stress in all areas and significantly more pressure in two areas, time constraints and promotion concerns.

African American feminists, relying on similar indicators have found that complex factors shape African American women's efforts and may influence discouragement or conflict. These factors relate on one hand to the elevation of African American males as symbolic of African American status by White society, while these same forces maintain a myth that African American women's roles are almost exclusively in domestic and community settings (Sanchez-Hucles, 1997; Kennelly, Misra, & Karides, 1999). This kind of environment is described by Gilkes (2001) in her analysis of complexity of African American women seeking leadership roles in African American community work and in the church.

Once legal barriers were dropped beginning in the 1960s, enough gains were made by women to change the characteristics of the doctoral pool. This diversification however, did not translate into expanded hiring and promotions for women and minorities as would be predicted by the traditional human capital model (Fosu, 1992; Hayes, 1990; Johnsrud & Jarlais, 1994;

AAUP Committee W, 1996; Vetter, 1994). Instead, a long slow process ensued underscored by the ebb and flow of affirmative action politics, rarely reaching the objective "meritocracy" model.

In responding to the lack of market response to changes in the quality of human capital, research on women faculty increasingly found that qualifications which accumulate along the way to shape achievement, such as traditional productivity, are more likely to determine faculty status than traditionally defined human capital such as educational achievement, research participation or other experience (AAUP Committee W, 1996). Such productivity indicators include formal output such as research grants, publications in scientific journals, academic conference papers and offices held in professional organizations and on prestigious committees. Such formal output, however, is achieved not by faculty status, but by informal means such as mentoring, network contacts and research connections (AAUP Committee W, 1996; Ferber & Nelson, 1993).

For women, research suggests other types of barriers, including traditional norms and rules governing secret committee votes, and informal, but stable cultural artifacts unrelated to actual productivity as well as personal attitudes and behavior of individual participants in personnel decisions (Magner, 1996). Some research found that otherwise qualified women were systematically barred from access to tenure track appointments or hobbled from earning tenure (Sarkees & McGlen, 1999). Finally, by the 1990s, after two decades of improvement in the status of women and minorities, a growing academic "backlash" similar to that of general employment, challenged academic affirmative action programs as "reverse discrimination" against White male academics (Kennelly et al., 1999).

4. THE HIRING EXPERIENCE OF AFRICAN AMERICAN WOMEN FACULTY

According to the U.S. Department of Education data, African American women made up 2.6 percent of higher education faculty of all institutional types in 2003–2004. This represented about 6.8 percent of all women faculty, and around 50.9 percent of total African American faculty. Hiring patterns are difficult to assess because of the lack of available data.

Data are also limited to examine the extent to which African American women have lost or gained in annual faculty hires over time, but U.S. Department of Education statistics for 1992 show that African American women represented 7 percent of senior female faculty and 7.2 percent of new female faculty hires. Although this pattern is better than the case of White female faculty who hold 87.3 percent of senior female faculty positions, but only 84.1 percent of new female faculty hires, hiring rates for African American females lag substantially behind African American men who represent 3.6 percent of senior male faculty, but 4.6 percent of new male hires (U.S. Department of Education, 1998). Employment of African American women faculty has proved more difficult in doctoral and research institutions than for other populations, particularly White women and African American men. African American women are likely to be hired in less prestigious two and four year institutions than others as well as in positions off tenure tracks and/or part time or temporary and in non-academic settings, particularly government (National Science Foundation, 2000). Despite competitive credentials, including degrees from prestigious institutions, African American women are far less likely to be recruited by similar institutions, contributing further to poor career prospects (Hayes, 1990; Johnsrud & Jarlis,1994; Long, Allison, & McGonnis,,1993; Moses, 1989).

5. INSTITUTIONAL AND DEPARTMENT DISTRIBUTION OF AFRICAN AMERICAN WOMEN FACULTY

Increasing the number of African American women faculty requires two key changes: First, increased work in traditional academic disciplines and research activities and second, more aggressive hiring by prestigious doctoral and research institutions. Discipline changes are in part dependent on choices of individual African American women themselves. Creating a stronger presence of African American women in more prestigious institutions must be undertaken by university efforts. Such hiring, however, is key to legitimizing African American women as scholars and reducing stereotypical views that African American women are weak performers (Kennelly et al., 1999; Bowen & Bok, 1998). As the 1996 AAUP Committee W study noted, research is crucial to careers in science and almost always involves negotiating support. Persons with the most promise to get external funding are generally favored in the faculty appointments process. The more highly ranked research institutions offer important visibility and play influential roles in setting research agendas, which in turn provide informal support for young scholars.

Evidence is limited on the distribution of African American women faculty in research and doctoral institutions by discipline, but there are indications that a disproportionally high concentration of African American female faculty are employed in two and four year colleges where teaching is a principal activity and support for research is limited (Moses, 1989). The 1993 U.S. Department of Education study of post secondary faculty further supports the view that African American women are less likely than African American men, White women or White men to be employed in doctoral and research institutions.

Additional preliminary data collected by the investigators through the Association of Black Sociologists (ABS) suggest that when African American women faculty are employed at doctoral and research institutions, they are likely to have appointments in African American Studies, Ethnic Studies, Women's Studies and other interdisciplinary departments. Many hold joint appointments between interdisciplinary programs and more traditional social and behavioral science departments (American Sociological Association, 1990). Interdisciplinary and joint appointments however, may limit the visibility of African American women in traditional areas of scholarship, including research activities and publications. The most respected academic research publications are primarily based in traditional disciplines. Less established interdisciplinary departments such as Afro-American Studies and Women's Studies, and joint appointments between disciplines may force African American women faculty into administrative and disciplinary conflicts, and cause problems in decisions on tenure and promotion.

Whether the hiring institution is a two or four year college, or a doctoral university will play a significant role in the progress of African American women in academia. Prestigious universities and departments dominate the awarding of research grants from leading government and private sources. This in turn increases the likelihood of publications in well-respected journals as well as enhances the national visibility and status of individual faculty. The rates of hiring African American males and White females by top institutions accelerated beginning in the 1970s, but two decades later failed to increase the number of African American women hired when the doctoral pool changed mainly from male to female (U.S. Department of Education, 1992).

Efforts by African American women to diversify specializations beginning in the 1970s did not easily translate into "mainstream" research and teaching job placements (U.S. Department of Education National Center for Educational Statistics, 1997). This has proved a particularly serious problem for African American women in the social and behavioral sciences. The

National Science Foundation Report on *Women, Minorities and Persons with Disabilities in Science and Engineering* citing 1989–1990 data noted that African American women had a mixed record in tenure track appointments. Overall, African American women with doctorates in all fields were more likely (68 percent) to be in tenure track positions (either already tenured or waiting for tenure) than were White women (58 percent) or Asian women (42 percent) (National Science Foundation, 1992). But in the social sciences where doctoral growth has been strongest, African American women faculty were more likely to be untenured at the assistant professor level (35 percent) compared to 28 percent of White women and 27 percent of Asian women (National Science Foundation, 1992). Table 3 corroborates these differences, although these data were not reported with specialization breakdown or for the type of institution, particularly doctoral and research institutions.

Productivity is a crucial issue in the tenure process because the output of faculty is assumed to be a primary factor in promotion and compensation. Research productivity is generally measured in terms of research appointments, presentations of papers at key discipline and professional conferences, publications in top ranked, peer reviewed journals, publication of books at prestigious presses, the receipt of research grants and serving on scientific committees and grant review bodies. The standard measure of faculty productivity, research and publications, however has not been studied extensively in the case of African Americans. One study of economics departments compared output in the number of students eventually obtaining PhDs against department faculty performance in publications in leading journals (Agesa, Granger, & Price, 1998). The researchers found that a few departments dominated and these were likely to have PhD programs, suggesting that economics undergraduates were more likely to pursue and complete a doctorate in economics if it were offered in the same institution where scholarship by African American faculty was high (Agesa et al., 1998). There is little conclusive research on how productivity in research and publications, the standard measures of faculty productivity, however, is actually rewarded in faculty status or compensation.

In the case of African American women, there is little evidence available on how research productivity shapes careers, or on the level of output in scholarly work. Evidence which is available indicates that African American women have problems in gaining access both to academic research appointments and to standard research grant support, which may be reflected in relatively low publications and professional organization participation. In the case of research appointments, African American women fair worse than other populations. Data from the National Science Doctoral Survey,

Table 3. Full-Time Instructional Faculty in Degree-Granting
Institutions, by Race, Academic Rank, and Gender (Fall, 2003).

Academic Rank	Total	Black	White
Professor			
Men	127,049	3,427	110,561
Women	39,366	1,916	34,363
Associate professor			
Men	82,758	3,863	67,479
Women	50,203	3,341	41,816
Assistant professor			
Men	83,564	4,276	60,166
Women	69,500	5,188	52,754
Instructor			
Men	44,984	2,809	35,474
Women	48,039	3,942	37,780
Lecturer			
Men	11,175	570	8,778
Women	12,273	629	9,695
Other			
Men	33,278	1,325	24,628
Women	29,407	1,851	22,954
All ranks			
Men	382,808	16,270	307,104
Women	248,788	16,867	199,362

Source: U.S. Department of Education, National Center for Education Statistics (2003),
Integrated Postsecondary Education Data System (IPEDS): Winter, 2003–2004. (This table was
prepared March 2005.)Available: http://nces.ed.gov/programs/digest/d04/tables/dt04_228.asp
Accessed 9/11/06. Also at http://chronicle.com/weekly/almanac/2006/nation/0102602.htm
Note: Excluded from the table are the numbers for other race/ethnic groups.

for example, indicate that of full time faculty, the percentage of time African
American faculty who engaged in research only (i.e. not teaching) was
equivalent to 0.7 percent, compared to 1.6 percent for Whites and 6.6 percent for Asian Pacific Islanders. Furthermore, only 1.4 percent of African
American women were engaged in research compared to 2 percent of
African American men (National Science Foundation, 1999). Available data
indicate that few government research grants have been awarded African
American women investigators (National Science Foundation, 2000). A
listing of NSF grants received by African American scholars over the past

five years obtained by the authors show only five of hundreds of grants were received by African American women and only three were awarded in social and behavioral sciences (National Science Foundation, 2000). Finally, while imperfect, a preliminary literature review by the authors of this paper turned up few authored studies and publications, editorial board participation and professional organization section or committee chairs by African American scholars in the social sciences in general, or African American women in particular.

At least one rigorous study undertaken by Merritt and Reskin (1997) was based on detailed data to explore the influence of departments – in this case law faculties – on faculty appointments and promotions examined and compared the status of African American women faculty to other populations. The findings documented differential treatment in law faculty appointments of African American women particularly compared to African American men. After controlling for productivity in research and publications and other faculty responsibilities, African American women were found to have fewer tenure track appointments, and suffer lower status titles and tenure compared to African American males, despite evidence of higher performance in research and publications (Merritt & Reskin, 1997). The authors conclude that the selection process itself, not objective performance criteria, left African American women underutilized on law faculty.[3]

Barriers to career progress of African American women academics in research institutions include a number of indirect and direct factors. Overt racial and gender discrimination have faded, but more subtle discrimination constituting what women call the "chilly atmosphere" in the university are as devastating and may be on the increase. Causes of the chilly atmosphere range from the lack of senior faculty mentors to an environment which discourages research on women or feminist perspectives to blatant "passes and inappropriate sexual behavior". As recently noted, mentors are particularly critical to advancement in higher education careers, but White males, the dominant senior faculty, are far less likely to take risks to mentor women (Sarkees & McGlen, 1999). In part, this may be to avoid the appearance of sexual relations, but as well it may reflect the desire to "keep the department a men's club". As pointed out by the American Sociological Association's Committee on the Status of Women in Sociology (1990), socialization into prevailing norms and values regarding research publications, grants and teaching and other professional activities are important to undercut misconceptions regarding expectations for research productivity, tenure and promotion. Second, academic research success requires participation in established networks of disciplines, including attending professional meetings, participating on committees, becoming familiar with leading trends and issues and having colleagues to review and discuss manuscripts and grant proposals. Most importantly, collaborators on grants and publications figure increasingly in productivity in social sciences as well as in physical and life sciences. Finally, African American women may be handicapped in participation in many external professional activities or in developing collaborative relationships by the demands made on them because they are African Americans. Such demands, which have little bearing on tenure and promotion include adding diversity to university committees, providing community services and playing extra-advisory roles to minority and women students.

Other more recent problems may reflect new circumstances related to the decline in African American males in the faculty recruitment pool. There is limited but growing evidence, that academic institutions are increasingly likely to hire males of African or Caribbean background than fill positions with African American women. National Science Foundation data, report that a higher percentage of employed African American male doctoral scientists is composed of non-U.S. born individuals than is the case with African American women, White men or women or other minorities (National Science Foundation, 1998).[4] For some observers, this suggests that institutions may deliberately seek and prioritize hiring of males, whether African American or those of African or Caribbean origin, passing over equally qualified African American women.

In the case of African American males other phenomena, a "competitive bidding process" by mainly White institutions may contribute to the problem of decreased attention to African American female scholars. Given the growing scarcity of African American male scholars, a "star" system may be created wherein a few leading African American male scholars dominate the idea of an "African American scholar". The concept is not unique to African Americans, but to the extent that high-prestige universities indulge in elevating African American male scholars to star status, limits are placed on attention to the contributions of African American women. The trend may also be supported by the success of the collegial networks among African American men which are effective in undercutting the isolation and racial barriers of individual institutions. This added to the higher visibility of African American men nationally in the media, politics and sports, acts to reinforce the invisibility of and negative image associated with African American women. Participants in a national conference on African American women in academia noted that the lack of a presence of African American women in academia results in a skewing of African

American Studies departments and scholarship toward male dominated views of African American cultural life and achievement (Collison, 1999). This trend, added to the recent practice noted above of recruiting foreign Black males from Africa and the Caribbean to "fill the African American male gap" caused by declines in native born African American male PhDs, has added to the complexity of discrimination faced by African American women faculty.

Little data exist examining the impact of the presence of African American women faculty in university and departmental cultures, African American student enrollment, performance and completion as well as on female students and other issues. A few researchers have explored the relationship between the presence of African American faculty and African American student academic performance. Without distinguishing possible male–female differences, Blackwell's (1987) study of factors contributing to African American student performance in a sample of professional and graduate programs, found high correlations between success and a presence of African American faculty. Another study using data from the National Study of African American College Students, however, found more mixed results (Braddock & Trent, 1991). These researchers suggested that preparation and commitment of students were the more important determination of program completion rates by African American students. Neither study directly tested the impact of African American female faculty on the presence or performance of African American students of either sex, however. It is highly likely that African American faculty, particularly women, can provide more appropriate role models and mentors for young African American women. The impact may be complex, but it is a combination of symbolic value, practical support and reinforcement particularly of doctoral research by African American women where questions raised are likely to differ substantially from those traditionally asked by White researchers. Experience further suggests that as African American women faculty increase in numbers, women student increases tend to follow (Vetter, 1994; Rayman & Brett, 1993).

6. CONCLUSION: CAN AFRICAN AMERICAN WOMEN CRACK THE ACADEMIC GLASS CEILING?

African American women have encountered both opportunity and obstacles in a long road to equal opportunity in academic careers. Although, beginning in the 1970s, African American women made rapid gains in completing doctoral degrees at the nation's most prestigious institutions, the payoff in faculty appointments has been less than stellar compared to other populations, particularly African American males who despite contractions in completion of doctoral degrees continue to dominate the high-prestige appointments of African Americans in U.S. doctoral and research institutions. The recent trend of recruiting foreign "Black males", further contributes to discrimination against African American women. American universities appear to have skirted the issue of affirmative action for African American women doctorate holders. This pattern contrasts with the case of White women who have been aggressively recruited and hired during the same period since passage of the Civil Rights Acts of the 1960s. One negative outcome, visible in the social sciences where African American women made the most impressive gains in completing doctorates, is the poor experience on the hiring and promotion front. Until special efforts are made to recruit and hire African American women doctoral degree holders, the African American presence on teaching faculties and in research of influence can be expected to continue to decline. The cost of the glass ceiling is high. The continuing lack or miniscule presence of African American women scholars in doctoral and research universities translates into opportunity costs in research, both theoretical and applied in social sciences. When African American women scholars are not included in meaningful numbers, it remains to be seen how a meaningful discourse on racial inequalities and the role and future of the African American community can proceed and inform serious debate? For these reasons, it is important that the university and research community wage an aggressive effort to increase the presence of African American women faculty in America's influential institutions to assure that payoffs for their efforts are comparable to those earned by African American men, White women and White men.

NOTES

1. According to the U.S. Department of Education's Integrated Postsecondary Educational Data Systems (IPEDS), in 1989–1990, African American females earned 61.9 percent of undergraduate degrees awarded African Americans. The distribution included 29.9 percent in business and management; 9.7 percent in health sciences; 5.6 percent in science and mathematics; 3.3 percent in computer science/information services and 1.8 percent in engineering. This compares to 8.5 percent in education.

2. The authors have been substantially frustrated by the current lack of easy access to disaggregated data, which displays minority women including African American women, separately from White women and minority males. At the same

time, contracts are extended to academic researchers who appear less than interested in understanding basic market questions, as well as the nature of bias in higher education institutions, including reporting systems.

3. This is especially troublesome for the potential negative impact on the entry of African American women into academic legal careers at a time when African American female law degree attainment increased from 840 to 956, between 1988–1989 and 1989–1990, compared to a decline from 780 to 762 for African American males during the same two-year period. Source: Table 259, "Completions Survey" (1991) IPEDS, U.S. Department of Education, Washington, DC.

4. According to NSF, of employed doctoral scientists and engineers surveyed in 1997, 58.7 percent of African American males were U.S. natives, compared to 86.5 percent for African American females; 91.5 percent White males and 92.9 percent White females. The highest percentage of non-U.S. citizens were among African American males at 21.2 percent of the total, compared to 4.2 percent for African American females and 3.3 percent White males and 2.7 percent White females. Of this same population, 32.5 percent of African American males were African, compared to 4.4 percent of African American females. Caribbean Blacks comprised 6.7 percent of both African American males and African American females (see National Science Foundation, 1998).

ACKNOWLEDGMENTS

Many thanks to Dr. James Blackwell for his comments and editorial help. The conclusions are our own. Our appreciation is also extended to Sharon Kibwana for her assistance with the data preparation.

REFERENCES

AAUP Committee W. (1996). *Women in Science.* Report of a Subcommittee of Committee W on the Status of Women, Washington, DC.

Agesa, J., Granger, M., & Price, G. N. (1998). Economics research at historically African American colleges and universities: Ranks and effects on the supply of African American economists. *The Review of African American Political Economy, 256*(4), 41.

American Sociological Association, Committee on the Status of Women in Sociology. (1990). *Unique Barriers Women of Color Faculty Encounter in the Academy.* Washington, DC: American Sociological Association.

Anastasia, I., & Miller, M. D. (1998). Sex and gender: A study of university professors. *Sex Roles, 38*(7–8), 675(9).

Berry, M. F. (1996). Why it is under attack. In: G. E. Curry (Ed.), *The affirmative action debate.* Reading, MA: Addison-Wesley Publications.

Bergmann, B. (1974). Occupational segregation, wages and profits when employer discriminate by race or sex. *Eastern Economic Journal, 1*(2), 103–110.

Bielby, D. D., & Bielby, W. T. (1988). She works hard for the money: Household responsibilities and the allocation of work effort. *American Journal of Sociology, 93,* 1031–1059.

Black Issues in Higher Education. (2005). Study finds women faculty experience more stress than men in higher education. *Black Issues in Higher Education, 22*(3), 2.
Blackwell, J. E. (1987). *Mainstreaming Outsiders: The production of African American professionals* (2nd edition). Dix Hills, NY: General Hall.
Blau, F., & Ferber, M. A. (1986). *The economics of women, men and work.* Englewood Cliffs, NJ: Prentice-Hall.
Blau, P. M. (1973). *The organization of academic work.* New York: Wiley.
Bowen, W. G., & Bok, D. in collaboration with Shulman, J. L., Nygren, T. I., Dale, S. B. & Meserve, L. A. (1998). *The shape of the river: Long term consequences of considering race in college and university admissions.* Princeton, NJ: Princeton University Press.
Bowles, E. D. (1923). Opportunities for educated colored women. In: E. L. Ihne, (Ed.), *African American women in higher education* (pp. 107–108). New York: Garland Publishing (1992).
Braddock, J. H., & Trent, W. (1991). Correlates of academic performance among black graduate students on racially different campuses. In: W. Allen, E. Epps & N. Haniff (Eds), *College in black and white: African American students in predominantly white and historically black public universities* (pp. 161–174). Albany, NY: State University of New York Press.
Bradley, C. (2005). The career experiences of African American women faculty: Implications for counselor education programs. *College Student Journal, 39*(3), 518–527.
Brown, D. R., & Keith, V. (2003). The epidemiology of mental disorders and mental health among African American women. In: D. R. Brown & V. M. Keith (Eds), *In and out of our right minds* (pp. 23–58). New York, NY: Columbia University Press.
Burbridge, L.C., (1997). Economics and American African American women. In: T.D. Boston (Ed.), *A different vision: African American economic thought.* (Vol. 1). London, UK: Routledge.
Cooper, A. J. (1891). Higher education for African American women: A justification. In: E. L. Ihne, (Ed.), *African American women in higher education* (pp. 57–60). New York: Garland Publishing (1992) (Excerpted from "The Higher Education of Women", The Southland, April, pp. 199–202).
Collison, M. (1999). Race women stepping forward. *African American Issues in Higher Education, 16*(7), 24.
Committee on Science, Engineering and Public Policy. (2006). *Beyond bias and barriers: Fulfilling the potential of women in academic science and engineering.* Washington, DC: National Academies Press.
Drago, R., & Williams, J. (2000). A half time tenure track proposal. *Change, 32*(6), 46.
Fairweather, J. S. (1995). Myths and realities of academic labor markets. *Economics of Education Review, 14*, 179–192.
Ferber, M. A., & Nelson, J. A. (1993). Introduction: The social construction of economics and the social construction of gender. In: M. A. Ferber & J. A. Nelson (Eds), *Beyond economic man* (pp. 23–37). Chicago: University of Chicago Press.
Fosu, A. K. (1992). Occupational mobility of African American women, 1958–1981: The impact of post 1964 and discrimination measures. *Industrial and Labor Relations Review, 45*(2), 281–294.
Gilkes, C. T. (2001). *If it wasn't for the women...African American women's experience and womanist culture in church and community.* Maryknoll, NY: Orbis Books.
Hayes, M. (1990). Minority women in higher education: Status and challenges. Paper presented at the annual meeting of the comparative and international education society, Anaheim, CA (ERIC Document Reproduction Service No. ED 363 236).

Jacobsen, J. P., & Newman, A. E. (1997). What data do economists use? The case of labor economics and industrial relations. *Feminist Economics, 3*(2), 127–130.

Jencks, C., & Reisman, D. (1968). *The academic revolution.* New York: Doubleday.

Johnsrud, L., & Jarlais, C. (1994). Barriers to tenure for women and minorities. *The Review of Higher Education, 4,* 333–335.

Journal of Blacks in Higher Education. (2006). JBHE completes its count of Black students and faculty at the Nation's flagship state universities. *Journal of Blacks in Higher Education, 51,* 54–59.

Keller, E. F. (1985). *Reflections on gender and science.* New Haven, CT: Yale University Press.

Kennelly, I., Misra, J., & Karides, M. (1999). The historical context of gender, race and class in the academic labor market. *Race, Gender and Class, 6*(3), 125–155.

King, M. C. (1992). Occupational segregation by race and sex, 1940–1988. *Monthly Labor Review, 115*(4), 30–37.

Kulis, S., & Miller, K. A. (1988). Are minority women sociologists in double jeopardy? *The American Sociologist, 19*(4), 323–339.

Kulis, S., Shaw, H., & Chong, Y. (2000). External labor markets and the distribution of African American scientists and engineers in academia. *Journal of Higher Education, 71*(2), 87.

Long, J. S., Allison, P. D., & McGonnis, R. (1993). Rank advancement in academic careers: Sex differences and the effects of productivity. *American Sociological Review, 58,* 703–722.

Magner, D. K. (1996). The new generation. *The Chronicle of Higher Education,* February 2, p. A17.

Malveaux, J. (1982). Recent trends in occupational segregation by race and sex. Paper presented to the committee on women's employment and related social issues, National Academy of Sciences, Washington, DC.

Merritt, D., & Reskin, B. (1997). Sex, race and credentials: The truth about affirmative action in law school hiring. *Columbia University Law School Review, 97*(March), 199–311.

Moses, Y. (1989). *African American women in academe: Issues and strategies.* Report *HE 022* 909, Association of American Colleges, Washington, DC (ERIC Document Reproduction Services, NO ED 311 817).

National Science Foundation. (1998). Employed Doctoral scientists and engineers by demographic characteristics, race/ethnicity, and sex 1997. *Survey of Doctorate Recipients* (p. 55). NSF, Division of Sciences of Science Resources Studies, Washington, DC (Table 33).

National Science Foundation. (1992). *Women, minorities and persons with disabilities in science and engineering.* Arlington, VA: National Science Foundation.

National Science Foundation. (1999). *Characteristics of doctoral scientists and engineers in the United States: 1997.* NSF 00–308, Table 48. Project Officer, Kelly H. Kang. Arlington, VA. Available at: http://www.nsf.gov/statistics/nsf00308/

National Science Foundation. (2000). Data tables provided to authors upon special request.

Power, M., & Rosenberg, S. (1997). Race, class and occupational mobility: African American and White women in service work in the US. *Feminist Economics, 3*(2), 40–59.

Rayman, P., & Brett, B. (1993). *Pathways for women in the sciences.* Wellesley, MA: Wellesley College Center for Research on Women.

Sanchez-Hucles, J. V. (1997). Jeopardy not bonus for African American women in the workforce: Why does the myth of advantage persist. *Journal of Community Psychology, 25*(5), 565(16).

Sarkees, M. R., & McGlen, N. E. (1999). Misdirected backlash: The evolving nature of academia and the status of women in political science. *PS: Political Science and Politics, 32*(1), 100–108.

Shaw, S. J. (1996). *What a woman ought to be and to do*. Chicago: University of Chicago Press.

Sokoloff, N. J. (1992). *African American women and White women in the professions*. New York: Routledge.

Thompson, C. J., & Dey, E. L. (1998). Pushed to the margins: Sources of stress for African American college and university faculty. *Journal of Higher Education, 69*(3), 324(22).

Trent, W.T. (1991). Focus on equity: Race and gender differences in degree attainment 1975–1976; 1980–1981. In: W.R. Allen, E.G. Epps, & N.Z. Haniff, (Eds), *College in African American and White*. Albany: State University of New York Press.

U.S. Department of Education. (2004). Integrated Postsecondary Education Data System (IPEDS): Fall, 2004. Washington, DC: National Center for Educational Statistics.

U.S. Department of Education, National Center for Educational Statistics. (1997). *Instructional faculty and staff in higher education institutions: Fall 1987 and fall 1992*. NCES 97-447, R. J. Kirshstein, N. Matheson and Z. Jing. Available at: http://nces.ed.gov/pubsearch/pubsinfo.asp?pubid=97470

U.S. Department of Education (2004). National Center for Education Statistics, Integrated Postsecondary Education Data System (IPEDS).

Vetter, B. M. (1994). *Women in science, mathematics and engineering: Myths and realities presented at the Sloan conference on women in science, mathematics and engineering*. Wellesley, MA: Wellesley College.

Wallace, P. A. (1980). *African American women in the labor force*. Cambridge, MA: MIT Press.

Williams, J. (1999). *Unbending gender: Why family and work conflict and what to do about it*. London, UK: Oxford University Press.

Woody, B. (1992). *African American women in the workplace*. Westport, CT: Greenwood Press.

PART VI:
CLASS AND RACIAL TRANSFORMATIONS IN AFRICA, THE CARIBBEAN, AND LATIN AMERICA

RECENT TRENDS IN U.S.–AFRICAN RELATIONS: ASSUMPTIONS, CONTEXT AND POLICY IMPERATIVES ☆

L. Adele Jinadu

SOME BASIC ASSUMPTIONS

I want to begin by indicating a number of central assumptions around which we can begin to discuss the relations between the United States of America and African countries in the next millennium.

The Intersection of Foreign Relations and National Interests

My starting point is the timeworn but still popular assumption that international or foreign relations provide a meeting-point for the interplay of the national interests of various state actors or nation states. It is of course problematic how "national interests" is to be defined, discovered, consensus

---

☆ Paper prepared for the special session, "African perspectives on U.S.–African Relations in the New Millennium," at the Fourth African–African-American Summit, Harare, Zimbabwe, 23 July 1997.

The New Black: Alternative Paradigms and Strategies for the 21st Century
Research in Race and Ethnic Relations, Volume 14, 237–264
ISSN: 0195-7449/doi:10.1016/S0195-7449(06)14011-8

achieved over its meaning and content, and pursued as policy. In this sense, "national interest" is a contested concept. It is not immune from the ambiguities and subjectivity which are inherent in contested concepts. Nonetheless, the general assumption is that the pursuit of its national interests is or should be a major objective of a country's foreign policy or relations with other countries.

If we are, therefore, to discuss U.S.–African relations, it may be useful to view such relations from the prism of the dynamic interplay and interface of the national interests of the U.S. and of individual African countries, in such a way that we can talk of the convergence or lack of convergence of such national interests.

In other words, the task before the analyst of U.S.–African relations is to focus on the opportunities, challenges and constraints which the national interests of the United States and individual African countries, as defined and pursued by policy-makers in the U.S. and Africa, impose on U.S.–African relations. Can these national interests be reconciled or managed, such that U.S.–African relations can be justified to and support for them canvassed from the U.S. and African publics, on the ground that they promote or should promote each other's national interests?

I think this will be an important consideration in the evolving U.S.–African relations in the next millennium. This is because developments and changes within the U.S. and Africa and in the world generally, particularly the trend towards globalisation and the hegemonic thrust of neo-liberalism on a world scale, indicate a need for a redefinition of what constitutes "national interests" in the context of U.S.–African relations.

Foreign Relations as a Mirror of Domestic Politics

My second assumption is that U.S.–African relations must be viewed within the background of the domestic politics, or if you like the political economy of the U.S. and of individual African countries. This assumption derives from the hypothesis that a country's foreign relations constitute an extension of its domestic politics, of its structure of governance and of the way economic and political power is organised within it.

It is of course possible that events outside a country's boundaries can and do often influence and shape its domestic politics but in the specific case of the conduct of a country's foreign relations, it is always useful to view it is an extension of its domestic politics. Thus as we focus on the possible direction of U.S.–African relations in the new millennium, we must begin to assess the implications of the changing structure of domestic politics in Africa and the United States for U.S.–African relations.

The Role of Non-State Actors in U.S.–African Relations

My third assumption is that in looking at and projecting U.S.–African relations in the next millennium we should place as much or perhaps more importance on the complementary roles of non-state transnational actors (private sector organisations, individual citizens, civil society institutions, etc.) as we place on state actors. These non-state transnational actors must be cultivated and encouraged because they constitute a potential source that can be co-opted, with radical effect, to promote, strengthen and advance U.S.–African relations, as we begin the new millennium.

Mutuality and Reciprocity as Foundations of U.S.–African Relations

My fourth assumption is that we begin to view U.S.–African relations in terms of a presumed mutuality of respect and reciprocity between the U.S. and individual African countries. This does not necessarily mean upholding a rigid principle of non-interference in each other's affairs, under which gross violations of universally accepted norms of behaviour are or can be committed by governments. But it does mean, particularly on the part of the U.S., and in view of its strategic predominance and power in the world, respect for Africa's independence, acceptance of cultural relativism and the curtailment of imperial reflexes, what the late U.S. Senator William J. Fulbright once characterised in an elegant phrase, as "the arrogance of power."

Building U.S.–African Relations on the Basis of a "Special Relationship"

My fifth assumption is that we must begin to build U.S.–African relations in the new millennium more aggressively on what I prefer to call certain shared similarities between the U.S. and Africa: their shared colonial experience and their common break with colonial rule; the cultural, including ethno-communal and racial pluralism which they share as a fact of political and economic life; and their shared exercise in nation-building as a post-colonial process or project.

In other words, these shared similarities should provide the basis for a new policy of "special relationship" between the U.S. and Africa. This is more so with the significant presence of over 22 million black and African–Americans as a major minority ethno-racial group in the U.S.

This observation acquires more relevance if we take into consideration the historical impact on Africa and on African development of the African Diaspora in the U.S. and the Caribbean, and the equally important accelerating and radicalising impact which the African independence movement, in theory and in practice, had in the decade 1950–1960 on black radical nationalism in the United States. No less important has been the living and lived cultural heritage of Africa in the U.S., in the form of African survivals in music, dance, aesthetics and the arts and religion.

THE CHANGING CONTEXT OF U.S.–AFRICAN RELATIONS

In addition to these assumptions, we need to focus on the changing policy context or environment within which U.S.–African relations will be forged and pursued in the new millennium. The changes in this policy environment will give rise to new challenges, opportunities and problems in U.S.–African relations.

Impact of Globalisation and the End of the Cold War on U.S.–African Relations

The trend towards globalisation and the shift in the structure of world politics from a bipolar or multipolar one to a unipolar one, with the consequential end of the cold war, is an important change that is bound to affect the nature of U.S.–African relations in the new millennium. The satellisation of Africa, which had hitherto in the cold war years characterised external perceptions of Africa should now give way to an informed view among policy-makers in the U.S. of Africa as a global partner in securing peace and security.

As the U.S. government formulates its post-cold war foreign policy objectives and goals, and resists neo-isolationist domestic pressures within the U.S., it becomes imperative, therefore, to use the opportunity to bring Africa to the centre-stage of the U.S. foreign policy process and to review or rethink the cold war era assumptions and expectations which had hitherto shaped U.S. African policy. This review should link a reconfigured U.S.–African relations to an enlightened conception of the mutuality and congruence of U.S. and African national interests, and in doing so reject neo-isolationist arguments that the U.S. should withdraw from Africa or relegate it to the "backburner."

Building U.S.–African Relations on a New Basis

To illustrate the concern with U.S. security and military interests and the containment of communism that tended to inform U.S. African policy during the cold war years might be replaced by concern with issues of democratisation, trade, economic liberalisation and human rights in Africa. These are issues around which to build coalitions of state and non-state transnational actors in Africa and the United States in pursuit of common objectives that are grounded in mutually reinforcing national interests.

From another perspective, it could be that the end of the cold war would see the U.S. playing a more independent role in Africa than it did during the cold war years when, in the light of a multipolar conception of the world, it tended to view Africa as the "sphere of influence" or the "back waters" of its western allies. The approach of the new millennium, coinciding as it does with the end of the cold war period, therefore, provides a good opportunity and a propitious basis for the U.S. to seize the initiative in pursuing an imaginative African policy on the basis of the convergence of U.S. and African national interests.

Changes and Critical Realignments in the Structure of Political Power in the U.S.

Another recent historic change or shift in the policy environment of U.S.–African relations has its source in the structure of domestic politics and the critical realignments of political and socioeconomic forces in the U.S. and in Africa. Let us begin with the U.S., where Congress plays an important role in the formulation and execution of foreign policy.

The 1994 and 1996 congressional elections in the U.S. resulted in the control of both the House of Representatives and the Senate by the Republican Party, in what was in each case a partisan shift to the conservative and fundamentalist right. The implications of this shift for U.S. African Policy are the following:

First, as a rule, Republican Congressmen generally tend to show less interest in Africa than their colleagues in the Democratic Party. Second, the conservative resurgence and control of the U.S. Congress in 1994 and 1996 have combined in their effect to weaken the political strength and influence of the Congressional Black Caucus, which had hitherto used its position within the majority party in the U.S. Congress, the Democratic Party, to advance and promote Africa and African interests in the U.S. Congress.

In other words, with the decline in its political clout within the U.S. Congress, the Congressional Black Caucus, a historically important African constituency within the U.S. Congress, has been weakened. To this must be added the loss through retirement of a number of critical and influential congressmen like Charles Diggs, Mervyn Dymally, Steve Solarz and Howard Wolpe who were successful in placing African issues on the congressional legislative agenda. The congressional leadership of the Black Caucus has now fallen upon Donald Payne who has continued to champion the cause of Africa in the U.S. Congress.

Third, the ideological emphasis of the right-wing Republican majority in the U.S. Congress on reducing the budget deficit, on downsising and on less government is likely to have a negative impact on U.S. aid and technical assistance to Africa, in so far as much if it depends on annual budgetary allocations which require Congressional approval.

The final report of the Ninetieth American Assembly (1997, pp. 5–6) has summed up not only the negative implications of this Republican resurgence and control of the U.S. Congress for U.S. African policy, as the Democratic Party-controlled Executive Branch strategically beats a retreat, but also the concern of the African constituency in the U.S. foreign policy elite groups for the consequences of the retreat, as follows:

> paradoxically, notwithstanding these dramatic developments that present both opportunities and challenges, recent years have witnessed not the expansion of American engagement with Africa, but in effect a retreat from the continent. U.S. policy has been characterised by a dangerous sense of drift. Many embassies and consulates, United States Agency for International Development (USAID) missions and United States Information Agency (USIA) offices have been closed or reduced to a token presence. Assistance levels have fallen to the point that the United States is becoming a minor player compared to other donors. It would be a tragedy if the end of the cold war and the emergence of new African governments that share U.S. values and economic principles were to be met by the withdrawal of the United States from Africa.

Changes in the Structure of Domestic Politics in Africa

Within Africa, no less significant changes have taken place in the domestic policy environment of the various African countries. Firstly, there is the wave of democratisation sweeping through the continent. The impetus for much of this particular change is internal, reflecting popular and grassroots-based demands for empowerment and democratisation, although it is complemented and in some cases encouraged and strengthened by external forces.

Furthermore, this change has shaped the evolving nature of U.S.–African relations. The result, for example, is that democratisation and commitment to market liberalisation by individual African countries now seen to be guiding considerations in determining the quantum of U.S. aid to them. This is clearly reflected in current U.S. aid programmes in Botswana, Ghana, Mali, Namibia, South Africa and Uganda. It is also clearly out spelt in the recent African policy package passed by the U.S. Congress, where democratisation and market liberalisation are put forward as the litmus tests for securing U.S. aid by African countries.

In so far as the democratisation agenda is advanced and demanded by civil society groups in Africa, it also poses a challenge to the U.S. to move beyond a policy of "quiet diplomacy" and moral suasion targeted at recalcitrant African regimes to active support of pro-democracy and opposition groups and the open criticism of and the imposition of sanctions on African regimes, including "friendly" ones that are obdurately resisting democratisation.

This policy thrust is necessarily at the risk of the U.S. being accused by African regimes at the receiving end of such overt "carrot and sticks" policy of supporting "subversive" organisations or of interfering in the internal affairs of their countries. This has been well-illustrated in the face-off in recent years between the U.S. government and the governments of Kenya and Nigeria over the support given to pro-democracy and opposition groups by the U.S. embassies in the two African countries.

The Significance of the New South Africa for Africa

Secondly, the independence of South Africa, coinciding with the end of the cold war era, has opened up a new phase in U.S.–African relations. This is reflected in the change in U.S. policy towards Angola and Mozambique, especially in the decline or cessation of U.S. support to UNITA in Angola; and in U.S.-brokered reconciliation and reform efforts in these two African lusophone countries. As it has turned out, the U.S. seems to be warmly embracing South Africa as a regional power and Nelson Mandela as the model African leader.

The defeat and surrender of apartheid, and the consequential emergence of black majority rule in South Africa, under universal adult suffrage, must be viewed also against the gradual weakening of the political presence and influence of the former colonial powers, France, Great Britain and Portugal, in Africa, and their preoccupation with European unity and the anti-immigration movement in these former imperial powers, which is generally anti-African and anti-Arab. The apparent retreat of the erstwhile imperial powers from Africa is a development which favours a much higher profile U.S. involvement in Africa through political, economic and cultural *links.*

The Salience of Internal Wars in Africa

Thirdly, in spite of the end of the cold war, internal wars in Africa may continue to pose serious threats to U.S. security interests on a global scale and to world peace and security in general. The civil war in Liberia and the ethnic wars in Rwanda, Burundi and Somalia have shown, from the humanitarian point of view, the need for limited or low profile U.S. military presence in peacekeeping activities in African troubled spots.

The lesson of Somalia, particularly its experience there, has made the U.S. wary or hesitant of getting involved militarily in imposing, or in the search for, a solution to internal wars in Africa. In such circumstances, the emerging trend may well be for the U.S. to use African proxies to find solutions to these problems, as in the Liberian civil war and the on-going attempts to bring the new military regime in Sierra Leone to its knees.

The recent policy pronouncement by the U.S. government to provide training and funding for an African Peacekeeping Force, drawn from Ethiopia, Ghana, Malawi, Mali, Senegal, Tunisia and Uganda is reflective of this trend in official U.S. thinking, although the U.S. government has been criticised for bypassing the Organisation of African Unity (OAU).

The Political Significance of Transnational Non-State Actors

I have referred already to the potential positive role of transnational non-state actors in moving U.S.–African relations in new directions, in the next millennium. In both the U.S. and Africa, these non-state actors are now more aggressively seeking to influence policy. It is in this sense that they constitute a critical dimension of the changing policy environment of U.S.–African relations.

Religious groups, professional associations, other civil society groups, private sector voluntary organisations and institutions in the U.S. and Africa are all actively seeking to influence U.S. African policy. They are helping to focus domestic and international attention and pressures on developments in Africa. At the same time, they are also seeking to influence the domestic policies of African regimes, to provide support for African domestic pro-democracy groups, and more importantly to challenge and confront authoritarian regimes, especially in the area of democratic transitions or governance and human rights.

The political significance of these non-state actors is that they are transnational actors who have not only created powerful linkages and networks between the U.S. and Africa but also have vigorously turned critical searchlight on the direction and content of U.S.–African relations. While much of this searchlight is channelled in the U.S. through avenues and processes of mainstream competitive electoral and legislative politics, in the case of Africa the continued closure of the political space, combined with the virtual redundance of legislatures in many countries has meant that much of the effort of these non-state actors is directed towards agitational and confrontational politics outside the political mainstream.

To put it in other words, while the institutionalisation of democratic politics in the U.S. has provided clear channels for the articulation and implementation of domestic and foreign policies, the personalisation or privatisation of political processes in much of Africa by political leaders has not made it easy either to determine where to apply pressure to influence policy, and with what effect, or even to engage in public discussion of policy, especially in the foreign policy area. It is in this respect that non-state actors have stepped in to fill the gap by acting as informal pressure groups to draw attention to inadequacies in the domestic and foreign policy of African governments.

POLICY IMPERATIVES: HUMAN RIGHTS AND DEMOCRACY

Given the assumptions and the policy context set out above, what policy imperatives should underline U.S.–African relations, as we approach the year 2000? What is the African agenda and how should the U.S. respond to it? What is required of African countries, if they are to ensure the salience of such an agenda in U.S. domestic and electoral politics?

Defining the African Agenda as Basis for Structuring U.S.–African Relations

What is the African agenda? If there is indeed an African agenda, it is a response to the economic and political crisis of the African state, reflected in low- and slow-growth rates, rising inflation, huge balance of payment deficits, declining agricultural productivity, food famine, fall in output and services in the productive sectors, political instability and authoritarian tendencies. All of this can be subsumed under the broad category of a crisis of good governance.

The Policy Dimensions of the African Agenda

The broad outline of the African agenda as a response to this crisis of good governance is provided by the Lagos Plan of Action, which was later substantially amended because of neo-liberal-inspired counter pressures from donor countries and the Bretton Woods institutions. The resultant policy document is "Africa's Priority Programme For Economic Recovery" (APPER). At the level of economic integration it has found expression in the African Economic Community Treaty which was formally adopted at the 27th Ordinary Assembly of Heads of State and Government of the OAU in Abuja, Nigeria in June 1991 and which was the subject of an international conference in Abuja in January 1992.

At the level of political liberalisation or democratisation, the African agenda was articulated by various African heads of state and government at the 27th Ordinary Assembly of Heads of State and Government of the OAU, held in June 1991 at Abuja, Nigeria, where the unequivocal case for democratisation and plural politics in Africa was made in the various speeches and addresses. This political aspect of the African agenda also finds much earlier eloquent articulation in the OAU-initiated African Charter on Human and People's Rights, to which virtually all OAU member-states have subscribed.

Recent Development in the Political Dimension of the African Agenda

More recently, at its 1997 Ordinary Assembly of Heads of State and Government, in Harare, Zimbabwe, the OAU for the first time condemned in the strongest terms, the military takeover of government in May 1997 from the democratically elected civilian government in Sierra Leone and called on its member-states to ensure the restoration of the democratically elected civilian government to power in that country. The significance of this development needs emphasis: for, with the end of colonial rule in Africa, marked by the defeat of apartheid and the accession to black majority rule in South Africa, the logic of the OAU's principled opposition to colonial rule and apartheid is now being applied to political developments within independent African countries.

It should be noted that this African agenda has also been put forward, adopted and pursued at the level of African sub-regional functional organisations like the Economic Community of West African States (ECOWAS) and the Southern African Development Coordinating Conference (SADCC). For example, in the Southern African sub-region, swift action a few years back by a consortium of governments in the sub-region led to the restoration of the democratically elected civilian government which had been overthrown in a military coup in Lesotho. In West Africa, ECOWAS is on record for having called on its member-states to ensure the return of the democratically elected civilian government overthrown by the military coup in Sierra Leone to power.

In short, at the level of African regional (continental) and sub-regional organisation, the African agenda for political liberalisation and decompression is now more than ever being actively pushed and promoted while at the same time military rule and unconstitutional or authoritarian rule is under considerable siege, in a marked departure from the earlier practice of inaction and toleration.

The Complementarity of Economic and Political Liberalisation

Broadly conceived the African agenda, in its original form in the Lagos Plan of Action and as adumbrated in the African Economic Community Treaty underscores the complementarity of economic and political liberalisation in charting new developmental paths and options for Africa on the basis of national and collective self-reliance and self-sustaining development. The emphasis is on "seeing development as a task that must involve everyone and every sector, private and public, agriculture and industry, labour, capital and peasantry" (Ake, 1996, pp. 24–25). At one and the same time, the agenda emphasises the primacy of sustainable development, commerce and trade, industrialisation, peace and security, education and culture, and democracy and human rights in moving Africa forward.

Policy Imperatives for U.S. Response to the African Agenda

It is within the parameters provided by this African agenda in its original form in the Lagos Plan of Action and in the African Economic Community Treaty and in the emphasis at the level of African regional (continental) and sub-regional organisations on political liberalisation and decompression that U.S. African policy, as we approach the new millennium, must be formulated and appraised. In other words, the U.S. must be seen to be responding to African initiatives, even as it seeks to pursue its own national interests in Africa. Put differently and in terms of one of the assumptions stated above, the African agenda should provide a meeting point, a conceptual map for the reconciliation of U.S. national interests with those of individual African countries.

In what follows, I shall focus on two aspects of the political component of the African agenda – human rights and democracy – and indicate how they touch upon U.S.–African relations. Let us begin with human rights.

Human Rights and African Politics

The notion of human rights is based on the assumption of a natural law that stipulates that there are certain immutable rights that belong to man qua man and which, in virtue of man's humanity, should be guaranteed to everyone and secured against anyone and the state. According to Maurice Cranston (1973, p. 7) human rights "are not rights which derive from a particular station; they are rights which belong to man simply because he is a man."

In Africa, the rhetoric of human rights was a central plank on which pre-independence agitational nationalist politics rested. The sources from which this aspect of the language of African nationalism sprang were partly U.S. in origin: Jeffersonian, Madisonian and radical Afro-American, although other sources included indigenous African, western and Asian influences.

Postcolonial Africa has witnessed substantial derogation from this human rights heritage in African nationalist thought, particularly in the curtailment of and siege laid on the civil and political rights of individual citizens of African countries by their governments. This development has arisen inspite of the fact that a number of African countries, like Nigeria, have a bill of rights entrenched in their constitutions.

The Collectivist: Cultural and Economic Components of the African Definition of Human Rights

In terms of an African agenda, it must be stated that, apart from the entrenchment of a bill of rights in some African constitutions, the OAU has adopted its own Charter of Human and Peoples' Rights that is binding on its member states. This OAU Charter of Human and Peoples' Rights, like the bill of rights in some African constitutions, goes beyond the liberal definition of human rights as primarily civil and political rights to include cultural, ethno-communal, social and economic rights.

This collectivist extension or definition of human rights is alien to the dominant notion of human rights in the U.S. As a result, U.S. African policy has over the years, but particularly more so under President Jimmy Carter, been preoccupied with human rights as civil and political rights (see Jinadu, 1980, Chapters 3–4). The reason for this has been primarily ideological, deriving from the dominant liberal conservative tradition in American politics.

However, broader U.S. policy concerns with the alleviation of poverty and development assistance sometimes draw on or imply collectivist notions of economic and social rights. In such cases, the justification has tended to be more on humanitarian and solidarity grounds than on the collectivist or social democratic grounds of the economic rights of the poor in African countries.

Articulating and Enforcing Human Rights in U.S. African Policy

In focusing on the enforcement of human rights in Africa, however, successive U.S. administrations have had to moderate their idealism with pragmatism and realism. As Warren Christopher once put it, ... *human rights, while a fundamental factor in our foreign policy, cannot always be the decisive factor* (Quoted in Jinadu, 1980, p. 47).

Considerations that could mitigate and which on occasions had diluted emphasis on human rights in U.S. African policy include the security interests of the U.S., on the one hand, and the welfare of the poor and hungry who should not suffer from or be penalised for the excesses and abuses of their governments, on the other hand. For example, in February 1977, in an appearance before the Senate Appropriations Committee, U.S. Secretary of State Cyrus Vance was categorical in insisting that U.S. aid to South Korea would not be eliminated or suspended, in spite of that country's poor human rights record (Jinadu, 1980, p. 61).

The reason he gave was that the overriding U.S. security interests and commitments in that strategically placed country necessitated such a posture. This was also why for a long time, the U.S. supported the regime of Mobutu in the former Zaire on grounds of U.S. security interests in the region, in spite of gross human rights violations that his regime committed. Another mitigating factor was characterised by Deputy Secretary of State Warren Christopher before the House Foreign Affairs Subcommittee on International Operations, in these words: *economic assistance that directly benefits the needy is rarely disapproved, even to governments with poor human-rights records* (Jinadu, 1980, p. 65).

These two mitigating considerations point to the dilemma that a human rights-oriented U.S. African policy continues to face in the light of rampant violations of the human rights of its peoples by African governments. This is why U.S. governments have also been accused from time to time of inconsistency or of applying double standards in the application and enforcement of their human rights policies in Africa. As the dilemma is likely to persist, the challenge of U.S. African policy in this area, as we approach the new millennium, is for the U.S. government to move towards more consistency and more aggressiveness in enforcing its human rights policy in Africa.

The U.S. Congress, Non-State U.S. Actors and Human Rights in Africa

It should be pointed out, however and in view of the policy context described earlier on, that it is because of this inconsistency in the application of a human rights policy in Africa by the executive branch in the U.S. that initiative in the human rights area has tended from time to time to pass on to the U.S. Congress, where pressure for sanctions against African regimes with poor human rights records is exerted on congressmen by transnational non-state actors. The resultant legislative action has usually taken the form of laws not only requiring that U.S. aid and foreign assistance policy take into account recipient countries' human rights and worker rights performance but also authorising the denial of U.S. aid to and the imposition of sanctions on countries which are adjudged to have committed "gross" human rights and worker rights violations.

This is also why the initiative has, oftentimes, passed to civil society groups in the U.S. in mobilising public opinion to bring pressure to bear on the executive branch and the Congress to penalise African countries guilty of "gross" human rights violations.

All of this presupposes that it is easy to measure human rights violations, assign weights to the human rights scale and to determine who or which regime is culpable. Is there, indeed, an acceptable level of human rights violation? What incentives are to be offered to induce the enforcement of human rights by African governments? How much support and encouragement should the U.S. give to internal dissidents and oppositional elements who are harassed and persecuted for demanding the enforcement of human rights? To what extent should the U.S. distance itself from governments and agencies engaged in the violation of the human rights of their citizens?

Some of these difficulties are reflected in the annual review and report of the human rights situation in countries that receive U.S. foreign assistance and in some other foreign countries, submitted to Congress by the Department of State, as required by the Foreign Assistance Act of 1961 and the Trade Act of 1974, as amended. Under the administration of President Jimmy Carter, an Liter-Agency Committee on Human Rights and Foreign Assistance, whose task is to review, from a specifically human rights perspective, all aspects of U.S. economic and financial assistance to other countries was created.

This institutional innovation in the human-rights area has since been strengthened. For example, the Bureau of Human Rights and Humanitarian Affairs was restructured and replaced in 1994 by a new Bureau of Democracy, Human Rights and Labour, under an Assistant Secretary of State.

The emphasis on human rights in U.S.–African relations has also witnessed the creation of a transnational network of human rights activists and monitors in the U.S. and Africa to highlight human rights abuses in Africa and to canvass for their protection, promotion and enforcement. The activities of this network constitute a desirable complement to the concern and interest of the U.S. and African countries in the human rights area. As we approach the next millennium the activities of these transnational networks will assume more critical levels of importance in U.S.–African relations, especially in providing independent data from those of state bureaucracies and agencies on the human rights situation in Africa, and also in bringing to the top of the policy agenda issues of children's rights, women's rights, worker rights and of the human rights of other marginalised and oppressed sections, like ethnic minorities of African societies.

Targeting Human Rights Violations by the Private Sector and Other Non-Governmental Actors

While the focus on the record of African governments in the human rights area has been a necessary development in U.S.–African relations, there is need, however, as we approach the next millennium, to turn the searchlight also on human rights violations by various civil society groups and the private sector in Africa. It is too readily assumed, and with good reasons, that governments are the only or even major violators of the human rights of their citizens. This itself is a reflection of the highly commandist character of the African state.

Yet, there is need to mount a general public enlightenment campaign on human rights across various strata of African societies. At the level of African civil societies, there are in a number of cases historically deep-rooted cultural, religious and social practices which derogate from the individual human rights of African peoples, especially of children, widows, women and workers. At another level, the deleterious effects of some private sector activities and those of multinational corporations on the enjoyment of human rights by the poorest sectors of African societies have been well-documented, as in the case of oil exploration in Nigeria and in recent international concern with the dumping of waste by multinational companies in Africa.

The giant multinationals, the organised private sector and other non-governmental agencies operating in Africa must be subjected to the same standards of accountability and transparency in the human rights area, as are African state actors. The recent boycott of Shell products in Western Europe, organised by environmental civil society groups, as well as political action against multinational corporations by indigenous communities in affected areas, as in oil exploration in the Delta area of Nigeria, is an illustration of how private sector accountability in this area can be brought to the attention of the international community.

Limitations on Enforcing Human Rights Accountability by the Private Sector

There can be little doubt that some of these multinationals continue to collude with various African governments in derogating from the human, social, cultural and economic rights of their peoples. For this reason, perhaps, and in view of the political power wielded by African governments to make life difficult for the multinationals, through local legislation, much more strenuous and vigorous pressures should continue to be applied on African governments to conform with internationally accepted human rights standards, in addition to those mounted on the multinationals by transnational non-state actors. African governments must set the example for the private sector to follow, and where necessary must impose sanctions on defaulting private sector organisations. This is an important policy area which U.S.–African relations, particularly U.S. African policy must address, as we approach the new millennium.

U.S. African Policy and Support for Economic Rights as Human Rights in Africa

The linkage between economic reforms, including the redistribution of wealth at the national and international levels, and the individual capacity of the African underclass for enjoying human rights should be high on the emergent U.S.–African relations in the 21st century. This requires concern with issues of social justice and a commitment to a redefinition of human rights to include the economic rights of the individual which the U.S., on ideological grounds, may not readily accept.

It also presupposes an activist and socially conscious view of the African state, which the U.S. government, under political domestic pressures from neo-conservative and neo-liberal ideologues in the U.S. may not readily subscribe to. But this need not be the case since there is a strong residual attachment, within the liberal left of the Democratic Party, to the tradition of Keynesian state interventionism which characterised the New Deal and the Great Society programmes of previous democratic party administrations in the U.S. under Franklin D. Roosevelt, John F. Kennedy and Lyndon B. Johnson.

What this collectivist and economistic notion of human rights also suggests is that such agenda of African economic reforms as the donor-driven structural adjustment programmes can, in the medium term, deepen the poverty of the African underclass. U.S. African policy in the new millennium should accept the fact that World Bank-driven structural adjustment programmes in Africa have failed. U.S. African policy should now be concerned with assisting African countries not only to lay the ghost of structural adjustment but also to adopt and implement short-term macro-economic strategies to combat and attenuate its more painful and reprehensible consequences.

U.S. Response to African Human Rights and the New World Order

The notion of human rights as social and economic rights also suggests the need to link the possibilities for human rights in Africa to structural reform of the character of the world economy. It is in this area that U.S. policy in the next millennium should seek to advance the demand of African countries for better terms of trade, for debt forgiveness and for a general redistribution of global wealth in favour of African countries.

There is already an historical basis for a shift in U.S. African policy along this line. For example, Dr. Henry Kissinger's 1975 address as U.S. Secretary of State to the United Nations General Assembly on 1 September 1975 (Veenhoven, 1977: 237–276), read on his behalf by Daniel Moynihan, then U.S. Ambassador to the U.N., indicated U.S. acceptance of the need to restructure the international economic system in a more equitable direction.

In another speech before the Fourth Ministerial Meeting of the United Nations Conference on Trade and Development in May 1976, Dr. Kissinger (UNCTAD, 1976, p. 15) re-emphasised the U.S. commitment to a restructured international economic order. He argued for rapid progress in four key areas: renewed efforts on commodity issues, including problems of resource invest-ment and trade; the application of technology to development; action to tackle the balance of payments and debt problems of developing countries; and focus on the special and urgent needs of the poorest countries in the world.

If there were doubts as to the sincerity of U.S. commitment to a restruc-tured international economic order, as indicated by Henry Kissinger, such doubts were confirmed by the contrary position taken by Kissinger's cabinet colleague and Treasury Secretary, William E. Simon (1976, p. 16) who, taking a neo-liberal stand, extolled the virtue of competition and the free market in the following words: *expropriation, indexation, cartellization – these are the false gods of many who seek a New International Economic Order. They are not the answer for either the developing nations or the industrialised nations …*

The Imperative of Unequivocal U.S. Support for a Restructured World Economy

As we approach the new millennium, U.S. African policy must stand out unequivocally in its support of African and third world demand for a reform or restructuring of the world economy. The argument in support of such a policy shift is that the structural reform of the world economy along lines demanded by African and other third world countries is in the long-term national interests of the U.S. and the industrial and developed world, in that it will conduce to peace and security in the world.

The recent initiative by the Clinton administration and senior congressional leaders to push through the U.S. Congress a joint Africa package is a welcome effort at the national level in the U.S. in this respect. Its goals are basically to shift U.S. African policy in the direction of trade and investment, to assist reforming African economies gain easier access to U.S. markets and to extend more debt forgiveness to them. It is expected that the initiative of the U.S. in this area will have a positive effect on other members of the G-8 to act collectively at the global level to advance African interests.

The expectation of the U.S. government is also that this policy initiative will create a favourable climate within the recipient African countries for the enjoyment of human rights by their citizens. However, the initiative still falls short of the extension to Africa of a modern-day version of the Marshall Aid to Western Europe. A small but significant step, it indicates the wave of the future in U.S.–African relations in the new millennium.

Keynesianism and African Development

The direction that this wave should traverse must be Keynesian and must draw on the Lagos Plan of Action: it should place high premium on more social investment in people, in primary health and water, in public transportation and in education by both the public sector and the private sector. U.S. African policy must involve Africans as partners in charting this direction; it must not just be handed down to them. There must be consultation and a meeting of minds.

In this respect an institutional framework similar to that provided by the Global Coalition for Africa must be established to bring together the U.S. government, African governments, eminent United States citizens and Africans out of government and representatives of the private sector and non-governmental organisations in the U.S. and in Africa, to set the agenda for a Keynesian-informed African development agenda that will serve the national interests of African countries and the United States.

Democratisation Trends and Tendencies in Africa

Let us now turn to issues of the democratisation project in African countries. What has been the trend? What has been its impact on U.S.–African relations?

The past decade or so has seen an upsurge of popular demands for plural and competitive electoral politics in various parts of Africa. These demands for a "second independence" underscore grassroots-based disappointment and even disillusionment with the colonial settlement, with the successor African inheritance elite or political class and with the economic and political performance of the post-colonial state in Africa. It is an indictment of the kleptocratic and politically "irresponsible" behaviour of the political ruling class generally in Africa. Informed by the democratic principles of accountability, participation, self-determination and political responsibility, these popular and grassroots-based demands constitute a critical reflection of, and response to what I have described earlier as the crisis of good governance in Africa.

The imperative need to democratise political and social processes in Africa, in reaction to these grassroots-based demands and in response to exogenously induced pressures from donor countries for political liberalisation, is now, as I have already indicated earlier on in this paper, a major item on the African agenda, as accepted and formulated by the OAU and by sub-regional groupings on the continent. The same concern with democratisation has been central to the course and direction of U.S.–African relations in recent years. It is likely to assume even more prominence in the coming years.

The current democracy debate in and about Africa has been conducted against the background of the collapse of Soviet communism, although the roots and the trajectories of the African movement for a "second independence" are autochthonous and predate the current resurgence of neo-liberalism and neo-conservatism in the west, following upon the fall of Soviet communism.

The Liberal Democratic Model and its Limitations in Africa

However, the dominant model or paradigm of democratic transitions now in vogue in Africa is liberal democracy and its market assumptions, and with emphasis on "good governance." This latter term, "good governance" extends the liberal democratic model in two interrelated senses: in an administrative-managerial sense to cover sound, i.e., transparent and accountable, administration, as used by the World Bank, for example; and in the Schumpterian sense of competitive or plural electoral politics, organised around periodic elections, under universal adult suffrage and with the assumptions of the indeterminacy of the elections, of the rule of law, due process, separation of powers and respect for human, particularly civil and political rights.

It is, therefore, in the context of the institutionalisation of liberal democratic politics that U.S.–African relations will take on significance in the next millennium. While the U.S. will want to push the model of liberal democracy, adapted to local circumstances, but without much diminution of the fundamental liberal democratic market assumptions and the principle of the periodicity and indeterminacy of elections, it must accept the need within Africa for a much more activist role for the state than may be warranted by the market assumptions of the liberal democratic state.

The U.S. and Prospects for Democratisation in Africa

The pattern of U.S.–African relations in the new millennium has already been set by aggressive pressures mounted by the U.S., in the last several years, on regimes in Benin Republic, the Cameroon, Gambia, Kenya, Niger, Nigeria, Zaire and Zambia to liberalise the political space in their respective countries and to move in the direction of liberal democratic politics. These pressures have included the combination of moral suasion, incentives and the threat or actual use of sanctions to move recalcitrant regimes towards decompression and democratisation.

U.S. African policy, in this respect, has been pursued in cohort with other members of the G-8 and other international organisations. It has consisted mainly at the level of the executive branch and the U.S. Congress of demanding for competitive elections, electoral reform, including creation of an independent electoral body and assistance with the logistic requirements of elections. In feet, at the level of Congress, democratisation is an inherent aspect of its concern with compliance with internationally recognised human rights by other countries. This aspect of U.S. African policy has on occasion created tension between the U.S. government and a number of African governments, like Kenya, Nigeria and Zimbabwe which have accused it of meddling in their internal affairs, of inciting their citizens against them and of providing support for oppositional elements.

U.S. Civil Society Groups and Democratisation in Africa

Civil society groups in the U.S. have served a complementary role to that of the U.S. government and the U.S. Congress in sensitizing U.S. and world opinion to the need for democratisation. Some of these groups, like the Washington, DC-based DFES and the National Democratic Institute, have also been involved in the assessment of the electoral needs of African countries, in providing necessary electoral assistance and in advising on election logistics and in election monitoring activities in individual African countries.

As in the human rights area, these civil society groups have created networks of pro-democracy groups and advocates on both sides of the Atlantic, serving as pressure groups to place the issue of democratisation in Africa high on the policy agenda in the U.S., in Africa, and in other parts of the world.

This trend is likely to continue into the next millennium and should be encouraged, but again with the caveat that the activities of U.S. pro-democracy groups in Africa must not appear patronising, unduly missionary in zeal. In other words they must not betray residual imperial reflexes, as has been the African experience with some election observer groups from the west.

Assessing Effect of U.S. Policy on Democratisation in Africa

The concern of the U.S. government and civil society groups in the country with democracy in Africa is often expressed as part of the "manifest" destiny of the U.S. to champion the cause of democracy in the world. The end of the Cold War has made it more comfortable and easier for the U.S. government to "jettison" or "desert," and to demand more vigorous commitment to democratisation from such regimes as Arap Moi's in Kenya and Mobutu's in the former Zaire that used to serve U.S. security and military interest well.

But how effective has U.S. policy been in achieving the deserved result? It is difficult to measure this; but whatever its short- or long-term effects, it must be viewed in the broader context of other exogenous pressures and more importantly of the home-based popular struggles of pro-democracy and oppositional groups within Africa, who continue to bear the brunt of oppression and who yet keep the democracy torch burning incandescently. Indeed, the solidarity effect of U.S. policy in this area on the social psychology of African pro-democracy and oppositional groups is so incalculable as to be unquantifiable. This must be the ultimate test of the effect of the policy, which is still unravelling in its longer-term impact and consequences.

What has been the record so far in Africa? It is mixed but encouraging, in Ghana, Kenya, the Cameroon and the Gambia disputed elections have been conducted, and in Kenya new elections are due by the end of 1997. In Nigeria, the transitions under President Babangida, after successful elections at the local government level and the state level and the election of National Assembly members, got stuck with the annulment of the popularly acclaimed 12 June 1993 presidential elections. In that country too, the current transition to civil rule programme under General Sard Abacha remains controversial. In Algeria, the Benin Republic, Botswana, Cape Verde, Ethiopia, Guinea-Bissau, Malawi, Mauritius, Mozambique, Sao Tome and Principe, Sierra Leone, South Africa, Zambia and Zimbabwe, elections were successfully concluded and with little controversy. However, there have been reversals in a number of cases: in Sierra Leone, the democratically elected civilian government in the country was recently overthrown; in Algeria, elections earlier being conducted in 1991 were aborted to forestall the apparent electoral victory of a fundamentalist, Islamicist party, the Islamic Salvation Front (FIS); and in Zambia, the euphoria created by the return to multiparty politics seems to have given way to disappointment with the politics of President Chiluba and the trend towards authoritarianism under him.

The extent to which U.S. policy on democratisation in Africa has shaped or contributed to these developments is difficult to assess. But in critical and strategic countries like Nigeria and Kenya, the outcome of U.S. policy has been to put great stress and strain on U.S. relations with these countries, while it has not succeeded in dislodging them from power or moving them along lines preferred or demanded by the U.S.

It seems, as these two cases show, that the nature of the critical social forces in contention at the domestic level is a more important dimension of the transition process than outside pressures. But pressures from the U.S. and other sources on these countries to decompress have served to deepen the antinomic contradictions between democratisation and authoritarianism in these countries. Such pressures carry with them the potential to catalyse the resolution of the contradictions in favour of the pro-democracy forces, in the long run.

What also seems to be the trend is that sometimes African oppositional and pro-democracy groups in the civil society place too much expectations on the ability of the U.S. government to bring about democratic change, only for them to realise the limitations on the ability of the U.S. to do so. Such limitations reflect the tardy and unpredictable effectiveness of moral suasion and sanctions on recalcitrant regimes, as was clearly evident in the case of Rhodesia under Smith after the unilateral declaration of independence (UDI) and apartheid South Africa; and also in the disinclination of the U.S. government, in view of its own domestic legislation, to be seen to be actively engaged in bringing down or subverting such governments.

The long-term effectiveness of U.S. policy in this area, as I have already indicated, is likely to be in its conscientization role, and in assisting to build an African-based pro-democracy constituency that will tap on the ground-swell of grassroots demand and the many popular struggles for participation and accountability in governance in Africa.

Strengthening the Psychosocial Dimensions of Democracy and Democratic Institutions in Africa

As we enter the next millennium, U.S. African policy should also seek to work with African regional and continental organisations to lay the foundations for the psychosocial (or attitudinal) and institutional correlates of democracy in Africa. Tolerance and promotion of diversity, commitment to due process, respect for the rule of law and human rights, and transparency in public life are some of these psychosocial correlates of democracy. At the institutional level, these correlates will include decentralization of constitutional power, with devolution to ethnic communities and to local governments, and multiple layers of authority.

There should be provisions for countervailing sources of power to prevent abuse and concentration of power in one person or institution. Thus there should be an independent judiciary and legislative oversight; independent electoral commissions or bodies to conduct periodic elections on a multi-party basis; and the reform of the civil service to make it more open, more performance-oriented, accountable and transparent.

These provisions should not be merely "dignified" paper provisions. In addition, processes should be designed and institutions created for their enforcement and to give them "teeth." In this respect, concern with democratisation and human rights should not begin and end with multi-party elections. The reversal in Zambia, to which reference was made above, is a telling case in point. Policy in this area should be pursued as a continuous attempt to nudge and pressure African regimes and the political leadership and their followership to show practical adherence to, and work for the effectiveness of these countervailing polycentric sources of power, which by definition and design are not concentrated in one person or institution.

The long tradition of separation of powers, informed by the Montesquean and Madisonian thesis that, since absolute power tends to corrupt absolutely, power must be used to check power. This same thesis, at another level, finds expression in the notion of home-rule which governs constitutional and political relations between federal, state and local governments in the U.S.

The thesis that continues to provide the bedrock for the peculiar type of federal government in the U.S. is a model which the U.S. must seek to project for adoption by democratising African countries. The common tendency among African rulers towards the absolutisation and the personalisation or privatisation of power, itself a hang-over inherited from absolutist colonial rule, and the winner-takes-all assumptions which have characterised electoral politics and the practice of parliamentarism and presidentialism in Africa, continue to be extremely salient impediments to the democratisation project in Africa.

Polycentric Solutions to Threats to Democracy in Africa

This is why the U.S. model of liberal democracy, modified by its system of separation of powers and federalism, and adapted to the peculiar circumstances of Africa, especially its pluralist ethnic mosaic and the need for an activist state to provide and invest in social infrastructures, is highly relevant to Africa. This bears repetition, if only because of the African predilection against federalism. Yet decentralised or peripheralised federalism is relevant, especially in its constitutionally entrenched devolution and deconcentration of power, as a solution to fears of ethnic domination that continue to be the bane of African politics. Federalism is relevant to Africa in another respect: it presupposes a polycentric solution to the problem of the absolutisation and personalisation of power, by constitutionally diffusing political power.

The polycentric institutions and processes referred to above are not easy to achieve in the short or medium term. This is clear from the sad and chequered experience of Nigeria which, more than any other country in Africa, has, at the level of constitutional and political theory, tried to design a political system which hi some important respects bears affinity to that of the U.S., from which it also bears striking dissimilarities. Rather, these institutions and processes should be viewed as long-term objectives which require short-to-medium-term strategies for then attainment. U.S. African policy hi the new millennium must be directed towards strategies for their attainment.

Democratisation, as I have already observed, involves much more than competitive plural politics and the conduct of elections. There is need to shift focus also to a concern with the conditions for its sustenance. This is an area where U.S. policy in the new millennium should be directed towards not only African governments but also to the civil society in Africa in a partnership for democratic consolidation.

CONCLUSION

Let me in conclusion make the following observations on the role of African-Americans in shaping and influencing U.S.–African relations. It is all the more important to do this in the context of this special session of the Fourth African–African-American Summit.

The Heavy Burden of the "Benign Neglect" of the Past

Traditionally, African-Americans have been excluded from the formal and informal foreign policy elite groups in the U.S. Moreover, as Donald Rotchild (1973, p. 215) once observed, the "benign neglect" which for much of the immediate postwar years up to the early 1960s characterised U.S. African policy was due partly to the absence of a volatile domestic constituency to place Africa on the domestic agenda in the U.S. This 'benign neglect" is itself symptomatic of the relationship between the domestic and foreign politics of a nation, to which I referred at the beginning of this paper.

To put it differently, "the benign neglect" of Africa in an earlier phase of U.S. African policy was a mirror reflection of the "benign neglect" which African-Americans suffered for a long tune in the U.S. The marginal and disadvantaged position of African-Americans in the political economy of the U.S. and its institutions was also reflected in their lack of political power to influence electoral outcomes.

In this respect, Rupert Emerson (1970, p. 167) has pointed out that "the Negro attitude in the United States towards Africa has only a marginal bearing on American policy there ... To put it in crude terms, there is no reason to assume that anybody can deliver a sufficiently substantial Negro vote on African issues to affect the outcome of significant elections."

Impact of the Radicalisation of Black Nationalism and Great Society Programmes in the U.S.

Much has, of course, changed since the mid-1950s and the 1960s in the U.S. We have since then witnessed the radicalisation of black nationalism in the U.S., including neo-Garveyite back-to-Africa movements. There have been and continue to be massive black voter registration exercises, consequent upon judicial and legislative action at the federal level, to remove restrictive measures whose effect was to effectively disenfranchise millions of African-Americans of voting age. The Great Society programmes and compensatory measures like quota and affirmative-action type ones, designed to integrate African-Americans into the U.S. "melting-pot," and into the economic and political mainstream of the country, were initiated and implemented to compensate for centuries of their "benign neglect" and the discrimination against them.

The African-American constituency in the U.S. has grown more volatile, and with it the political and electoral significance of its vote. The African-American leadership has also increasingly shown interest in Africa and in influencing U.S. African policy (Diggs, 1976, pp. 4–8). The activities of the Congressional Black Caucus and private sector black organisations and institutions like TransAfrica and Africans are illustrative of this interest.

The Challenge for African-American Input into U.S. African Policy

The changes in the structure of U.S. domestic politics and the opportunities presented for a new direction in U.S. African policy by changes in Africa and in the structure of world politics, to which reference was made in sections "Some Basic Assumptions," in above, pose a particular challenge of relevance to African-Americans in the articulation and implementation of U.S. African policy, as we approach the new millennium. The challenge can be summed up in the form of the need for an African-American agenda for U.S. African policy. The agenda must derive from the policy imperatives I have set out in section "Policy Imperatives: Human Rights and Democracy" of this paper.

Defining an African-American Agenda for U.S. African Policy

Let me set out briefly a framework for articulating and pursuing such an agenda.

First, linkages between Africa and the African-American community need to be strengthened through the building of transnational and transcontinental networks of professional groups, business groups, educational institutions, religious groups and the mass media. These linkages are critical for no other reason than that European propagated racist prejudices about Africans and about African-Americans still divide Africans and African-Americans. These prejudices continue to create, and indeed strengthen wrong and divisive stereotypical impressions on both sides, making it all the more difficult for Africans and African-Americans to realise the potential contributions they can and should make to each other's development.

Second, African-Americans must seek representation at high levels of the foreign policy establishment as a way of influencing from within the formulation and implementation of U.S. African policy. More and more of them should seek congressional and diplomatic careers.

Third, African-American leaders like Vernon Jordan and C. Payne Lucas who currently have access to the innermost recesses of presidential power in the U.S. are strategically placed to influence a more sympathetic and Afrocentric U.S. African policy, and should be encouraged to do so.

ACKNOWLEDGMENT

The author is grateful to H.E. Ambassador Walter C. Carrington, United States Ambassador to Nigeria and to Dr. Okechukwu Ibeanu of the Centre for Advanced Social Science, Port Harcourt, Nigeria for their perceptive and useful comments on the initial draft of this paper.

REFERENCES

Ake, C. (1996). *Democracy and development in Africa.* Washington, DC: The Blockings Institution.
American Assembly. (1997). *Africa & U.S. national interests: The ninetieth American assembly, March 13–16.* New York: Columbia University.
Cranston, M. (1973). *What are human rights.* London: The Bodley Head.
Diggs, C. (1976). The Afro-American stake in Africa, *The Black Scholar.* January.
Emerson, R. (1970). Race in Africa: United States foreign policy. In: G. W. Shepherd (Ed.), *Racial influences on American foreign policy.* New York: Basic Books.
Jinadu, L. A. (1980). *Human rights and U.S. African policy under President Carter.* Lagos: Nigerian Institute of International Affairs.
Rotchild, D. (1973). Engagement versus disengagement in Africa: The choices for America. In: A. M. Jones Jr. (Ed.), *U.S. foreign policy in a changing world.* New York: David McKay.
Simon, W. E. (1976). The core of U.S. international economic policy. In: F. W. Neal (Ed.), *Pacem in Terris IV: American foreign policy and the third world.* Santa Barbara, CA: Fund For The Republic, Inc.
UNCTAD. (1976). UNCTAD IV: Expanding cooperation for global economic development. Washington, DC: Department of State, Bureau of Public Affairs.
Veenhoven, W.A. (Ed.), (1977). *Case studies on human rights and fundamental freedoms* (Vol. 5, pp. 237–276). The Hague: Martinus Nijhoff Publishers.

BLACKNESS AS BLUEPRINT: RADICAL BECOMING AND SOCIAL TRANSFORMATION

João H. Costa Vargas

ABSTRACT

The contours and transformative potential of a mode of black politics that I analyze in this essay derive from what black people in the African diaspora have necessarily always been engaged with: becoming. Radical becoming offers both a vital critique of our colonization and a blueprint for the formation of new, ethical, and anti-fascist subjectivities and soci-abilities.

Focusing a theoretical discussion about the political constitution and consequences of black radical becoming, this chapter systematizes the theories and praxes of black activists in grassroots organizations in Los Angeles and Rio de Janeiro. It draws on ethnographic data and it engages with black feminists and critical race theorists. The radical nature of this specific form of black politics is based on three axes: its constant self-critique and reformulation; its Afrodiasporic transnationalism; and its commitment to social justice. The resulting political vocabulary and practices emphasize race as an energizer of political identification and action that moves beyond traditional identity politics. Such worldview offers crucial and necessary alternatives to our ever conservative, fearful, and genocidal political climate.

The New Black: Alternative Paradigms and Strategies for the 21st Century
Research in Race and Ethnic Relations, Volume 14, 265–285
Copyright © 2007 by Elsevier Ltd.
ISSN: 0195-7449/doi:10.1016/S0195-7449(06)14012-X

BLACKNESS AS BLUEPRINT: RADICAL BECOMING
AND SOCIAL TRANSFORMATION

At its most basic formulation, blackness is a result of at least two sets of processes: on the one hand, the various vectors of historical racialization emanating from hegemonic institutions and practices, and on the other, the acquired historical consciousness and praxis of what it means to be black. Blackness is thus itself a process; it is always in the making, defined by its intrinsic dynamism as it is inflected by and simultaneously affects the contexts we live in.

Let us focus on blackness as a result of our own agency. We are black insofar as, having more or less survived the constant assaults on our humanity, we recognize and draw on a collective reservoir of resistance, pride, and hopes. Thus, because blackness is a process marked by time, space, and power, and because this collective reservoir is not only constantly changing but can be accessed through countless routes (organizing, art, and spirituality, for example) we are always *becoming* black. On the basis of this simple truth, I will present an argument about the radical nature of black politics that is based precisely on what we have necessarily always been engaged with: becoming. By emphasizing becoming rather than the being, this mode of black politics offers both a vital critique of our colonization and a blueprint for the formation of new, ethical, and anti-fascist subjectivities and sociabilities.[1]

Developing a theoretical discussion about the political constitution and consequences of black radical becoming, this essay derives from the theories and praxes of black activists in grassroots organizations in Los Angeles and Rio de Janeiro with whom I have been collaborating since 1996 (Vargas, 1999, 2003). Drawing on ethnographic data as well as engaging with black feminists and critical race theorists, this essay suggests an argument about the radical nature of a specific form of black politics that is based on (a) its constant self-critique and reformulation, (b) its Afrodiasporic transnationalism, and (c) its commitment to social justice. While thoughts based on race are central to this politics, the dangers of race-thinking are permanently debated. The resulting political vocabulary and practices emphasize race as an energizer of political identification and action that embrace while moving beyond traditional identity politics whose political programs reflect the consciousness and experience of belonging to discrete (racialized, gendered, sexed, national) groups (Kelley, 1997; Lipsitz, 1997). How can black identity politics be utilized as both a tool emerging out of the epistemic privilege of the experience of blackness (Mohanty, 2000), and also as an energizer of insights that is critical of and extrapolates the particularities of being black? In this text, I describe how a certain modality of black identity politics – what I call radical becoming – builds on the knowledge created and developed in sites of imposed racial marginality, as well as is attentive to the dangers immanent to the uncritical reliance on the necessary limitations of experience. I contend that black radical becoming offers a blueprint of political consciousness and organizing that is potentially able to both draw on the cognitive advantages the experiences of blackness generate and establish bridges with non-black progressive movements. Furthermore, such perspective, as it takes up a self-critical gaze, is equipped to critically challenge the various hierarchies of social class, gender, color, sexuality, and nationality, among many others, which occur both within black movements and between members of multiracial alliances. Black radical becoming, building on the acceptance of our necessary vulnerability as cognitive and political strength, offers a blueprint for liberation.

I will start by focusing on the following question: can definitions of race be defended as basis for ethical reasoning and political organizing? As, for example, Paul Gilroy (2000) would have it, is the idea of race so anachronic and dangerous that we must strive toward postracial modes of thought and action?

Although the ethnography I conducted in South Central Los Angeles between 1996 and 1998 while working at the Coalition Against Police Abuse (CAPA) as well as other works sympathetic to the struggles of Afrodiasporic peoples document the traps of the concept of race, these same works suggest grounds for ethical race-thinking that challenges and moves beyond the essentialist and fascist results that race-thinking can generate (Collins, 1991; Sudbury, 1998).[2] Racializing thoughts and practices, as weapons of resistance, as intellectual tools, and as transformative catalyzers point to both the reaffirmation of race-based, collective identities, and the need to constantly question the necessarily provisory, temporary, and partial racialized truths that are produced. Racialized truths, for reasons I will explain, are always this: vital, but limited.

As I will argue, the worldviews that have the greater potential for achieving social justice, while recognizing the necessity and the dangers of race-thinking, have in common their need for constant self-reinvention: they embrace motion, mutation, search; and they recognize the connection between the many social problems we face today – especially those occurring among blacks – and our resistance against self-criticism. Black activists and artists in Los Angeles and Rio de Janeiro recognize we are all colonized – blacks, browns, whites, all of us. This, of course, is not to diminish the gains whites accrue by simply being white in a white supremacist society, nor the advantages secured to non-whites when we possessively invest in whiteness (Lipsitz, 1997). As members of this western culture, our cognitive and moral architecture tends to value hierarchy, permanence, boundaries (Spivak, 1999). We are materialistic, selfish, power-driven, dependent on (our small yet) permanent and excluding truths. As Barbara Smith (2000) reminds us, our own racism, sexism, and homophobia continue to divide us. Our thinking about race is part of this colonial matrix, and as such limits our understanding of the social world and our strategies for change. So why do blacks in organizations committed to social justice insist on race-thinking?

As the historical objects of racialization, we have developed multifaceted visions and practices about race. One of the consequences of our marginal location vis-à-vis systems of material production and ideology is that we have learned how to use the master's tools – in this case race-thinking – to our own benefit (Collins, 1991; Robinson, 2000[1983]). Our condition as racialized beings obviously cannot be explained without recourse to race. Furthermore, race-thinking has enabled communities of color to find references in history, explanations for suffering, and hopes for a better future that are necessarily connected to race. Challenging the dehumanization of racism involves the remaking of our own history – one that is not dependent on the occidental, white-dominated discourses, and one that, more importantly, reaffirms our agency, intelligence, beauty, and will to persevere and transform (Robinson, 2000[1983]). Race is thus altered into an index of tradition, pride, and strategies for change, from the first slave revolts to the latest forms of liberatory rap music in the contemporary African diaspora. Afrocentrism's uncritical use and abuse of the master's tools aside – its frequent defense of gender hierarchies, for example – its greatest contribution is the much needed love ethic toward black people (Collins, 1998).

Race has also become indispensable to theories of oppression, especially in polities of the African diaspora. Activists and academics have argued convincingly for the centrality – if not the primacy – of race in determining one's relation to society, especially in the case of African Americans.[3] Social class is effectively lived through race, which is to say: persons of color experience this society's power structures and everyday interactions primarily though our racialization. Our racialization, in turn, gives meaning to, translates, and is inflected by, not only our class position, but also our political convictions, nationality, gender, and sexual orientation (Hall, 1980). Claims of solidarity, based primarily on social class, as the old left makes them, will obviously not work (Kelley, 1997).

Still, as struggles for justice depend on the strategies, solidarities, and hopes that race-thinking generates, we must recognize, as several social movements already have, that while these types of struggle are absolutely necessary, they are not sufficient. Race-thinking is not sufficient because, at best, persons of color coalesced around identity politics will accrue greater access to resources and juridical recognition while the racialized matrix of thinking, perpetual source of oppression and dehumanization, will remain intact (Crenshaw et al., 1995, Lorde, 1984). The oppressor within and without will not be fully challenged. Indeed, if race-thinking is part and parcel of the hegemonic apparatus – one that necessarily depends on multiple hierarchies that include gender, class, age, nation, among many others – the victories that it generates can only be partial victories.

Black activists such as the ones at CAPA know that while the racialized struggle against the police and social injustices is vital, it is only part of a broader battle in which a new society, a new culture will have to be formed. Existing modes of identity politics may save our lives, but will not save our minds and souls. Similar to the bricoleur's modi operandi, new forms of political organizing and participation can and will emerge from the cutting and pasting and rearranging of the existing structures (Lévi-Strauss, 1989). But these seemingly new forms of doing politics will be necessarily constrained by what is already in place, what is already known, and the socially shared cognitive maps. The range of possibilities, while theoretically vast, is in reality compressed by previously existing and unchallenged assumptions and bureaucratic processes. Identity politics, when uncritically engaged in the possible gains that the existing cultural, legal, and political structures can yield, is necessarily restricted by how we conceptualize difference. Current differences in race, gender, color, sexuality, class – modalities from which identity politics emerge – unless recognized as hegemonic cognitive tools and subsequently deconstructed, will never dismantle the oppressive mental and political structures. Audre Lorde (1984) recognized such dilemma, and defined it in terms of "the master's tools will never dismantle the master's house" (p. 112).

Race is a political and therefore plastic, manipulated and manipulating category. One that is immersed in history, sanctioned in society, and one that constitutes an arena of dynamic struggle. Not only are we objects of racial classifications, but we are also subjects of our own racial making. As subjects of race-thinking, we draw boundaries according to which individuals, communities, and histories are more or less valued, more or less taken into account, more or less considered as potential allies. It is up to us, then, to make sure this dangerous weapon is utilized in productive ways. How do we know when we are productive? Social justice and liberation are the necessary parameters. Insofar as race-thinking helps us elucidate the roots of our oppression, as well as construct alternative futures, its use is warranted. Blackness is born out of personal experiences of dehumanization, but is best expressed and rendered effective when connected to collective histories and strategies of struggle (Marable, 1997). A route out of complicity with the master (house, tools, narratives, race-thinking) is radically accepting our necessary and endless process of transformation as we envision and work for liberation. Black radical becoming suggests possibilities of liberation that are both immersed in the historical experiences of racialization and the constant transformative dynamics that characterize such experiences. At once identity politics (because rooted in the black experiences) and transcendental (because ever dynamic, self-reformulating, and utopian), black radical becoming indicates an approach to and a vision of politics that puts the accent on the process, rather than on the end result.

In parallel to the politics of bricolage – to the politics done with the master's tools in the master's house – sometimes feeding from it, sometimes influencing it, there is another, less perceptible but nevertheless crucial mode of politics that aims more drastically at the construction of an ethical, just future. This sometimes quieter, more plastic – fragile even – and not so obvious yet radical politics wants to construct a new polity: a new vocabulary, new modes of sociability, new cognitive tools, new ways of understanding our racialized world while moving beyond the need to think within, and contingent to our racialized world (Kelley, 1997).[4] This mode of politics is not as dependent on the already given, and it projects a future whose content it refuses to define. In Lévi-Strauss's terms (1989) – notwithstanding the so-ethnocentric, often male-centered, technocratic and therefore so questionable metaphor – this politics is akin to what the engineer does, that is, she visualizes realities that are not yet announced, that have not been thought about. This politics of transfiguration (Gilroy, 1993) struggles for the construction of a new house, set of principles, and political culture that, while recognizing the abuses and uses of race, will continually strive to deconstruct and reconstruct our subjectivities, sociabilities, dreams, and desires for justice.[5] This politics ceaselessly affirms the need to imagine a world yet to be realized.[6]

The radical experiments I am talking about belong to the political traditions of the African diaspora (Robinson, 2000[1983]). Positions and concepts and hierarchies of authority are dismantled (as the deconstructivists want), but collective problems, collective solutions, and collective struggle are the ultimate parameters, thus distancing this type of politics from the bourgeois, liberal individualism-derived postmodern project (Collins, 1998, Mohanty, 2000).

Like that of the Combahee River Collective (1995), this political praxis refuses easy solutions and permanent truths. It operates under and around conventional, occidental communications and understandings. It depends on (political, artistic, personal) performances that happen out of the reach of our colonized perceptions: nonlinear, multinational, linking the past, present and future in improvised and profound ways, little preoccupied with Cartesian logic. Spend a day at CAPA, participate in the discussions between former Panthers, interact with ex-gang members, listen to the stories of their travels to Europe, Africa, South America, engage with their metaphysics, their notions of death and life, try to capture the significance of the role music plays in their lives, witness their search for new modes of relating to people of non-African American backgrounds, their commitment to a just society, to liberation. You will notice *something* that runs parallel to the detailed legal knowledge accumulated and documented; something that is of a distinct nature than the discussions about and practices of the strategies of community organizing that are necessary in order to help black women and men survive in times of genocide. This something is very distinct from – even though not necessarily antagonistic and certainly complimentary to – the techniques whose value is precisely guaranteeing survival in the master's house. This something develops through visionary hopes, international travels, dialogues and dreams across languages, experiences, sexualities, and races. This something stems from identity politics as it is informed by the experience of blackness, but it moves beyond identity politics as it recognizes both the possible limitations of identity politics and the cognitive kinship between identity politics and how social differences are conceptualized – and therefore always already suspect – by hegemonic forces. Mostly unnamed, this something is utopian, it is transformative, liberatory, and speaks of a state of mind and spirit that sees the limitations of playing – and sometimes winning – the master's games.

Becoming: this is the radical principle organizing the politics of transfiguration. Because it is not dependent on stable definitions, it is able to incorporate race-thinking as a moment of the struggle, as a stage, as a concept that is constantly calling for revision, expansion, and erasure. Becoming means a commitment to a permanent process of metamorphosis. It is fitting that in the fight for decolonization (of the self, our everyday lives, worldviews, politics), we comprehend that our theoretical and practical shortcomings in the struggle for justice are in great measure derived from our dependence on categories that restrict our horizons that confine us to the master's house. The master's house is not only the structure of power, ideologies, and exclusions that define polities. The master's house is also within each one of us, and hence the need to be constantly directing our critical gaze to our most profound thoughts and tendencies (Lorde, 1984; Sandoval, 2000). Still, there are no guarantees. The work for radical change is by definition empty of assurances. The cultivation vulnerability, necessary for the permanent self-critique, as well as moral principles and committed and open activism – these are some of the antidotes to the vertigo of permanent search, deconstructions, and reconstructions.

What are the characteristics of the activism that is effective in promoting the methodology of the oppressed, the politics of transfiguration? It is clear that if we are to move beyond the master's house and find appropriate tools to decolonize ourselves, we need to establish the conditions of possibility for self-critique, dialogue, understanding, and organizing across the lines that define bourgeois hierarchies: race, gender, sexuality, age, place of residence, social class, and nationality, just to name the more obvious. Coalitions are the only means to promote radical transformation (Smith, 2000).[7] No oppressed group has a complete perspective on the various facets of oppression, both imposed on us and operating within ourselves. Our perspectives are necessarily partial, our truths are limited (Collins, 1998; chapter 11). This is not to say all perspectives are equally valid, nor that one oppressed group will have a clearer vision than another. Oppression, however, does create oppositional consciousness – it is the challenge of transfigurative politics to recognize our localized truths for what they are and what they offer while learning to comprehend other truths generated in sites of marginality. The ensuing dialogue will expand our views as it necessarily transforms our initial perspectives, reaches a new, amalgamated, temporary understanding, in a hermeneutic circle informed by collective ethics of justice. Black people in the African diaspora are particularly well prepared for such dynamics: excluded from, yet a part of western modernity, Afrodiasporic communities have a privileged understanding of the need to be innovating, deconstructing, creating – on the run, so to speak. The alternatives are domestication, cooptation, death.

One of the main obstacles to an activism informed by such (temporary) principles is identity politics. Don't get me wrong: race-thinking is often crucial, especially among the most oppressed, and justifies the strategic employment of particular identities and experiences in the effort to demand the fulfillment of the master's house's promises, or in the struggle to simply make it to the next day. Much unlike those who advocate the new anti-essentialist orthodoxy (Appiah, 1992; Gilroy, 2000), my ethnography

(Vargas, 1999) as well as other works have shown how strategically effective essentialist assumptions and modes of solidarity are in promoting not only critical reflection and organizing, but above all, survival (Lipsitz, 1997; Sudbury, 1998; Chapter 4; Tyson, 1999; Williams, 1998[1962]). Without the racial solidarity laboriously woven in contexts of deprivation and often of desperation, black women and men would not have survived to this day. Among activists and persons just trying to survive anti-black racisms, racial solidarity is fundamental when confronting genocide.

Yet, as many of the strategies described in works focusing on black organizations show (Collins, 1998; Kelley, 1997; Smith, 2000), essentialism is necessary, but not enough for deeper and more complete liberation. Identity politics will not be sufficient for alliance building and for dismantling the master's house and building a new one.

How, then, can we, if not move beyond, then complement identity politics, prevent it from reifying the very cognitive and political grammars that are utilized to marginalize people as colored, women, gays, lesbians, non-nationals? I will reflect on the question through the experiences of organized groups of people of color in Los Angeles as they both combat their looming extinction and project a more just and solidary future. Activists in oppressed communities hold insights that are crucial for everyone's emancipation. CAPA is an example of a wider movement reaching the local, national, and transnational levels that, while recognizing the effectiveness of identity politics, is nevertheless proposing a new perspective on how we conceptualize the relationship between identity and politics.

The point I want to develop is how a specific Afrodiasporic transnational sensibility (and the results it generates) subordinates the formation of new identities to a politics of radical liberation. In contrast to identity politics – yet clearly emanating from a particular modality of black identity politics – the new type of politics makes the transformative, ethical, unfinished, and dialogical nature of the revolutionary project the very basis for the formation of new identities. Our colonization renders it imperative that we keep questioning and searching for structures of sentiment and sociability that will allow complete liberation. As Robin Kelley (1997) wrote, "the struggle is to remake culture itself, to develop new ideas, new relationships, and new values that place mutuality over materialism and collective responsibility over 'personal responsibility,' and place greater emphasis on ending all forms of oppression rather than striving to become the oppressor..." (p. 126). The ensuing politics of identification – complementing, questioning, and ultimately reconstructing identity politics – offers blueprints for radical justice (Sudbury, 1998; 179).

When CAPA organizers established a political connection with black activists in Rio de Janeiro, Brazil, in 1993, they put many of these concepts to work. Since then, the collaborations between African Americans and black Brazilians have shown how racial solidarity, experienced in a diasporic transatlantic setting, becomes a fundamental tool for overcoming social injustice while claiming full citizenship through appropriation, decolonizing, and re-elaboration of popular conceptions about blacks and the poor, state polices, and public spaces. One of the motives that led US blacks to seek connections with Rio community organizers was their conviction that Brazil has the second largest population of African-descended people in the world, behind only Nigeria. This clearly points to the importance of race classifications (and related expectations) in the relations between African Americans and Brazilians.

In Rio, CAPA activists interacted mostly with inhabitants of one of the poorest, most violent, stigmatized, and dilapidated neighborhoods, the Jacarezinho favela, where more than 150,000 people live under the despotism of drug dealers and state-sanctioned brutality exercised by the police.

African Americans were at first disturbed by the variety of race and color classifications utilized by Brazilians. Brazilians of color, on their part, were puzzled with US blacks' overarching and rigid racial categories.[8] This initial tension is still generating conceptual developments. On the Brazilian side, the persons and organizations who were part of the initial contact seem today, after much initial hesitation, more willing to identify as black (negro/a or Afro-Brasileira/o) and acknowledge a common history and set of political agendas with blacks in the US and other countries of the diaspora than they were a decade ago. LA black activists have also relativized their views on race. As a consequence, alliances with Latina/os and other potential allies, mostly non-African American, were revitalized.

The phenomenon of increasing black self-identification is part of a wider, contradictory process taking place in Brazil. In a context marked by a greater connection to the world market as implemented by elite-oriented, neo-liberal policies of presidents Fernando Collor de Mello (impeached in 1992) and Fernando Henrique Cardoso (elected in 1994 and reelected in 1998), black cultural workers, politicians, community activists, and non-governmental organizations have been able to influence and feed from the growing debate around race. Black beauty, interracial marriage, affirmative action, quotas, land rights, and reparations now feature prominently in mass communication media, public fora, and everyday conversations. Hip hop, especially in Rio, São Paulo, Belo Horizonte, and Salvador has politicized the condition of black favela youth.[9] The considerable interest in and participation generated by the preparatory meetings, state and national, for the 2001 Durban, South Africa conference against Racism throughout Brazil are indications of how valued and important the debates around race have become. High-school and college students, workers of all backgrounds, academics, professionals, and party members were in attendance during four days of intense debates and negotiations.[10]

The contact between US blacks and Rio favela activists happened at the cusp of a changing political atmosphere in which the traditionally muted discussions about Brazilian racial relations were invigorated (Hanchard, 1994, 1999; Sheriff, 2001; Twine, 1998). Inspired by CAPA's relentlessness in confronting the ongoing genocide of black people in the US, Rio activists incorporated and modified a US conceptual framework that further complexified their already radical stance. Before African Americans arrived, some of Rio's activists had been involved in organizing favela residents to protest the recurring deaths of their neighbors in the hands of the police. The protests reached a zenith when several buses were burnt and activists declared favelas were just demanding what was their right – and they would descend to the asphalt if it were necessary.[11] By adapting the discourse of racial injustice – fine-tuned in various discussions with US blacks – to the demands of full citizenship fuelling the protests, Rio activists constructed an analysis that presented new elements vis-à-vis the conventional radical discourses in Brazil. This is not to say that racial consciousness all of sudden became a catalyst for community organizing. Nor that Brazilians of color immediately felt compelled to identify as black. But the adoption of race-specific language that connected police brutality, unemployment, and lack of public services to being black certainly impacted the manners in which such problems had hitherto been talked about. Today's greater motivation, among favela dwellers and activists, to embrace a racialized perspective and identify as black must be connected to both the globalizing black US commodified cultural products (Gilroy, 2000), and the dialogues with African American community organizers. These two processes have interacted with and been modified by already-existing tendencies in Brazil that point to the affirmation of politicized blackness, as the case of favela activists illustrates.

Afrodiasporic transnational alliances constitute a fundamental aspect of the favela struggle insofar as they provide what no Brazilian organization or individuals can offer, that is, an expanded ideological and practical horizon of possibilities. The favela movement's adversaries are powerful and deadly. The symbolic and practical effects alliances with CAPA activists (themselves former Black Panthers) have on the local police, politicians, and drug dealers cannot be underestimated. Because of their well-known history of confrontational politics against law enforcement in particular and oppressive, racist institutions in general, black US militants give Brazilians a tactical edge insofar as they provide, not only crucial moral, financial, and psychological support, but also embody a tradition that has proven to be effective in fighting institutionalized forms of power.

As importantly, the alliances with progressive black Americans work to diffuse the common accusations of involvement with drug commerce waged against new favela representatives. These accusations have become a pattern since the end of the dictatorship. Whereas during the military regime politicized communities and their leaders were tagged as communists (and thus, from the state's perspective, justifiably harassed, imprisoned, and killed), beginning in the 1980s, representatives of the favelas that do not automatically subscribe to official party guidelines and discourses are frequently dismissed as spokespersons for drug dealers. The irony is that even leftist parties such as the Worker's Party (Partido dos Trabalhadores – PT), through some of their members in Rio, were quick to condemn the efforts by Jacarezinho's neighborhood association to curb police brutality in these same terms (Braga, 2001; Petry, 2001; Vargas, 2003).

By deepening and publicizing international political liaisons, the men and women of Jacarezinho shift the focus away from the local scenes to the deep political roots that bind their perspectives with that of fellow US black community organizers. As they protest against the social conservatism of the right (of which racism is a prominent yet mostly silent aspect) and the race blindness of the left, Jacarezinho organizers assert their political views that make race a central category of their lives and analyses. Transnational alliances in the black diaspora therefore provide counternarratives that are crucial in maintaining and expanding liberation movements.

You may ask whether the politics embraced by favela activists are still within the master's house. In what measure do Brazilian organizers challenge institutional powers and established grammar as they utilize racialized discourses that, as we have seen, can unselfconsciously feed from and therefore reproduce hierarchies? As favela activists challenge the police and the multiple facets of social exclusion, and attempt to transform race into a galvanizer for solidarity and mobilization, are they not engaging in traditional politics of fulfillment?

The fact that such questions cannot be answered unequivocally reveals, first, how context determines the effectiveness of identity politics, and second, how race-thinking is at times – if not at *most* times – necessary to advance black people's pursue of justice. In the case of Rio, the novelty of race-based thinking constitutes an open confrontation to a form of established power that negates the validity of racial categories as explanation for Brazilian social reality. In the context of racial democracy,[12] the open articulation of race as a central element determining distribution of resources, access to decision-making spheres, interactions with representatives of the state, and everyday interactions constitute a clear attempt to formulate a new, alternative political consciousness. While this new consciousness is obviously attuned to the promises of bourgeois society – and in this sense within the confines of the master's house – it establishes a rupture with forms of domination that, even though clearly racialized, silence their very racial determinants.

In the Brazilian case, therefore, identity politics is encouraging a politics of identification among Afro-descendants who, through their elaboration of discursive and practical tools that render effective their solidarity, are making necessary demands to the state and to civil society seeking to guarantee a base for, not only the minimum conditions for citizenship but, in the last analysis, plain and simple survival. Blacks in Brazil, as in the US, although by different means, are attempting to outlive their respective country's forms of genocide. Jacarezinho activists are demanding that the state fulfills its promises of universal citizenship but at the same time are searching for new subjectivities and modes of solidarity that allow their practitioners to struggle for a future not yet imagined.

The dialogues with African Americans are contributing to the elaboration of hopes of a just society that is not yet known. These less defined desires are expressed in the willingness to question (while utilizing) newly found, provisory truths about race, in the engagement with alternative strategies of organization, and in the discussion of political and cultural traditions of the African diaspora. Jacarezinho organizers are skeptical of hierarchies and concentration of power, much like CAPA activists. Rio activists have embraced the challenges of questioning taken-for-granted assumptions while developing strategies to cope with the daily assaults on dignity and life. Their politics are both in and outside the master's house – fulfillment and transfiguration. Such politics are at once based on the bricoleur's and the engineer's modus operandi; and they utilize race solidarity with blacks of the African diaspora as well as with peoples of color of varied nations (Cuba, Ecuador, and Colombia, for example).

This process of decolonization, for all its transformative potential, has barely started. Among favela activists, race-thinking is incipient; thinking beyond race is just as embryonic. Hierarchies and exclusion, while more evident when imposed by institutions and individuals, sometimes remain blatantly unchallenged. Reflecting a trend in the Left, gender relations continue to be problematic. Sexism and homophobia, and the attending patriarchy, are common particularly among black activist men. Women in the neighborhood association continue to be relegated to traditional functions such as cooks, cleaners, secretaries, and overall invisible roles. Such reality became shockingly clear during a meeting of various Rio favela organizations I attended in 2001. The great majority of speakers were men while women were in the kitchen, serving coffee and food, and in the background. The difficulties in approaching sexism and homophobia are an indication of how much farther and deeper we must go if our desires for radical transformation and destruction of hierarchies are going to materialize. While the struggles against racism are central, they will be unfinished and self-defeating if not accompanied by active engagement against all forms of oppression and exclusion.

The political character of the African diaspora emerges clearly out of the experiences analyzed so far. While strategies that can be classified as inside the master's house are prevalent and necessary, the deeply revolutionary aspects of the black diasporic politics are those which are in sharp contrast to the already-known, or to the politics of fulfillment that a bricoleur's approach would generate. The revolutionary Afrodiasporic politics is a distinct yet shared political sensibility and know-how that is categorical in its wishes for a non-hierarchical, solidary social world. In the same way that historically black peoples have seldom employed the weapons and the violence of our oppressors when given the opportunity, the radical politics informing the search for a new house refuses to limit itself to the politics of fulfillment, to the bricoleur's (even if surprising) rearrangements, to the vocabularies and strategies of identity politics (Robinson, 2000[1983]; p. 168). The love supreme that constitutes this politics' method blueprint is not restricted by already existing projects of society, vocabularies, and sociabilities. The reference – or should I say, the non-reference – is outside of our material world, even though concrete justice and decision-making powers in this material world are vigorously fought for. This politics of transfiguration is a renunciation of our actual existence for the struggle toward a collective existence of which we will probably not be a part. We renounce our individual being for the collective being; we renounce our actually existing being for an ontological being to be realized in an indeterminate future. This politics of transfiguration is a politics of renouncing, but not only. The renouncing is an indeterminate moment that, guided by the dignity of those who have put the collective good above all else, is itself the model of the social world yet to be constructed.

Renouncing the master's house means renouncing our small and temporary truths, our provisional comforts derived from our episodic successes in using the master's tools against the masters and (willingly or not) against ourselves. What surfaces with the methodologies of the oppressed is a firm commitment to a historical consciousness that has been successful in opposing our objectification by emphasizing a metaphysical reservoir predicated on our ultimate integrity. We are in this corrupt, hierarchical, racialized, patriarchal, and exclusive capitalist world, but we are not reducible to it. As I learned from activists, poets, musicians, and in conversations in South Central and Jacarezinho, some of our fundamental values are just different than what defines the world we live in (see also Kelley, 2002). In the same way enslaved Africans were not solely the product of slavery – they were African first – we are not merely the product of the contemporary systems of power, production, and representations. We must struggle against the very obvious injustices of which blacks are the preferential targets, but ideally we must also look beyond the immediate fights for survival.

The black radical tradition that informs the endless search for liberation, although modeled in a metaphysical structure of sentiments, has materialized itself in alternative sociabilities, or at the very least, in theories about such sociabilities. Palmares, Haiti, Rastafarian communities in Ethiopia, Black Power: in all these instances, theoretical or practical, the refusal to be dominated by actual material and psychological realities has characterized the drive to innovation. It is either physical and moral death, or the necessary and liberating pain of stepping out of and imagining beyond the already known. The enslaved had no choice; blacks and other oppressed groups today have no choice. Hence the continuing significance of the metaphysical and the accent on the structures of thought still dominating black diasporic politics.

The black radical tradition also lives in a frequency that is mostly not perceptible to the historical police state and social organization, from the slave master to the contemporary panopticon-like types of control. I am obviously not talking about black self-defense efforts and radical liberatory movements more generally – those have been surely confronted by the powerful with all their might and means. I am speaking about that which remains even after the dismantling of maroon settlements, lynchings, the persistence of the most destructive and hard-to-locate forms of racism, FBI's COINTELPROs (old and new), and our own tendencies to love our chains and to enchain others. This historical responsibility, this imagination and spirit of freedom, because it is not material and cannot be produced and located in social isolation, cannot be appropriated and dialectically transformed into capital's own weapons of domination. The point I am making is that, whereas it can be argued, with Hardt and Negri (2000), that existing institutions of power, or Empire, are the result of bourgeois society's response to proletarian internationalism, such argument becomes fragile, or limited, when we consider that blacks and other racialized groups have, on the one hand, not been fully recognized as parts of this internationalism, and on the other, have operated through spirituality, metacommunication, poetry, have dared to imagine the unimaginable, and have survived. Which is to say, by claiming the end of metaphysics, the self-containment of our actual world, Hardt and Negri reproduce European-centered perspectives that silence the non-discursive, non-material contributions peoples of color have made, shared, preserved, and metamorphosed in a critique of world capitalism and its contradictory ideologies. At the very least, Hardt and Negri automatically assume people of color's social movements have been phagocytized by Empire. Hegel's aphorism about the temperate zones of Europe as the stage of history can be applied to *Empire* insofar as Hardt and Negri's narrative racializes – whitens – the struggles thought to be the most relevant to the advancement of international socialism.[13]

The politics of the Afrodiasporic peoples and organizations analyzed here present us with a radical utopia. It is radical because the new adamantly unsettled and freed imagined polity is neither in defined time and space coordinates, nor is it an already formed mental construction. The dreams, the imaginations that inform the most revolutionary aspects of the struggles in the US and Brazil refuse to settle for the provisory utopian societies they evoke. It is as if the activists/intellectuals/artists engaged in revolutionary politics are saying that any and all imagination and forms of liberation need to be constantly readjusted. No revolution is final; and the (provisory) accomplishments are in the struggle itself.

One of the provisory accomplishments of the LA/Rio connection has been the construction of a lingua franca that, while encumbered by language differences,[14] builds on a set of shared sentiments and practices that make revolutionary communication possible. This vocabulary has at its core not only the recognition of a common enemy, but also, and more importantly, a common passion of and method toward justice, equality, and freedom. The common enemy is accessed through the analysis of police brutality, poverty, marginalization, and white supremacy that, although occurring in different forms in LA and Rio, reveal a set of irreducible principles, the more obvious of which are the maintenance of hierarchies and their ideological justifications. Activists have noted how the influx of sophisticated arms, drugs, and the opening of the markets to international capitalism has also meant more unemployment, more state violence, more prisons, more racism against

Afrodiasporic communities, more sexism and homophobia applied to the new labor divisions, more Aids/HIV, more genocide. The emerging common vocabulary is able to deconstruct the logic of neoliberal transnational capitalism, trace its continuity from at least the expansion of colonialism and slavery to its role in the genocidal present-day policies, and project alternatives to such policies that draw on the necessary wisdoms that made it possible for Afrodiasporic communities to endure to this day. This lingua franca lends itself to envisioning new realities and remaking our selves and our sociabilities. Because it is on the move, embracing change, adaptation, it never ceases to explore new possibilities. The lingua franca of freedom is embedded in semantics of endless self-making and of radical social transformation.

Radical dreams of justice require searching for deep historical roots and broad social structures, and connecting these to personal and collective action aimed at building alternative modes of sociability. What alternative modes of sociability? We cannot know because we should not know. Opposed to the crystal certainties of fascism (Arendt, 1979[1948]; Lefort, 1981), to quick-answers, homogeneity, stability, and prediction, radical wishes of freedom cannot settle – they need to operate on the provisory. There is no radical enough, already-formed revolutionary syntax. We need to keep imagining beyond the strict geographical, ideological, and cognitive confines defined by race essentialism while preserving our racial pride and wisdoms; we need to continue with the construction a new house, with new tools, even if it means we will have to rebuild it soon thereafter, with new inputs and insights coming from new alliances. The continuing and global significance of race only attests to the urgent need of coming to terms with its manifestations so that the essential but always limited benefits accruing from its use can be harvested while its powerful traps can be avoided.

ACKNOWLEDGMENTS

I would like to thank Moon-Kie Jung, Jemima Pierre, Edmund T. Gordon, Charles Hale, Mohan Ambikaipaker, Jafari Allen, and Nichole Rustin for helpful comments and suggestions.

NOTES

1. A related notion of becoming is in the following: "Identity, like a river, is always changing, always in transition, always in nepantla. Like the river downstream, you're not the same person you were upstream. You begin to define yourself in terms of who

you are becoming, and not who you have been." (Anzaldúa, 2002, p. 556). While I certainly value the emphasis on the becoming, I am also aware that for Afrodiasporic persons, the amplitude of identity possibilities is not infinite; black radical becoming is thus a political possibility that speaks to both agency and structural constraints.

2. Founded by Black Panther Party members who survived the FBI's Counter Intelligence Programs (COINTELPROs), CAPA has been in South Central Los Angeles since 1976. It was formed primarily in response to the historically persistent waves of police shooting, beatings, and harassment that define predominantly black neighborhoods. Michael Zinzun, a nationally known community activist and former Black Panther Party member, today coordinates CAPA. The institution embraces a variety of causes that are both the result of CAPA's historical antecedents of community-related political activity and its analysis of and intervention in emerging events such as the 1980s' great wave of immigration from Latin and Central America, the Reaganomics-generated unemployment crisis, gang activity, and large-scale, high-tech, militarized, publicly sanctioned police repression. For more information on CAPA, see Vargas (1999, 2003).

3. Regardless of class, blacks are more segregated than poorest Latino/as (see Massey & Denton, 1993). Intergenerational transmission of income, wealth, and occupational status continue to constrain blacks' perspectives vis-à-vis other racial groups in the US (see Oliver & Shapiro, 1997; Labor/Community Strategy Center, 1992).

4. The need for the *new* would place such radical politics in the modernist tradition, as described by Berman (1988), Schorske (1981), Habermas (1990), and Andrade (1981), among others. However, while its kinship with modernity is apparent, this radical politics constitutes a critique of the modernist project as it unravels the contradictions of bourgeois society, so obvious from the perspective of enslaved blacks and their descendants (see Gilroy, 1993).

5. Patricia Hill Collins (1991) located two interdependent dimensions of black women's activism: one is concerned with group survival, and does not challenge structures of oppression; the other is the struggle for institutional transformation. While the wishes and practices of transformation I describe go beyond institutional transformation, the characterization is compatible with the argument I am developing.

6. Charles Lawrence III (1995) asserts the need to dream and imagine a world yet not realized. This radical, transfigurative project accepts the dream but cannot settle. To settle would be to give up on the fundamental need of constant reinvention.

7. For Black US communities, the condition of possibility of forming viable coalitions across race has been, first of all, coming together as autonomous black people (Carmichael & Hamilton, 1967).

8. Abdias do Nascimento (1989) provides useful explanations of Brazilian racial categories and their social consequences. For comparisons between Brazilian and US race relations see the volume edited by Michael Hanchard (1999). Robin Sheriff (2001) challenges the widely accepted notions concerning the multiplicity of racial classifications in Brazil by examining the everyday lives of people living in a favela in Rio.

9. MVBill, Os Racionais, O Rappa, Cidade Negra: these are some of the musical performers whose lyrics openly challenge racism in the largest Brazilian cities.

10. The Brazilian delegation and final document almost totally excluded favela blacks and their proposals. I speak based on the experience of having participated in both the state of Rio de Janeiro's preparatory meeting and the national convention

that also took place in Rio. In those occasions I worked with a group of favela activists – connected to CAPA – attempting to have their perspectives on racism and how to improve the lives of those living in the most neglected areas in the country taken into account. The simple fact that the established black intelligentsia, contrary to business as usual, had their views challenged by Afro-Brazilians of the favelas is a good indication of the vitality of the contemporary debate around race in Brazil.

Another example of this vitality was the last televised debate on September 2002 among the presidential candidates, when a question regarding the use of racial quotas by the federal government was posed to all the contestants. This is certainly the first time such a debate is raised at this national level. Lula, the Worker's Party candidate, not surprisingly (given the Left's poor record in approaching racism) declared that, if elected, his party would utilize 'scientific criteria' to determine who is black. Ciro Gomes, another center-leftist candidate otherwise inexpressive, seized the moment to criticize Lula (then far ahead in the vote intention polls) and stated his position that blacks are all that consider themselves to be so.

11. "Descend to the asphalt" was a phrase utilized by black favela activists to express their intention of protesting their exclusion and discrimination in Rio's elite areas (the asphalt) and there claim what was theirs – that is, jobs, education, and respect. The activists calculated that suggesting high concentrations of people of the favela in elite areas would generate panic among the well off. See the following newspapers: *O Globo*, 25 May 2000; *Extra*, 22 August 2000; *Jornal do Brasil*, 22 October 2000.

12. Racial democracy, the hegemonic, prevailing ideology about Brazilian race relations that asserts the absence of race-based social exclusions (as in the US and Apartheid South Africa), derives mostly from the work of Gilberto Freyre (1951, 1964). Elsewhere, I suggest that Brazilian social relations are marked by a dialectic according to which the hyperconsciousness of race and is always accompanied by its negation (Vargas, 2004).

13. Spivak (1999) has located this structure of thought in Kant, Hegel, Marx, and Foucault, among others. Such a reading of Hardt and Negri, especially their silent assumptions about the 'native informant,' key conceptual tool for Spivak's deconstructions, will reveal their racialized (albeit, and not surprisingly silent) analytical matrix.

14. This apparent contraction between a lingua franca and language barriers is not lost by the activists, who often joke about how they can communicate humor and dreams of freedom *without utilizing a strict set of* communicative tools. The resulting lingua franca, based on dreams of freedom, utilizes not only syncretic words and phrases made up of English, Portuguese, and Spanish, among others, but also gestures, musics, touches, and facial expressions.

REFERENCES

Andrade, M. de. (1981). *Macunaíma: o Herói sem nenhum Caráter*. Brasília: CNPq.
Anzaldúa, G. (2002). Now let us shift... the path of conocimiento... inner work, public acts. In: G. Anzaldúa & A. Keating (Eds), *This bridge we call home* (pp. 540–577). New York: Routledge.
Appiah, K. A. (1992). *In my father's house: Africa in the philosophy of culture*. New York: Oxford University Press.

Arendt, H. (1979[1948]). *The origins of totalitarianism.* San Diego: Harcourt Brace.
Berman, M. (1988). *All that is solid melts into the air: The experience of modernity.* New York: Penguin.
Braga, É. (2001). Favela trancada a cadeado. *O Dia, 8*(July), 4.
Carmichael, S. [Kwame Ture] & Hamilton, C. (1967). *Black power: The politics of liberation in America.* New York: Random House.
Collins, P. H. (1991). *Black feminist thought: Knowledge, consciousness, and the politics of empowerment.* London: Routledge.
Collins, P. H. (1998). *Fighting words: Black women and the search for justice.* Minneapolis: University of Minnesota Press.
Combahee River Collective. (1995). A Black feminist statement. In: B. Guy-Sheftall (Ed.), *Words of fire: An Anthology of African-American feminist thought.* New York: The New Press.
Crenshaw, K., Gotanda, N., Peller, G., & Thomas, K. (Eds) (1995). *Critical race theory: The key writings that formed the movement.* New York: The New Press.
Freyre, G. (1951). *Brazil, an interpretation.* New York: Knopf.
Freyre, G. (1964). *Casa-grande & senzala: Formacão da familia Brasileira sob o regime da economia patriarcal.* Rio de Janeiro: José Olympio.
Gilroy, P. (1993). *The Black Atlantic: modernity and double consciousness.* Cambridge, MA: Harvard University Press.
Gilroy, P. (2000). *Against race: Imagining political culture beyond the color line.* Cambridge, MA: Harvard University Press.
Habermas, J. (1990). *The philosophical discourse of modernity: Twelve lectures.* Boston: MIT Press.
Hall, S. (1980). Race, articulation, and societies structured in dominance. In: *Sociological theories: Race and colonialism.* London: Unesco.
Hanchard, M. (1994). *Orpheus and power: The Movimento Negro of Rio de Janeiro and São Paulo, Brazil, 1945–1988.* Princeton: Princeton University Press.
Hanchard, M. (Ed.) (1999). *Racial politics in contemporary Brazil.* Durham: Duke University Press.
Hardt, M., & Negri, A. (2000). *Empire.* Cambridge, MA: Harvard University Press.
Kelley, R. D. G. (1997). *Yo' mama's disfunktional! Fighting the culture wars in urban America.* Boston: Beacon Press.
Kelley, R. D. G. (2002). *Freedom dreams: The Black radical imagination.* Boston: Beacon Press.
Labor/Community Strategy Center. (1992). *Reconstructing Los Angeles from the bottom up.* Los Angeles.
Lawrence III, C. (1995). The word and the river: Pedagogy as scholarship as struggle. In: K. Crenshaw, N. Gotanda, G. Peller, & K. Thomas (Eds), *Critical race theory: The key writings that formed the movement.* New York: The New Press.
Lefort, C. (1981). *L'Invention democratique: Les limites de la domination totalitaire.* Paris: Fayard.
Lévi-Strauss, C. (1989). *O pensamento selvagem.* Campinas: Papirus.
Lipsitz, G. (1997). *The possessive investment in whiteness: How White people profit from identity politics.* Philadelphia: Temple University Press.
Lorde, A. (1984). *Sister outsider.* Trumansburg, NY: Crossing Press.
Marable, M. (1997). Rethinking black liberation: Towards a new protest paradigm. *Race & Class, 38*(4), 1–14.

Massey, D., & Denton, N. (1993). *American apartheid: Segregation and the making of the underclass*. Cambridge, MA: Harvard University Press.

Mohanty, S. P. (2000). The epistemic status of cultural identity: On *Beloved* and *The Post-colonial Condition*. In: P. M. L. Moya & M. R. Hames-Garcia (Eds), *Reclaiming identity* (pp. 29–66). Berkeley: University of California Press.

Nascimento, A. (1989). *Brazil: Mixture or massacre?* Dover: The Majority Press.

Oliver, M., & Shapiro, T. (1997). *Black wealth/White wealth: A new perspective on racial inequality*. New York: Routledge.

Petry, S. (2001). Morro Carioca cria condomínio-favela. *Folha de S.Paulo, 25*(July), C1.

Robinson, C. (2000[1983]). *Black marxism: The making of the Black radical tradition*. Chapel Hill: University of North Carolina Press.

Sandoval, C. (2000). *Methodology of the oppressed*. Minneapolis: University of Minnesota Press.

Schorske, C. (1981). *Fin-de-siecle Vienna: Politics and culture*. New York: Random House.

Sheriff, R. (2001). *Dreaming equality: Colour, race, and racism in urban Brazil*. New Brunswick: Rutgers University Press.

Smith, B. (2000). *The truth that never hurts: Writings on race, gender, and freedom*. New Brunswick: Rutgers University Press.

Spivak, G. (1999). *A critique of postcolonial reason: Toward a history of the vanishing present*. Cambridge, MA: Harvard University Press.

Sudbury, J. (1998). *Other kinds of dreams: Black women's organizations and the politics of transformation*. London: Routledge.

Twine, F. W. (1998). *Racism in a racial democracy : The maintenance of white supremacy in Brazil*. New Brunswick, N.J.: Rutgers University Press.

Tyson, T. (1999). *Radio free Dixie: Robert F. Williams and the roots of black power*. Chapel Hill: University of North Carolina Press.

Vargas, J. H. C. (1999). Blacks in the city of Angels' dust. PhD dissertation, University of California, San Diego.

Vargas, J. H. C. (2003). The inner city and the favela: Transnational Black politics. *Race & Class, 44*(4), 19–40.

Vargas, J. H. C. (2004). Hyperconsciousness of race and its negation: The dialectic of white supremacy in Brazil., *Identities, 11*, 443–470.

Williams, R. (1998[1962]). *Negroes with guns*. Detroit: Wayne State University Press.

THEORIZING HETEROGENEITY: SOCIAL AND ECONOMIC WELL-BEING OF NATIVE BLACKS, AFRO-CARIBBEAN AND AFRICAN IMMIGRANTS IN THE U.S. ☆

Sherrill L. Sellers, Hiu Ha Florence Chong, and Michelle Harris

ABSTRACT

This study presents three theoretical perspectives to explore the patterns of social and economic well-being among native blacks, Afro-Caribbean, and African immigrants in the US: the assimilation model which emphasizes individual performance and views immigration as a process of human-capital enhancement; the cultural model which suggests that immigrant groups have cultural capital that allows for greater upward mobility and improved well-being; and the ethnic penalty model which suggests race as preeminent in determining social-economic well-being. Using census data from 1990 to 2000, we find modest support for each perspective. We

☆This research was made possible through a grant from the Worldwide University Network (WUN).

The New Black: Alternative Paradigms and Strategies for the 21st Century
Research in Race and Ethnic Relations, Volume 14, 287–305
Copyright © 2007 by Elsevier Ltd.
ISSN: 0195-7449/doi:10.1016/S0195-7449(06)14013-1

concluded with a call for additional research that models the heterogeneity within black communities.

Over the last decade, blacks have become an increasingly important part of the United States immigrant flow. In 2001, blacks from Africa and the Caribbean represented 11.6 percent of the total US foreign-born population. Census data indicate that African and Afro-Caribbean immigrants contributed to nearly 25 percent of the growth in the black population in the 1990s (Nasser, 2003). The number of immigrants from the sub-Saharan countries of Africa grew more than twofold, and those immigrants with Afro-Caribbean roots increased over 60 percent. These demographic changes hint at considerable heterogeneity within the US black community.

In recent years, Caribbean immigrants have received some attention (Butcher, 1994; Heron, 2001; Kalmijn, 1996; Model, 1995; Model, Fisher, & Silberman, 1999; Waters, 1999), and a small body of research on African immigrants is taking shape (Arthur, 2000; Dodoo & Takyi, 2002; Kposowa, 2002; Sellers, Ward, & Pate, in press; Kasinitz, 1992; Takyi, 2002). Few studies, however, have compared the experiences of native blacks, Afro-Caribbean, and African immigrants in the US (Dodoo, 1997).

A main thread that ties these few studies together is the view that African and Afro-Caribbean immigrants outperform or out-earn native-born blacks in America (Butcher, 1994; Dodoo, 1997; Heron, 2001; Model et al, 1999; Waters, 1994). Theoretical explanations for these disparities rely heavily on assimilation models and cultural perspectives, which suggest that human or cultural capital characteristics are the main contributors to within and between group variation (Butcher, 1994; Sowell, 1978; Waters, 1994).

However, neither human nor cultural capital perspectives adequately account for "blackness,"i.e., of the role of race in shaping mobility experiences. Native blacks, Afro-Caribbeans, and African immigrants are historically situated at the intersections of two different concepts of American racial identity – "race" – the ascribed concept and –"ethnicity" – how groups define themselves. Yet, research on blacks in the US has often made few distinctions between native blacks, African immigrants and Afro-Caribbean immigrants (Dodoo, 1991; Freeman, 2002; Lim, 2001).

This paper considers two questions: (1) what are similarities and differences in social and economic well being among native blacks, Afro-Caribbean and African immigrants? and (2) to what extent do existing theoretical frameworks account for this variation?

THEORETICAL PERSPECTIVES

To address the aforementioned questions, we consider three frameworks – assimilation models, cultural capital models, and the ethnic penalty model. We then examine census data to assess explanatory power of these theoretical perspectives.

Assimilation Models

The classic straight-line assimilation model assumes that assimilation works in a linear trajectory. All immigrants or ethnic minorities will ultimately integrate into white middle class US society (Gordon, 1964). Immigration is therefore a process of human capital enhancement. Human-capital characteristics such as English language proficiency, education, years of residence, and other specific skills relevant to the country of residence, determine disparities among individuals, natives and immigrants, as well as within and between racial groups. The less human capital a group has the lower the returns to social and economic attainment. New immigrants are usually on a lower position on the social stratification ladder, and may be less economically competitive compared to their native-born counterparts by virtue of lower human capital. Higher levels of social and economic well-being can be achieved as length of residence increases and as language proficiency, educational attainment, and other dimensions of human capital improve (Borjas, 1994; Chiswick, Cohen, & Zach, 1997; Clark & Lindley, 2004). Assimilation theory emphasizes individual-level performance and views immigration as a process of human capital enhancement in which black immigrants acquire skills relevant to the destination country. It assumes that black immigrants' disadvantage will disappear as length of stay in the US increases.

Several limitations to the straight-line assimilation model have been identified. First, immigrants do not necessarily start from the bottom and work themselves up the socioeconomic ladder. The issue of selection bias in immigration partly explains this. According to Butcher (1994), not all residents in a sending country are equally likely to emigrate. Those potential immigrants with higher levels of education, stronger language skills and increased employability (e.g., advanced technical skills) are much more likely to leave than their less advantaged counterparts, therefore placing them not at the bottom but somewhere higher up on the receiving country's stratification ladder. Second, the straight-line assimilation model provides little insight into the role of geographic distance in the assimilation of immigrant groups. Compared with Caribbean immigrants, African immigrants are more likely to encounter greater obstacles for relocation (because of the greater distance they must travel) and therefore experience an even larger selection bias. The well-known 'brain drain' phenomenon that refers to inflow of highly educated, skilled and achievement-orientated Africans to the US (Arthur, 2000; Dodoo, 1997) may support this argument. From this point of view, it will be reasonable to suggest that African and Caribbean immigrants, rather than native black Americans, will have better social and economic well-being. Further, because African immigrants are the most geographically distant, they will outperform Afro-Caribbean immigrants.

Findings on the impact of human capital characteristics on black immigrant economic well being are inconsistent. Some studies found that new immigrants experience an initial economic disadvantage (Heron, 2001). Others found that this economic set-back disappears as length of stay in the US increases (Borjas, 1994; Chiswick et al., 1997). Other findings suggest that both Caribbean and African immigrants were indeed better off than their native counterparts regardless of the duration of residence and their immigrant status (Butcher, 1994; Dodoo, 1997; Djamba, 1999). Yet, in the case of black African immigrants, similar or even higher human capital as that of blacks from the Caribbean does not necessarily lead to equal outcomes on economic attainment (Dodoo, 1997). It should be noted that the classic assimilation model was developed based on the 'successful' acculturation and assimilation of white European immigrants rather than ethnic-racial minorities (Wildsmith, 2004). Thus, the model does not adequately address racial and ethnic differences and a variety of contextual condition such as the existence of structural barriers, historical background, and power imbalances and inequality among racial and ethnic groups that might impede upward social mobility (Karas, 2002; Ostine, 1998). Further, it simplifies complex human activities into a 'uniform mechanism' (Ostine, 1998).

Addressing these critiques, segmented assimilation theory (Portes & Zhou, 1993) emphasizes multiple trajectories of assimilation. Social capital, such as social networks and the presence or absence of ethnic community, is viewed as a main trait that predicts differential social outcomes among various groups. The theory argues that immigrants or minority ethnic groups do not necessarily or automatically assimilate into white mainstream society. The diversity of socioeconomic characteristics and reasons for migration results in diverse adaptive trajectories. The outcome of social and economic well-being depends on which sector – the ethnic community, white middle class or black inner-city underclass – into which immigrants assimilate (*ibid*). Different sectors have different levels of human and social capital resources at their disposal. For example, an ethnic community may be a convenient market for an individual to sell goods and services. Individuals with start-up capital, business and social networks, and other resources can find a place in the market. This can lead to upward social mobility. Conversely, deficiency of these resources impedes individuals' progress and can lead to a downward trajectory, and social and economic distress. A few studies provide some support for the segmented assimilation theory, finding that low socioeconomic status immigrants and their offspring are more likely to assimilate into the downward mobility trajectory at the bottom of society by virtue of the level of racial segregation in the US and the concentration of poverty among minority Americans (Gans, 1992; Portes & Zhou, 1993).

Ethnic enclaves play an important part in the immigrant and minority groups' socioeconomic attainment although it is controversial for its role in hindering the integration of immigrants in the broader society. An ethnic enclave may reflect social distance among immigrants and natives as they serve and attract immigrants sharing the same ethnicity, but drive away natives (Freeman, 2002). Accordingly, an ethnic enclave may function as an alternative for immigrants or ethnic minorities to participate in the economic mainstream, and as a way for immigrants to avoid potential adversarial encounters in the wider society by taking advantage of the social network among their own ethnic group (Heron, 2001; Freeman, 2002). Ethnic enclaves may protect immigrants from exposure to discrimination – racial or otherwise (Portes & Zhou, 1993). Nonetheless, enclave residents are more likely to move out of the area after their socioeconomic circumstances improve. It is possible that in doing so, these residents remove valuable economic resources from the community.

Assimilation theories offer concepts – human/social capital and ethnic enclave – that enable us to hypothesize that: (1) as they have the longest length of stay, native blacks will have highest levels of social and economic well-being; (2) a group with the greater human capital, such as higher levels of education and English language proficiency, will have the better social and economic well-being; (3) the well-being of a group which is highly concentrated in a certain area will be worse off than those who reside in more racially mixed environments; and (4) over time there will be a convergence such that as immigrants acquire more social capital their social and economic trajectories will improve.

Cultural Theoretical Perspectives

Scholars who endorse cultural explanations suggest that norms and values are the key influence in determining social and economic attainment of ethnic groups and immigrants. For instance, Sowell (1978, pp. 41–48) argues that "color alone, or racism alone, is clearly not a sufficient explanation of the disparities within the black population or between the black and white populations" (in Butcher, 1994). Sowell (1978) suggests that cultural traditions provide the most straightforward explanation. At its simplest, this perspective suggests that cultural traditions of US-born blacks impede their economic progress.

Scholars who endorse cultural explanations emphasize that race and racial discrimination are no longer important in determining social and economic attainment of ethnic groups and immigrants. Rather, historical and contemporary cultural background and cultural characteristics such as attitudes toward work and school lead to differential outcomes within and between groups. Native blacks are disadvantaged because of historically harsh slave experiences and racial minority status after liberation and these have lead to the stigmatization of "blackness" in the US (Dodoo, 1997). By contrast, the legacy of slavery was less violent and of shorter duration for Afro-Caribbean and African immigrants (Sowell, 1978). Further, higher cultural capital, such as high motivation and achievement orientation, diligence, better work ethnic and frugality, enable Afro-Caribbean and African immigrants to overcome discrimination and immigrant status (*ibid*).

The ethnic identity model is a variant of Sowell's cultural perspective. The model focuses on distinguishing one's racial-ethnic group through expressions of strong ethnic identity and focuses on the differences between groups. Mary Waters (1994, 1999) hints at this perspective as she articulates the views of Afro-Caribbean immigrants vis-à-vis US-born blacks. US-born blacks are often viewed as disorganized, lacking a work ethic, and obsessed with race (Waters, 1994). Caribbean immigrants are often perceived by whites as culturally superior to native-born blacks and this opens up opportunities for upward social mobility for Afro-Caribbeans. The advantages of being a 'model minority' are maintained through preserving unique customs, culture, and accents that distinguish Afro-Caribbeans from their native counterparts (Ostine, 1998).

The comparison between native-born blacks and Caribbean immigrants gives rise to questions regarding how the cultural perspective applies to African immigrants. We note that it is impossible to speak of one "culture" for an entire continent, with 53 different countries, and hundreds of spoken languages. We suspect that what appear to be cultural differences between native blacks and African immigrants may be less related to cultural differences between the groups and more related to improper comparisons. A full range of native blacks (across the social and economic spectrum) are compared to immigrants who are the best and brightest of the sending country. Further, the long and expensive journey traveling from Africa to the US, indicate high possibility that African immigrants have high motivation for success (Arthur, 2000; Dodoo, 1997).

Overall, the cultural perspective provides paradoxical explanations on the disparities of black populations by underplaying race and claiming the outcome of social and economic well being as the product of differences in cultural capital. The perspective blames native black Americans for their lower social and economic standing and ties it to the cultural characteristics of the group. The discourse of the cultural perspective, therefore, perpetuates a form of racism by denying the relevance of race, the barriers of racism, and the special position of 'blackness' in the US (Pierre, 2004). In this sense, acknowledging the heterogeneity of the black community in the US underscores the limits of the cultural perspective.

Ethnic Penalty Model

Partly as a corrective to the assimilation and cultural capital theoretical perspectives, the ethnic penalty model focuses particular attention on the role of ethnicity in a group's mobility experiences. The ethnic penalty perspective derives from the many observations and studies of communities of color, which find that these communities can have similar human capital as whites but gain much lower returns on their investment (Bobo, Kluegel, & Smith, 1997; Pattilo-McCoy, 1999). The concept of ethnic penalty presents a crucial hint at the impact of race and racial discrimination on the social and economic well being of people of color. Variation in social and economic well being of different groups can be attributed to social stratification, stereotyping, discrimination and racism. The key point of the ethnic penalty model is that, relative to whites, all blacks should have lower levels of economic well being. One extrapolation of the model suggests that the differences within black populations would not be that great. It is possible that all blacks encounter a penalty in the host society but that penalty is not equally distributed – it varies among ethnic groups. The question is how the ethnic penalty model differentiates the disparity among native-born blacks, African and Afro-Caribbean immigrants.

The notion of "multicultural racism" provides an alternative view for explaining social and economic heterogeneity within black populations in the US (Gladwell, 1996). Coined by essayist Malcolm Gladwell, the phrase captures race-related divisions within groups that are the function of different trajectories for success depending on ethnic identity. People of Caribbean descent are perceived to be "better Black" people than native-born blacks and therefore are afforded more employment and economic opportunities that lead to better socioeconomic outcomes for this group. Aracelis Francis (2000) observed tensions between African immigrants and native-born American blacks and suggested that these divisions may contribute to the exploitation of both groups by pitting the groups against each other rather than joining as allies in efforts to overcome racial discrimination. In the similar vein, Jackson and Cothran (2003) hinted that the relationship among these three ethnic groups is tense. They assert that Afro-Caribbean and African immigrants have little contact with each other in American life. In particular, African immigrants seem reluctant to befriend Afro-Caribbean and native American blacks. Their findings indicate that each group harbored stereotypes, misconceptions, and myths about the others. Jackson and Cothran point out that the misconceptions have been perpetuated as a way to continue rivalry for economic and social advantages. The irony is that the groups are at times competing for the "the crumbs," that is, the low-wage service jobs in the secondary labor force.

Based on the above discussion, the ethnic penalty model predicts that native blacks' well being may be worse off than either Afro-Caribbean or African immigrants because native black Americans are under the heaviest penalty. The model is less able to predict relationships for Afro-Caribbean and African immigrants. The concept of multiculturalism racism is relatively new and there is very little research evidence on the perceptions of Americans, in general, and black communities, in particular, toward African immigrants. Hence, it is less-well known to what extent the ethnic penalty model explains the level of penalty of African immigrants. However, if Caribbean immigrants benefit more from multiculturalism racism for their economic well-being, then, predicting that African immigrants will be at the similar position with Caribbean immigrants, is reasonable.

To summarize, the assimilation perspective suggests that native blacks might have better social and economic outcomes but the trajectories may converge as immigrants acquire human and social capital. The cultural theoretical perspective suggests that African and Afro-Caribbean immigrants hold cultural values that facilitate social and economic success, hence native black Americans will be lest well off on social and economic outcomes. The ethnic penalty model suggests that native blacks are disadvantaged compared to the other two groups due to differential penalties and unwitting participation of the groups in their systematic disadvantage and structurally reinforced strife. Interestingly, both the cultural perspective and the ethnic penalty model do not easily suggest a difference between Afro-Caribbean and African immigrants.

To examine the strength of these claims, we examine census data from 1990 and 2000. We note at the outset that these analyses are very preliminary. Our aim is to advance the conversation about heterogeneity within black populations. Further research with longitudinal data collected specifically to investigate the merits of the three theoretical perspectives is needed.

DATA SOURCES

Data were drawn from multiple sources, although the primary data sources are the 1990 and 2000 US Census.[1] Data from one study (Table 1) mainly focus on a specific age range of male respondents while the other (Tables 2 & 3) focus on all blacks in a metropolitan area and enable us to compare the three ethnic groups in two different census periods.

Descriptive Data

As shown in Table 1, African immigrants are about five year younger than Afro-Caribbean immigrants and native-black American. The number of African immigrants who hold college degree (either attained in the US or abroad) is 58 percent, which is about fourfold that of Afro-Caribbean immigrants and of native-black Americans. Although fewer African immigrants hold degrees granted by US institutions, the percentage is still higher than the other two groups. Compared to African immigrants, Afro-Caribbean immigrants have more years in the US (experiences and longer duration of immigration). The 1990 census data shows that 76 and 57 percent of African immigrants and Caribbean immigrants, respectively, arrived in the US after 1975. Almost all native-black Americans and 60 percent of Caribbean blacks speak only English at home. Conversely, the majority of African immigrants speak languages other than English at home. In terms of geographical location, the three ethnic groups vary considerably. More than six out of ten native-black Americans reside in Southern USA, while 71.5 percent and 92.8 percent of African and Afro-Caribbean immigrants reside in the Southern and Northeastern portion of the US. Further, the modal residential area suggests that both African and Afro-Caribbean immigrants are more likely to concentrate in metropolitan areas in comparison with native-born blacks. Native-black Americans have the lowest earning capacity and worked fewer hours in 1989 compared to African and Afro-Caribbean immigrants.

Table 1. Socioeconomic Characteristics of Black Males in America: the 1990 Census.

	African American	Afro-Caribbean	African
Age	40.2	40.9	35.7
College degree (%)			
American degree	13.1	7.6	24.8
Foreign degree	NA	7.0	33.2
Year of experience			
American experience	22.0	13.1	9.9
Foreign experience	NA	10.1	5.4
English ability (%)			
Speaks only english	97.0	60.1	22.8
Very good	2.1	17.0	60.4
Good	0.6	12.4	14.3
Poor	0.3	8.7	2.4
None	0.0	1.9	0.1
Spatial location (%)			
Nonmetropolitan	15.4	1.6	2.0
West	10.5	4.2	17.1
Midwest	17.1	2.8	11.4
Northeast	10.7	58.1	26.0
South	61.7	34.7	45.5
Year of immigration (%)			
Native born	100	NA	NA
Pre-1965	NA	9.6	3.1
1965–1974	NA	33.4	20.9
1975–1984	NA	41.8	56.7
1985–1990	NA	15.2	19.3
Annual (1989) earnings ($)	21,919	23,261	24,562
Hourly (1989) earnings	12.09	12.98	13.36
Hours worked in 1989	1,907	1,921	1,982
Total number	14,347	7,346	1,973

Note: (1) The data were from 5% PUMS of the 1990 census, selected only males whose age were between 25–64 years and who were employed in 1989. 10 percent of African Americans were randomly selected from the 5% PUMS due to their relatively big sample.
Source: Adapted from Dodoo (1997, Table 1, p. 534).

Table 2. Socioeconomic Characteristics of Non-Hispanic Whites and Non-Hispanic Black Populations in Comparison: the 1990 and 2000 Census.

	1990 Census				2000 Census			
	Non-Hispanic Whites	African American	Afro-Caribbean	African	Non-Hispanic Whites	African American	Afro-Caribbean	African
Foreign born (%)	3.9	1.8	72.4	72.1	4.2	2.2	68.3	78.5
Education level (years)	12.9	11.7	12.1	14.3	13.5	12.4	12.6	14.0
Median household income ($)	47,481	29,251	42,927	35,041	53,000	33,790	43,650	42,900
Unemployment rate (%)	4.7	12.5	9.4	8.5	4.0	11.2	8.7	7.3
Poverty rate (%)	11.3	32.8	17.8	24.7	11.2	30.4	18.8	22.1

Note: (1) Sampling includes Black populations from 331 metropolitan regions.
(2) Data were from the 5% PUMS of the 1990 census and the 1% 2000 PUMS.
(3) Afro-Caribbeans are those people who report their ancestry and/or country of birth in the predominantly black islands of the Caribbean, including such places as Jamaica and Trinidad, but not Guyana. People reporting their ancestry and/or country of birth as a specific sub-Saharan African country are classified as African. African Americans are black people born outside Africa.

Source: (1) Logan and Deane (2003, Table 4, p. 6.) http://mumford1.dyndns.org/cen2000/BlackWhite/BlackDiversityReport/black-diver-sity01.htm
(2) Statistics for non-Hispanic Whites adopted from Lewis Mumford Center (2001) *Ethnic Diversity Grows, Neighborhood Integration Lags Behind.* http://mumford1.dyndns.org/census2000/wholePop/Wpreport/MumfordReport.pdf

Table 3. Residential Patterns and Neighborhood Characteristics of Non-Hispanic Black Populations in Comparison, the 1990 and 2000 Census.

	1990 Census				2000 Census			
	White	African American	Afro-Caribbean	African	White	African American	Afro-Caribbean	African
Exposure[a] to whites	85.3	33.4	33.5	56.7	80.2	33.3	29.9	46.3
Segregation[b] from black	64.4	NA	NA	NA	59.9	NA	NA	NA
Segregation from white	NA	68.6	74.1	69.6	NA	65.0	71.8	67.8
Isolation (exposure to own group)	NA	54.3	12.5	1.8	NA	49.4	15.3	3.3
Exposure to blacks	5.7	56.1	47.3	23.3	6.7	51.8	47.3	28.3
Segregation from African American	NA	NA	46.6	68.9	NA	NA	42.5	59.2
Segregation from Afro-Caribbean	NA	62.3	NA	66.7	NA	56.3	NA	60.3
Segregation from Africans	NA	75.8	66.1	NA	NA	66.7	60.0	NA
Median HH income of neighborhood ($)	47,683	31,548	39,970	44,715	52,637	35,679	41,328	45,567
Education of neighborhoods (college or above %)	23.8	14.0	17.5	28.8	29.0	17.5	20.3	29.3

See Note in Table 2.

Source: (1) Logan and Deane (Lewis Mumford Center) (2003, Table 5.8, pp. 7.11, 2), http://mumford1.dyndns.org/cen2000/BlackWhite/BlackDiversityReport/black-diversity01.htm, and Statistics for non-Hispanic Whites adopted from Lewis Mumford Center (2001) *Ethnic Diversity Grows, Neighborhood Integration Lags Behind.* http://mumford1.dyndns.org/census2000/wholePop/Wpreport/MumfordReport.pdf

[a]Exposure and isolation indices refer to the racial/ethnic composition of a tract where the average member of a given group lives. For example an isolation score of 80.2 for whites means that the average white lives in a neighborhood that is 80.2% white. An exposure score of 6.7% for white-black exposure indicates that the average white lives in a neighborhood that is 6.7% black.

[b]The standard measure of segregation is the Index of Dissimilarity (D). The index ranges from 0 to 100; a value of 60 or above is considered very high, e.g., a D score of 60 for black-white segregation means that 60% of either group must move to a different tract for the two groups to become equally distributed. Score at 40–50 is considered moderate levels of segregation while values of 30 or less are considered low (see the two reports from Lewis Mumford Center).

Table 2 shows that the socioeconomic conditions of Afro-Caribbean and Africans differed from that of native black Americans over the two decades. An average African immigrant has 14.3 years of education, which is over two years more than native-black Americans and Afro-Caribbeans in the 1980s. The 2000 census showed that the gap in educational attainment among the three groups diminished. The education level of native-black Americans and Afro-Caribbeans increased 0.7 and 0.5 years becoming 12.4 and 12.6 years, respectively, while African immigrants decreased 0.3 years becoming 14 years. African immigrants have the lowest unemployment rate (8.5 and 7.3 percent), while the unemployment rate of native-black Americans was 12.5 and 11.2 percent in the two periods of the census. In terms of household income, 1990 census indicates that Afro-Caribbean immigrants with $42,927 a year household income earned far more than the other two groups, although the 2000 census shows that earning gap is narrowing. Further, the poverty rate for Afro-Caribbean is the lowest among the three groups, but the rate increases one percent to 18.8 percent in the 2000 Census. Almost one in three native-black Americans is poor, although the percentage drops from 32.8 percent to 30.4 percent. Overall, the 2000 census shows a narrowing of disparities between the three groups. However, the differences remain substantial. Further, it appears that less educated Afro-Caribbean immigrants outperform African immigrants on household income and poverty rate. Compared to Afro-Caribbean immigrants, African immigrants seem to gain fewer returns from their higher educational attainment and lower unemployment rate.

Table 3 sketches a picture of black residential patterns in which blacks are highly isolated from one another. This is particularly true for Afro-Caribbean and African immigrants due, in part, to their small size of population. Turning to exposure to whites, African immigrants have the highest exposure percent among the three groups, but their exposure dropped dramatically from 56.7% to 46.3% over the decade. Native-born black Americans' exposure to whites remained about the same over the decade, while the exposure of Afro-Caribbeans to whites declined to 29.9 percent becoming the lowest among the three groups. This means that less than one-third of people in the neighborhood where an average Afro-Caribbean person lived were whites.

The percent of Africans or Afro-Caribbeans living in neighborhoods with others of their ethnic group increased slightly in the 2000 census compared to the 1990. Native-born black Americans had the highest percent of exposure to their own group and to other blacks although the exposure declined in 2000. Afro-Caribbeans were highly exposed to blacks as well even though this group is much smaller than the native-black American group. Nearly half of the people in the neighborhood where an average Afro-Caribbean person lived were black. Conversely, Africans lived in neighborhoods where whites outnumber blacks. Further, the score of isolation from one's own group is high for African and Caribbean immigrants, but particularly high for African immigrants. An average African immigrant lived in a neighborhood in which 1.8 percent (in 1990) and 3.3 percent (in 2000) of the neighbors were also African immigrants.

The three ethnic groups are highly segregated from one another, particularly from African immigrants, even though segregation declined over the decade. African immigrants tended to live in more advantaged neighborhoods, (where their neighbors reported median incomes of $44,715 in the 1990 and $45,567 in the 2000, and higher education levels) than the neighborhoods in which native-black Americans and Afro-Caribbeans resided. The average African immigrant in 2000 lived in a neighborhood where 29.3 percent of residents had a college education. By contrast, only 17.5 percent of the residents in an average native-born Black American neighborhood were college educated.

DISCUSSION

The descriptive data consistently highlight disparities among native-born Black Americans, Afro-Caribbean and African immigrants. African and Afro-Caribbean immigrants have better social and economic well being compared to their black American counterparts; also, Caribbean immigrants' well being seems to be slightly better than African immigrants. We note four interesting patterns among the three groups. First, despite their higher education level and lower unemployment rate, African immigrants experience higher levels of poverty and lower median household income than Caribbean immigrants. This suggests that African immigrants have lower returns to their human capital. Second, the three groups are highly segregated from whites and from one another, and have their own modal concentration areas although African immigrants are least exposed to other blacks and to members of their own group. Third, there is a narrowing of the gap between the three groups between 1990 and 2000. Last, the improved socioeconomic status of blacks across the three groups did not decrease the segregation from whites, but did increase the integration between groups.

The data suggest that the straight-line assimilation model for explaining the heterogeneity among the three groups is problematic. The assimilation model predicts that immigrants would have lower levels of economic success. This is not the case; native-born blacks have the lowest levels of economic well being. Neither years of residence in the receiving country nor years of experience appear to be important factors in determining the disparity. Other factors, such as education, seem to better predict the differences between natives and immigrants. Yet, questions regarding why African immigrants have lower returns to human capital characteristics compared to Afro-Caribbean immigrants remains unexplained. While straight-line assimilation model fails to explain the disadvantage of African immigrants, we need to seek other plausible explanations from other theoretical frameworks.

To what extent is an explanation based on a segmented assimilation model viable? For their higher individual and social resources such as education and higher neighborhood quality, one would expect African immigrants' well being to be parallel to or even exceed that of Afro-Caribbean immigrants. Yet, this is not the case. The different level of exposure to and segregation from whites between the two black immigrant groups might offer us a hint of a plausible explanation for this contradiction. A modal resident area with higher segregation from whites and higher exposure to blacks suggests that Afro-Caribbean immigrants are highly concentrated. Afro-Caribbeans might draw on an ethnic enclave to protect against discrimination and to foster social, cultural and economic support. This speculation does not hold for native-blacks who are also highly concentrated in specific areas and segregated from whites. It is possible that Afro-Caribbean immigrants assimilate into an ethnic community while native blacks integrate into a black inner-city 'underclass.'

It is difficult to trace how far the cultural perspective fits the data because we did not directly measure the cultural capital of the three groups. However, proxies for cultural capital, such as working more hours, lower level of welfare participation rate, English language proficiency, higher level of education, and lower unemployment rate, may inform the discussion. If the proxies enable us to generalize cultural characteristics among the three groups of black, African immigrants are expected to be favored. Using these measures, it is difficult to support the cultural argument as the data shows that Afro-Caribbean, not African immigrants, have better social and economic outcomes. We therefore, find that cultural differences as the principle explanation of group well being are inadequate.

The ethnic penalty perspective suggests that all blacks will have lower levels of economic well being relative to whites and that within group differences are a function of differentiated discrimination and multicultural racism. From the data, we find this perspective is more persuasive than the other perspectives. As indicated in Table 2, all three groups of blacks have lower income, higher poverty, and higher unemployment than whites. Yet the three groups are not similarly disadvantaged. For native-black Americans, given the small gap in education, but the massive household-income gap, much higher poverty rate, and high level of segregation from whites, racial discrimination seems to be a factor. For African immigrants, attributing the outcome of social and economic well being to discrimination is more complicated. One plausible explanation is that the job mismatch of African immigrants is due to the lack of options in the job market, which might force an African immigrant to take a low-paying job over no job at all (Katende, 1994; Dodoo, 1997). Further, perhaps media images that portray African nations as sites of poverty, AIDS, starvation, and strife, to some degree, contribute to negative stereotypes of Africans in the receiving country.

All too often blacks in the US are presented as a monolithic, flat community where differences are hidden, left unexplained, or are unaccounted for by both theories and methods. Such theoretical and methodological ambiguity lies at the heart of much of the confusion, unresolved questions, and lies (of both omission and commission), which currently clouds mobility research with regards to American blacks. This study, identifying three theoretical perspectives, provides descriptive evidence of the utility of investigating a more robust characterization of blacks. The models –assimilation, cultural capital, and ethnic penalty – suggest that greater upward mobility and improved well being observed between Afro-Caribbeans, are not easily explainable by a single perspective. The perspectives provide at least minimal explanatory power for either African immigrants or native blacks. We are left with more questions than answers. Most importantly we see a need to develop a more comprehensive theoretical perspective, one that blends the three models here explored.

As we look toward future theorizing, we envision a model, which allows for contextual and historical antecedents that suggest multiple mobility streams. At the very least, such a model would suggests that timing of entry into the US market, type of entry, and resources (both within the community and external to the community) available would be of interest. This model must account for the changing racial ethnic landscape. Finally, we note that the mere presence of racially designated similarities does not mean that such similarity actually exists. It would appear that just as we note among whites there are preferences for certain types of whites, there are preferences for certain types of blacks. Hence, we note that white immigrants who are Anglo Saxon, French, or German (i.e. Northern Europeans) tend to have higher relative mobility trajectories (all things being equal) then those white immigrants who are Irish, Italian, or Polish (i.e., Southern Europeans). Such variable mobility streams are often lost when we discuss race writ large, and hence the value of this paper is that it calls us to reassess our notions of homogeneity, and look toward an increasing heterogeneous society.

NOTE

1. The data came from two studies. (1) We drew indicators in socioeconomic characteristics from '*Assimilation Differences among African in America*' by F. Nii-Amoo Dodoo in 1997. The study used the 5% Public Use Micro Samples (PUMS) of the 1990 census to look at those aged 25–64 year old black male respondents. For those African Americans, due to their relatively big sample, the study randomly drew 10% sample from PUMS. Human capital and economic outcome earnings are the key information of the study. It should be noted that individual male is the analysis unit. (2) The second study was from '*Black Diversity in Metropolitan America*' by John R. Logan and Glenn Deane in 2003. The study extracted information of 331 metropolitan regions in America from four census data files, including the 5% PUMS of the 1990 census, the Census 2000 1% PUMS(2000 PUMS), and summary files of the 1990 (STF4A) and the 2000 Census (SF3). The study further divided the black populations into African American, African and Afro-Caribbean in accordance with the information on their ancestry and/or country of birth and race. Key information available from this report includes education, poverty rate, unemployment rate, median income of household, residential patterns and neighborhood characteristics. Accordingly, these data are sample estimates based on census returns from one of every six households, rather than population enumerations.

REFERENCES

Arthur, J. A. (2000). *Invisible sojourners: African immigrant diaspora in the United States.* Praeger.

Bobo, L., Kluegel, J., & Smith, R. (1997). Laissez-Faire racism: The crystallization of a kinder, gentler, antiblack ideology. In: T. Steven & M. Jack (Eds), *Racial attitudes in the 1980s* (pp. 15–42). Westport, CT: Praeger.

Borjas, G. J. (1994). The economics of immigration. *Journal of Economic Literature, 32,* 1667–1717.

Butcher, K. F. (1994). Black immigrants in the United States: A comparison with native Blacks and other immigrants. *Industrial and Labor Relations Review, 47*(2), 265–284.

Chiswick, B. R., Cohen, Y., & Zach, T. (1997). The labor market status of immigrants: Effects of the unemployment rate at arrival and duration of residence. *Industrial and Labor Relations Review, 50*(2), 289–303.

Djamba, Y. K. (1999). African immigrants in the United States: A socio-demographic profile in comparison to native Blacks. *Journal of Asian and African Studies, 34*, 210–215.

Dodoo, E-A. F. (1991). Immigrant and native Black workers labor force participation in the United States. *National Journal of Sociology, 5*, 1–17.

Dodoo, E-A. F. (1997). Assimilation differences among Africans in America. *Social Forces, 76*(2), 527–546.

Dodoo, E-A. F., & Takyi, B. K. (2002). Africans in the diaspora: Black-white earnings differences among American's Africans. *Ethnic and Racial Studies, 25*(6), 913–941.

Francis, E. A. (2000). Social work practice with African-descent immigrants. In: P. R. Balgapal (Ed.), *Social work practice with immigrants and refugees* (pp. 127–166). New York, NY: Columbia University Press.

Freeman, L. (2002). Does spatial assimilation work for Black immigrants in the US? *Urban Studies, 39*(11), 1983–2003.

Gans, H. J. (1992). Second generation decline: Scenarios for the economic and ethnic future of the Post-1965 America immigrants. *Ethnic and Racial Studies, 15*, 173–192.

Gladwell, M. (1996). *Black like them*: http://wwwgladwell.com/1996/1996_04_29_a_black.htm, June 25, 2005.

Gordon, M. (1964). *Assimilation in American life*. New York: Oxford University Press.

Heron, M. P. (2001). *The occupational attainment of Caribbean immigrants in the United States*. LFB: Scholarly.

Jackson, J. V., & Cothran, M. E. (2003). Black versus Black: The relationships among African, African American, and African Caribbean persons. *Journal of Black Studies, 33*(5), 576–604.

Kalmijn, M. (1996). The socioeconomic assimilation of Caribbean American Blacks. *Social Forces, 74*(9), 911–930.

Karas, J. (2002). Bridges and barriers: Earnings and occupational attainment among immigrants. In: C. Suarez-Orozco, & M. Suarez-Orozco (Eds), *The new Americans: Recent immigration and American society*. LFB: Scholarly Publishing.

Kasinitz, P. (1992). *The new immigration – Caribbean New York: Black immigrants and the politics of race*. NY: Cornell University Press.

Kposowa, A. J. (2002). Human capital and the performance of African immigrants in the U.S labour market. *The Western Journal of Black Studies, 26*(3), 175–183.

Lim, N. (2001). On the back of Blacks? Immigrants and the fortunes of African Americans. In: R. Waldinger (Ed.), *Strangers at the gate: New immigrants in urban America* (pp. 186–227). University of California.

Logan, J. R., & Deane, G. (2003). *Black diversity in metropolitan America*. http://www.uchastings.edu/wingate/PDF/Black_Diversity_final.pdf

Model, S. (1995). West Indian prosperity: Fact or fiction? *Social Problems, 42*, 535–553.

Model, S., Fisher, G., & Silberman, R. (1999). Black Caribbeans in comparative perspective. *Journal of Ethnic and Migration Studies, 25*(2), 183–208.

Nasser, H. E. (2003). Black America's new diversity: Immigrants from Africa, Caribbean making their voices heard. *USA Today, February 17*, http://www.usatoday.com/news/nation/2003-02-16-black-america-diversity-usat_x.htm, October 20, 2006.

Ostine, F. (1998). Caribbean immigrants and the sociology of race and ethnicity: Limits of the assimilation perspective. *African American Research Perspectives, 4*(1), http://www.rcgd.isr.umich.edu/prba/perspectives/spring1998/rostine.pdf

Pattillo-McCoy, M. (1999). *Black picket fences: Privilege and peril among the black middle class*. Chicago: University of Chicago Press.

Pierre, J. (2004). Black immigrants in the United States and the 'cultural narratives' of ethnicity, identities. *Global Studies in Cultural and Power*, *11*, 141–170.

Portes, A., & Zhou, M. (1993). The new second generation: Segmented assimilation and its variants. *The Annals of the American Academy of Political and Social Science*, *530* (November), 74–96.

Sowell, T. (1978). *Three Black histories. Essays and data on American ethnic groups* (pp. 41–48). Washington, DC:The Urban Institute.

Takyi, B. K. (2002). The making of the second diaspora: On the recent African immigrant community in the United States of America. *The Western Journal of Black Studies*, *26*(1), 32–43.

Waters, M. (1994). Ethnic and racial identities of second generation Black immigrants in New York city. *International Migration Review*, *28*(4), 795–820.

Waters, M. (1999). *Black identities: West Indian immigrant dreams and American realities*. Cambridge: Harvard University Press.

Wildsmith, E. (2004). Race/ethnic differences in female headship: Exploring the assumption of assimilation theory. *Social Science Quarterly*, *85*(1), 89–106.

TWO NATIONS OF DISCOURSE: MAPPING RACIAL IDEOLOGIES IN POST-APARTHEID SOUTH AFRICA ☆, ☆☆

Amy E. Ansell

ABSTRACT

This paper presents an analysis of 154 written submissions to the Head Office of the South African Human Rights Commission invited as part of the consultative process leading up to the South African National Conference on Racism 2000. The submissions demonstrate a fundamental lack of consensus regarding what racism is and how to combat it. Although the submissions reveal a variety of perspectives on racism within each self-identified racial group, a significant racial dimension – even bifurcation – is clearly manifest. Black and White South Africans approach the questions that were the topic of the National Conference on Racism in

☆This paper was first prepared for the conference "The Burden of Race? 'Whiteness' and 'Blackness' in Modern South Africa", History Workshop and Wits Institute for Social and Economic Research, University of Witwatersrand (5–8 July 2001).
☆☆*Source*: Two nations of discourse: Mapping racial ideologies in post-apartheid South Africa by Amy E. Ansell, Politikon: *South African Journal of Political Studies*, *31*(1) (2004) 3–26. http://www.tandf.co.uk/journals

The New Black: Alternative Paradigms and Strategies for the 21st Century
Research in Race and Ethnic Relations, Volume 14, 307–334
ISSN: 0195-7449/doi:10.1016/S0195-7449(06)14014-3

meaningfully different ways, suggesting the existence of 'two nations of discourse'. In mapping racial ideologies in post-apartheid South Africa, the paper outlines the benefits of a structural approach in its engagement of a range of sociological debates from an international perspective: (1) the distinction between racial attitudes and ideologies; (2) the production and nature of new forms of racial identity, discourse, and racism; (3) the social construction of whiteness; and (4) the politics of non-racialism in the context of political projects such as nation-building and reconciliation.

INTRODUCTION

Most of us knew from the time democracy won the day, back in 1994, that factors such as racism will still be with us ... More and more people are feeling the sting of the evil silent racism that we are subjected to, today. (W. M. L.)

I had hoped that we South Africans would start on a new non-racist path into the future and stay away from the apartheid era methods where every activity had a racial connotations. (sic.) Sadly this has not happened and government, educational institutions and many other organisations and institutions have perpetuated it and even refined the process ... in the name of affirmative action or setting right the wrongs of the past. (Charles S)

The two statements above are taken from files of public submissions to the South African Human Rights Commission collected as part of the consultative process leading up to the National Conference on Racism held in Johannesburg in 2000. The Conference was intended in part as a precursor to the United Nations Conference on Racism held in Durban in 2001. Its significance proved to be more on the national level, however, in provoking debate concerning the nature, extent and purchase of race and racism in the post-apartheid context and in signalling the end of the honeymoon period of the 'rainbow nation'. Although much of the world continues to look to South Africa as a miraculous model of racial reconciliation, debate around the Conference theme revealed the extent and depth of the racialised fault-lines just below the surface of the saccharine non-racial political dispensation.

Non-racialism was a laudable and integral goal of the anti-apartheid movement in exile and remained a central and constitutive part of the ANC's ideology as party to the negotiated settlement of the 1990s under the leadership of Nelson Mandela (Price, 1997). Although non-racialism remains a cherished ideal inscribed in the Constitution, in practice it has emerged as a much more contested and contradictory canon during the period of democratic consolidation presided over by Thabo Mbeki. For example, with respect to the use of apartheid-era racial categories for the purpose of redress in the context of Employment Equity, debate has emerged over what constitutes the proper scope and limits of non-racialism and the consequences of its violation.[1] The abstract ideal of non-racialism that served so well during the period of *transition* has run up against the imperatives of *transformation*, leading to a much more messy terrain wherein race has been juridically outlawed as a moral basis of citizenship and government but legislatively reinscribed for strategic purposes of redress. Moreover, post-apartheid racial identities have proved resilient to continuing appeals to forge a common, national South African identity and remain existentially salient in all sorts of affective expressions of cultural and political belonging and taste.[2] The fact of the continuing significance of race despite the formal end of apartheid should come as no surprise except to the most ardent 'post-racist'.[3] Apartheid was a society so structured in racial dominance that its transformation demands from Government and necessitates on the part of all South Africans an ongoing engagement with the legacies and continued purchase of race.

The transition in ANC leadership from Mandela to Mbeki roughly coincided with a shift of emphasis from national unity and reconciliation to a more race-conscious imperative to address the profoundly racialised *socio-economic* dimensions of post-apartheid South African society left relatively untouched by the elite-pacted *political* transition to democratic rule. In 1998, then Deputy President Thabo Mbeki delivered a speech to Parliament, in the context of the opening of the debate on reconciliation and nation-building, in which he described South Africa as 'two nations':

> South Africa is a country of two nations ... One ... is white, relatively prosperous, regardless of gender or geographic dispersal. It has ready access to a developed economic, physical, educational, communication and other infrastructure ... The second and larger nation of South Africa is black and poor, with the worst affected being women in the rural areas, the black rural population in general and the disabled. This nation lives under conditions of a grossly underdeveloped economic, physical, educational, communication and other infrastructure. It has virtually no possibility to exercise what in reality amounts to a theoretical right to equal opportunity.[4]

The speech proved exceptionally controversial in its race-conscious explosion of the metaphor of the 'rainbow nation' and alleged implicit appeal to a more divisive African nationalism.[5] In the language of academia, the two nations metaphor was essentialist, reductionist, not messy enough. Much of the debate centred on whether race or class was the more important variable in the new South Africa. While Mbeki's speech refused such a choice and instead focused on their mutual interaction, many critics charged that recent census data demonstrated that newly salient class differences within the black community were more important than racial differences between black and white South Africans.[6] Whether expressed as adherence to liberal non-racialism or radical class politics, the response to the two nations thesis suggested that, in a context wherein every major indicator of life chances and well-being continues to be cleaved by race, many South Africans remain willfully blind to its continuing significance. In the midst of such controversy and a brewing racialised conflict at the University of Witwatersrand commonly referred to as the 'Makgoba Affair',[7] Mbeki cautioned that such blindness represents an obstacle to the nation-building project:

> [T]he only escape for those who seek the absence of turbulence, and strive to maintain their position of privilege by stealth, will be the artificial imposition of social amnesia, until the next conflict emerges above the gentle waves. I do not believe that any one of us wants to live in fake and unreal world peopled by ostriches with heads hidden in the sand. (Mbeki, 1998)

It is from within this broad context that President Mbeki called for a National Conference on Racism. The South African Human Rights Commission (SAHRC) – as the national institution established to entrench constitutional democracy and promote non-discrimination-invited public submissions via leaflets and media/web advertisements and held hearings throughout the country in order to achieve a national consensus on what racism is and how to combat it. Although the Head Office in Johannesburg did not hold public hearings (hosted instead by the Gauteng Provincial Office), it did receive a total of 154 written submissions unique in that they were divided almost equally between white and black South Africans.[8] The racial demographics were unique in the sense that white South Africans by and large did not participate in SAHRC Provincial processes. Sent in by post or e-mail and ranging from between a paragraph and 20 or more pages in length (the average being 1–2 pages), these Head Office submissions provide the data for the mapping of contemporary racial ideology below.

The meaning of the two nations metaphor is extended in this paper beyond its socio-economic reading to address the more existential dimensions of racial discourse, ideology and worldview. Indeed, this broader reading is true to its original usage by Benjamin Disraeli who characterised the rich and poor of his Victorian England as: "Two nations, between whom there is no intercourse and no sympathy; who are as ignorant of each other's habits, thought, and feelings, as if they were dwellers in different zones, or inhabitants of different planets."[9] Given the deliberate structuring of separate worlds by the architects of apartheid, and persistent differences in socio-economic conditions experienced by subordinate and dominant races in the post-apartheid era, it seems reasonable to expect that black and white South Africans would develop competing perspectives or ideologies to explain their relative positions in society. How South Africans write about racism emerges as much from a mix of ideology and politics shaped by differing group position and experience in the racial order as from the structure of the problem itself.

Analysis of SAHRC Head Office submissions does not claim to be representative of white and black *attitudes* towards racism; rather, the goal is to map contemporary racial *ideologies* extant as companion to the transformed racial structure of the post-1994 period. The distinction between the study of racial attitudes and the study of racial ideologies itself relies on what sociologists refer to as a structural theory of racism.[10] Developed as a self-conscious challenge to the common-sense view of racism as a static package of irrational prejudice exhibited by individuals, the structural approach understands racial ideology as a framework of beliefs or worldview expressed by racialised social groups in an effort to explain and justify (dominant race) or challenge (subordinate race or races) relations of racial dominance and inequality.[11] To the extent that divergent racial ideologies are expounded in the submissions, therefore, requires examination of how such competing discursive or interpretative repertoires are linked to and fundamentally shaped by differences in group position, economic and political interest, everyday experience, and even psychological wages within the context of the current racial order.

Whereas the prejudice model of racism associated with attitudinal research is often quite static and limited by methodological individualism, the structural account is dynamic in foregrounding interactions between new forms of racial ideology and changing racialised social systems. To the degree that attitudinal research does engage change, in the South African context, it is most often through the narrow lens of questioning whether prejudice has increased or decreased since the transition to democratic rule. The structural approach, by contrast, engages the question of how racial ideology has been transformed or produced anew in the post-apartheid context in order to speak to the challenges, struggles, and dilemmas of the current historical juncture. Conceptions of race, the performance of racial identity, and notions of racism are no longer so closely bound to apartheid strictures; rather, they are each rearticulated around new axes of the local post-transitional moment and increasingly global racial politics. It is here that our analysis engages the international literature on 'new racism' in probing contemporary racial ideological constructions that tend to be sanitised, ostensibly non-racial, and couched within liberal democratic discourses of human/individual rights but nevertheless work to shore up white privilege under challenge.[12]

Finally, a structural theory of racism provides a fresh lens on the production and performance of post-apartheid *racial identities* (as distinct from
racism above). Public submissions on the topic of racism reveal at least as
much about the forging of their authors' racial identities in a context of
dramatic unfixing as about their content on the ostensible theme (i.e., racism). Read as an opinion poll on the proper definition of racism, the SAHRC
files hold little interest or value (in that they are not intellectually rigorous or
coherent, nor a representative sample in strict methodological terms and in
the sense that it is likely submissions are skewed towards the most strongly
opinionated). Much more productive is a reading as an innovative performance of blackness and whiteness in the new South Africa replete with new
characters, plot lines, and settings. Whiteness and blackness as constructed
categories of identity developed and evolved together throughout the centuries of colonialism and apartheid, constituting imagined notions of 'selfhood' and 'other'. Today these notions are changing, as whiteness and
blackness no longer refer to the same meanings as under apartheid, creating
'dilemmas of selfhood' as identities become dislocated and reconstituted in a
new context (Nutttal, 2001). White-authored submissions hold particular
interest in this vein as the production and performance of whiteness has
undergone profound alteration with the loss of political power. Here the
paper intersects with the burgeoning international literature on whiteness in
highlighting the attempts by white South Africans to re-moor their identities
and guard privilege in the context of changing power relationships.[13]

SAHRC HEAD OFFICE SUBMISSIONS: A
DISCURSIVE GEOGRAPHY OF TWO NATIONS

The remainder of this paper presents an analysis of the total of 154 written
submissions to the Head Office of the SAHRC collected in July and August
of 2000. The submissions demonstrate a fundamental lack of consensus
regarding what racism is and how to combat it. Although they reveal a
diversity of perspectives on racism associated with varying class, gender,
age, religious and other variables, a significant racial dimension – even bifurcation – is clearly manifest. On a variety of topics that serve to organise
the discussion to follow – ranging from the meaning attributed to the legacy
of apartheid, competing definitions of racism, allegations of new forms of
racism, descriptions of institutional racism, and articulation of rival meanings of non-racialism – black and white South Africans approach the questions that were the topic of the National Conference on Racism in

meaningfully different ways, suggesting the existence of 'two nations of discourse'.

The Legacy of Apartheid

Since after 1994 elections we thought we were free but it seems as if the white man still have the authority to press a black man even further down. (S. S. R.)

Afrikaner nationalism has now been replaced by the much vaunted Black consciousness, which is as destructive and evil as any other racism. (R. O. B.)

The meaning and purchase of the legacy of apartheid emerges in many submissions as a central concern. The SAHRC files evidence that how the past is remembered is far from consensual in the new South Africa. Despite the attempt by the Truth and Reconciliation Commission (TRC) to write a new national narrative of the apartheid past as part of the nation-building project, the submissions reveal that South Africans selectively draw upon the past in conflicting ways as they negotiate and claim their place in the new racial order (Statman, 2000; Nuttal & Coetzee, 1998).

The belief that white racism against black people remains a part of contemporary South African society and politics despite the demise of apartheid is expressed in several submissions by self-identified blacks. Lurike F. writes: "Many people feel that they are still suffering under the yoke of apartheid. Although no one will attempt to say it out loud, we do still have racial barriers ... even a blind man will be able to tell you there is definitely such a thing as racism." Several submissions detail how the racism of apartheid continues today in new, more subtle, and sometimes more entrenched forms. W. M. L. remarks: "Most of us knew from the time democracy won the day, back in 1994, that factors such as racism will still be with us ... More and more people are feeling the sting of the evil silent racism that we are subjected to, today." Contributors describe how racism continues to impact negatively on people's consciousness. 16-year-old Thando S. offers a poem entitled 'Transparently Opaque':

Wait a minute mister, you mispronounced my name.

You didn't wait for all the information before you

Turned me away.

You kind of hurt my feelings

Pretending I'm transparent.

You see me, a thieving shadow with unclean thought

And filthy words. Why, when you're the real devil?

You see right through me, you go right through me.

Your Thoughts, your words.

I feel like I'm invisible.

Why, mister? You kind of hurt my feelings.

Judging me from the outside and not looking in.

Contributors also describe how the residues of apartheid inequities and
structures continue to limit the meaning of the metaphor of the 'rainbow
nation'. Nolwazi M. from Soweto writes of "A black soul in denial":

> Although South Africans are now learning to laugh at their diversity in race, colour and
> culture, the rainbow is not quite as shiny or as bright as it should be. In fact, the very
> mention of the word 'rainbow' provokes nervous twitching and hollow laughter ... On
> the one side of the rainbow you find white people sitting comfortably on the pot of gold,
> staring curiously at the other races, trying to grab their fortune on big Bucks Bonanza
> and Bambanani. On the other side, you find black people who boast that "Black is
> beautiful", which means that white is ugly ... Racial prejudices, stereotyping and igno-
> rance tend to always creep into our thinking.

The role of whites in the reconciliation process is viewed sceptically. Sanele
D. comments : "The reconciliation process seems to be emanating from one
end (Africans) whereas the other faction (specifically whites) either do not
want it and do not even see the need for it ... These Whites should be very
apologetic after so many thousands black people died because of their ill-
doing and even today they have the guts to frustrate more blacks."

In a distinctly different vein, several submissions by self-identified white authors caution against the pitfalls of dealing with the apartheid past. Some argue
that in the spirit of reconciliation South Africans must forget about the divided
past and focus instead on building a common future. One submission states:

> The solution or the way forward to build this country is to join hands together share the
> views and experiences. My dearest friend if you remove that old statue of Paul Kruger
> and put Mandela's statue, I am telling you that you are practicing the black apartheid
> when the whites come into power they will take that statue of Mandela and put it away
> because he is black and brings back their white apartheid. But if you put these statues
> together Mandela's statue next to Paul Kruger, then the whites will take De Klerk's
> statue and put it next to Mandela's then in that way the nation will come up and there
> will be no more racism.

M. S. M. cautions that politicians who comment on the injustices of the
past cause "more bad feelings like all the commissions and recrimina-
tions ... Why keep bringing up the past, forget what happened, who was

wrong and who was right, just get on with the job and work together instead of causing a state of reverse apartheid."

Others assert that while statutory racism ended in 1994 with the transition to democracy, the legacy of apartheid racial classifications is dangerously present in contemporary ANC rule. Among self-identified whites, a central concern is that Afrikaner nationalism is being replaced by African nationalism, with all the attendant negative consequences in terms of a racially divided and hostile society. Gerhard P. writes:

> You would agree with me that two wrongs do not make a right, but distort matters even further. I certainly do acknowledge the serious wrongs of apartheid, and have in fact opposed it all my life. I continue to be against it, also now that the role players have been swapped around and the policy of race differentiation is being labeled "affirmative action". Under the policy of apartheid, particularly the Afrikaners sought to obtain certain privileges and protection for themselves. Today the black majority seeks to do likewise.

The silence here with concern to identification with or support for the apartheid regime is noteworthy and very positive vis-à-vis the prospects for reconciliation. Far from representing a simple denial of the past, these authors acknowledge the injustices of the past and state their objection. But the acknowledgement is selective in the sense that commitment to redress the socio-economic legacies of apartheid is avoided, indeed trumped, by rhetorical commitment to non-racialism. So it is a particular kind of denial; denial of the cumulative benefits of being white. In her study of white identity in a changing South Africa, Melissa Steyn writes:

> ... a desire to close the discussion on the past is one strand within a general pattern of denial. The appeal to let sleeping dogs lie hides the crucial issue of which dogs are still holding onto the bones. It is an evasion of the extent to which the past permeates the present, of how the legacy of social injustice continues into the future. It is a refusal to acknowledge that sustaining 'normal' white life perpetuates the disadvantages of others. Complacency, even indifference, is passed off as liberality.[14]

By contrast to those who want to wish the past away or blame the ANC for its continuing impact are those who advocate the therapeutic or healing aspects of investigating the past. With respect to the TRC, Mrs. Greta T. writes: "Many people believe that the TRC harmed race relations by digging up hurt and pain from the past. I disagree. I believe that true healing cannot take place when resentment, bitterness, guilt and fear lie buried." While debate can be entertained about whether white guilt is in fact therapeutic, appropriate, or politically desirable,[15] such sentiment clearly moves away from denial of the past and avoidance of culpability. And further along the spectrum of white-authored responses are perspectives that sociologist Ruth Frankenberg would classify as 'racially cognisant', meaning that they acknowledge racial difference and racism and the meaning it has for people's lives and society as a whole.[16] One submission states: "I can really understand the bitterness that many black people still experience. They were hurt very deeply by apartheid. Most of the scars are on the souls of millions. Whites must remember that 99% of the forgiveness must be granted by our fellow South Africans of colour, and we whites must have the humility to ask for that forgiveness."

The meaning of the apartheid past vis-à-vis its effects on the present is still very much up for grabs. Far from denying or celebrating the apartheid past, all contributors – black and white – share in its condemnation. Yet the lessons to be taken for the future are far from agreed upon. For some, mostly self-identified black South Africans, the legacies of apartheid continue to structure their lives both materially and psychologically. In the current climate of race conciliation, the race-conscious expression of critical sentiment about the past and continuing realities of white racism represents what Grant Farred (1997) refers to as a "battle to retain memories of oppression". Other submissions, by contrast, most from self-identified white South Africans, articulate commitment to a non-racial future and deride the extent to which the ANC in their view is contributing to the re-racialisation of society along lines similar to – but a reversal of – the apartheid past. Although white responses are far from uniform, ranging from a certain type of denial of the past to race cognisance, a new pattern of meaning construction on the part of white South Africans is evident. Rhetorical accommodation to non-racialism is combined with denial of the continuing impact of the legacies of the apartheid past beyond political processes of the so-called re-racialisation. Such a combination allows white South Africans to claim the moral high ground of being 'beyond race' while refusing sacrifice of the accumulated benefits of racial privilege inherited from the past.

Defining Racism

... racism is the discrimination of one group of people upon the other for the purposes of subjugation or maintaining that subjugation. (Frank A.)

[A]ny definition of racism that is based on specific racial categories is itself racist and should not be countenanced. (George E.)

The submissions make clear that the challenge today is less to prove whether racism has increased or decreased in measure since apartheid than to dominate the ideological or symbolic struggle to define what constitutes racism and, by extension, the most effective means by which to combat it. Several submissions define racism as an inescapable product of human nature.

Cassandra L. writes: "racism is everywhere because originated in the deepest recesses of the human mind. Fear of the unknown and a suspicion of anything different is a characteristic of a typical human attitude." Tony H. remarks: "Whether we live in South Africa, Britain, the United States or Russia the issue of race will always be with us. It is a human condition and racism occurs in all societies." Other submissions regard racism as a product of the intolerance or greed of white people: "... racism is rife ... whites do not want to be equal to blacks. That won't happen in South Africa." Each of the above submissions represents a cynical view regarding the elimination of racism, whether the cynicism is grounded in human nature, universal appearance, or an essentialist view of white people's inability to change, respectively.

Only one of the 154 submissions intimated that racism had to do with biology, or notions of white superiority and black inferiority so characteristic of traditional forms of overt white racism. An anonymous submission verging on hate mail ridicules the attempt by the SAHRC to eliminate racism, remarking that such a project is "perfectly naïve coming only from black mind! The blacks will always be inferior ... more ferocious than animals ... rejoicing about crimes, murder and rape." All other submissions share an underlying assumption that racism can be eliminated or effectively challenged, although the consensus shatters once one probes into what exactly such challenge would necessarily entail. At issue here is whether one defines racism asymmetrically as having to do with unequal structures of power and advantage, or universally as entailing inalienable rights on the part of the individual to be free of barriers based on race, colour, or creed. I characterise the tension between these two tendencies below as a debate between the structural and idealist views. Which view predominates carries significant implications for who can be considered racist and how to most effectively combat racism.

Defining racism in structural terms involves a focus on poverty, inequality, political economy, and discriminatory practices/outcomes. A minority of submissions, most of them but not all authored by self-identified blacks, strike an economic register in defining racism. Sesheka M. remarks: "Just like HIV/AIDS poverty ... is the cause of racism". Isaac D. similarly writes of the economic basis of racism:

> Racism in South Africa is based on the haves and the have not. When we talk about reparation, the haves say, no, we were not fighting for money. That is racism in itself because the people of this country fought for human and economic rights for which they were denied. We were tortured, detained, maimed, that is why we are starving today ... Our economic system is wrong.

Frank A. argues that Black people cannot be racist "because racism ... does not just mean discrimination of one group of people upon the other, it presupposes subjugation ... We black people as a people do not have economic power therefore we cannot be racist." The focus on power and political economy, rather than simple prejudice, is associated in the submissions with a demand for structural redress as the most effective way to combat racism. One human rights NGO campaigns for the need "to dismantle the racial structure as it exists, then society could enjoy power and prestige that is evenly distributed."

The idealist tendency, by contrast, relies more on abstract, universalistic themes in defining racism as any and all unfair treatment based on skin colour, irrespective of whether the colour is white or black. The tendency found expression in white-authored submissions that self-consciously deferred to transitional rhetoric. George E. argues that the idea that only whites can be racist denies essential human equality and universal treatment and so flies in the face of what he refers to as the "whole point of the democratic transition". In this view, racism is not a structural problem in need of redress but a psychological condition that can best be eliminated through programmes of re-socialisation, multicultural education, and opportunities for inter-cultural exchange. For some, combating racism calls for the fostering of dialogue to facilitate empathetic communication and to counter racial conditioning. Robert M. proposes implementing a national 'Dialogue Project' in order to provide "the opportunity and the process for people to engage empathetically on the issue of racism." Connie D. suggests that "getting to know each other" socially is important and that people of different racial groups need to intermarry. Others such as Faith G. employ religious metaphors in pleas for love and inter-racial friendship. Johann B. writes of the importance of Ubuntu as a tool to reduce racist attitudes: "If all people abide by and live out the world view of Ubuntu which is a reference to the basic values of humannes love, intense caring and sharing, respect and compassion South Africa and the whole global world would be freed of all forms of racism." Dr. G. concludes: "racism ... is a mind set problem ... I think we need to accept one another first as human being."

It appears from the submissions that South Africa now finds itself in a definitional interregnum: between a structural definition of racism revolving around an economic register and an idealist one grounded in a moral language of human sameness. The interregnum is also racialised to the extent that the structural view is strongly associated with black contributors, while the idealist view is expressed predominantly by white South Africans. The two competing definitions take on political meaning as black contributors draw upon the structural view to distance themselves from metaphors of race conciliation, while whites employ non-racial transitional rhetoric compatible with the idealist view as a benchmark against which to measure their displeasure with the current political dispensation. Especially, relevant to the study of whiteness is how the vocabulary of non-racialism serves to impoverish the political imagination so that acting against racism means changing mind-sets and not structures of power. Racism is not a mental quirk or psychological flaw, as in Fanon's characterisation, but a social edifice erected over racial inequality to reproduce systemic advantages.[17] From the perspective of a structural theory of racism, idealist definitions that reduce racism to a question of prejudice serve to elide or obscure issues of power and inequality and so contribute to a defence of the racially inegalitarian status quo.

The Many Faces of Racism

Nowadays, it seems that racism has taken on a more subtler undertone: one which is not violent but none-the-less demeans and humiliates the person on the receiving end. (N. O. L. H. R.)

I feel that after a history of more than 300 years in this country I am still being regarded as an unwelcome "settler" ... Can we claim that we have made any real progress on building better race relations, or have we simply changed into a mirror image of the same oppressive system of the previous regime. (M. F. B.)

A constituent part of the struggle to define racism is identification of a variety of forms of racism. Submissions detail numerous forms of racism, ranging from traditional racism (white against black), black-on-black racism, anti-Semitism, anti-immigrant racism, anti-Arab racism, and racism against other communities of color. For example, Sipho H. comments: "Racism is going very strong in our Country, the people who are racist in our country today are 'Indians' ... Indians are more racist than whites. They do not like Africans." In a similar vein, Sephiwo S. details what he believes to be racism towards blacks in the Muslim community: "The Muslim community is divided into two classes the rich and predominantly Indian and the poor predominantly African. Racism and discrimination is alive and rife in the Muslim community ...."

Particularly relevant to this study of competing nations of discourse is debate over *new* forms of racism. The majority of black authors assume a conventional model of white racism and express that its deleterious impact continues in new, more subtle and coded ways. Sandile M. writes:

The majority, being obviously Black people are tired of all these fancy, mind-boggling slogans such as "The Rainbow Nation, the African Renaissance, South Africa for All, Masakhane" ... Most white people we speak to ... are laughing at the Black Nation. Some of the things they say are absurd. I quote "You are jobless, (it used to be ... tell Mandela) now its "tell your ANC you put them into power"); comment ... price of

petrol is too high; reaction "it is your corrupt Government". Clearly these are irresponsible Racist comments made by the very White People who are enjoying the freedom and benefits made freely available to them as in the past. White people have
distanced themselves from anything that in their eye is negative because it is the result of
the Black Government and yet continue to enjoy a good lifestyle under the African Sky
with no conscience and participation other than loading up their pockets and taking
more control ... Racism has continued unabated.

Within the parameters of this nation of discourse, the newness of new racism
involves hiding, disguising, or coding white anti-black racism in ways that
are more culturally and politically palatable.

By contrast, several submissions by self-identified whites describe what
they label 'reverse racism', or anti-white racism. Many white South Africans
feel targeted as the new victims of race conscious social policy, or what is
identified as 'reverse apartheid'. Tales of reverse discrimination abound,
whether in the form of allegations of media bias against whites, not getting a
job because one is white, or discrimination on the job because of the same.
Such tales symbolically construct white innocence in decrying that the
present generation should not be forced to pay for the sins of the parent
generation.[18] Wendy M. feels she and her colleagues have been the victims
of open racism on the part of the SABC, which was allegedly not interested
in covering overseas victories in 1999 of a school pipe band:

I personally was told that as there were not blacks in the band they were very sorry but
they could not cover it. I have since then seen choirs and sports teams covered by the
SABC and they have all been almost exclusively black school children ... We all feel that
these children, no matter their race or colour work very hard to be the best ... and they
are being denied opportunities for exposure and even sponsorship on the basis of their
colour ... Give us what you promise – non racist treatment for ALL SOUTH
AFRICANS IRRESPECTIVE OF RACE OR COLOUR OR CULTURE. These
children did not have anything to do with the OLD REGIME OF APARTHEID and
most of us (their parents) were even too young to vote for the racist regime of the past.
They should not be made to suffer for the mistakes made by others.

Similarly, Mrs. M. F. B. identifies herself as a female white South African
who was overjoyed in 1994 but has since become cynical:

I feel myself part of a discarded minority who is getting blamed for all conceivable
wrongs in the country ... At present only one side of racism in South Africa is seen and
recognised as such, i.e. white-on-black racism. The existence of its mirror image and twin
brother, black-on-white racism, which is just as rampant, evil and destructive, is not even
acknowledged, let alone condemned. Thus, tragically, the very perception of racism in
South Africa is racist.

In a similar vein, Hugh W. writes: "It would be unthinkable in the new
South Africa for someone to form an Association of White Plumbers. But it

seems quite acceptable for there to be a Black Lawyer's Association ... and no-one calls that 'racist'."

The notion of reverse racism slides easily and often into another form, what Nancy Murray labels 'anti-anti-racism'.[19] Within the frame of this discourse, activities and policies geared towards racial redress (such as employment equity) are themselves regarded as racist. Hugh W. writes: "The most blatant example of reverse racism is 'Affirmative Action' in the 'transformation' process. There seems to be no shame for a Black person to hold a position which s/he is not competent to hold. Ability is less important than skin colour, provided the skin is black." Other submissions express a form of anti-anti-racism by targeting the National Conference on Racism itself (as one more opportunity to 'bash whitey') and/or the SAHRC (for allegedly enriching itself in the name of human rights and the ANC) as the focus of ire.

The submissions by self-identified whites further demonstrate that culture has taken over much of the ideological work that used to be supplied by race.[20] For example, Tony H. argues against affirmative action by insisting that the problem in South Africa is not one of race but rather cultural diversity: "The differences in this country are more than racial – they are tribal, they are also based on language, on rituals and on historic associations not easily amenable to modification ...." Mrs. M. F. B. writes: "Birds of a feather flock together" – it is only natural for people to feel more comfortable with the way their own race or culture group do things or perceive the world. Preference for one's own group is perfectly natural and need not be negative. Ray D. similarly employs such culture talk as a substitute for the taboo topic of race. Defining himself as a "Euro African of British decent and protectionist or culturalist when my cultural heritage is threatened ...", he remarks that "not all cultures are equal ... No Budda, no Michelangelo, no Newton, No Bach, No Shakespeare, etc. has ever come out of the (African) continent" and thus '"one side does have the right to discriminate". Ray D. concludes with a defence of colonisation and apartheid, remarking that without such civilising projects "Africa would still be a dark continent". Finally, in arguing against 'forced' integration, Paul P. aptly circumvents the multicultural demand for respect for cultural difference in claiming that whites are fast becoming the new victims of an illiberal racial agenda:

> Blacks and Whites will always stay with their own kind ... Just because Whites do not attend soccer matches does not mean we are racists. I have never seen or hardly see Blacks at Cricket or Rugby matches but this does not mean that Blacks are racists. We must accept that our cultures differ and live and let live otherwise there will never be harmony in this country.

Paul P. concludes that for "far too long the cry has been that we must adopt
and tolerate Black traditions (such as lobola, slaughter of cattle, ancestor
worship). But I think it is also fair that White traditions and customs should
also be tolerated."

So while consensus exists on the sentiment that racism endures in the new
South Africa, albeit in new form, there is profound disagreement over how
to identify it and exactly what qualifies it as new. Many black-authored
submissions assert that the same old anti-black racism of apartheid persists
today but is dressed up in new garb. Such sentiment is consistent with
findings from studies of white racial attitudes employing a subtle racism
scale.[21] By contrast, the majority of white South Africans writing on the
theme of new racism asserts that apartheid-style racism is relegated to the
past and that they are victims of new forms of anti-white racism being
institutionalised by the new Government.

In its encounter with such competing identifications of the new racism, the
structural theory of racism avoids the pitfalls of the attempt to ferret out
supposedly hidden prejudice or in some other way determine the extent to
which racial attitudes have genuinely changed.[22] Much more productive for
the purpose of mapping contemporary racial ideologies is an understanding
of how the battle to claim victim status serves to lubricate the racial order at
this particular historical juncture. The outcome of this battle carries meaningful consequences for democratic consolidation. One nation of discourse
sets up a logic that requires the further pursuit of racial redress, or challenge
to the power relations that presently adhere to the status quo. The other
claims the moral high ground of non-racialism and deference to abstract
principles of democratic liberalism that serve in the present context of
marked racial inequality inherited from the apartheid past to defend exclusive patterns of advantage and privilege. Whichever version of new racism
triumphs, it seems clear that what is at issue revolves less around the ghosts
of apartheid (whether in the form of allegations of coded anti-black prejudice
or 'reverse racism'), but rather novel forms of racism born out of a battle to
interpellate the liberal democratic tradition in the post-transitional context.

Whose Institutional Racism?

*Racism is so rife ... There is more racism in our work place now that before 1994 elections.
The Racists hide behind the fact that, we have Black CEO's, Principals, and Director-
Generals. The middle management is still controlled by them (whites). (Christian T.)*

*A Black man unfairly dismissed me in my employment ... The reason – he did not like me
because I am white!!! (J. P. D.)*

The most ostensibly neutral and descriptive submissions were on the topic of institutional racism, although even these reveal significantly different universes of meaning. Institutional racism is defined here as pervasive and systemic racism produced in institutional settings (the media, prisons, schools, health, military, law, etc.) as a function of values, customs, and informal cultures operating together with rules, regulations, and procedures that produce discriminatory outcomes (Bolaffi et al., 2003). The institutional contexts that invited the most responses (and the most racially bifurcated responses) are racism in the workplace and racism and politics.

Roughly, half the responses in these categories were sent in by self-identified black South Africans who complain that discrimination has not stopped in the new South Africa and, according to some, has even grown worse. One submission argues that discrimination experienced at work – in terms of white harassment of blacks and white team leaders calling black workers 'Kaffir' and 'Haare gat' – has grown worse since the introduction of the Employment Equity Act. A submission by a local Black Economic Caucus details discrimination within the local Chamber of Business and local banking and tourism industries: "We represent the constituency of Business People that was excluded from the mainstream of business because of past discriminatory legislation. The discrimination however has not stopped after the 'New South Africa' came into being." Similarly, Joel D. writes of his experiences of discrimination as a black small businessman. He claims that white managers at Anglo-American terminated his cleaning contract unfairly and practiced nepotism in awarding a new contract to a white company: "Here was a unit of Anglo American (the biggest company in the country) that has publicly pledged to support emerging black business cutting me out and giving my contract to a major white company."

Complaints of individual experiences of discrimination at work abound. Vivian N. is a senior typist with the South African Police. She complains of unequal treatment and asserts that the "sentiments of apartheid still exist" in the Service. An anonymous submission from a worker at Kopanang Mine, Vaal reefs writes of continuing racism in the mining industry (specifically Anglo Gold), citing discrimination in training schedules, criteria for promotion, working conditions, disciplinary code procedures, and undermining relations with white supervisors. Such alleged experiences of racism and discrimination seem equally rampant among black middle-class professionals. An architect details his experience of unfair dismissal by a former employer, citing experiences (as the only black in the company) of excessive amounts of denigration in relations with his white employers, offensive and unequal treatment concerning corporate benefits, overtime pay, profit sharing, and leave policy. He quotes his boss as remarking at the time of

dismissal that it would be better for him to work for a company where there
are people of the same race, reasoning that he does not "quite understand
the way of life of a white person" and as a result is always 'misinterpreting
issues'.

Similar themes as expressed above are manifest in submissions on the
topic of racism and politics. Complaints about discrimination within government departments are to be found, as are comments that racism is rife in
Parliament. One chief animal health technician employed by the KZN
Department of Agriculture complains of racism, lack of transformation
(7 of 13 senior positions are held by whites), and a culture of intimidation
within the Department: "Mostly the problem we are facing is that the whites
who were advantaged in the past and holding high positions are still holding
them. Therefore in middle management positions they place less experienced
and less educated whites, ignoring more qualified and experienced blacks."
Chris M. asks rhetorically: "... does Tony Leon like black people?" He
continues: "I remember somebody in Parliament saying that 'equity bill and
affirmative action' is apartheid in reverse. Whites do not want to be equal to
blacks."

Most of these submissions conclude with a call for National Government
intervention to monitor/stop discrimination and accelerate affirmative action in the workplace and local government structures. A repetitive theme is
that companies remain white at the top and that affirmative action has been
used 'for window dressing' only. White management is commonly portrayed
as obstructionist vis-à-vis corporate and governmental transformation. For
example, with regard to educational transformation, Christian T. complains
of racism, sabotage, and 'dirty tricks' at Technikon Northern Gauteng:

> The Racists hide behind the fact that, we have Black CEO's, Principals, and Director-
> Generals ... They seek in many occasions to promote Black mediocres above Blacks who
> have what it takes to succeed, just to show how blacks are incompetent ... The only ones who
> get promoted are the blacks they perceive do not threaten their continued grip on power.

By contrast, an almost equal number of submissions on these topics were
authored by self-identified whites who assert that employment and political
career opportunities are stacked against them, especially white males who
are the alleged new victims of affirmative action. J. P. D. writes of her
suffering for 12 years because of her politically active husband who was
forced into exile, returning to South Africa in 1994 only to be "met with so
much prejudice in the job market because he was one of the 'privileged
group'. He was turned down for every job because he was white." Most
common are complaints that unskilled individuals are filling corporate and

political positions because of the colour of their skin rather than demonstrated merit. Brian M. is a computer programmer who has just returned to South Africa from the U.S. only to find himself "always fighting against a wall of 'affirmative action'". He alleges that such walls create racism and put hatred in people's hearts, concluding: "... Our problem is not so much racism anymore, but unskilled individuals filling positions."

In the wake of the eradication of the legal barriers that kept South African institutions segregated in the past, several submissions register complaint about the informal yet hostile cultures and often demographically skewed desegregated environments in which whites must operate today. Jo-ke. E. N. writes:

> My daughter is a student at the Pretoria College and studying a course in hairdressing. White pupils are a minority at the college and it happens frequently that they are described as 'Whities' with ugly hair and ugly eyes. This is detrimental to the cause we are all working for – to create a workplace in which we are all treated equally and respect each others cultures and differences.

Pat F. recounts her experience of 'incredible racism' as a white woman working in a predominantly black and Indian organisation. "Indians discriminated against me for the food I eat (beef and pork), the fact that I'm not married and over 30 years old. They have called me 'white cockroach' or 'whitey' and used the colour of my skin whenever I tried making suggestions or contributions in any way ...."

With regard to politics, a common complaint is that Government is benefiting one race at the expense of the other. Mrs. M. F. B. writes: "Unfortunately the present government is deliberately playing a major role in dividing and polarising the South African society along racial lines, thereby ... encouraging colourcoded violence." In explaining who benefits most from keeping racism alive, she remarks: "[T]he answer is obvious: by keeping the South African society divided on racial lines (and labeling opposition parties accordingly as 'white' parties) the ruling ANC stands the most to gain ... the fight against racism should not be used as a political tool to create racial solidarity behind the ruling party."

Gerhard P. derides the present government's stance on affirmative action, saying that it risks loosing what he calls "the moral basis of impartiality so important to stamp out racism in the country" as the policy is similar to apartheid in its focus on racial criteria. According to Gerhard P., affirmative action nourishes racism, causes increased animosity, fuels white emigration, harms the economy, and impacts negatively on every citizen. "All this could be avoided by giving all the citizens of this country, be they black, white or green, similar opportunities to unfold their talents." The submission author continues to rehearse a familiar theme in British and American neoconservative discourse; that is, that affirmative action is also harmful to black beneficiaries in terms of stigmatisation and negative self-esteem.[23] Affirmative action also harms the white youth: "Penalising them for the policy of their fathers would be the surest way of calling for conflict." He concludes: "I would want to summarise by saying that any government involvement benefiting one race at the expense of the other is bound to effect negatively on the racial harmony of the country. I fail to understand why the authorities do not learn from the past and avoid making the same old mistakes all over again."

Competing meanings are therefore registered in the submissions on the topic of institutional racism. Rather than attempt to figure out the truth content of vying claims of advantage or disadvantage in a variety of institutional contexts, the mapping of contemporary racial ideologies highlights the powerful emotional issues at stake as the racial order loosens from its apartheid-era moorings. Those previously disadvantaged during apartheid express disfavour that the pace of transformation is too slow and the changes too superficial or tokenistic as a result of the obstructionist practices of the beneficiaries of the old order. White South Africans express feelings of marginalisation and victimisation in the face of equality-promoting programmes and experience their loss of privileged status not only as discriminatory against them but also, in diasporic identification with global whiteness, as deleterious in signalling falling standards, increasing corruption, and the end of meritocracy.[24] Despite celebration of the 10-year anniversary of the first democratic election, tremendous conflict persists in all sorts of smaller, more local, and institutional contexts over who shall call the shots with concern to the nature, extent, and pace of societal transformation.

Non-Racialism in Black and White

Differences need to be recognised and dealt with before we can become one people. To try to live and work together harmoniously while denying differences is like trying to heal a wound that has not first been cleaned. (Greta T.)

Racism will only start to disappear once we stop calling one another by our skin colours and not by our name or where we come from ... I get very angry seeing reports on TV and in the press referring to black people or white people when they mean South Africans. You will only stop seeing colour once you stop saying the colour. (Colin W.)

Characteristic of both nations of discourse charted above is selective engagement with transitional rhetoric and the nation-building framework in articulating competing notions of the meaning and usefulness of non-racialism. Among the more colour-conscious commentators, acknowledgement of racial difference is understood as a necessary ingredient of progress towards racial equality. One female mental health professional articulates clearly the distinction between notions of sameness or equality as articulated in the notion color blindness, on the one hand, and notions of difference and redress as articulated in theories of anti-racism on the other:

> [T]he one issue/example of racism bothers me the most is the ANC's stance of Non-Racialism being confused with Color Blind model ... (the latter) is when people are treated the same. I have had very good and caring colleagues say to me "I make no difference I treat all my clients the same". The tendency with this method of assessment emphasis the Similarities in people and overlooks the Differences ... Our aim as anti-racist workers should be to clarify the oppression that the black individual has experienced in relation to conventional mental health/illness services and seek ways of confronting and changing the service.

For those who understand non-racialism in universalistic or colour-blind terms, the principle is lauded as a central building block of the rainbow nation. One 15 year old from Germiston writes: "... god make man in His image, which means that before the eyes of God we are the same. No one has ever heard of a white, black or a coloured God. As South Africans ... Let us stand up and build our non-racial rainbow nation. Together we can do it but divided we can't." Such liberal evocation of humanist notions ("I don't care if you are yellow, green, purple or pink – we are all human") is common in the call for a shared South African national identity to replace identities based on race or ethnicity. Within this nation of discourse, it is argued that while non-racialism may be a positive ideal, it is not in fact being put into practice. Charles S. derides the present government for corrupting the ideal:

> I had hoped that we South Africans would start on a new non-racist path into the future and stay away from the apartheid era methods where every activity had a racial connotation. Sadly this has not happened and government, educational institutions and many other organisations and institutions have perpetuated it and even refined the process. This is now done in the name of affirmative action or setting right the wrongs of the past ... how many times are we not still asked what our race is? ... The point is that every time the question is asked there is a reinforcement of the concept of race and racial differences ... My thesis is that until we remove the words Black and White and all other similar connotations from the South African vocabulary we will not eradicate the evil that is racism ... This consciousness and awareness of race is fundamental to the problem of racism and must be avoided and banished completely.

South Africa is far from the only country to engage in such symbolic conflict over the meaning of non-racialism. Fundamental disagreements exist throughout the world on the role and status of race vis-à-vis social and governmental policy. Non-racialism as a term seems to be particularly ambiguous and contested in the South African context, in part because of the changing role of the ideal throughout the decades of the liberation struggle and the nature of the compromise that underlies the negotiated settlement. For some, non-racialism means that no account of race should be taken whatsoever. Any notice of race contributes to processes of re-racialisation and policies of 'reverse apartheid'. For others, and consistent with the structural theory of racism outlined above, such myopia around race contributes to the effect (intended or unintended) of eliding the inter-section of race and power, and the benefits which have historically accrued from that intersection, thereby entrenching apartheid inequities and white privilege. According to this view, racial difference must be acknowledged and used as a basis of government policy if race-based inequities from the past are to be effectively redressed. It is vital to contest the equation of racial projects that pay attention to race in the pursuit of greater equality with those which historically employed race in order to keep the social terrain radically uneven.

CONCLUSIONS

What racism is and how to combat it evokes broad disagreement in South Africa today. The submissions to the SAHRC surveyed in this paper reveal a fundamental lack of consensus on such topics and instead evidence ide-ological bifurcation to the extent that one would be remiss not to note racial differences in perspectives. A majority of submissions by black South Africans express that the racism of apartheid continues in a variety of new forms and contexts, while white contributors by and large decry the use of race as a valid criteria of analysis or redress, complaining that such (mis)use facilitates dangerous trends towards 're-racialisation' and even 'reverse apartheid'. Whether or not one agrees with the characterisation of such ideological bifurcation as "two nations of discourse", it is beyond debate that black and white South Africans approach the questions that were the topic of the National Conference on Racism in meaningfully different ways. Such bifurcation has less to do with purported essential racial difference than with differential group position and experience in the post-apartheid racial order.

Far from being eliminated along with the transition to democratic rule, racial meanings, racial/ethnic identities, and racialised state practices are recreating themselves anew precisely in and through the exit from apartheid and the struggle to forge a new hegemonic racial order. The transition to democracy has itself enhanced the salience of race and racism, and aspects of the current exit from apartheid rule heighten the salience and popular appeal. In this view, far more interesting than the question of whether *attitudinal* racism has increased or decreased in salience or, by extension, how can it be eliminated, is analysis of the ideological role of race as a 'nodal point' of transitional politics.[25] The concept of race as a nodal point of the transition directs attention to the process by which the racial idea is used – to construct moral authority for oneself and to undermine that of the opposition – as various racial projects scramble to dominate the terms, nature and pace of the transition. The hegemonic struggle over racial meanings is not only political or ideological, but material as well; for each racial project mobilises a set of meanings (vis-à-vis apartheid's legacy, the definition and forms of racism, the nature of institutional racism, and the proper interpretation of non-racialism) which serve to either defend, naturalise, reify, and rationalise *or* challenge, expose, and upset existing relations of power.[26]

It is precisely this link between meaning and power that informs the sociological literature on new forms of racism. More conventional studies of racism which assume the existence of prejudice, mean-spirited affect, and expressed belief in white supremacy are not up to the task of charting the new forms of racism; forms which disavow racist intent and work via circumvention of anti-racist and transitional or nation-building rhetoric but nevertheless mobilise meaning in defence of the racially inegalitarian status quo. Indeed, if there is a new racism in South Africa, it is one produced among competing interpretations of the liberal democratic tradition, not one that penetrates the mainstream in stealth from the outside.

Numerous black-authored submissions assert that the old racism of apartheid persists in the new South Africa but is camouflaged or sanitised due to the strength of taboos against racism accompanying the new dispensation. But little evidence exists in the submissions surveyed of apartheid-style racism or attempts to disguise it. Indeed, only one out of 154 submissions expresses outright race hatred, mean-spiritedness, and an attitude of racial superiority. Methodologically one is presented with a difficulty as it is virtually impossible to accurately detect that which is effectively disguised. But what is clear is that mostly all attempts to articulate race in the SAHRC files work in and through the lens of transitional rhetoric. Even the extreme Afrikaner right wing has for the most part jettisoned apartheid-style discourse of white supremacy in favour of a discourse that engages the multicultural right to protect and defend its (white) culture in a multiracial democracy. Identifying the newness of today's new racism is therefore a much more difficult task than simply ferreting out hidden prejudice. Such detective work falls into the trap of an ahistorical essentialism by equating white with racist. Racism resides less in the white (or black) mind than in the socio-historical context, which gives it purchase. Anti-racist efforts, by implication, must be directed not at finding the outright bigot in our midst who employs code-words in order to appear respectable, but rather towards identifying the process by which racism adapts and changes in order to speak to the dilemmas and challenges born of the context of democratic consolidation.

The majority of white-authored submissions similarly assume that racism is something that exists external to the liberal democratic tradition and so fail to see the potential for racism to be recast in their expressed views on a range of questions related to the role of race in democratic societies worldwide: Do we treat people the same or differently? Are rights universal or specific, individually or group-based? Is a non-racial society colour blind or race conscious? Those interventions grounded in universalistic principles of liberal humanism, which deride programmes of racial redress and distributive justice as 'reverse apartheid' elide continuing patterns of racial power and powerlessness and, in so doing, put these very same principles in the service of a politics of white backlash. In equating race-conscious strategies to achieve racial equality with racist strategies to block that very same goal, such discourses of moral symmetry arguably mobilise ostensibly benign and race-neutral meanings in the service of preserving unequal relations of racial power and advantage.

Finally, the burgeoning international literature on the social construction of whiteness dovetails with the findings of this study in arguing for the need to study racism not only from the perspective of its object or victim, but also its subject or perpetrator.[27] Whether in the form of denial of culpability for the apartheid past, complaints of victimisation in the face of ANC re-racialisation, or race cognisance, the submissions demonstrate that South African whites are also involved with racism. Although not representative of white opinion, the submissions reveal a tendency towards amnesia in dealing with the past and myopia with respect to the continuing impact of apartheid's legacies. "I never voted for the Nats", assert so many, "I stand innocent and inappropriately laden with responsibilities to redress wrongs for which I am not myself responsible" (Statman, 1999). The very ideology of non-racialism that fuelled the struggle against apartheid is thereby being appropriated and circumvented by its beneficiaries in order to oppose corrective measures to redress relations of racial inequality inherited from the past.

A structural view of racism provides a compass of power by which to judge the messy terrain of competing narratives on racism contained in the SAHRC files. Racial ideology is not simply an attitude of racial prejudice free-floating in people's heads. Rather, it is a framework of beliefs or worldview expressed by differentially positioned racialised social groups that mobilises meaning in the service of defending and justifying (dominant race) or challenging (subordinate race or races) relations of racial dominance and inequality. As the struggle to forge a new post-apartheid hegemonic racial order proceeds, it is the task of those committed to a society of diminished racial inequities to examine the production and defence of new racial ideologies that freshly articulate with the challenges and dilemmas of the new order. This study is but one contribution to that task.

NOTES

1. The deleterious consequences of the violation of non-racialism constitute the main theme of Paul Gilroy's (2000) new work. For elaborated discussion of apartheid racial categories and their reification and usage in contemporary South African politics see Posel, "What's in a Name? Racial Categorisations under Apartheid and their Afterlife", paper delivered at the Conference "The Burden of Race? 'Whiteness' and 'Blackness' in Modern South Africa", History Workshop and Wits Institute for Social and Economic Research, University of Witwatersrand (5–8 July 2001); Posel (2001).

2. For a terrific study of racial identity in post-apartheid South Africa see Nadine Dolby (2001). For empirical data on the residues of apartheid racial thinking see Gibson and Macdonald (2001); quoted in Posel, *op. cit.*, p. 1.

3. The term 'post-racist' refers to conservative thinkers in the U.S. and elsewhere who claim that the juridical abolition of institutional racism (such as Jim Crow or apartheid) has meant the end of racism and that any appeal to race is therefore regressive in the contemporary period. For a classic statement of this position see D'Souza (1995).

4. Thabo Mbeki, "South Africa: Two Nations", Statement of Deputy President Thabo Mbeki at the opening of the debate on reconciliation and nation-building, National Assembly, 29 May 1998; quoted in Hadland and Rantao (1999, p. 188).

5. For an elaboration of this line of argument see Marks Chabedi, "Whither the Rainbow Nation? The ANC, the Black Middle Class and Changing Perceptions of 'Blackness' in the Post-Apartheid South Africa", paper presented at the Conference "The Burden of Race? 'Whiteness' and 'Blackness' in Modern South Africa", History Workshop and Wits Institute for Social and Economic Research, University of Witwatersrand (5–8 July 2001).

6. Interpretation of the census data itself was racialised, with the black media focusing on the racial differences between black and white and the liberal, predominantly liberal media focusing on intra-black-class differences.

7. For an analysis of the Makgoba Affair see Statman and Ansell (2000).

8. The terms white and black are employed here as racial constructions, with black referring inclusively to those who self-identify as African, Coloured, and Indian. Although most of the submissions by authors who self-identify as black in the Head Office files are from Africans, submissions to various Provincial Offices are characterised by much higher percentages of Coloured and Indian authors. Future research is needed to understand better intra-black differences in the context of such an inclusive definition, especially as Coloured and Indian perspectives and identities are beginning to show signs of selective alignment with South African whites. For more on this latter point see Dolby; *op. cit.*

9. Benjamin Disraeli; quoted in: Andrew Hacker (1992). Hacker applies the 'two nations' metaphor to his widely read study of contemporary race relations in the United States.

10. For elaboration of the structural theory of racism see Ansell (1997) and Bonilla-Silva (2001).

11. Ansell, *ibid.*, pp. 70–73; Bonilla-Silva, *ibid.*, p. 12.

12. The phrase 'new racism' refers to a shift away from traditional forms of racism based on presumed 'natural' hierarchies of white superiority and black inferiority (based in biology) to new forms oriented more around culture and nation. For more on 'new racism' see Ansell (1997), Barker (1982), Taguieff (1990), Balibar and Wallerstein (1991), and Bonilla-Silva (2003).

13. The literature on whiteness is voluminous and too broad to reference here. The most important recent works with concern to South Africa include Steyn (2001b), Goodwin and Schiff (1995), and Statman (1999).

14. Steyn; *op. cit.*, pp. 112–113.

15. Debate exists on the productivity of white guilt. Melissa Steyn argues that white guilt is perhaps a necessary process of self-examination leading to heightened anti-racist consciousness, while Ruth Frankenberg argues that it leads to political paralysis. Steyn; *op. cit.*; Ruth Frankenberg (1993).

16. Frankenberg; *op. cit.*, pp. 157–190.

17. Fanon writes, "The habit of considering racism as a mental quirk, as a psychological flaw, must be abandoned." Quoted in Bonilla-Silva (1996).

18. The symbolic construction of white innocence in the context of U.S. debates on reconciliation and apology is developed and elaborated in Ansell and Statman (1999).

19. See Ansell (1997). The term 'anti-anti-racism' was first coined by Nancy Murray (1986).

20. For more on the new cultural forms of racism, see Balibar (1991), Taguieff (1990), and Ansell (1997).

21. Studies of white racial attitudes using a subtle racism scale include Gunnar Theissen (1997), Gibson and Macdonald (2001), and John Duckitt (1991). Consistent with findings in the context of the United States is the finding that equality-promoting policies are supported by whites in principle only, not in implementation. For more on this in the U.S. context see Schuman, Steeh, and Bobo (1985). Another interesting finding is that whites support racial integration yet oppose affirmative

action, leading authors of both the IJR and CSVR study to conclude that whites feel less threatened by integration than a policy that acts directly upon correcting racial inequality. These sentiments are then linked to subtle forms of racial attitudes.

22. The attempt to determine the extent to which white racial attitudes have genuinely changed is what drives the CSVR study referenced above. The author identifies a 'post-apartheid syndrome' characterised by "a desire to forget about the past, low human rights awareness, racist views, a denial of the right to compensation for apartheid victims, an unwillingness to undo the legacy of socio-economic justice, and a residual desire to glorify apartheid." CSVR; *op. cit.*, p. 13. Rather than characterise such sentiment as a psychological syndrome, this paper approaches contemporary white racial attitudes within the context of sociological studies of ideology.

23. For elaboration of the neo-conservative position see Ansell (1997).

24. For elaboration of the notion of diasporic identification see Melissa Steyn (2001a).

25. The phrase 'nodal point' is used effectively in Anna Marie Smith's analysis of New Right discourse in Britain (Smith, 1994).

26. Such a link between meaning and power is formulated by John B. Thompson in his more general theory of the operation of ideology (Thompson, 1990).

27. This particular formulation of the task of critical whiteness studies is developed by Toni Morrison (1992).

REFERENCES

Ansell, A. E. (1997). *New right/new racism: Race and reaction in the United States and Britain.* New York: New York University Press.

Ansell, A. E., & Statman, J. M. (1999). 'I never owned slaves': The Euro-American construction of the racialized other. In: P. B. Lippe & J. Feagin (Eds), *Research in politics and society,* (Vol. 6, pp. 151–173). New York: JAI Press.

Balibar, E., & Wallerstein, I. (1991). *Race, nation, class: Ambiguous identities.* London: Verso.

Barker, M. (1982). *The new racism: Conservatives and the ideology of the tribe.* London: Junction Books.

Bolaffi, G., Bracelenti, R., Braham, P., & Gindro, S. (Eds) (2003). *Dictionary of race, ethnicity and culture* (pp. 147–151). London: Sage.

Bonilla-Silva, E. (1996). Rethinking racism: Toward a structural interpretation. *American Sociological Review, 62,* 467.

Bonilla-Silva, E. (2001). *White supremacy and racism in the post-civil rights era.* Boulder: Lynne Rienner.

Bonilla-Silva, E. (2003). *Racism without racists: Color-blind racism and the persistence of racial inequality in the United States.* Maryland: Rowman & Littlefield.

Dolby, N. (2001). *Constructing race: Youth, identity, and popular culture in South Africa.* Albany: SUNY Press.

D'Souza, D. (1995). *The end of racism: Principles for a multiracial society.* New York: Free Press.

Duckitt, J. (1991). The development and validation of a subtle racism scale in South Africa. *South African Journal of Psychology, 21*(4), 233–239.

Farred, G. (1997). Bulletproof settlers: The politics of offense in the New South Africa. In: M. Hill (Ed.), *Whiteness: A critical reader* (pp. 63–80). New York: New York University Press.

Frankenberg, R. (1993). *White women, race matters: The social construction of whiteness* (pp. 157–190). Minneapolis: University of Minnesota Press.

Gibson, J., & Macdonald, H. (2001). *Truth – yes, reconciliation – maybe: South Africans judge the truth and reconciliation process.* Cape Town: Institute for Justice and Reconciliation.

Gilroy, P. (2000). *Against race: Imagining political culture beyond the color line.* Cambridge, MA: Harvard University Press.

Goodwin, J., & Schiff, B. (1995). *Heart of Whiteness: Afrikaners face Black rule in the new South Africa.* New York: Scribner.

Hacker, A. (1992). *Two nations: Black and White, separate, hostile, unequal.* New York: Scribner p. ix.

Hadland, A., & Rantao, J. (1999). *The life and times of Thabo Mbeki.* Cape Town: Zebra Press.

Mbeki, T. (1998). Statement of Deputy President Thabo Mbeki on the occasion of the debate on the budget vote, national assemly, June 3; quoted in Hadland and Rantao (1999), *op. cit.*, p. 202.

Morrison, T. (1992). *Playing in the dark: Whiteness and the literary imagination.* Cambridge, MA: Harvard University Press.

Murray, N. (1986). Anti-racists and other demons: The press and ideology in Thatcher's Britain. *Race and Class, 3*(Winter), 1–26.

Nuttal, S. (2001). Subjectivities of whiteness. *African Studies Review, 44*(2), 115–140.

Nuttal, S., & Coetzee, C. (Eds) (1998). *Negotiating the past: The making of memory in South Africa.* Cape Town: Oxford University Press.

Posel, D. (2001). Race as common sense: Racial classification in twentieth-century South Africa. *Africa Studies Review, 44*(2), 87–113.

Price, R. (1997). Race and reconciliation in the New South Africa. *Politics and Society, 25*(2), 149–178.

Schuman, H., Steeh, C., & Bobo, L. (1985). *Racial attitudes in America: Trends and interpretations.* Cambridge, MA: Harvard University Press.

Smith, A. M. (1994). *New right discourse on race and sexuality: Britain 1968–1990.* Cambridge: Cambridge University Press.

Statman, J. M. (1999). The shape of the shadow: Mapping the dimensions of white amnesia and denial in post-apartheid South Africa. *ReVision, 22*(1), 35–41.

Statman, J. M. (2000). Performing the truth: The social psychological context of TRC narratives. *South African Journal of Psychology, 30*(1), 23–32.

Statman, J. M., & Ansell, A. E. (2000). The rise and fall of the Makgoba affair: A case study of symbolic politics. *Politikon, 27*(2), 277–295.

Steyn, M. (2001a). 'White talk': White South Africans and the management of diasporic whiteness. Paper presented at the conference "The Burden of Race? 'Whiteness' and 'Blackness' in the New South Africa", History Workshop and Wits Institute for Social and Economic Research, University of Witwatersrand, 5–8 July.

Steyn, M. (2001b). *Whiteness just isn't what it used to be: White identity in a changing South Africa.* Albany: SUNY Press.

Taguieff, P. (1990). The new cultural racism in France. *Telos, 83*(Spring), 109–122.

Theissen, G. (1997). *Between acknowledgement and ignorance: How White South Africans have dealt with the apartheid past.* Johannesburg: Centre for the Study of Violence and Reconciliation.

Thompson, J. B. (1990). *Ideology and modern culture.* Cambridge: Polity Press.

PART VII: EPILOGUE

THE NEW BLACK AND THE MAKING OF THE BLACK SOCIAL IMAGINATION

Rodney Coates and Rutledge Dennis

Several major themes permeate most of the articles in this volume. One theme focuses on the issues and problems, which distinguish old and new concepts of racism and discrimination; the other theme centers on the distinctions, ideal typically, of blacks as the "New Colored" and the "New Negro," and now, the "New Black." As we review the social history of the collective black population, there is a transparency in the black use of the social imagination to help structure the immediate world and to project ideas and ideals for a future world. This Black Social Imagination is embodied in the idea that human life and activity is collectively created, that Divine Providence exists, and that humans use their imagination to construct a world not yet born – one in which they hope to dwell, and one which offers the freedom and liberty they desire. This imagination suggests that those living in a state of un-freedom can still "imagine" freedom. After all, those entering the stages of un-freedom may well have remembered a time of freedom. Those born in the state of un-freedom have, no doubt, heard legends and stories of past generations which did not dwell in a state of servitude. In fact, one might assert that not having freedom makes one even more anxious, and more creative, in imagining both a time and a place where such a desired freedom might be obtained. This explains the appeal to

The New Black: Alternative Paradigms and Strategies for the 21st Century
Research in Race and Ethnic Relations, Volume 14, 337–343
ISSN: 0195-7449/doi:10.1016/S0195-7449(06)14015-5

divine Providence, and for blacks, the association of the slave experience to
the enslavement of the Hebrew people, both in Egypt and Babylon. One can
then make the case that people living in bondage can be said to live in two
worlds: First, they live in World One, the daily non-free world where they
must cope with the anxieties, slights, brutality, and hardships of being
un-free, and hence, dominated. In this world, the dominated must devise
strategies and tactics to ensure their survival, and thus avoid both physical
and emotional annihilation. Second, they live imaginatively in World Two,
the world of the non-free and the slave.

We now have available in-depth ante-bellum and post-bellum slave narratives, which provide an overture to the World One. In addition, we have
the works of W. E. B. Du Bois, Carter G. Woodson, and many others
who've painted a vivid landscape of the un-freedom of World One. Ironically, many have not given those in World One their due, often assuming
that those in this world accepted this world as it was, and refused to seriously
challenge it. However, reading the narratives and the socio-history of the era,
reveals to no small extent, a world of rebellion and resistance. The other side
of this dialectic reveals a world of patience, camouflages, masks, and play-
acting – all necessary for survival in a world bent on enslavement in body and
mind. Without doubt, the playing out of this dialectic, was necessary. That
they were not destroyed in the process speaks volume of the strength and
tenacity of those caught up in this world who were determined to survive and
have their survival serve as a beacon of light and hope to future generations.

World Two can be said to have co-existed with World One in that horrors
expressed in the narratives of World One were often a pretext for imaginative ventures into World Two in which a new and better world was
envisioned and projected. A classic example of such models for the future
can be seen in Du Bois' books, *Souls of Black Folk and Dusk of Dawn*, in
Washington's *Up From Slavery*, and Alain Locke's *New Negro*. In each of
these books we are given examples of both new and old racism and discrimination and new and old "ideal types" of "the Colored", "the Negro."
With each "ideal type" came an assortment of latent and manifest behavioral responses and projections. From the very beginning of the black presence in the United States until virtually the last third of the twentieth
century, World Two would be the world of the black social imagination in
which true freedom was longed for and continued to be a possibility in
which a model for the formerly oppressed would be that of citizens finally
taking their place along side other citizens in a free society. In the 1960s
Dr. Martin Luther King, Jr., envisioned and outlined models for American
freedom and democracy, not only for a future Black America but also for a

future America which would include all as partners in the great American democratic experiment. His models were carefully sketched on a foundation of religion, ethics, justice, and a sense of civic responsibility.

The sociological and philosophical assumptions that guided the logic of Dr. King, Locke, Du Bois and others were ideas associated with the principles of social and cultural pluralism as well as the concept of community. That there were features of black life that should be nurtured and preserved, and that there were attributes of black life, history, and culture of great merit which justified placement alongside features of white culture, life, and history. Indeed, these features representing black life, history, and culture comprised the inner layer of life for blacks, which made the machinations of World Two thinkable and obtainable. Thus, World Two was not simply an idle pie-in-the-sky projection. Rather, scholars such as John Blassingame, Eugene Genovese, Ira Berlin, John Hope Franklin, and Herbert Guttman, in addition to Du Bois, E. Franklin Frazier, and Carter Woodson, Charles Johnson, and others were already in the process of charting, outlining, and designing those social and cultural networks constructed in the nineteenth and twentieth centuries, which would incorporate the ideas and ideals of this black imagination and wrestle with it as they operated between, and had to live between, the invidious comparisons between the American creed and deed. These cultural experiences would assist in structuring World Two from the inside, just as from the outside, the abolition of social and legal restrictions would result in the coming together of the threads of the inner cultural world connecting to the social fabric of the world of whites.

The challenges for the New Black in the twenty-first century are somewhat different from those challenges faced by blacks in the eighteenth, nineteenth, and twentieth centuries. Though many might disagree, we can say with great assurance that massive and revolutionary changes have occurred within the black population over the past two centuries. With that said, we can still make the case, however, that additional revolutionary changes will be necessary before the case book is closed on the death of racism and discrimination in America and the rest of the world. The challenges for the New Black in this new century are many, and as there are still battles of freedom and democracy to be fought and won, those of us must understand that we, too, have our World One and World Two, though the issues are different, and though many of the models and visions for World Two as envisioned by men and women of the eighteen, nineteenth centuries, and now, the twentieth century. But, we must remember that there was no quick and revolutionary change-over from "the New Negro" to the "New Black," for the new black was evolving from the new negro long before conditions were ripe for the new black to emerge. Indeed, we can chart the slow evolution of the New Black from the eighteenth century when men like "Othello" and Peter Williams challenged slavery and social injustices. They were living in their eras, but sought to transcend their era in order to transplant their vision of a new life on the yet uncharted grounds of the future. Also, we need only to review the socio-history of the Black Reconstruction in the South following the defeat of the Confederacy and the immediate immersion of the newly freed slaves into the politics, economic, and education practices of that era. This transition into the world of the existing "possible" would have been unlikely had those visions and mental acting out been completely absent in World One.

The uniqueness of Black Americans can be seen in many ways when juxtaposed against the American racial and class canvas. Chief among this exceptionalism is the fact that blacks had almost 300 years of slavery, and for this reason, lived in World One. During the Reconstruction there was a decade in which blacks lived in World Two. Following the collapse of the Reconstruction, and from then until the mid- and late-1960s, blacks returned to World One, though this would mainly characterize the world of Southern Blacks, not Northern Blacks. But being forced to return to a highly restricted world under Jim Crow was not the same as living in the isolated World One behind the Cotton Curtain from 1619 to 1865. For much had happened between 1877 and the 1960s. W. E. B. Du Bois and Booker T. Washington, each in his own unique way, brought an intense racial consciousness to the black population, North and South; Washington with his emphasis on vocational education and the need for a black collective economic enterprise, and his strategy to place suffrage and civil rights as second-tier issues to provide breathing space for Southern blacks so as to enable them to develop an economic consciousness and create an economic base; Du Bois's gift of racial consciousness which he conveyed, was centered on higher education, the world of culture and literature, and how these qualities would come to fruition in the Talented Tenth, who would in turn convey that racial consciousness to the larger black population. This need for and use of this consciousness is clearly seen in Du Bois' *Souls of Black Folk and Washington's Up From Slavery.*

Following the colossal battles between Du Bois and Washington in which the basic differences were ideological on one hand and on the other centered on the world of the practical. Washington lived basically in the world of the practical, and in fact, can be said to have developed a theory of practicality as it relates to possible actions of a powerless people compromising a small percentage of the population; and what is practically possible that a small, but determined, percentage of the dominant group had historically demonstrated a willingness to kill members of that group, whenever necessary, to maintain total control and power. The artistic and literary works of the Harlem Renaissance illustrated the emergence of the "New Negro," but many believed that a new consciousness gotten within the contexts and constraints of racially segregated society would not solve the problem. At the end of the nineteenth century, Du Bois had hoped to connect Black Americans within a larger network African people with the Pan-African Movements. Garvey, coming to America to help Washington fulfill his, Washington's, program of constructing a black economic enterprise, moved far beyond Washington's plans by focusing on Africa and the possible immigration of blacks to the continent.

After the Harlem Renaissance with its focus on the "New Negro," and its simultaneous co-existence with the politics and economics of the Garvey Movement, racial consciousness was raised to a new level among many blacks. In addition, the theme of Africa in Black American life would resonate soon after World War II, first among those who fought the war in Europe and Asia. The Civil Rights Movement highlighted the fact that throughout the world, African people were under assault by Europeans, and in America, blacks were undergoing another phase of their historical struggle to end racial segregation and seek the social equality enjoyed by white Americans. The Nation of Islam had always pointed to the similarity of the struggles of African people throughout the world, and Malcolm X threatened to take the case of Black Americans to the United Nations. He viewed the struggle for racial justice in the U.S., not as a civil rights struggle, but rather, as a human rights struggle, a position Martin Luther King, Jr. would later adopt. But the victories of the Civil Rights Movement, as important as they were – school desegregation, voting rights, civil rights, etc., would not, perhaps could not, address the central core of the black existence in the United States: the sense that black life lacked a central thread that would etch a collective sense of peoplehood; that were movements toward a collective identity, one shaped by more than 300 years of collective suffering and the creation of a culture built upon exclusion, which blacks had managed to shape a collective life as the eternal outsiders. For this reason, it was inevitable that the concept of Black Power would emerge among many who became increasingly dissatisfied with the slow pace of desegregation and the even slower pace in which blacks would be structurally integrated into the economics and politics of American life.

The yearning for peoplehood, though, cannot be given by those who have historically excluded. So even with the civil rights battles won during the last

40–50 years of the twentieth century, some of the victories often seemed hollow, largely because with each victory, with each door opened, blacks peered in to see that there exists an emotional socio-cultural emptiness that in many ways may have had little to do with the civil rights and economic gains they fought for and won. If a look in the mirror by the collective black population did not reveal a collective cultural void and emotional and psychological disconnect and delimiting compartmentalization, it did suggest a collective puzzlement, by no means debilitating, but one promoting uncertainity and a lack of a forthright and clearly defined collective cultural resolve. This is why singularly structural analysis, which tends to overemphasize the predominant role of economics, may not be sufficient for a population, particularly, a population estranged from the cultural moorings of its historical past and not attached in any meaningful way to the culture of the larger and dominant society with which it lives; the situated is a culture which has oppressed it and continues to do so in large and small ways. That the structural explanation is insufficient suggests that humans cannot live by [bread] economics alone. This defect of structural explanation is based on two features largely absent from structural logic and sociology in general: the reluctance to introduce the element of values in human life and behavior, and the reluctance to analyze the role of religion in human life and relationships. The value component is largely omitted by liberals and radicals on the left because they are unable and unwilling to confront that argument as presented by conservative, and since their political and social concerns cover values only on the macro level as these relate to issues of social, political and economic justice, they have abandoned discussions of values on the personal and familial level. For this reason, liberals and left radicals are dismissive of discussions of values when applied to racial and ethnic sub-communities.

Religion is even more often dismissed as a force in sociological analysis by liberals and left radicals, especially when the focus is on racial and ethnic sub-communities. This omission parallels the fact that most academics and social researchers are either atheists or agnostics. My argument here is not that they should not be either. Instead, my argument is that in their dismissal of religion of a force in human life, though they may be unbelievers, they may be missing a central point in the lives of those whom they study. This appears to be one of the major differences between early social researchers such as Du Bois, Frazier, and Johnson and more contemporary researchers espousing structuralist perspectives. As anti-religious as Du Bois and Frazier may have been, each recognized the role of religion, either latently or manifestly, within black communities. This is why their studies present us with a more well-rounded view of black communities, and by doing so, we also have a more rounded view of individuals engaged in many series of social networks and social relations within those communities. This was also a defect in the works of Oliver C. Cox, especially in his last book that focused on race relations, nationalism, and black leadership. He was largely dismissive of religion and religious leaders in black communities, viewing them essentially as a collective negative force in community life.

The challenge to the New Blacks of the twenty-first Century is to move boldly into this century and to move swiftly into World Two and to make World Two an immediate reality. Social, political, and economic opportunities in the twenty-first century may better permit the New Blacks to do the following:

1. Challenge the idea that it is painful and impossible to be both Black and American.
2. Challenge the idea that only urban inner-city life and culture represent the Black perspective and experience.
3. Challenge the view that being middle class is merely an attempt to "act" and "be" White.
4. Challenge the view that Black music only covers the blues, jazz, and soul music, but not classical music or contemporary pop or standard.
5. Challenge the idea that capitalism is inherently bad or evil.
6. Challenge the idea that socialism is inherently bad or evil.
7. Challenge the view that all Blacks must think alike and express similar social views and values.
8. Challenge the view that the only political party for Blacks is the Democratic Party.
9. Challenge the idea that social integration offers the solution to the American racial dilemma.
10. Challenge the view that only social and racial separation offer the solution to the American racial dilemma.
11. Challenge the idea that Christianity is the only acceptable religious perspective for Blacks.
12. Challenge the idea that America belongs to Whites because Whites alone created the nation.
13. Challenge the One-Drop blood rule.
14. Challenge the idea that Black Americans cannot perform well in science and math.
15. Challenge the idea of White American ownership of the country with an extensive case for Black American ownership.

SET UP A CONTINUATION ORDER TODAY!

Did you know that you can set up a continuation order on all Elsevier-JAI series and have each new volume sent directly to you upon publication? For details on how to set up a **continuation order**, contact your nearest regional sales office listed below.

To view related series in Sociology, please visit:

www.elsevier.com/sociology

30% Discount for Authors on All Books!

A 30% discount is available to Elsevier book and journal contributors on all books (except multi-volume reference works).

To claim your discount, full payment is required with your order, which must be sent directly to the publisher at the nearest regional sales office above.